A Legacy Preserved

Contemporary Louisiana Decoy Carvers

A Legacy Preserved

Contemporary Louisiana Decoy Carvers

Harvey J. Lewis

University of Louisiana at Lafayette Press
2016

ISBN 13 (paper): 978-1-935754-83-1

University of Louisiana at Lafayette Press
P.O. Box 43558
Lafayette, LA 70504-3558
http://ulpress.org

Printed in China on acid-free paper.

Library of Congress Cataloging-in-Publication Data

Names: Lewis, Harvey J., author.
Title: A legacy preserved : contemporary Louisiana decoy carvers / Harvey J. Lewis.
Description: Lafayette, LA : University of Louisiana at Lafayette Press, 2016.
Identifiers: LCCN 2016025498 | ISBN 9781935754831
Subjects: LCSH: Decoy carvers--Louisiana. | Decoys (Hunting)--Louisiana.
Classification: LCC NK9712 .L48 2016 | DDC 745.593/60976309051--dc23
LC record available at https://lccn.loc.gov/2016025498

Cover image: a collection of pintail decoys by Bill Hanemann

I dedicate this book to my wife, Gail, my most ardent admirer and severe critic. Without her love, encouragement, and pre-editorial advice, this book would not have been written.

- Harvey J. Lewis

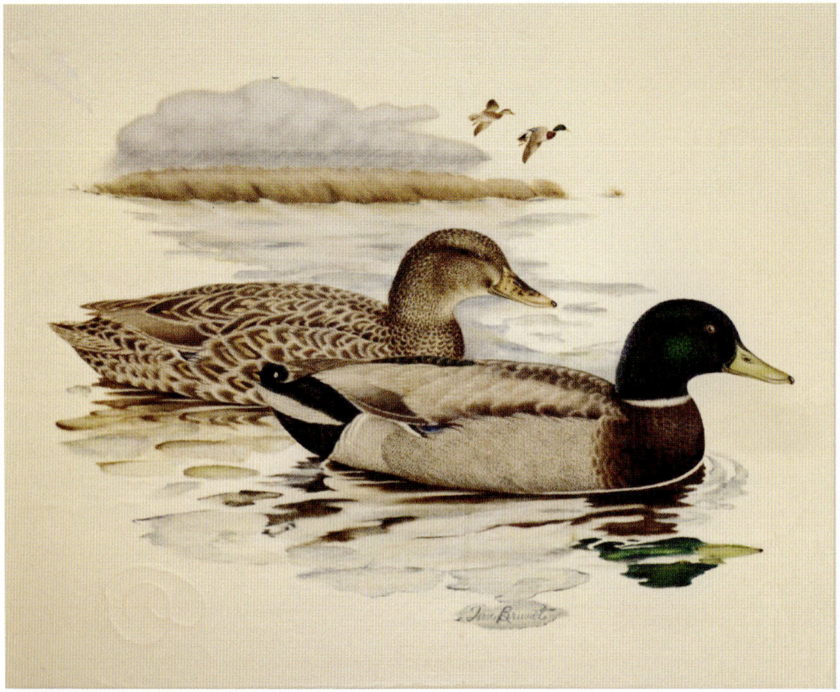

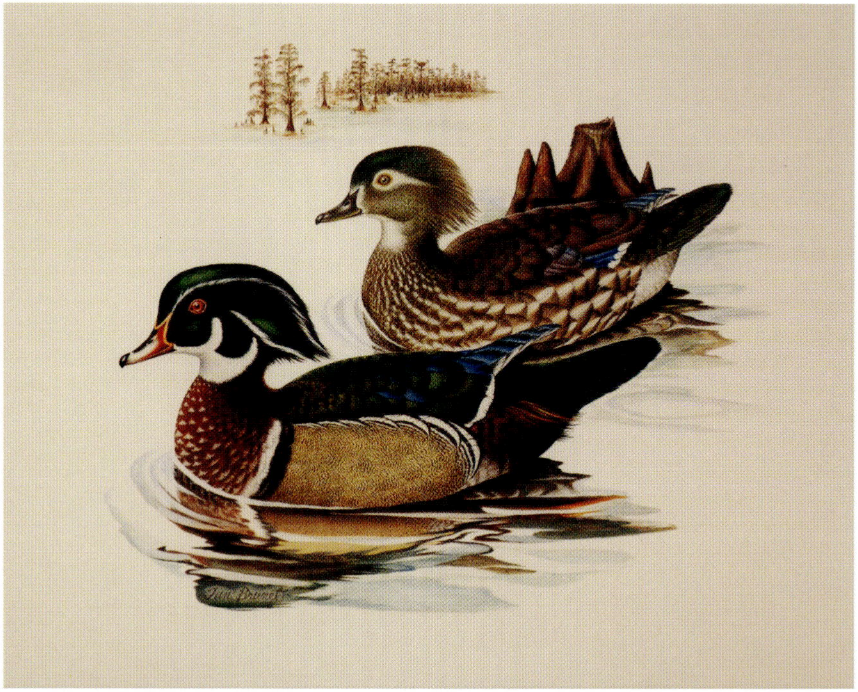

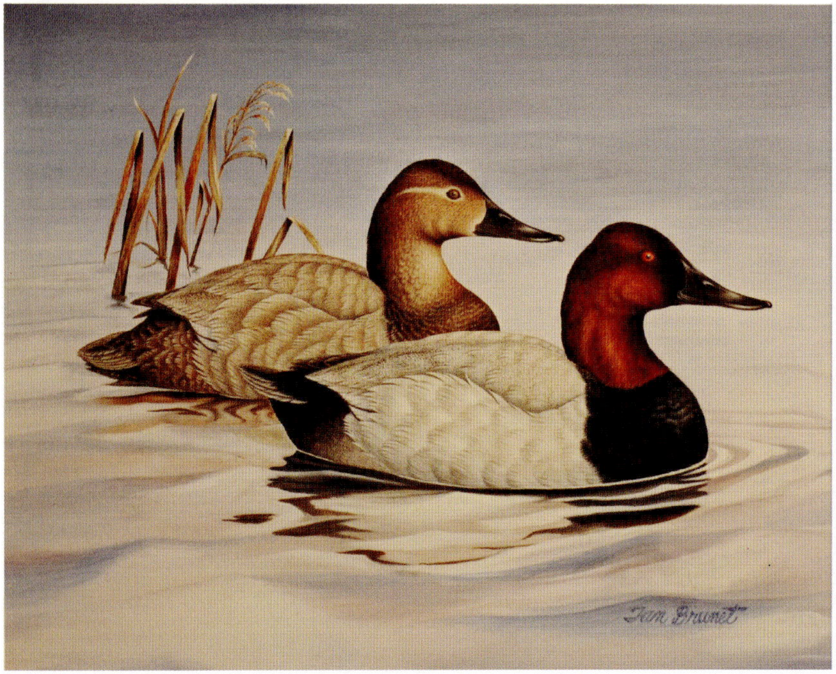

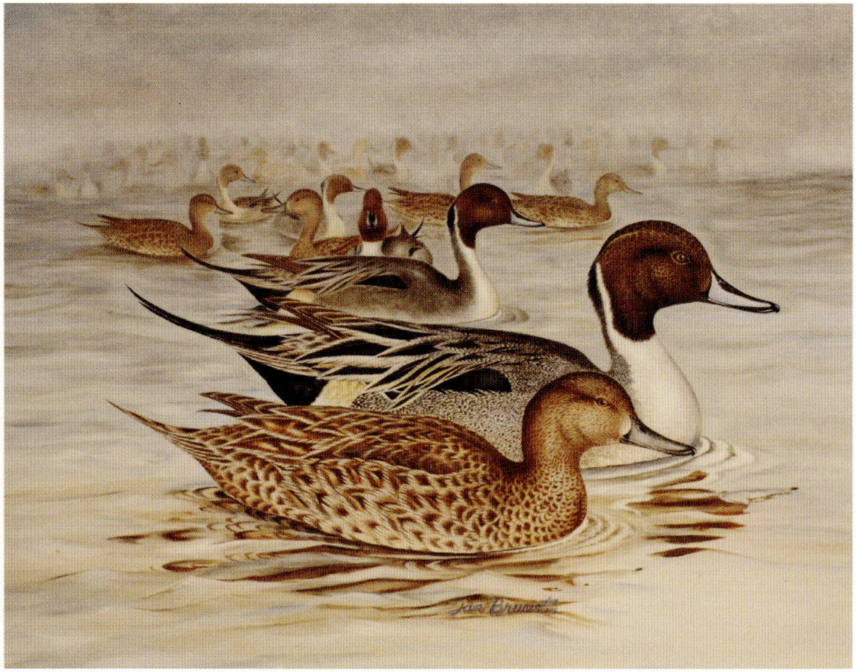

Table of Contents

Opposite page: Tan Brunet's wildfowl paintings

Acknowledgments

Special thanks to my wife Gail; Paul Bourgeois, whose photographs made my book so much better; and the featured carvers who made this project a most pleasurable and educational experience. Special thanks are also due to the UL Press, James Wilson and Michael Martin, my editors, who made this text better, and to Mary Duhé, the layout artist, who deserves full credit for making the book so attractive. Others, who provided invaluable advice, information, inspiration, or technical assistance, which I clearly needed and now thank, are:

Brian Cheramie, Dr. Ken Margolis, Bill Hanemann, Carl Danos, Jean Frank, Wally Gundlach, Peter Waters, Nancy Lewis Hawkins, Megan Lewis, Wendy W. Van Dusen, Chris Weaver, Richard Reeves, Martin St. Romain, Peter Wolf, Charles E. Hawkins IV, Andrew "Tan" Brunet, Willie Badeaux, Matt Lewis, Allan Kancher, Shelia Zeringue, Wayne Frady, and finally, my late brother, Stuart—his memory and our hunting trips together inspired me to write this book

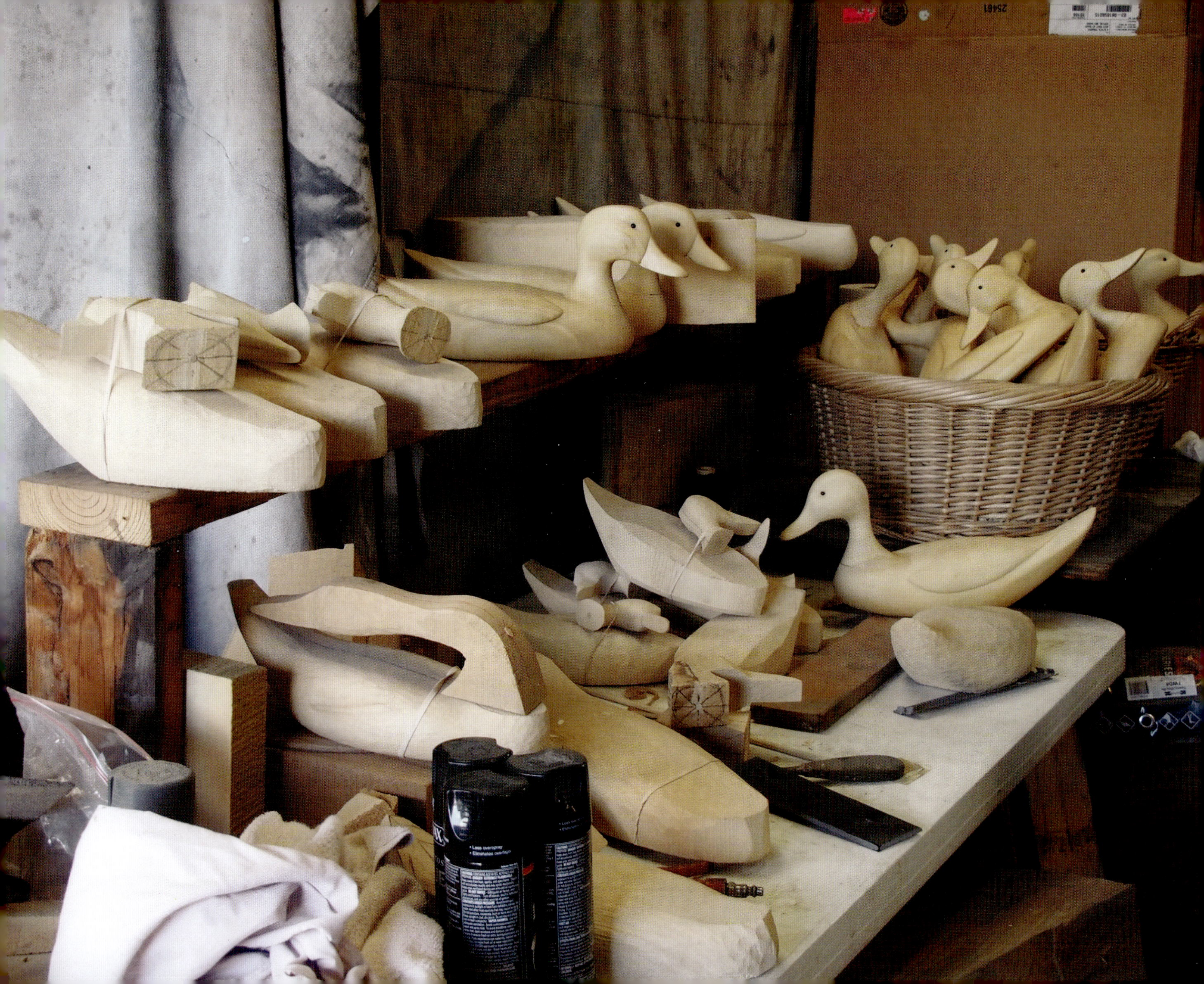

I A Legacy Preserved

Opposite page: Cal Kingsmill's assorted decoys in progress

For many years Louisiana has been known as the "Sportsman's Paradise." This is in large part because of the state's wildfowl hunting, a pervasive part of its heritage and culture. Alongside that hunting tradition there has also developed an artistic legacy carried on by Louisiana's wildfowl decoy carvers. Though their work dates back more than one hundred years, their artistic significance was not recognized until 1975, when Charles Frank released his classic book, *Louisiana Duck Decoys*. By that time, and certainly by the 1980s, most of the state's "old master carvers" had died or stopped carving. Fortunately, many of those old masters passed on their wildfowl artistry to a new generation that has since carried on Louisiana's decoy carving tradition with honor and distinction. Unfortunately, this group has done so largely without the recognition it rightfully deserves. Even decorative carvers who have achieved national prominence by winning state and national competitions have received little or no local press coverage. This book aims to change that.

My interest in and love for Louisiana hunting decoys began in 1975 when I went to buy my wife a bracelet at Adler's, New Orleans's oldest and most respected jewelry store. I don't remember buying my wife's gift that day, but I distinctly recall buying a first edition, paperback copy of Frank's *Louisiana Duck Decoys*, which I still have. I soon began collecting old Louisiana hunting decoys, a hobby that became a passion. Over many years I bought, sold, and traded hundreds of decoys. I stopped collecting old Louisiana hunting decoys in the 1990s when good ones became very scarce—and very expensive. Over the next twenty-five years I sold many of my prize decoys, and my collection is now down to about twenty old hunting decoys.

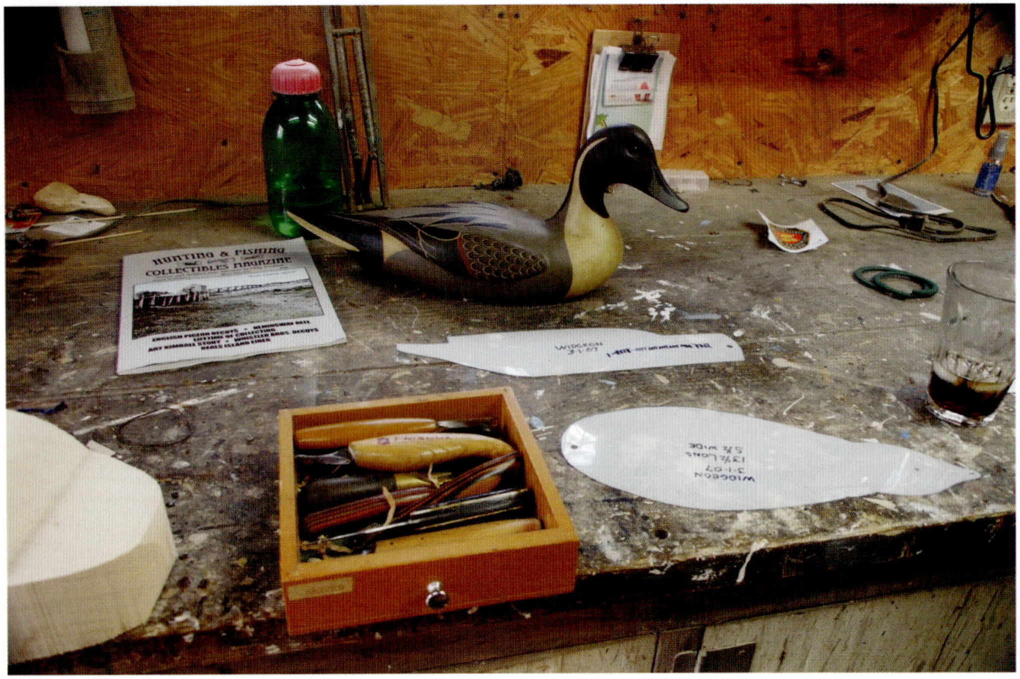

Above: The workshop of a contemporary decoy carver

In a perverse way, it was the remnants of my old hunting decoy collection that caused me to write a book about contemporary Louisiana carvers and their decoys. After I retired from actively practicing law several years ago, I visited my longtime friend Bill Hanemann and brought a Clovis Vizier mallard hen for him to repaint. Besides being a great contemporary carver, Bill is generally acknowledged to be the ultimate authority on Louisiana decoys. He encouraged me to write about contemporary Louisiana carvers and their decoys. At the outset, I knew little about this topic but I quickly became interested, and after meeting and getting to know the carvers I have written about, viewing their incredible artistry, and doing considerable research, I simply fell in love with contemporary Louisiana decoys. In my opinion, good contemporary hunting decoys (like those created by the carvers discussed in this book) are at least as well carved as the old masters' best and, invariably, are better painted. Contemporary decorative wildfowl carvings defy comparison primarily because Clovis Vizier is the only Old Master to carve in this style, and he did so in the 1950s in a very primitive manner.

Louisiana is blessed with many deserving contemporary carvers, and it is not possible to write in detail about all of them in one book. I have selected eighteen of Louisiana's contemporary carvers. Fourteen of those are thought to be a representative cross section of this state's "senior division," along with four of their very talented decoy-carving sons. The selected carvers are all great artists and even better people. A number of them are responsible for resurrecting decoy carving throughout the Gulf Coast in the aftermath of Hurricane Katrina and thus salvaging Louisiana's decoy carving tradition.

Early chapters of this book provide a historical overview of decoy carving in Louisiana and a review of the work of a number of the old master carvers whose work influenced many of the contemporary masters. These chapters also provide background on contemporary carving styles, the contemporary decoy era, and contemporary decoy collecting.

A separate chapter is devoted to each of the contemporary masters except for the three father-son (or -sons) combinations and a pair of brothers; the carver families each share a chapter. Another chapter is about the late Mike Frady, a great carver whose career started during the old masters' era and continued well into the contemporary period. Frady's decoys, his carving lessons, and to some extent his influence, bridges the two periods. Following the contemporary master carver profiles, the next to last chapter examines decoy counterfeiting, a very serious problem that threatens the value of wildfowl decoys, harming both carvers and collectors.[1] This book describes how trafficking in counterfeit decoys works in the real world and also contains suggestions about how to stop it. The final chapter is about the Louisiana Wildfowl Carvers and Collectors Guild, the organization devoted to preserving and promoting decoy carving in Louisiana.

Most of the "next generation contemporary carvers" are now in their late sixties and seventies. All are great wildfowl artists and have earned the right to be called Louisiana's "contemporary masters." Now is the time to spread the word of their exceptional artistry while all but a very few are still carving and their decoys are available to purchase. This recognition is needed before it is too late. Writing this book and collecting contemporary Louisiana decoys has been a gratifying and enlightening experience. It is my sincere hope that all who read this book will have a similar reaction, and that this book will do for Louisiana's contemporary masters what Charles Frank's *Louisiana Duck Decoys* did for the state's old master carvers.

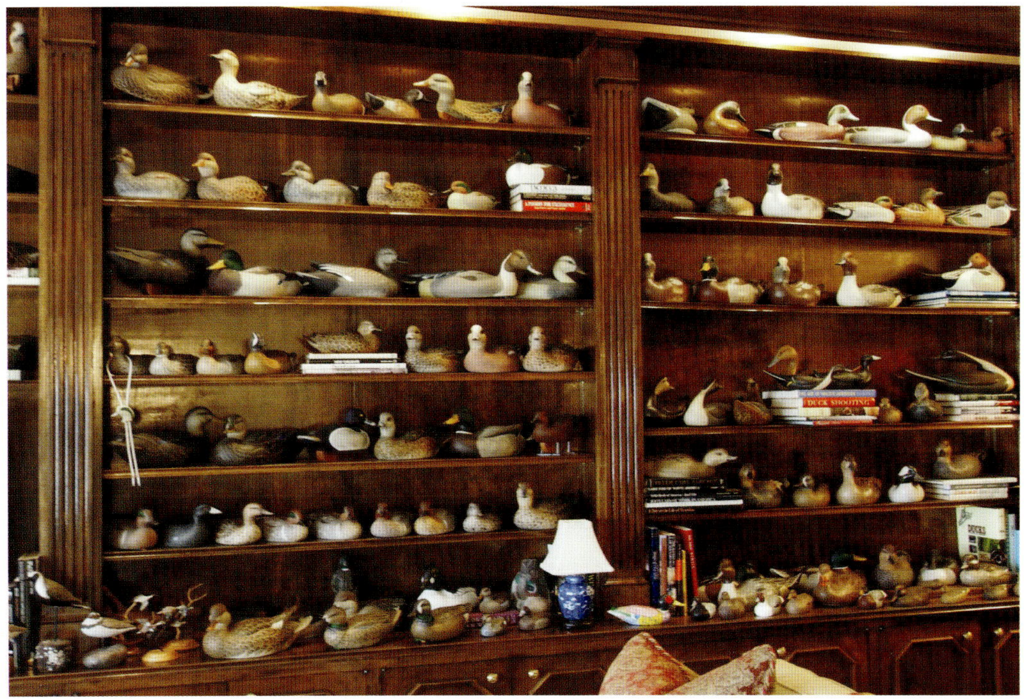

RIGHT: Private collection of contemporary decoys

ENDNOTES

1. Charles Frank Jr., chap. 22 in *Wetland Heritage: The Louisiana Duck Decoy* (Gretna, La.: Pelican Publishing, 1985).

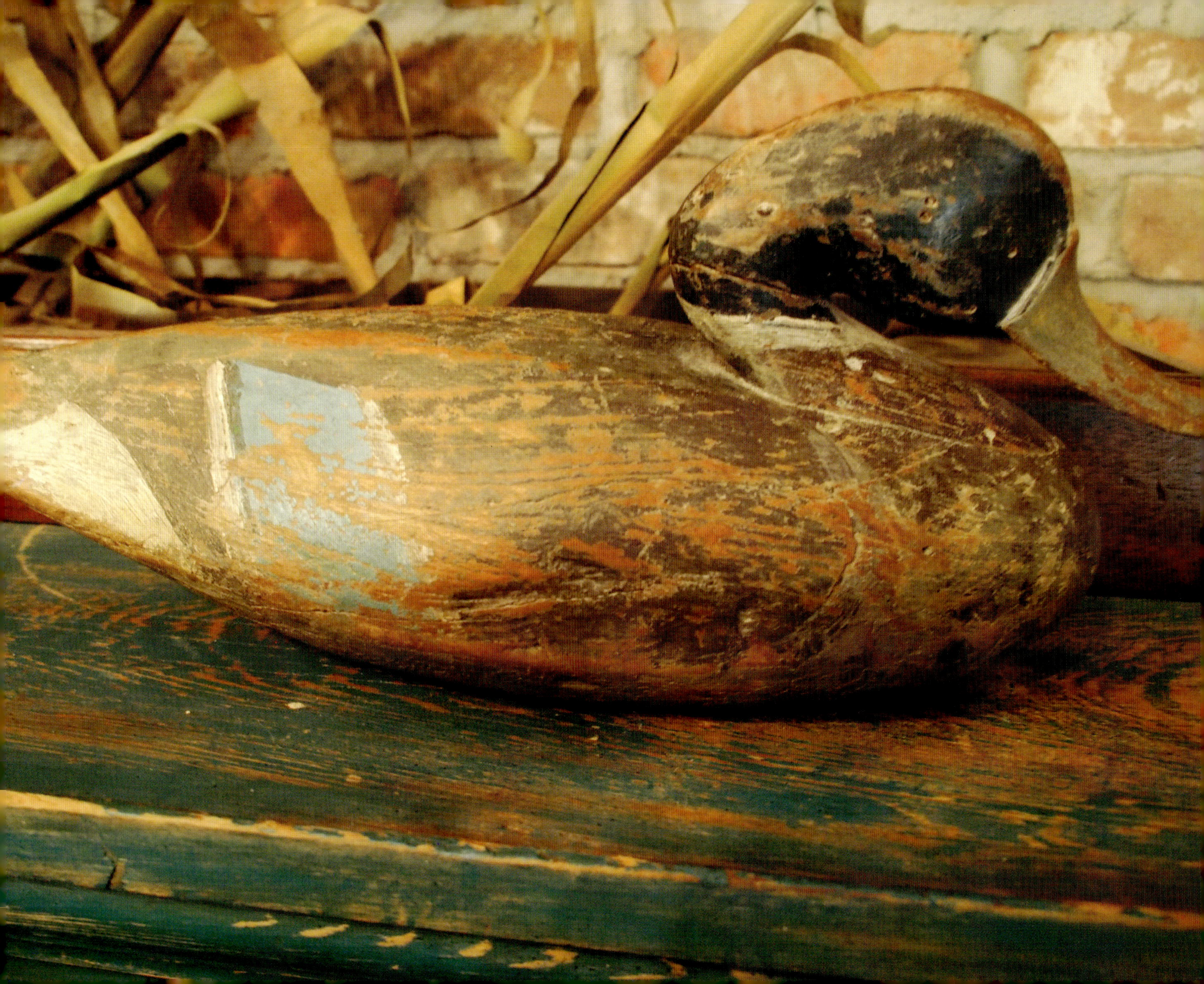

1 Louisiana Decoys
A Historical Overview

Opposite page: Marc Alcide Comardelle's mallard drake decoy

In order to better appreciate the work and motivation of Louisiana's contemporary masters, a basic understanding of the history of decoy carving in Louisiana is essential.

Ducks are sociable and curious creatures. To take advantage of those characteristics, waterfowl hunters for centuries have created decoys to lure ducks within range of their weapons. It wasn't necessary for a decoy to look much like the ducks being hunted—anything that fooled the wildfowl enough to come close enough to shoot was just fine. The first decoys were made by Native Americans thousands of years ago using reeds woven together and filled with feathers. The Native American decoys were crude, but they worked. By the mid-1960s, wildfowl decoys were regarded as museum quality, uniquely American folk art everywhere except Louisiana. Louisiana-made hunting decoys were denied like recognition at that time because two misinformed East Coast decoy authorities and their museum curator friend didn't think Louisiana carvers' decoys were worthy (as discussed below).[1]

In Louisiana, the earliest hunting decoys date back to the nineteenth century. These early decoys were made of either cypress or tupelo gum wood. The head and body were carved separately and, when finished, joined together with wooden pegs. The early Louisiana carvers' primitive tools included hatchets, hammers, files, rasps, and knives.[2] Some carvers used oyster shells like sandpaper to smooth their decoys and often used duck feathers to finish painting them. From the late nineteenth century onward, decoys produced by some Louisiana carvers rivaled the best of those carved anywhere in the United States, but the Louisiana carvers and their decoys were largely ignored beyond the state's boundaries until 1975, when Charles Frank Jr. published *The Louisiana Duck Decoy*.

In fact, as late as 1934 there was doubt that there were any decoy carvers in Louisiana at all. That year, Joel Barber, then America's foremost decoy collector and authority, wrote in his highly regarded book *Wild Fowl Decoys*: "That great region lying . . . west along the Gulf of Mexico has never gone in for native decoy making." Barber then said he never found any "decoys of hand hewn cypress [made] by denizens of the Bayous . . . or great marshes of the delta of the Mississippi."[3] Thirty-two years later, William F. Mackey Jr., Barber's successor as this country's greatest decoy collector and an even greater decoy authority, authored *American Bird Decoys*, in which he damned Louisiana decoys and carvers .[4] He explained that no Louisiana decoys were "shown [in his book] because their workmanship does not compare with that of the decoys from the areas included, which are generally recognized as collectible. Hundreds of crude Gulf coast cypress duck decoys have been reviewed and found wanting. Perhaps, some may be attracted by their crude form but the vast majority of this country's collectors have passed them by. They simply lack decoy appeal."[5]

Barber's belief that Louisiana had no indigenous decoy carvers and Mackey's later view that Louisiana's decoys were crude and lacked appeal were firmly refuted by Frank's *Louisiana Duck Decoys*, which even includes a chapter entitled "Why Louisiana Decoys Merit Our Attention." There, Frank points out where and why Barber and Mackey went wrong; including the fact that Mackey apparently quit looking for decoys somewhere north of Natchez, Mississippi. *Louisiana Duck Decoys* lists over 130 Louisiana carvers working before 1965 (many as far back as the latter part of the nineteenth century) who produced extraordinary decoys. In fact, in 1949 a mallard pair produced by Lifelike Lures, Bob Couret's decoy making factory in New Orleans, took first prize in the Professional Machine Made Class at the International Decoy Maker's contest

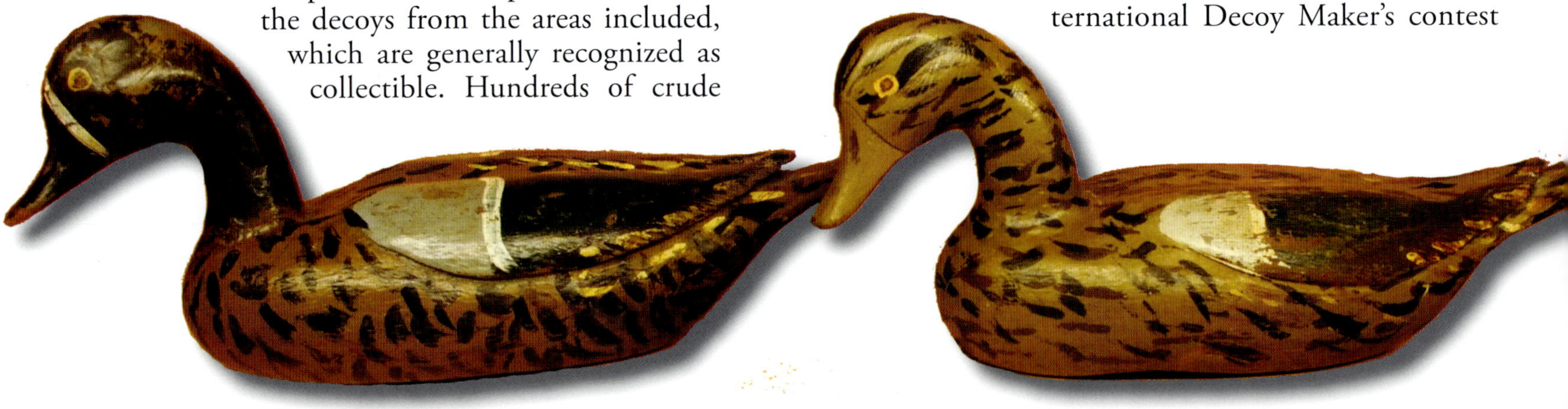

Blue-winged teal pair carved by Xavier Bourg

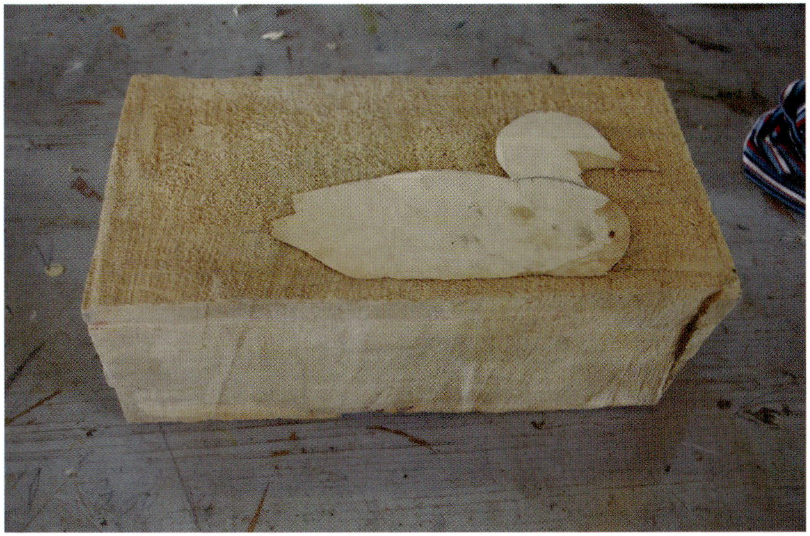

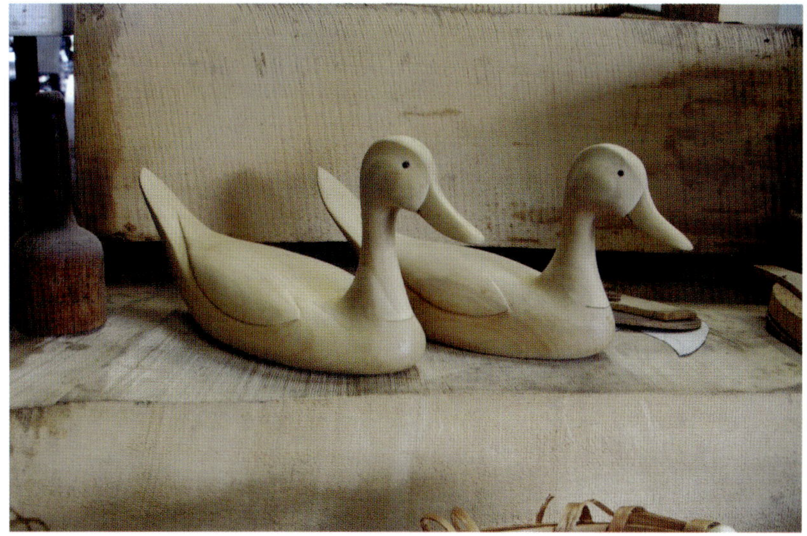

A decoy pattern is laid on a solid block of wood and eventually carved down to resemble the decoys that appear right

in New York.[6] Clovis Vizier, from Galliano, Louisiana, a small town on Bayou Lafourche, entered a pair of mallards in the 1951 North American Decoy Makers Contest and won second prize. In 1985, Frank authored another book, *Wetland Heritage: The Louisiana Duck Decoy*, which identifies additional Louisiana decoy carvers who made gorgeous decoys, many of whom were active long before and/or at the time of Mackey's book.

The most comprehensive and best-illustrated book on old Louisiana decoys is Brian Cheramie's *Louisiana Lures and Legends*, published in 1997. Cheramie is extraordinarily knowledgeable and owns the finest and likely the largest collection of old Louisiana decoys. His book depicts and describes the true artistry of Louisiana's old decoy carvers, and he too conclusively proves that Mackey was wrong in his assessment of their skill level.

Alan Haid, a nationally recognized decoy expert, published *Decoys of the Mississippi Flyway* in 1981. Haid's book contains a fully-illustrated chapter featuring Louisiana carvers and decoys that Haid describes with numerous superlatives, such as "fine," "high quality," and "superbly styled."

In 1983, Gene Kangas, another highly regarded national decoy expert, wrote *Decoys: A North American Survey*. It is described as "the first publication to encompass all of the major decoy making area of North America." This book gives an exceptional overview of hunting decoys nationwide. Chapter 18 is devoted to Louisiana decoys,

A fine, full-bodied pintail drake
likely carved by Charles Joefrau of the Lafrance Group

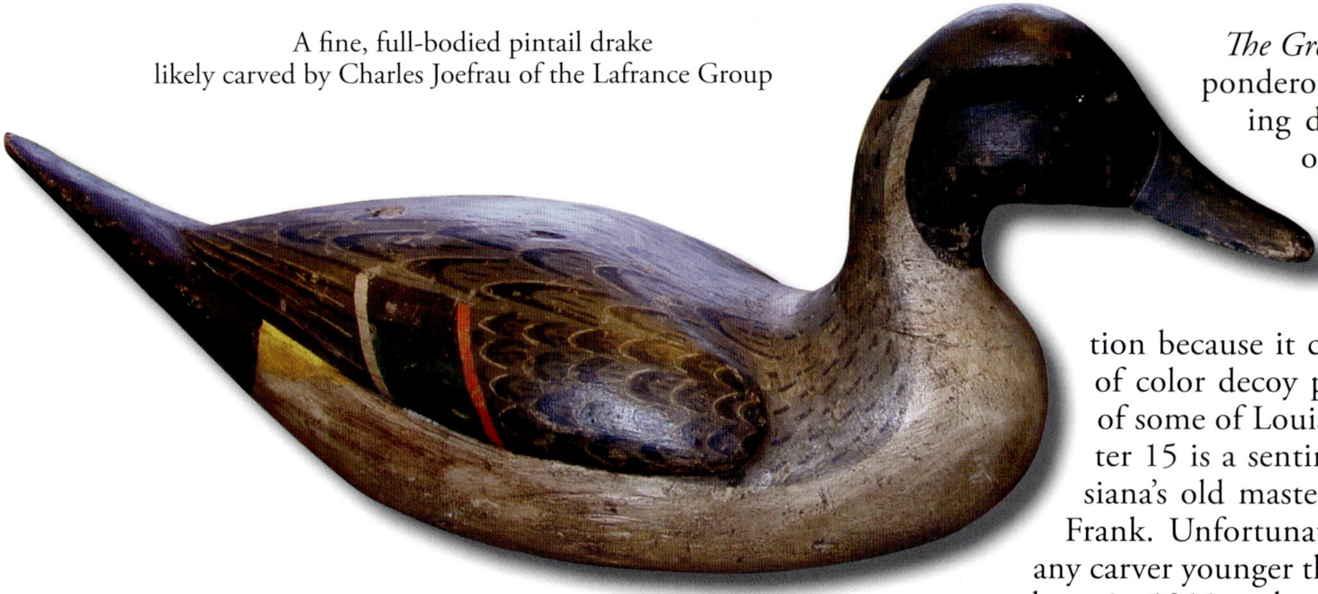

The Great Book of Wildfowl Decoys is a ponderous compilation of mostly hunting decoys from twenty-two states or areas in the United States, Canada, and Europe where decoy carving was popular. This book, published in 1990, deserves special mention because it contains an incredible number of color decoy photographs, including fifteen of some of Louisiana's very best decoys. Chapter 15 is a sentimental discussion about Louisiana's old master carvers authored by Charles Frank. Unfortunately, there is no discussion of any carver younger than James Curtis Roussel, who was born in 1911 and started carving in 1930, eighty-six years ago.

which Kangas describes as "Distinctly unique" and "one of the more 'recent' areas to be discovered . . . as being a major decoy producing region . . . teeming with extraordinary duck decoys." Kangas skewered Mackey for his negative view of Louisiana decoys.[7] He described Louisiana hunting decoys as having "exciting spontaneity of form and fluid painting patterns. . . . The typical Louisiana decoy was almost always carved solid due to their rather exotic woods (cypress, willow, and tupelo gum), which are extremely light in weight . . . the majority being small, low backed, and flat bottom designed for quiet water shooting. Relief carved wings are prevalent, paint styles are often bold and include detailed wing, tail, and feather patterns." Kangas's book beautifully illustrates this point with thirty-two black and white decoy photographs carved by virtually all of Louisiana's old masters.

Any lingering doubt that Louisiana's old hunting decoy carvers rank among this country's very best should be completely removed by Loy S. Harrell Jr.'s book, *Decoys: North America's One Hundred Greatest*, published in 2000. This authoritative text pictures decoys by Clovis "Cadise" Vizier, Nicole Vidacovich Sr., and Victor Alfonso, and lists them among the one hundred best ever carved in this country. Also included are decoys by Cobb, Shang Wheeler, the Ward brothers, Shourds, Crowell, Perdew, and Dudley—all acknowledged to be the best non-Louisiana carvers who ever lived. These men were contemporaries of the three Louisiana carvers whose artistic ability certainly matched, if not exceeded, theirs as did the other great old Louisiana carving masters discussed in the books previously mentioned.

Knowledgeable collectors of old Louisiana decoys believe that the era of the old masters and their decoys ended in the 1950s, done-in by synthetic decoys, a byproduct of the World War II. Decoy making in Louisiana continued in the years that followed, but by the mid-1980s almost all of Louisiana's great old master carvers had died or quit carving. As we shall see in the chapters that follow, their artistic talent was passed on to the next generation of carvers, especially those featured in this book. These and other fine Louisiana contemporary carvers took the art of the decoy to a whole new level. Their well-done decorative decoys were the wooden counterparts of any taxidermist's best work. In the view of many knowledgeable observers, their working decoys are better carved and painted than many of the old masters' decoys.

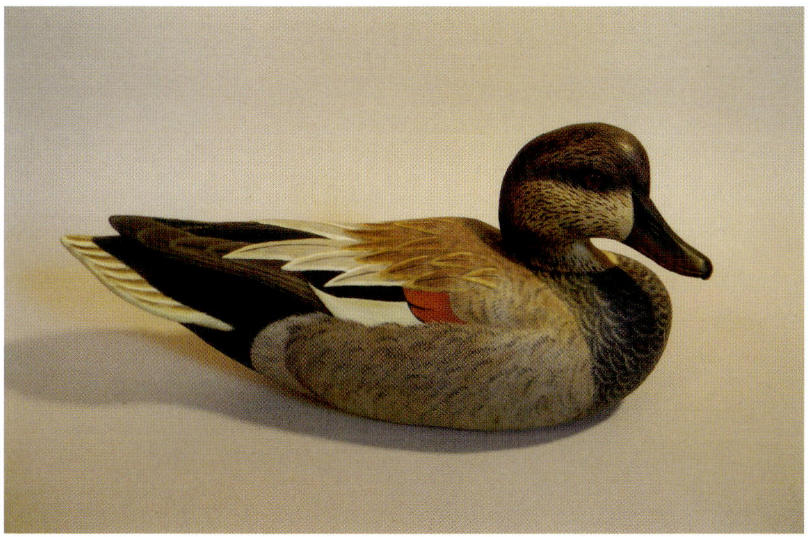

An example of a contemporary decoy,
a gadwall carved by Rock Zeringue

The most interesting recent development has been the significant increase in demand for wooden decoys to hunt over. Today, many Louisiana contemporary carvers are making the same style "no frills" hunting decoys that their artistic forbearers made well over a hundred years ago. Some hunters argue that these contemporary hunting decoys are more effective lures than the old hunting decoys because they are more realistic. There is little dispute that contemporary hunting decoys perform better than decoys made of rubber or molded plastic because they float more naturally and do not wobble in windy conditions like their non-wooden counterparts. Moreover, wooden decoys do not sink when hit by errant pellets. In any event, there is substantial demand for wooden hunting decoys and contemporary working decoy carvers are once again very busy filling orders.

Endnotes

1. Adele Earnest, *The Art of the Decoy: American Bird Carvings* (New York: C.N Potter, 1965), 38.
2. Frank, *Wetland Heritage*, 116.
3. Joel Barber, *Wild Fowl Decoys* (New York: Derrydale Press, 2000), 146.
4. William F. Mackey Jr., *American Bird Decoys: The Authoritative Story of Our Classic Bird Decoys and their Colorful Makers* (Bonanza Books, 1965).
5. Mackey, *American Bird Decoys*, 33.
6. 1996-97 Decoy Collector's Guide, 114.
7. Gene Kangas, *Decoys: A North American Survey* (Spanish Fork, Utah, Hillcrest Publications, 1983) 250.

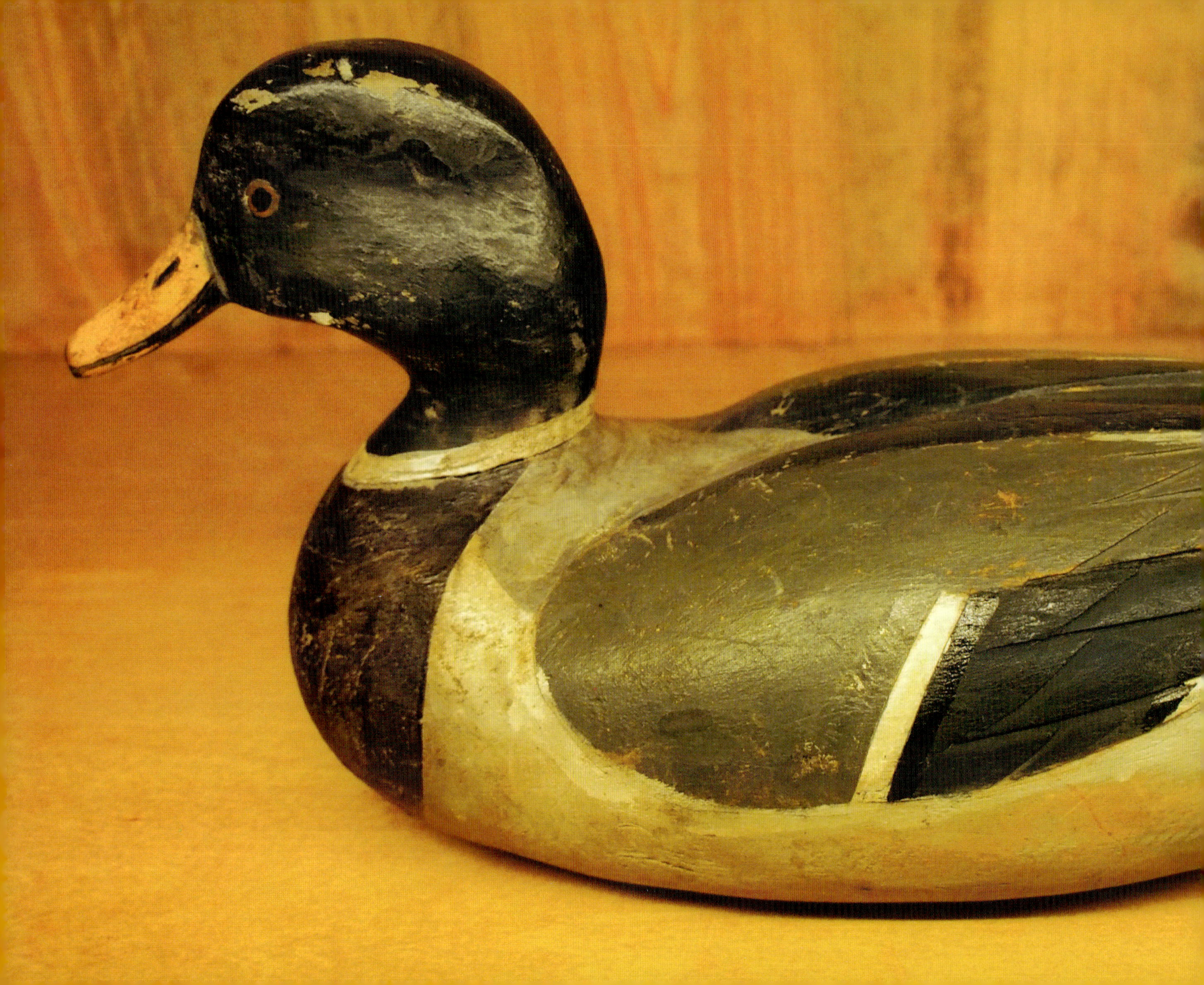

OPPOSITE PAGE: Clovis Vizier's mallard drake decoy

2 SELECT OLD MASTERS: *The Early Mentors*

The six old Louisiana master carvers chosen for discussion in this chapter are significant for not only their own work in decoy carving, but also for their tutoring and influence on many of the contemporary carvers discussed in later chapters. The selected old masters are:

- Clovis Vizier (1885-1975),
- Reme Angé Roussel (1903-1972),
- Marc Alcide Comardelle (1890-1955),
- Mark Whipple (1884-1961),
- the collaborative team of Mitchell Lafrance (1882-1979), George Frederick Jr. (1907-1997), and Charles Numa Joefrau (1913-1983),
- Nicole Vidacovich (1853-1945).

For the most part, these old master carvers were self-taught hunters and guides. Their classrooms were Louisiana's coastal marshes, where vast numbers of waterfowl spent the winter months feasting on aquatic plants that grew abundantly in the sweet water ponds. The large concentration of wildfowl provided food for the hunter/carver and his family and employment as a guide at one of the area's numerous private hunting clubs. Their day lasted as many hours as it took for them or the "swells," (the clients they were guiding) to kill as many ducks as they wanted, as there existed no limits then. These men spent countless hours over many years watching, at close range, ducks and geese floating on the ponds or approaching the blinds with wings cupped, ready to land. During the off-season those retained images

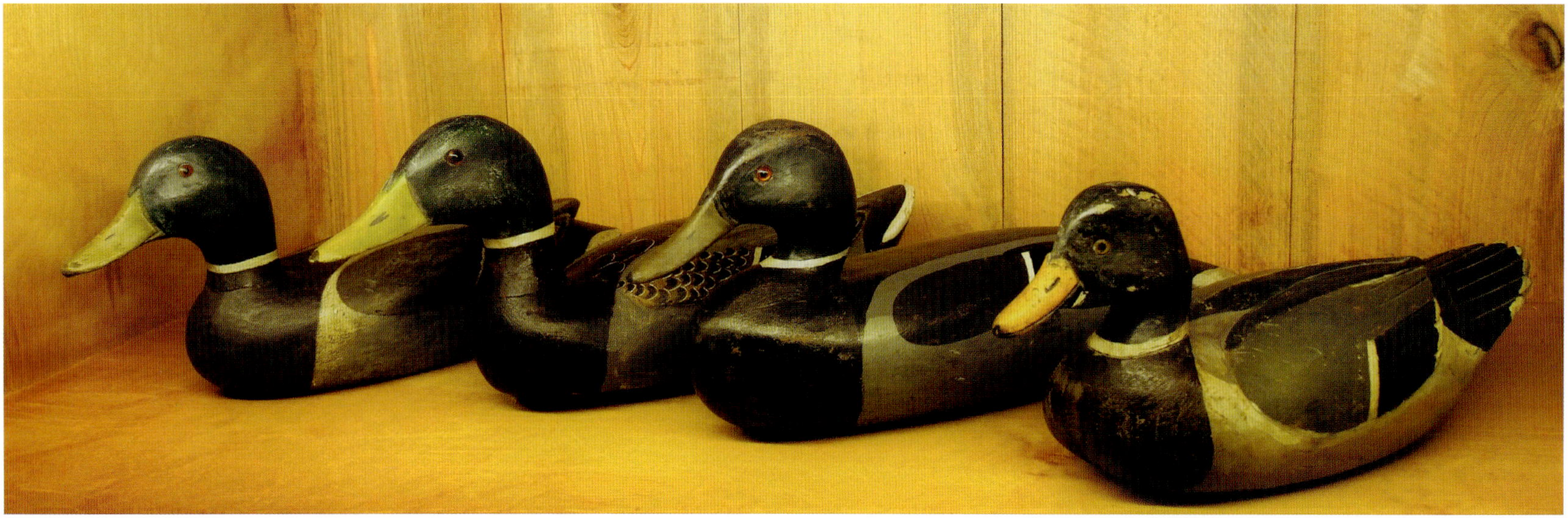

Mallard drake decoys carved by old master carvers, from left to right: Roussel, Lafrance, Whipple, and Vizier

guided the old masters' hands as they carved and painted their hunting decoys.

The main objective of all of the old masters was to carve and paint a decoy that lured the prey within gunning range. They had no intention of producing an identical replica of the real thing. Decoys were quite simply hunting tools—like a shotgun, shell bucket, duck call, or a pirogue. Their decoys were made to look how real ducks in the wild looked to them. In many respects, these old Louisiana decoy makers were the wood-carving equivalent of the French Impressionist Painters.

Study the accompanying photographs of the selected old masters' decoys, and it is unlikely that you will find many similarities. Their decoys were not intended as works of art but they certainly achieved folk art status and have been widely displayed in numerous prestigious museums, including the New Orleans Museum of Art and the Historic New Orleans Collection. Tragically, this recognition came after most of the old masters had died.[1]

Fortunately, this select group of the old master carvers shared their knowledge and carving techniques with younger men who perpetuated the decoy's hallowed place in Louisiana's culture. Most of the old master carvers' pupils were family members but some were just friends. Clovis Vizier and his brother Odee (1890-1969) taught Odee's son, Jimmy Vizier (1933-2010), and Jimmy's cousin, Tan Brunet, how to carve and paint hunting decoys. The two younger men transitioned into carving decorative decoys for which they earned world-class status and recognition. Tan continued the mentoring role with his two sons, Jett and Jude, who continued the family tradition by each winning multiple national decoy carving championships.

Clovis Vizier's decoys are generally smaller and more elaborately carved than those produced by his contemporaries. A pair of mallards shown in photograph 1 has been selected as representative of Vizier's duck decoys. Their bodies are full and the bottoms are flat, as was his carving style. Vizier did not use patterns. He let the size and shape of the wood, either cypress or tupelo gum, dictate the size and shape of the decoy he was carving.[2] Unlike many other carvers, Vizier typically painted the eyes on his decoys instead of using glass. The feathers on both of the decoys' wings, particularly the primaries and speculum (brightest colored wing feathers), were not only undercut but also rather deeply etched and raised above each decoy's body. The tail feathers on Vizier's mallard drake are even more deeply etched out. On close examination, one can see the outline of feathers on the wings and bodies of both decoys. The mallard hen has even more etched feathering, particularly on her head. The drake's tail feathers are rather deeply etched and the hen's less so. The detailed feathering, especially on the wings, gives Vizier's decoys a more decorative look than those of the other old master carvers and makes it easy to see why his decoys won second place in a 1951 national decoy carving contest and are greatly prized by knowledgeable collectors.

Vizier carved decoys in various poses, including some with turned heads, some preening, and others in full flight. He also carved boats and bald eagles.[3] While Vizier's protégés utilized and greatly improved upon this old master's detailed carving style, they did not adopt his practice of carving stout, flat-bottomed, and undersized decoys. Tragically, Vizier suffered a debilitating stroke in 1957 at age seventy-one and was no longer able to carve after that, although he lived another nineteen years.[4] Vizier was truly one of Louisiana's great carvers and mentors.

Raceland's Reme Angé Roussel Jr. was born, raised, and lived near Bayou Lafourche, about thirty-five miles upstream from Clovis Vizier's home in Galliano. Charlie Frank called Roussel "a master carver . . . whose artistry was held in universal respect. . . . He was a self-taught artist . . . [and] with the simplest of tools he fashioned the most magnificent floating sculpture."[5] Roussel's decoys were exquisitely carved with raised wings and detailed carving of the heads. While most other old master carvers depicted the decoy's nostrils with a simple thin painted line on the decoy's bill, Roussel often carved out the nostrils, as he did on the teal drake shown in photograph 2.

While the painting on his earlier decoys was much simpler, Roussel's later painting style included full body feathering and wing detailing, as shown in photograph 3 of a blue-winged teal drake and hen. Like virtually all other Louisiana carvers, Roussel used cypress and tupelo gum to make his decoys. Other masters used the shape of the wood to dictate the shape of their decoys but Roussel shaped his decoys by using patterns—simple pencil drawings on a sheet of paper. He would then lay the patterns on a block of wood and cut out the head and body separately with a band saw.

In *Louisiana Lures and Legends*, Brian Cheramie says that "Roussel's decoys had three distinguishing features that were common to all of the species he carved except his coots. The heads of his decoys are erect and looking straight ahead in

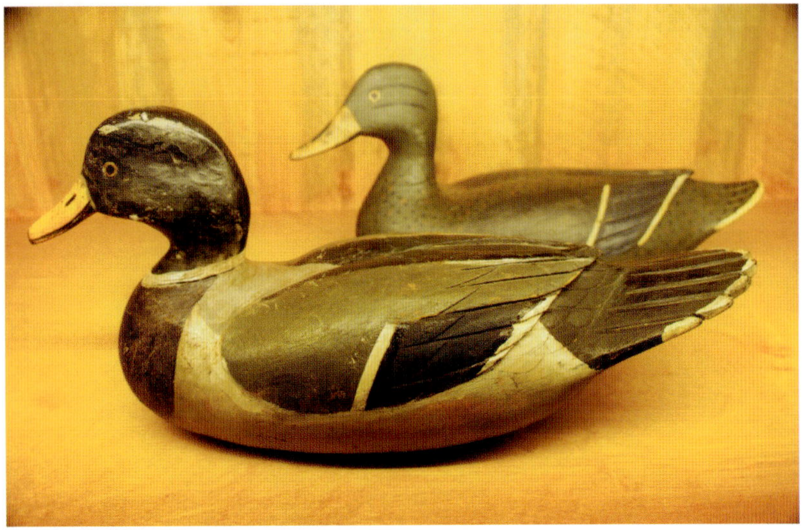

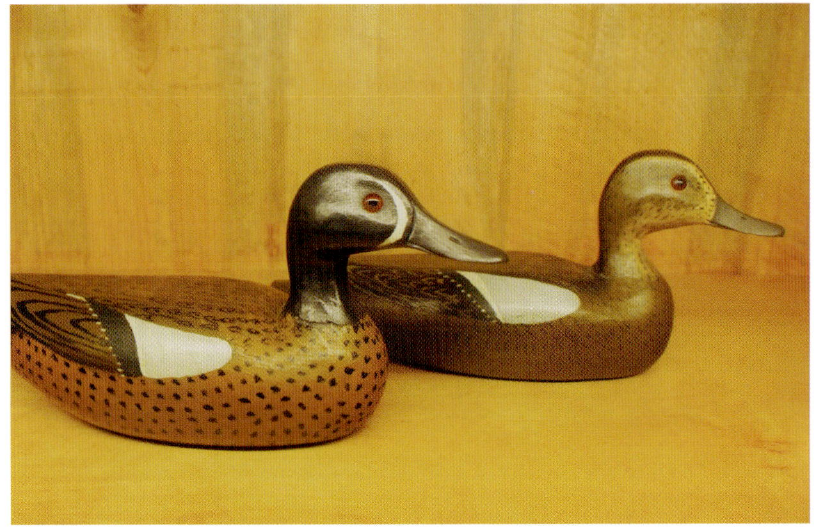

Left: (1) Pair of Vizier mallards
Above: (3) Pair of Roussel blue-winged teal

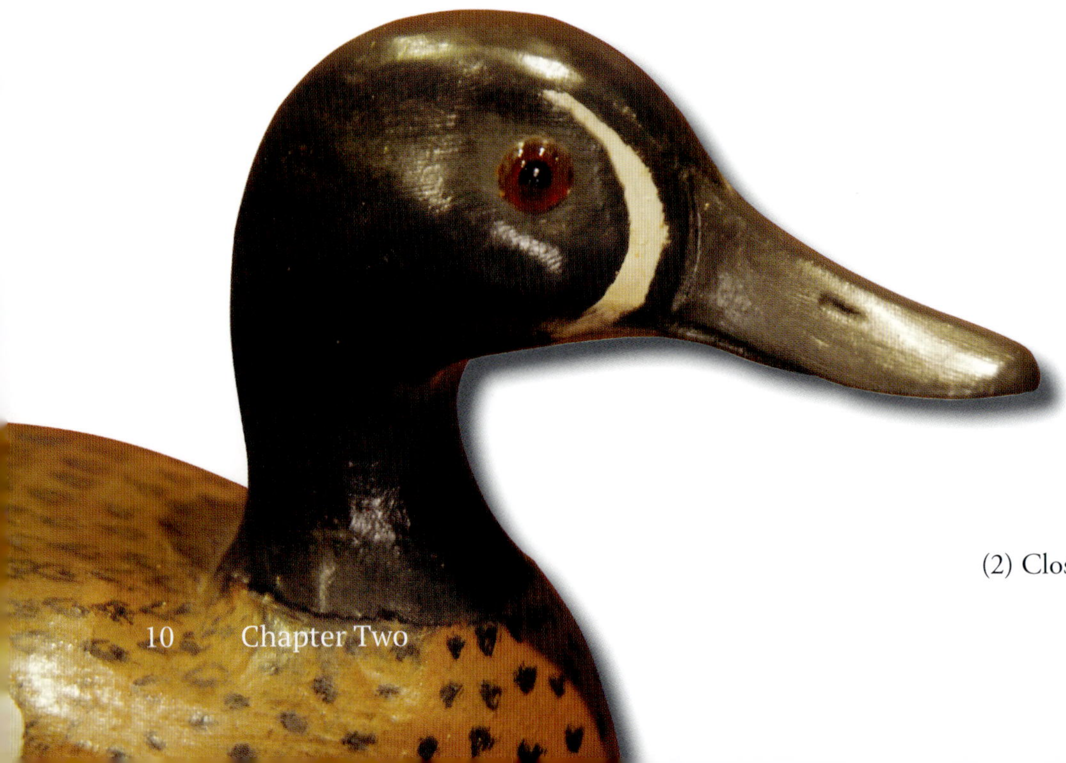

(2) Close-up of Roussel teal drake with carved out nostrils

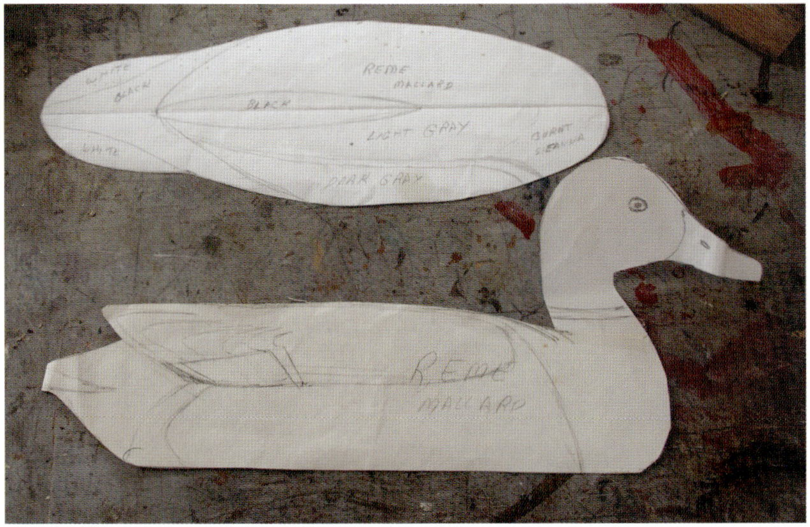

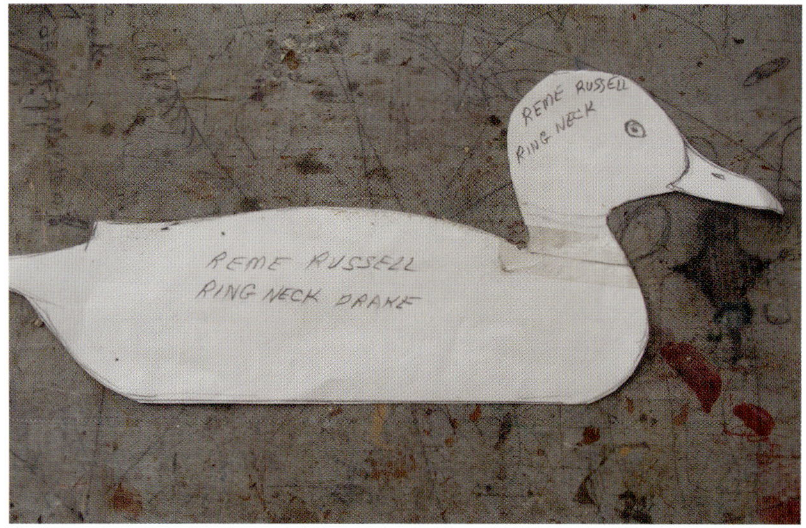

(4 & 5) Roussel's decoy patterns; (6) BOTTOM RIGHT: Badeaux's scaup

the so called 'gunner pose.' The wing tips are elevated and there is feather detailing over the decoy's entire body except on the bottom."[6]

One of Roussel's best—and probably his most successful—carving pupil, Willie Badeaux, is one of the contemporary masters featured in this book. The two men remained close until Roussel's death. Badeaux inherited many of this old master's patterns, some of which are shown above in photographs 4 and 5. Note the patterns containing painting instructions for the species to be carved. There is an understandable similarity in the two masters' carving style, seen particularly in Badeaux's early decoys. Badeaux's later decoys, however, are far more ornately carved and painted than his mentor's, as photograph 6 depicts.

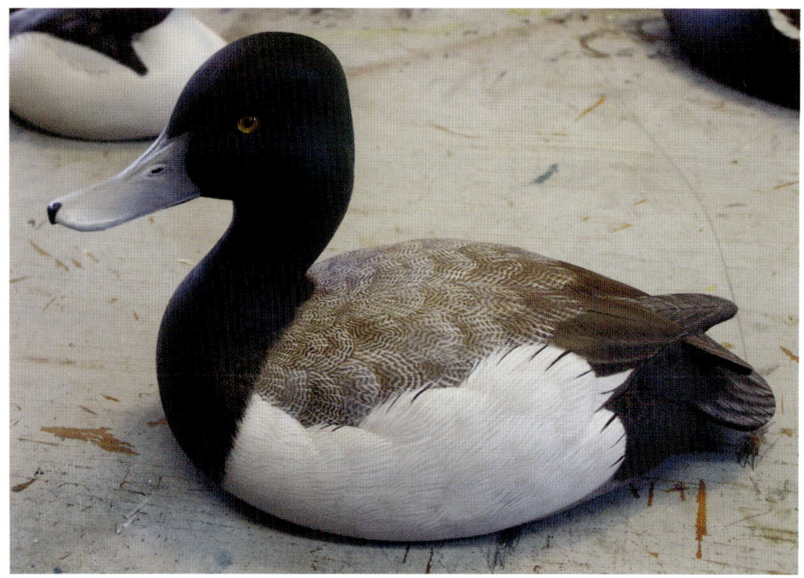

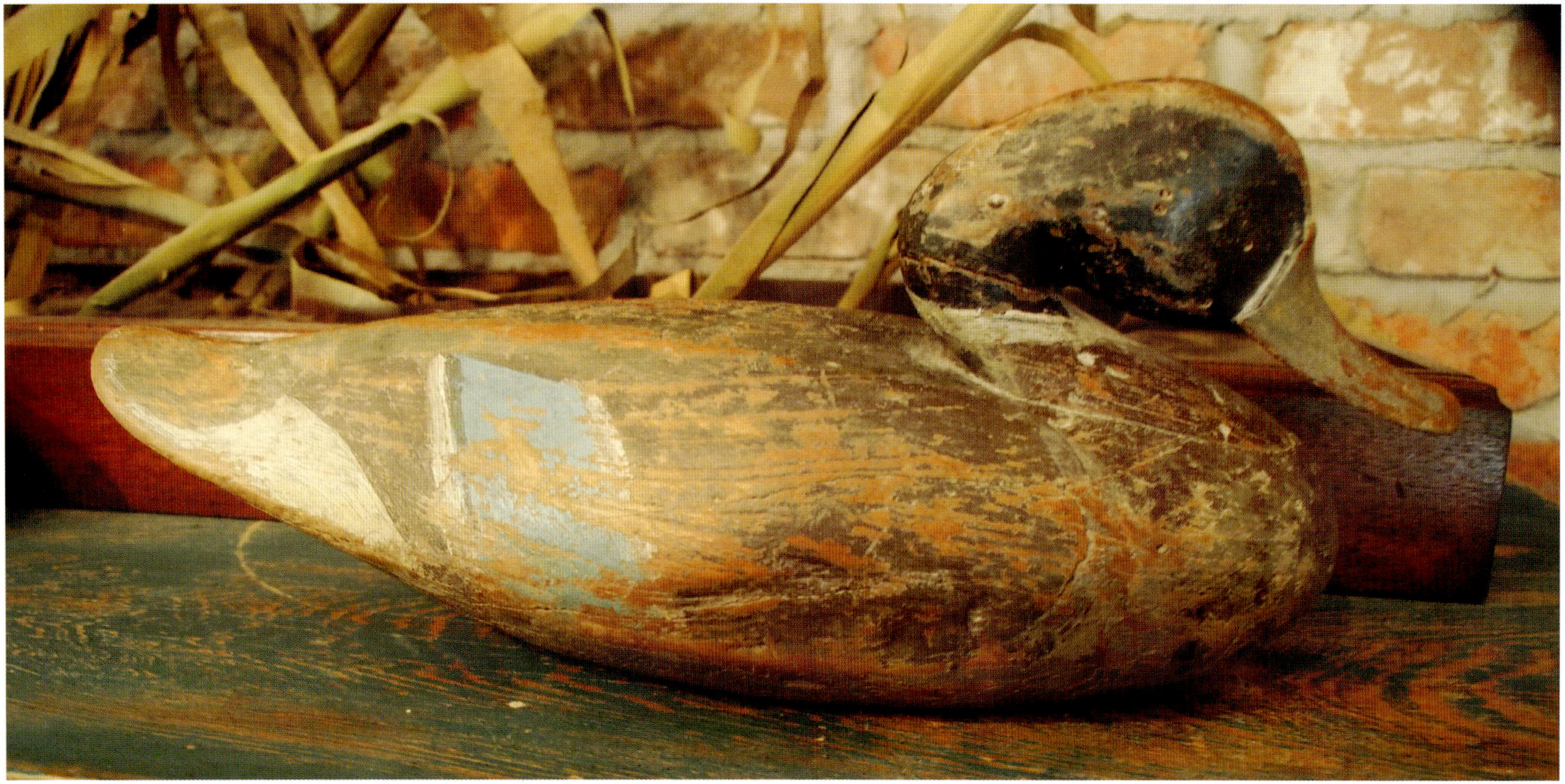

(7) A mallard drake decoy carved by Marc Alcide Comardelle

Badeaux was also influenced and inspired by his wife's uncle, Marc Alcide Comardelle, known to all as "Alcide." Comardelle was the head guide at a hunting club located at Simoneaux Pond. He was also a market hunter, trapper, fisherman, and decoy carver, and he frequently guided author Charlie Frank, who wrote a whole chapter about Comardelle in *Wetland's Heritage*.[7] "Many of [Alcide's] large decoys were carved with a curved neck as if the bird was oiling his breast feathers," Frank wrote. "He finished his decoys with a simple paint scheme in bold, natural colors. . . . His trademark crooked neck tilting to the back of the bird made for a compact decoy in the marsh."[8] The elongated, crooked neck on Comardelle's decoys resemble some of Victor Alfonso's decoys. The body of Comardelle's decoy is also reminiscent of Mark Whipple's because of the broad base head/body joint and the exaggerated breast as photograph 7 depicts.

Mark Whipple's decoys differ greatly in appearance from Vidacovich's and the other master carvers. Generally, the heads of Whipple's decoys were not as erect as the other carvers, and the breasts of his decoys were exaggerated and more prominent than in other carvers' style, perhaps except for Alcide Comardelle. These very distinguishing characteristics give Whipple's decoys the appearance of being at ease. More important, the extended breast had a practical purpose; it created a larger base where the head of the decoy was attached to the body. This feature allowed Whipple to make the strongest head-body joint of any of the old master carvers. It should also be noted that there is no carving on the body of Whipple's decoys and his paint patterns are very simple. He made no attempt to delineate the individual primary feathers, but he did paint the speculum on his mallards, pintails, and ring-neckeds using a slash of color between two white lines for this purpose. He also used two wider black lines in a "V" shape to separate the primary and the tail feathers. Photograph 8 shows a very fine pair of Whipple mallards and illustrates all of features described above.

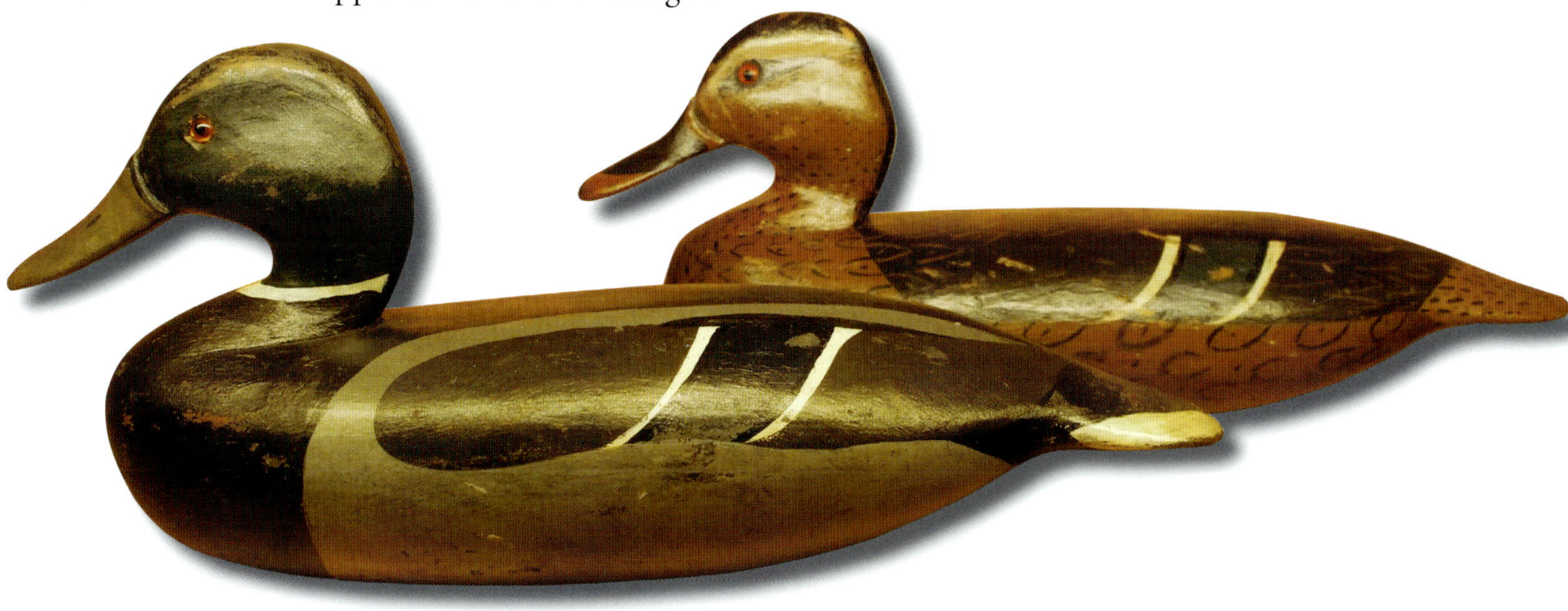

(8) A mallard pair carved by Mark Whipple

Mitchel Lafrance, Charles Joefrau, and George Frederick Jr. were three master carvers who frequently worked together. These men produced wonderful decoys of many species, especially mallards, pintails, and blue-winged teal. Their decoys came in varying shapes, poses, and sizes because they did not use patterns to cut out their decoys. Instead, the size and shape of the cypress and tupelo gum they chose dictated the decoys they carved. While most old masters put the head facing straight ahead or in "gunner pose," this group frequently carved their decoys with turned heads, or as "preeners," where the decoy's head and extended neck are turned back over the body. The trio also created the "minnie chaser" pose, where the decoy's neck is extended forward of the body just above the surface of the water. Another factor influencing the size, shape, and pose was which of the trio did the carving. Joefrau's decoys were generally more full bodied and frequently had upswept tails, especially his pintail drakes as demonstrated on page 4 and in photograph 9. LaFrance's decoys tended to have thinner bodies than those carved by Joefrau as shown in photograph 10.

Top: (9) Pintail drake by Lafrance group
Bottom: (10) Pintail hen by Lafrance group

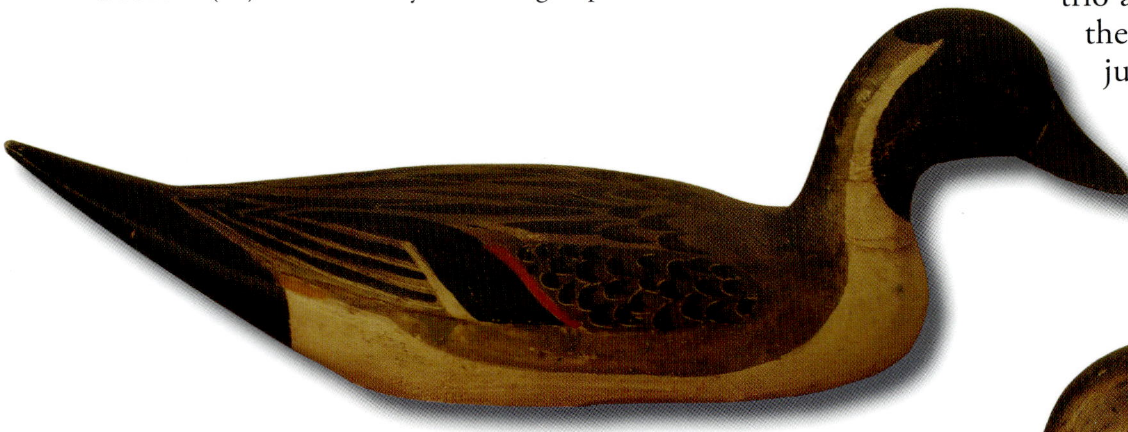

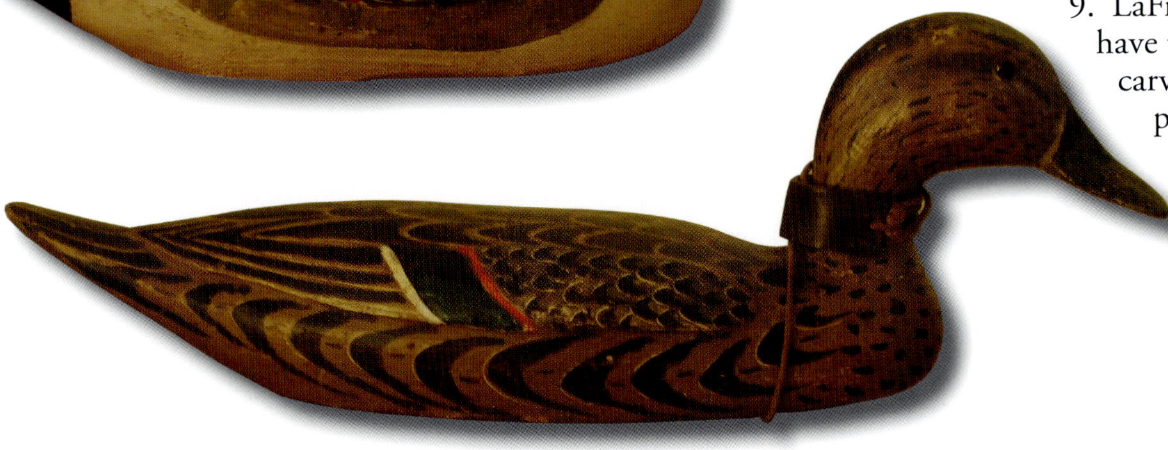

The trio perfected "scratch painting," certainly one of the most distinguishing features of their decoys. Scratch painting is a four-step process as illustrated in photograph 11. A white base coat is first applied and allowed to dry. Then a second coat of a slightly darker color is applied. While this second coat of paint is still wet, a sharp object like a heated ice pick is used to etch or scribe out different size semicircular shapes on the decoy's wings and body to simulate feathers. After the second coat dries, a very dark color, usually black, is applied to outline and emphasize these semicircular feathers. These features are clearly shown on the mallard hen shown in photograph 12.

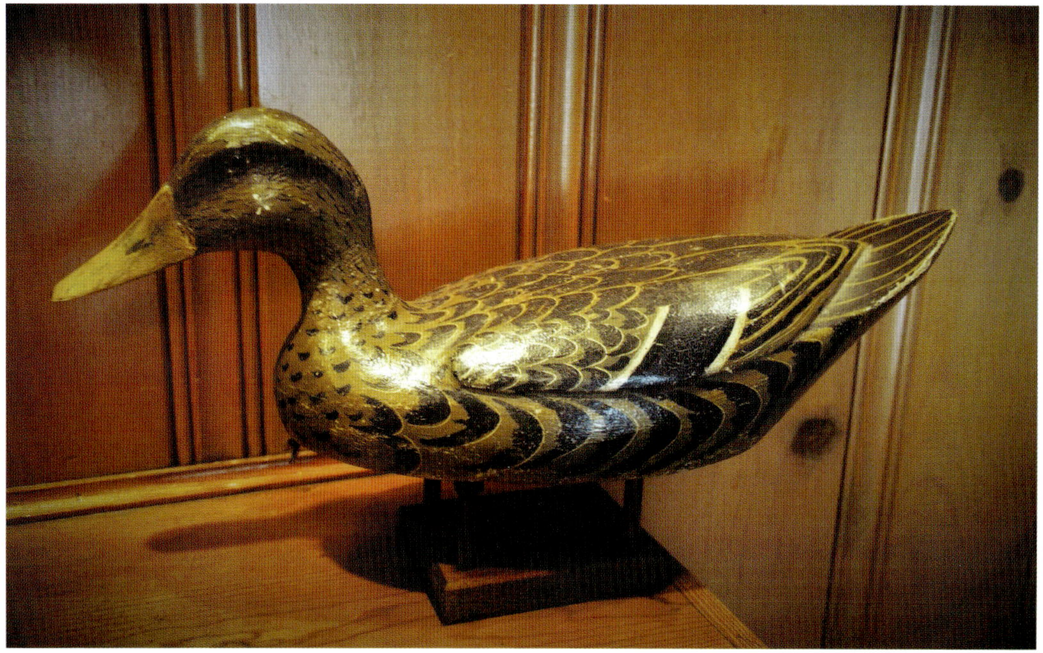

(12) Lafrance group mallard hen, likely carved by Joefrau

The trio, especially Lafrance, respectfully referred to as "Mr. Mitchell," greatly influenced two generations of the Hutchison family, brothers Rudolph and Charles, now both deceased, and Charles's son, Eric (born 1957), a contemporary master. Eric spent many hours in Mr. Mitchell's carving and painting classes. Besides Eric, contemporary masters Bill Hanemann and Cal Kingsmill were also influenced by this trio, as is clearly reflected in the scratch painting style that all three customarily use.

Nicole Vidacovich influenced the carving styles of all of the featured contemporary masters, especially Bill Hanemann and Cal Kingsmill. Vidacovich's decoys were elegantly shaped and simply carved as photograph 13 il-

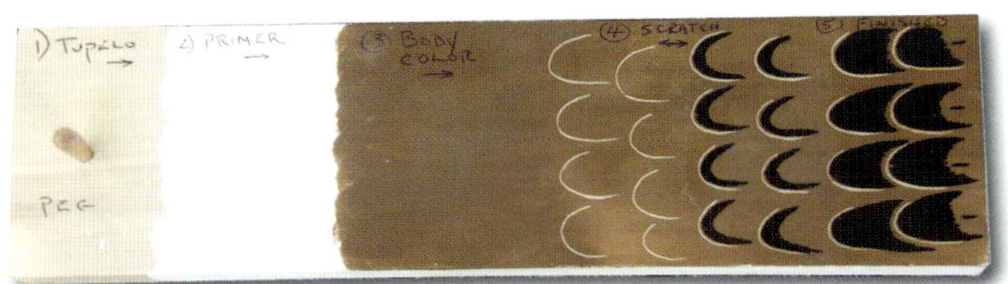

(11) Sample of the scratch painting process

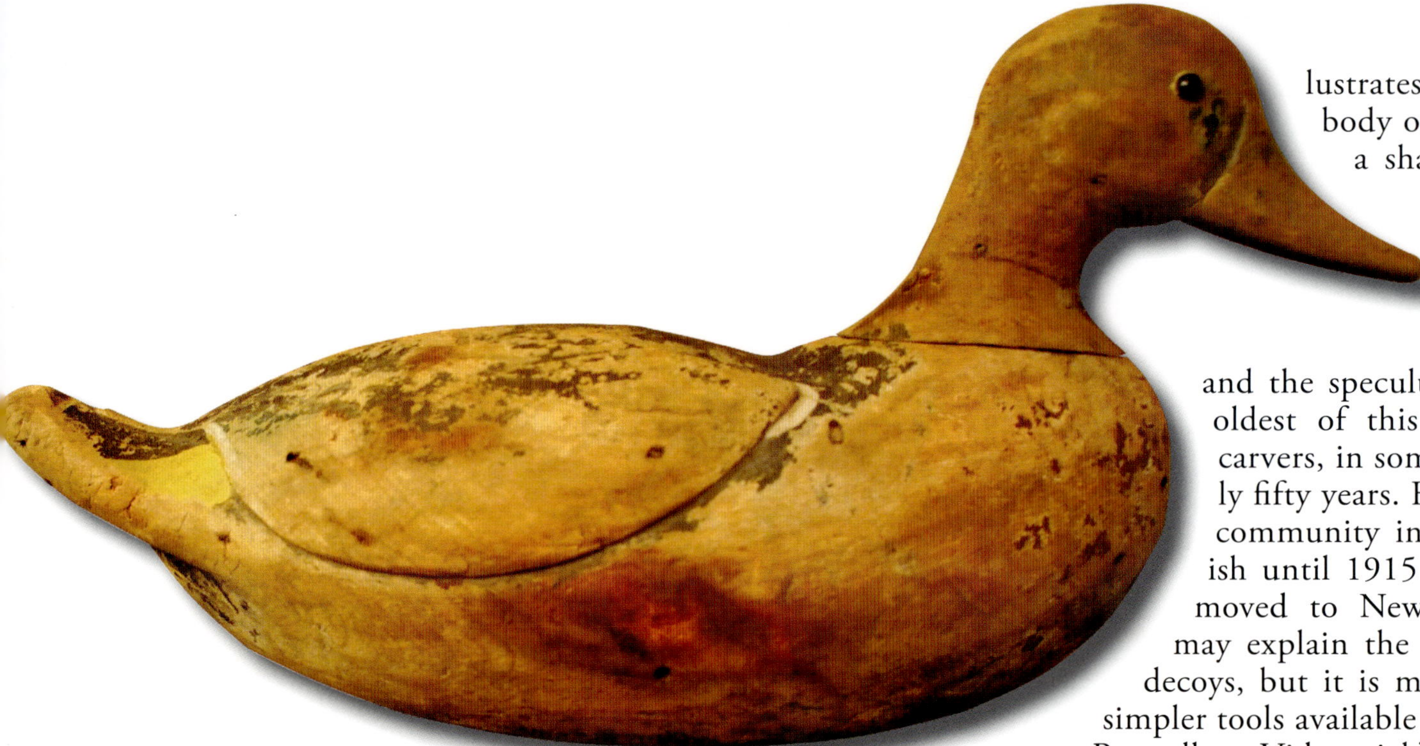

(13) Nicole Vidacovich decoy

lustrates. The only carving on the body of Vidacovich's decoys was a shallow undercut that outlined the wings. He used thick oil paint and sometimes he would texture the paint on the wing tip feathers and the speculums. Vidacovich was the oldest of this distinguished group of carvers, in some cases by thirty to nearly fifty years. He lived in a remote rural community in lower Plaquemines Parish until 1915 when he and his family moved to New Orleans. These factors may explain the relative simplicity of his decoys, but it is more likely a result of the simpler tools available in his day.

Regardless, Vidacovich's decoys are some of the most beautiful hunting decoys carved anywhere. On October 23, 2007, a major decoy exhibit named *Birds of a Feather: Wildfowl Carvings in Southeast Louisiana* opened at the Historic New Orleans Collection with Vidacovich as one of the featured carvers. The forty-four-page abundantly illustrated and informative catalogue for this exhibit is a must for any serious collector of Louisiana decoys, both old hunting and contemporary. The program notes Vidacovich "carved some of the most memorable early working decoys . . . [he] paid close attention to detail. . . . His use of patterns, artist-grade oil paint, and taxidermy grade glass eyes suggest that Vidacovich may have sensed the potential for decoys to transcend their functional status and, one day be recognized as a legitimate art form . . . his creation of what can only be described as decorative waterfowl decoys." Vidacovich's premonition proved to be incredibly accurate as the work of his artistic descendants, the contemporary masters, has proven.

By the mid-1950s, the "golden age" of Louisiana's old masters' decoy carving had come to an end, although their hunting decoys, if genuine and in good condition, continue to be treasured by traditional collectors. One need only look at the ever-increasing prices paid for the old masters' decoys in private sales, at auctions, and on eBay. By the 1980s, most of the old masters were no longer carving due to death or disability. The genuineness of old Louisiana gunners was frequently questioned as an increasing number of counterfeit decoys, newly carved and painted but aged to look just like ones carved by an old master, were being offered for sale or trade as the real thing. Retail stores in Louisiana no longer sold collectible quality old hunting decoys. Time, hurricanes, and collectors had effectively taken the old masters' decoys out of circulation.

The shrinking supply of old hunting decoys, the ever increasing prices for the few good ones available for purchase, and the concerns about counterfeits created opportunities for the next generation of decoy carvers. Decorative decoys were winning world-class carving competitions, garnering increased money prizes, and, most important, gaining the attention of a new and growing group of decoy collectors. These collectors appreciated the transition from wildfowl folk art to wildfowl fine art. The decorative decoy is made for display and not for hunting. As previously mentioned, there was also an increased demand for old-style hunting decoys from duck hunters who tired of using decoys made of synthetic materials and wanted to hunt over wooden ones. By the 1990s, many contemporary carvers had stopped making decoratives and increasingly produced old style hunting slicks. Once again proving that the more things change, the more things remain the same.

Endnotes

1. Charles Frank Jr., *Louisiana Duck Decoys* (Gretna, La.: Pelican Publishing, 1975), 18.
2. Brian Cheramie, Charles Connor, Mark Riseling, and Troy Glasgow, *Lures and Legends: The Decoy Collection of Brian Cheramie and Period Photography of David L. Hall* (Golden Meadow, La.: REM Corporation, 1997), 76.
3. Ibid., 76.
4. Ibid., 77.
5. Frank, *Wetland Heritage*, 131.
6. Cheramie, et al., *Louisiana Lures and Legends*, 48-57.
7. Frank, *Wetland Heritage*, 127.
8. Cheramie, et al., *Louisiana Lures and Legends*, 106.

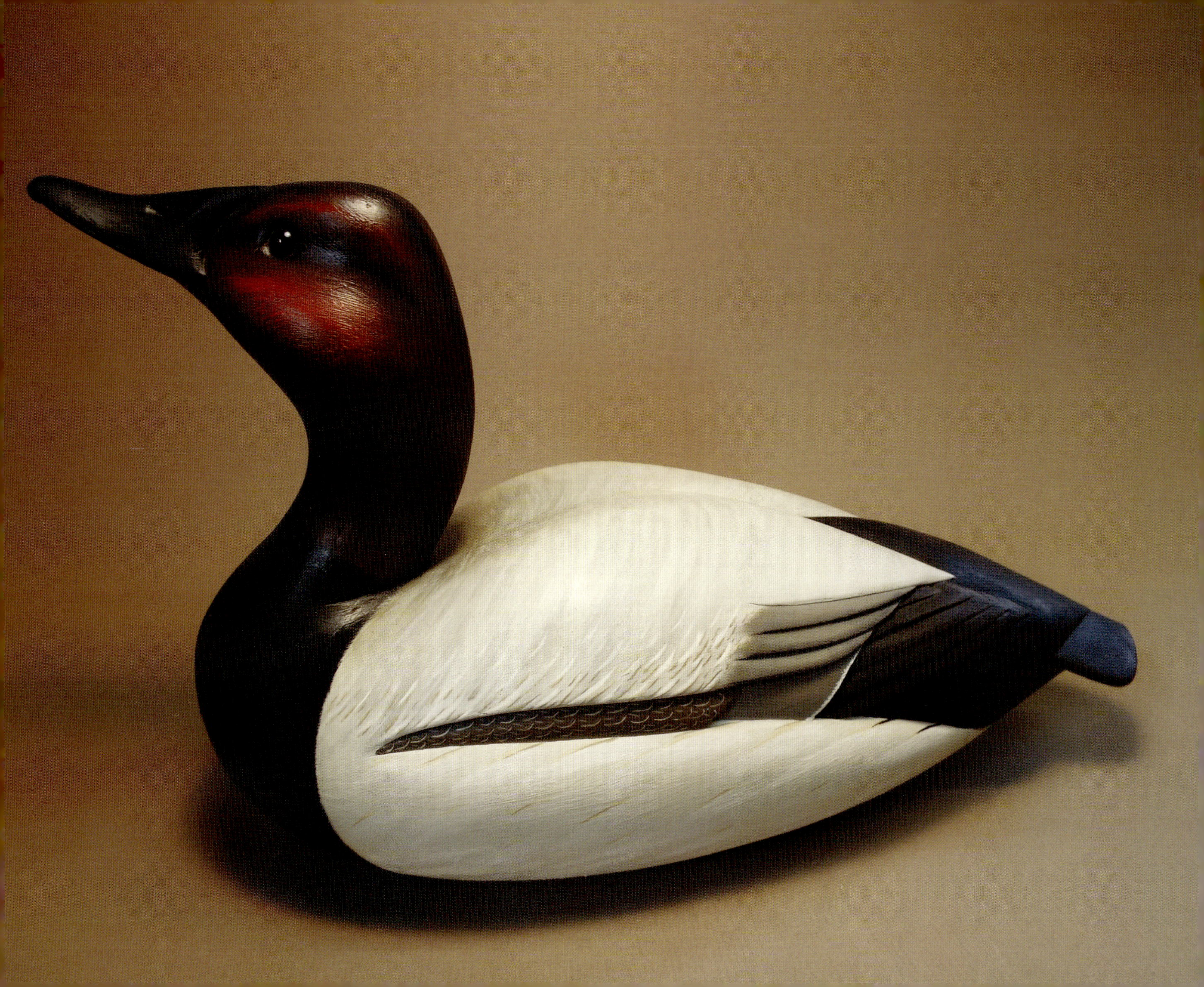

3 Classifying Contemporary Carving Styles

Opposite page: Bill Hanemann's canvasback drake decorative gunner

In Louisiana there are three basic contemporary decoy carving styles:

(1) the traditional hunting decoy, sometimes called a "gunner," a "working decoy," a "slick," or even a "contemporary antique"
(2) a decorative decoy
(3) a decorative gunner

A basic understanding of the differences between the three styles helps one to better appreciate them.

The hunting decoy is smooth-sided with minimal carving, simple paint patterns, and intended to be hunted over. Today, many decoys of this style, whether made by a contemporary carver or, especially, any carved by one of Louisiana's old masters, are put on display and never used to hunt.

A decorative decoy is a work of fine art, intended as a mantelpiece decoration or for decoy carving competitions. The decorative decoy is intended to be an exact replica of a real duck with elaborate carving of the feathers on the decoy's wings, body, and tail achieved with burning tools. At its best, it is very difficult, if not impossible, to distinguish between a decorative decoy and a taxidermist's good rendition of the same sex and species.

As the name suggests, the decorative gunner is a combination of the previously mentioned two styles and was created by contemporary carvers. It has more carving than a hunting decoy but less than a decorative. The wing feathers, primary and secondary, are usually elevated or at least undercut, and the painting is extremely detailed and frequently textured in this style.

Paintbrushes rather than burning tools are used to achieve the feather detailing.

Photographs of each of the three styles are displayed here. Photograph 1 is a typical slick contemporary hunting decoy: a mallard drake carved by Willie Badeaux. Photograph 2 is a decorative gunner: an English Caller carved by Carl Danos. Photograph 2a is another decorative gunner, a blue-winged teal drake carved by Mike Bonner. Photograph 3 is a decorative spoonbill drake carved by Richard Reeves that won a Ward World Championship.

There is an interesting variation of the three basic styles called "chip carving" which Donald Weaver Sr. originated many years ago, and his son Chris continues to use quite effectively. Chip carving is where the decoy is cut to the desired shape with a hatchet and then a knife. This leaves the decoy with shallow gouge marks that are not sanded smooth before it is painted (as is the standard practice). A chip carved decoy is esthetically pleasing. It is said to be a more effective hunting lure because it doesn't reflect the sun, which causes ducks to flare off as happens with many smooth painted hunting decoys. Photograph 4 shows Chris Weaver's chip carved decorative gunner pair of green-winged teal.

Another interesting variation was created by Carl Danos, who carved a decoy from a cypress root and then used a burning tool and a coat of bee's wax (a clear varnish) but no paint to fashion what is regarded as a decorative gunner decoy. Photograph 5 shows this very unique decoy.

The transitions from one style to another were not very orderly, nor was there a specific time when one carving style ended and another began. Old master carvers like Nicole Vidacovich and Clovis Vizier were carving ducks in full flight that would certainly fall into the decorative category

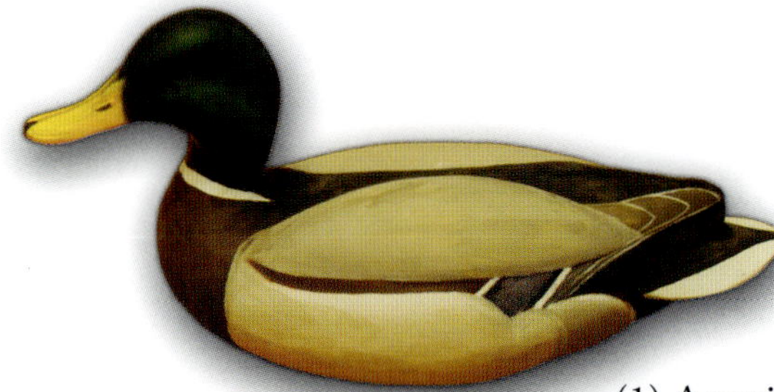

(1) A typical slick contemporary hunting decoy: a mallard drake carved by Willie Badeaux

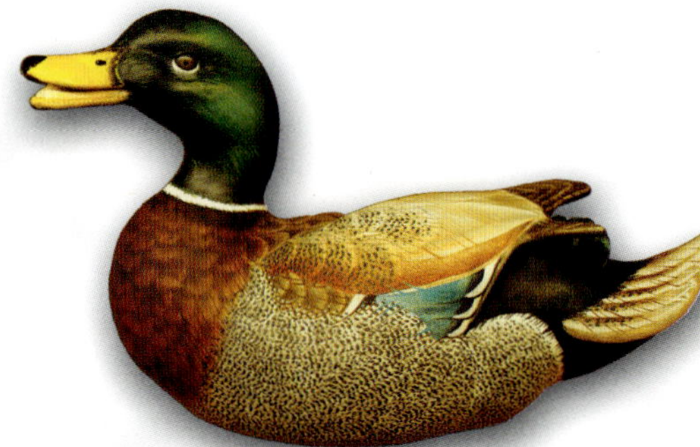

(2) A decorative gunner: an English Caller carved by Carl Danos

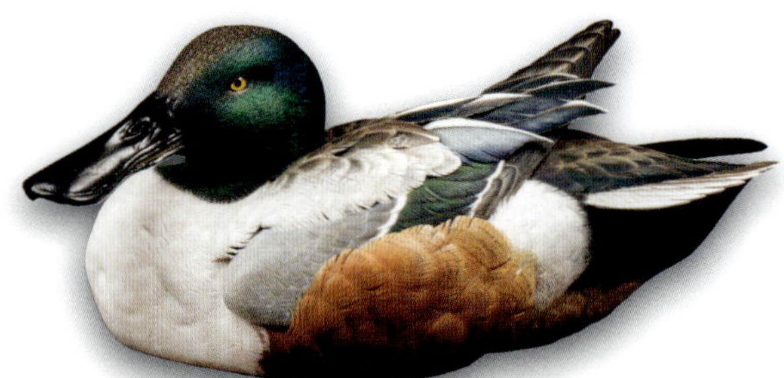

(3) A decorative: a spoonbill drake carved by Richard Reeves

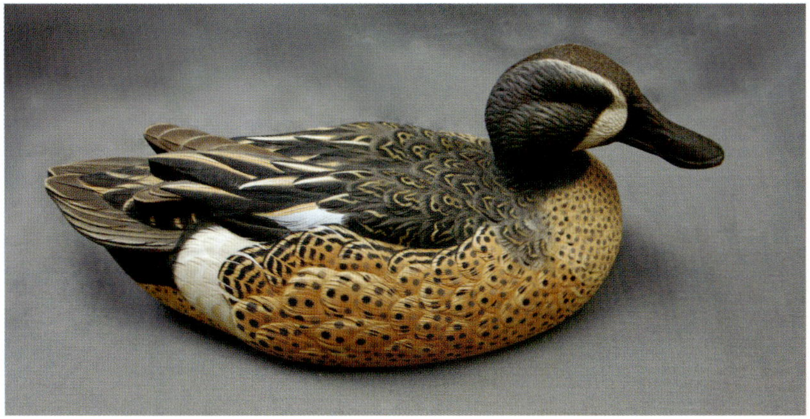

(2a) A decorative gunner blue-winged teal drake carved by Mike Bonner

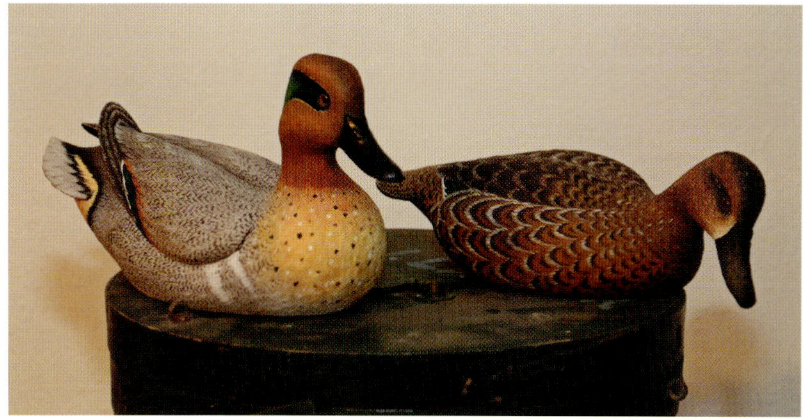

ABOVE: (4) A chip carved decorative gunner pair of green-winged teal by Chris Weaver

BELOW: (5) A Carl Danos decorative gunner decoy scribed with a burning tool

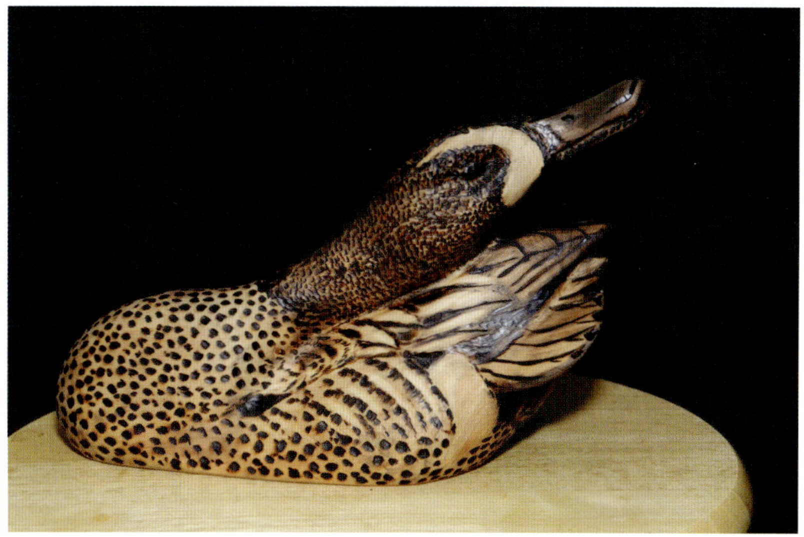

if one had existed fifty to a hundred years ago. Reme Roussel, another master carver of hunting decoys, also carved a larger than life-size eagle that adorned the roof of a building his hometown of Raceland.[1]

Nonetheless, the contemporary masters featured here are thought to be more artistically versatile than the old masters who rarely made anything other than working decoys that were intended to be hunted over. All of the contemporary masters in this book carve in more than one of the three described styles and a number carve things other than wildfowl. For that reason, no effort is made to fit them into a particular category.

ENDNOTES

1. Frank, *Louisiana Duck Decoys*, 27.

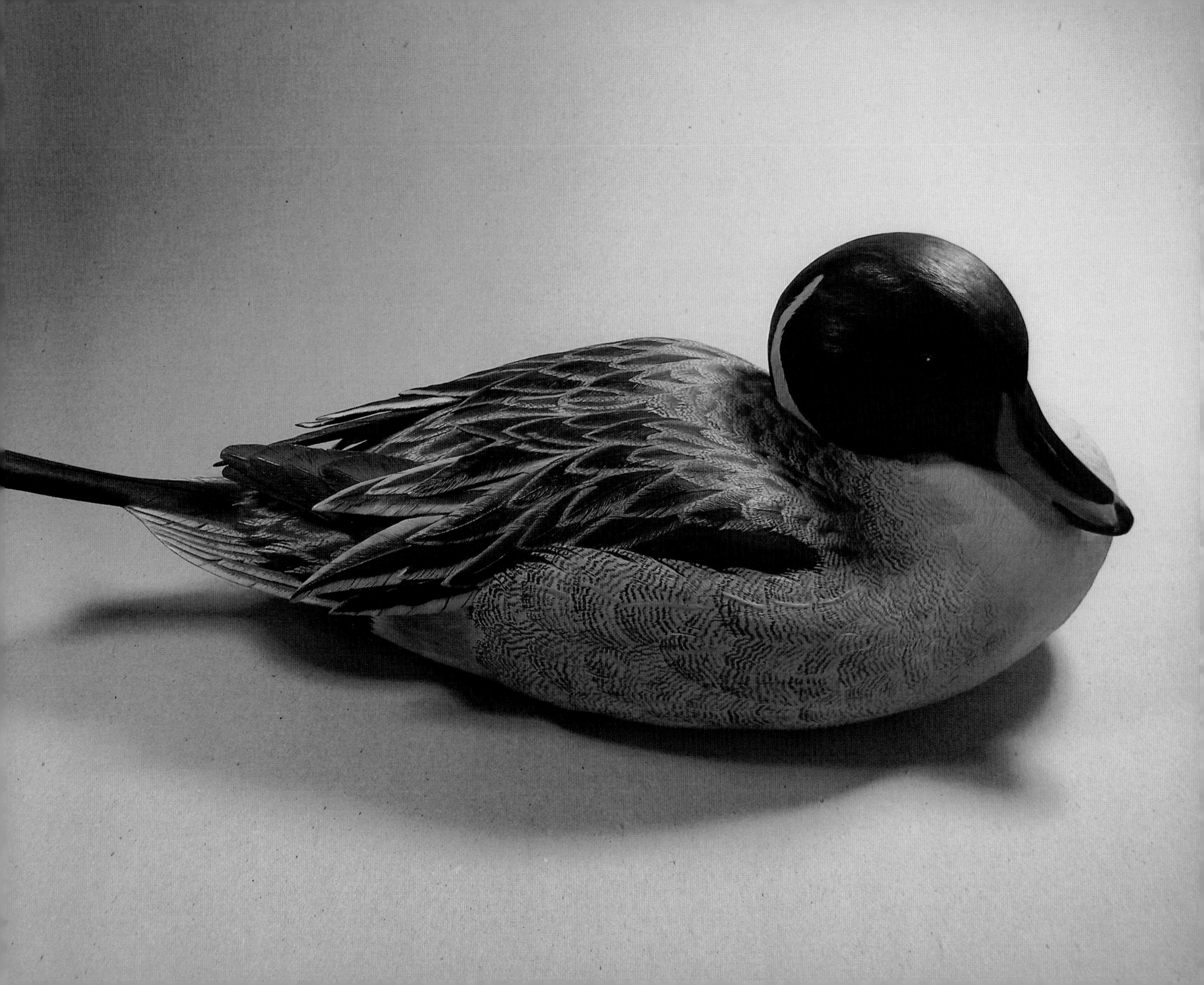

4 The Contemporary Carving Era

Opposite page: Pintail drake decorative gunner carved by Rock Zeringue and painted by Sheila Zeringue

According to the Louisiana Wildfowl Carvers and Collector's Guild (LWCCG) website, Louisiana is home to the largest number of Ward World Decoy Carving Champions and master carvers in the country. The Guild, founded in 1975, suggests that the contemporary decoy carving era began about sixty years ago. That coincides with the view of many collectors of old Louisiana hunting decoys. It also coincides with the year that Clovis Vizier's well-carved mallard pair won second place in the 1951 North American Decoy Makers' Contest held in New York City. Fittingly, in the 1970s and 1980s, Clovis Vizier's descendants Jimmy Vizier and Andrew "Tan" Brunet from Galliano, Louisiana, each won multiple Best in Show awards and also regularly won others at the Ward World Championships (the Super Bowl of decoy carving).

The success of these two men, their incredible artistry, their willingness to teach other Louisiana decoy carvers, and their active and continuing involvement in the LWCCG from its earliest days, played a major role in perpetuating the state's decoy carving tradition. Other great Louisiana decorative carvers soon began competing and winning top prizes at the annual Louisiana Wildfowl Carving Festival and the Ward and other national events. This group includes Willie Badeaux, Tan Brunet's sons, Jett and Jude, Mike Bonner, Bill Hanemann, Richard Reeves, and the Hutchisons, Charles, Rudy and Eric, as well as Carl and Reagan Danos.

As previously noted, the "golden age" of the old masters and their hunting slicks peaked in the 1950s. This is not to suggest that people stopped carving hunting decoys but, by the 1970s, a number of the then younger carvers turned to carving decorative decoys. They were lured by the prize money being offered at the carving shows and were fueled by a desire to compete to prove they were best. In a short time, decorative carving evolved from making a single or pair of ornately carved and painted decoys to producing large and complex wooden wildfowl sculptures. If the old masters' carving style can be called "Impressionistic," the new decorative style can be called "Photorealistic." The ultimate objective of the decorative carving style is to make something, be it a duck, bird of prey, or songbird that looks exactly like the real thing. Richard Reeve's kingfisher shown in photograph 1 is a very fine example. Decoratives were never meant to be hunted over. They were intended for display like any other form of fine art.

Did featuring decorative carvings at the competitions and festivals drive demand for that style? Or did the collectors' taste change and their demand for decoratives drive what the decoy shows featured? Regardless, beginning in the 1980s, the top decorative carvers' work commanded increasingly higher prices, and they could not fill all of the orders they received.

Artistically, some collectors believe that the contemporary decorative carvers' fine art trumped the old masters' folk art. Some of the improvements in the contemporary decoratives can be traced to new and better paint and carving equipment, including power saws and burning tools. This allowed talented decorative carvers to produce ever more realistic decoys with detailed feathering and luminescent painting. Other differences can be explained by the amount of time it takes to produce a competition-grade decorative. Richard Reeves, who just won the 2015 Ward's Best in Show award, estimates it takes a year and a half to produce a decorative decoy for a competitive event if the carver works

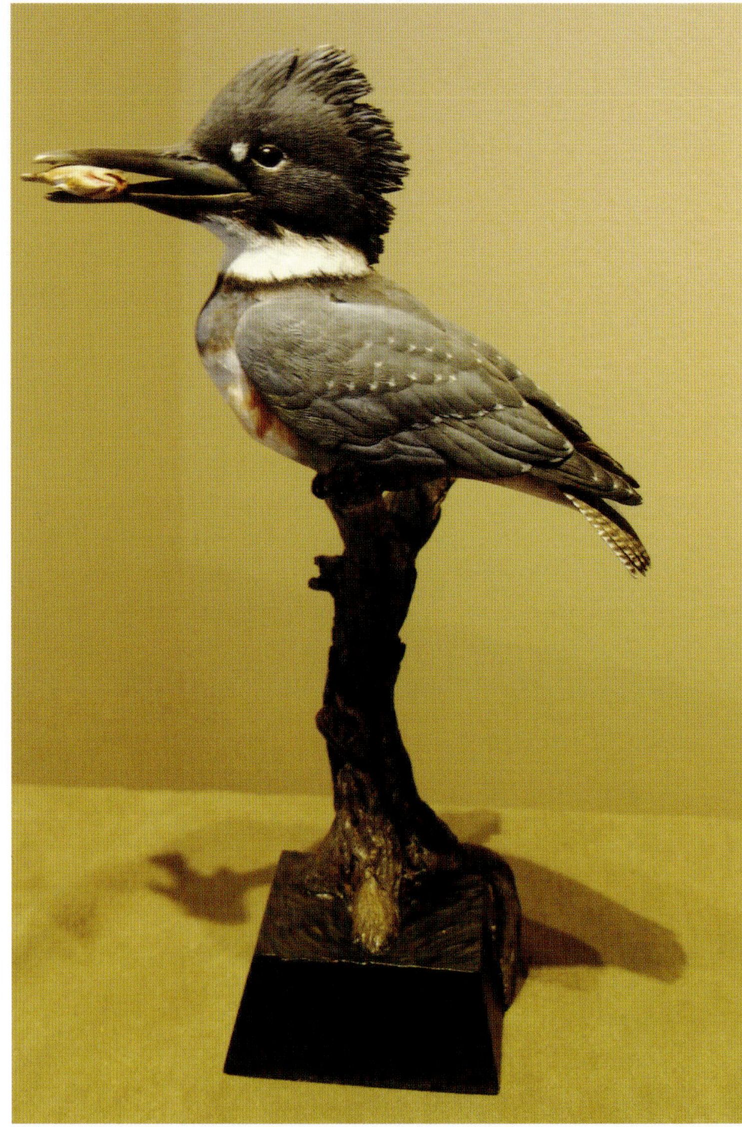

(1) Richard Reeves's kingfisher

diligently. Certainly no old master took anything like that amount of time to carve and paint a hunting slick. Incredibly, over the last thirty years, Louisiana decorative carvers have captured almost 50 percent of the annual Ward Best in World competition and/or top prizes in other major categories in that distinguished organization's annual contests.

One would expect that the evolution of contemporary carving styles would have started with better carved and painted hunting decoys, then progressed to more ornately carved and painted gunning decoratives, and ultimately to decorative sculptures. But it didn't happen that way. In the late 1970s, many carvers accepted the challenge to make the most realistic looking decoys possible and were rewarded with ever increasing prize money at the carving competitions and increased prices for their finished work.

Eric Hutchison recalls when he and his father, Charles, carved a complex and beautiful wildfowl sculpture and entered it in the second Louisiana Wildfowl Carvers' Festival, held in 1976. The consensus among the competing carvers was that the Hutchisons' work was a sure bet to be the festival's Best in Show selection and secure the accompanying $10,000 purchase prize that went to the winner. That didn't happen. The Hutchisons came in second. They received a far more modest monetary prize but got to keep their wooden sculpture, which they promptly put on display in Adler's Sports Art Gallery. Two weeks later, it sold for $25,000.

The golden era of decorative decoy carving in Louisiana peaked in the 1990s in terms of the prices that carving style commanded and the number of carvers producing that style of decoys. At that time, decorative decoys produced by the most well-known carvers regularly sold for $25,000 or more.

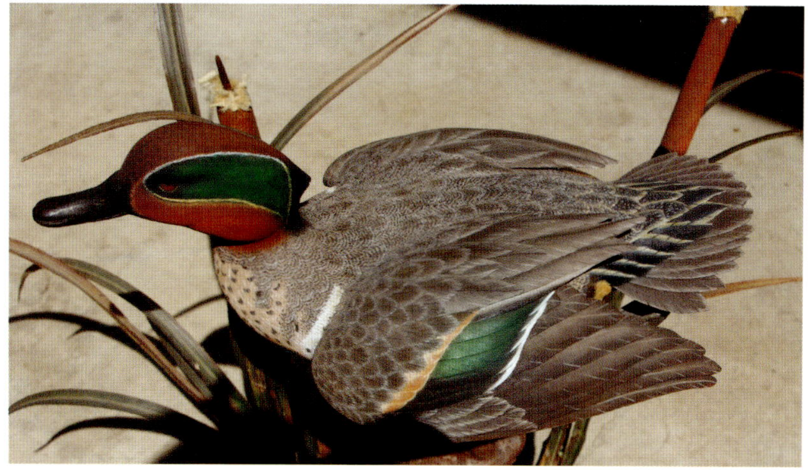

(2) Willie Badeaux's green-winged teal

Willie Badeaux, an award winning decorative carver, said he and his close friends Jimmy Vizier and Tan Brunet regularly went to and competed in the big decoy carving contests and shows in the East, as did Carl and Reagan Danos. Not only did this talented group regularly win top prizes at these competitions, they also sold every decoy they brought. Photograph 2 shows a beautiful decorative composition featuring a green-winged teal drake by Badeaux and is representative of the type of work that he and his Bayou Lafourche colleagues were taking east to show and sell.

Meanwhile, other and less expensive contemporary carving styles proved to be very popular in Louisiana. For example, exquisite miniature decoys carved by Dennis Treitler, Roy Legaux Sr., Tan Brunet, Willie Badeaux, and others were among the best selling items at the 1984 World's Fair in New Orleans. Photograph 3 shows a se-

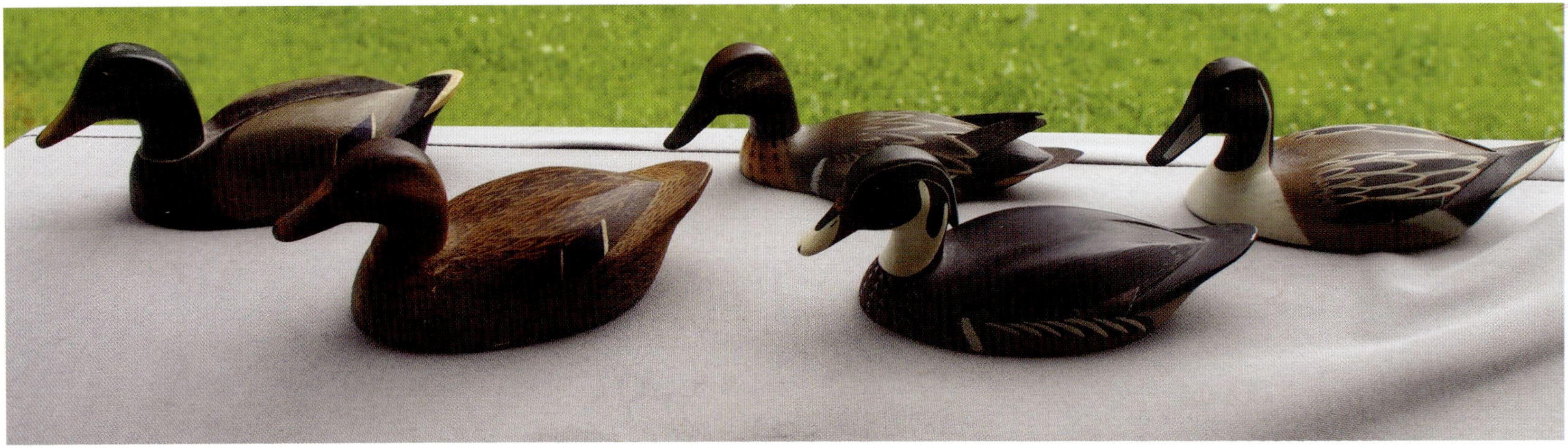

Above: (3) Dennis Treitler's assorted miniatures

Below: (4) Dick Bonner's assorted miniatures

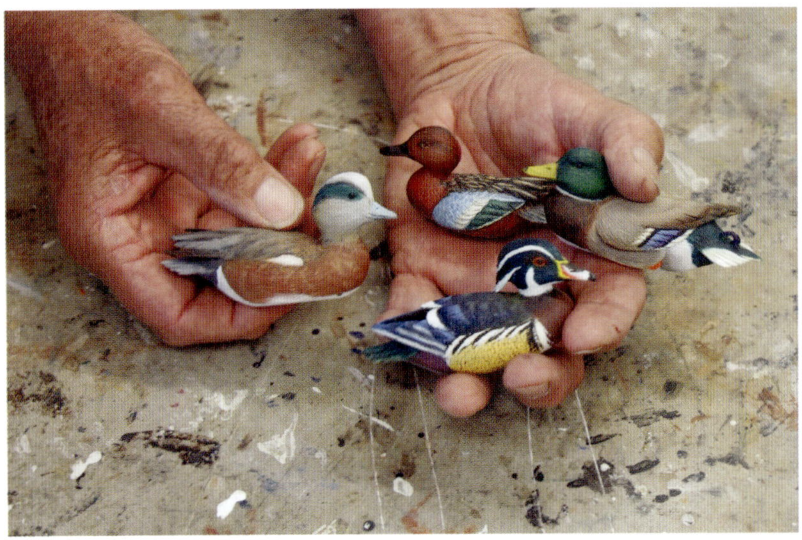

lection of Treitler's miniatures like those he sold at the '84 World's Fair. Dick Bonner and Bill Hanemann were also carving miniatures around this time and continue to do so. A sample of Bonner's recent miniatures is shown in photograph 4 and a very special trio of Hanemann's recent different size pintails is shown in photograph 5.

Badeaux and Tan Brunet put on carving exhibitions at the Fair and made two pirogues. One of those pirogues is on display at the Old State Capitol building (now a museum) in Baton Rouge, and the other one is on display at the Jean Lafitte State Museum in Thibodaux, Louisiana.

The golden era of decorative decoys slowly waned around 2010 even though Louisiana's decorative carvers were continuing to produce top quality work. Reagan Danos won a Best in Category award in 2014 at the Ward with the decorative green-winged teal hen shown in photograph 6. As previously mentioned, decorative carver Richard Reeves won the 2015 Ward Pairs Best in Show. Mike Bonner, another great Louisiana decorative carver, won the Best in

Show award at the 2014 Louisiana Wildfowl Festival, and Willie Badeaux and his son Gary, both fine decorative carvers, won first place awards in other divisions at that same competition.

There were several reasons for the change. The most significant was a sharp decline in the number of deep-pocketed collectors who were willing and able to pay the asking price for good decoratives. Moreover, there was a change in the public's taste for decorative decoys and wildfowl carvings. That carving style was no longer in favor. A number of Louisiana's better decorative carvers quit entering competitive events because they no longer wanted to be constrained to produce an exact replica or the judges' perception of one. They wanted the artistic license to make what they wanted without capricious judging. Others quit because they were teaching decoy carving and did not want to compete against their students. Many stopped carving decoratives because they could not sell what they made for enough money to compensate them for the time and effort required to produce a satisfactory product. Other carvers simply got "burned out" carving decoratives.

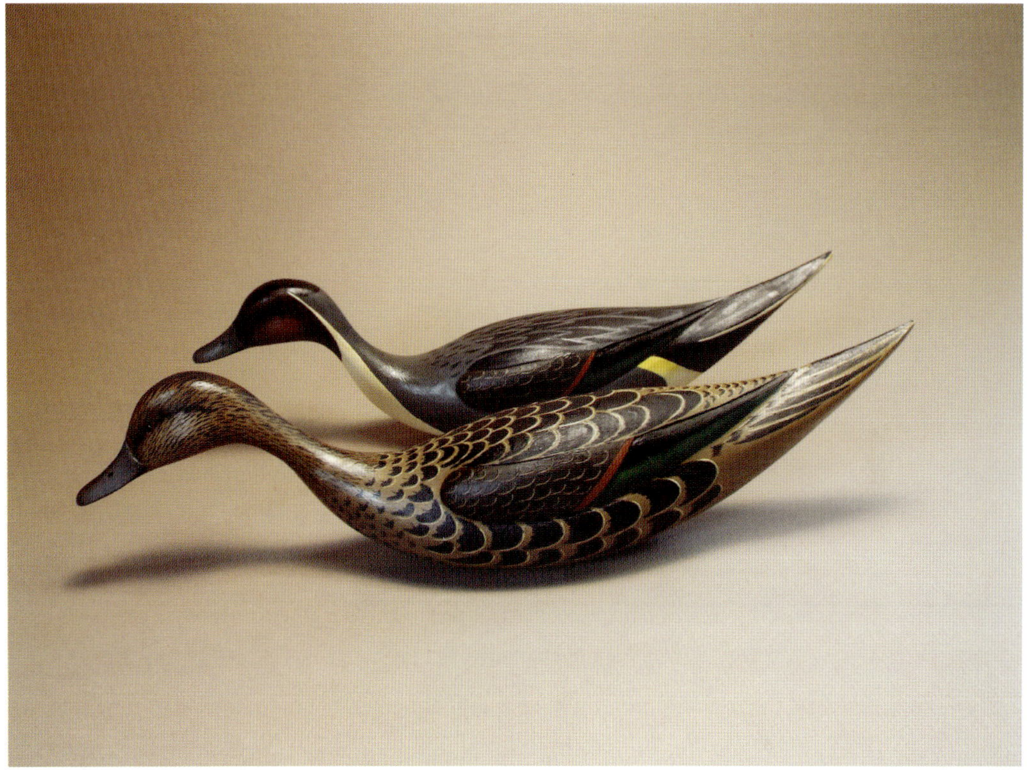

(5) Bill Hanemann's miniature pintail pair

While the decoratives declined in popularity, the other two contemporary carving styles flourished. Carvers were producing better carved and painted decoys and the line between contemporary hunting slicks and decorative gunners became blurred. Painting techniques continued to improve and there were new innovations. Roy Legaux Sr. perfected a texturing effect that results in making the feathers appear almost as realistic as those created by using a burning tool.

Carl and Reagan Danos as well as Dennis Treitler, Bill Hanemann, Willie Badeaux, and Rock Zeringue, all great carvers and painters, are making such beautiful decorative gunners that few collectors would think of hunting over them, despite Treitler's insistence that his decoys are made to be used. Today, the contemporary masters' decorative gunners sell for about $500 and up. Almost all of their work is done on a commission basis, and it usually takes months if not years to get delivery.

The most interesting recent development in the Louisiana decoy carving world is the increasing number of Louisiana wildfowlers who want to hunt over a large spread of wooden decoys. Today's hunting slicks costs from $100 up to $300 each and often more when made by one of the contemporary masters who sell all they can produce. It usually takes about a week or so to complete a hunting decoy. At least one contemporary master can complete a decorative gunner in as little as a day and a half. Despite the relatively short time it takes to make a contemporary hunting decoy, expect to wait to get delivery.

What is behind this recent surge in demand? Is it a nostalgic desire for hunters to use wooden decoys like those used by their ancestors? Is it because contemporary hunting decoys are more effective lures than synthetic ones? Has using a large and expensive rig of contemporary decoys become a hunting lodge status symbol? Hunters often say that wooden decoys look more like real ducks than synthetic ones when afloat and the wooden ones don't "wiggle" like the synthetics when it's windy. Regardless of the reason, contemporary hunting decoys are certainly not your father's old wooden decoys. A brief glance at Cal Kingsmill and Eric Hutchison's personal hunting rigs shown in photographs 7 and 8 quickly reveals that truth.

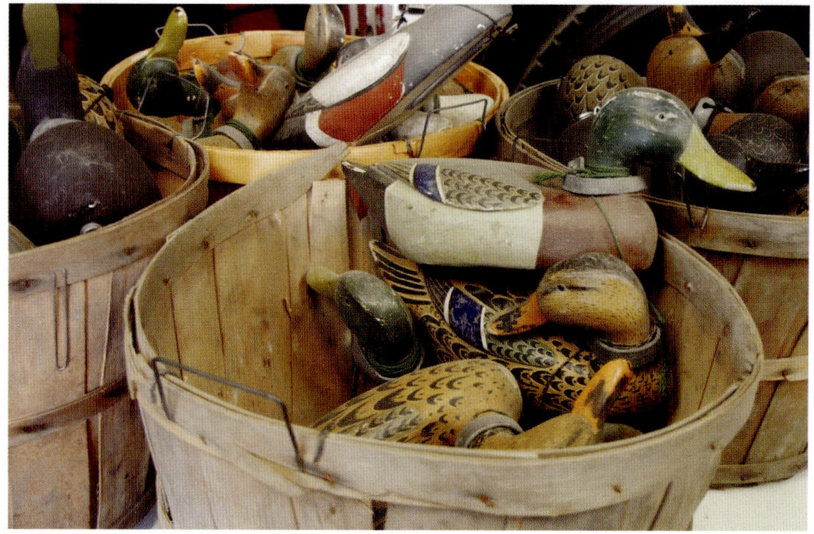

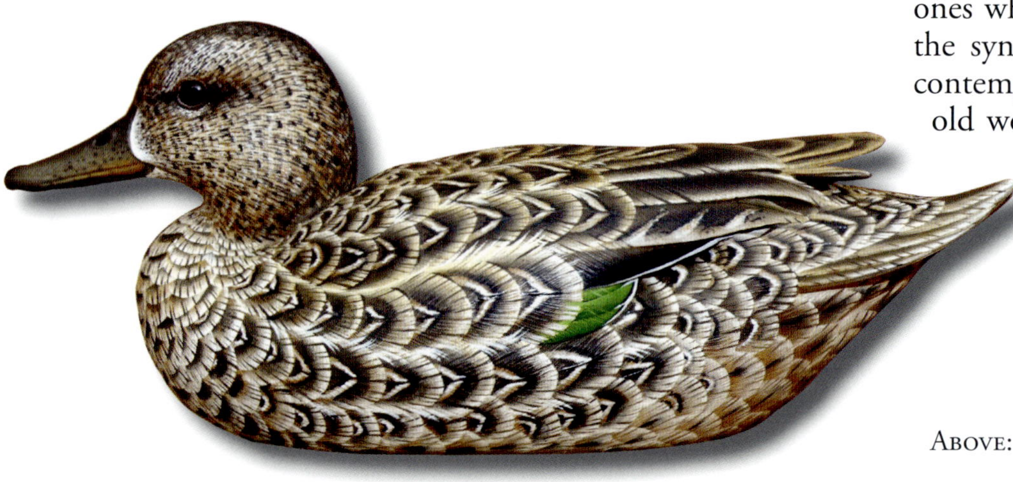

LEFT: (6) Reagan Danos's green-winged teal

ABOVE: (7) Cal Kingsmill's assorted hunting slicks

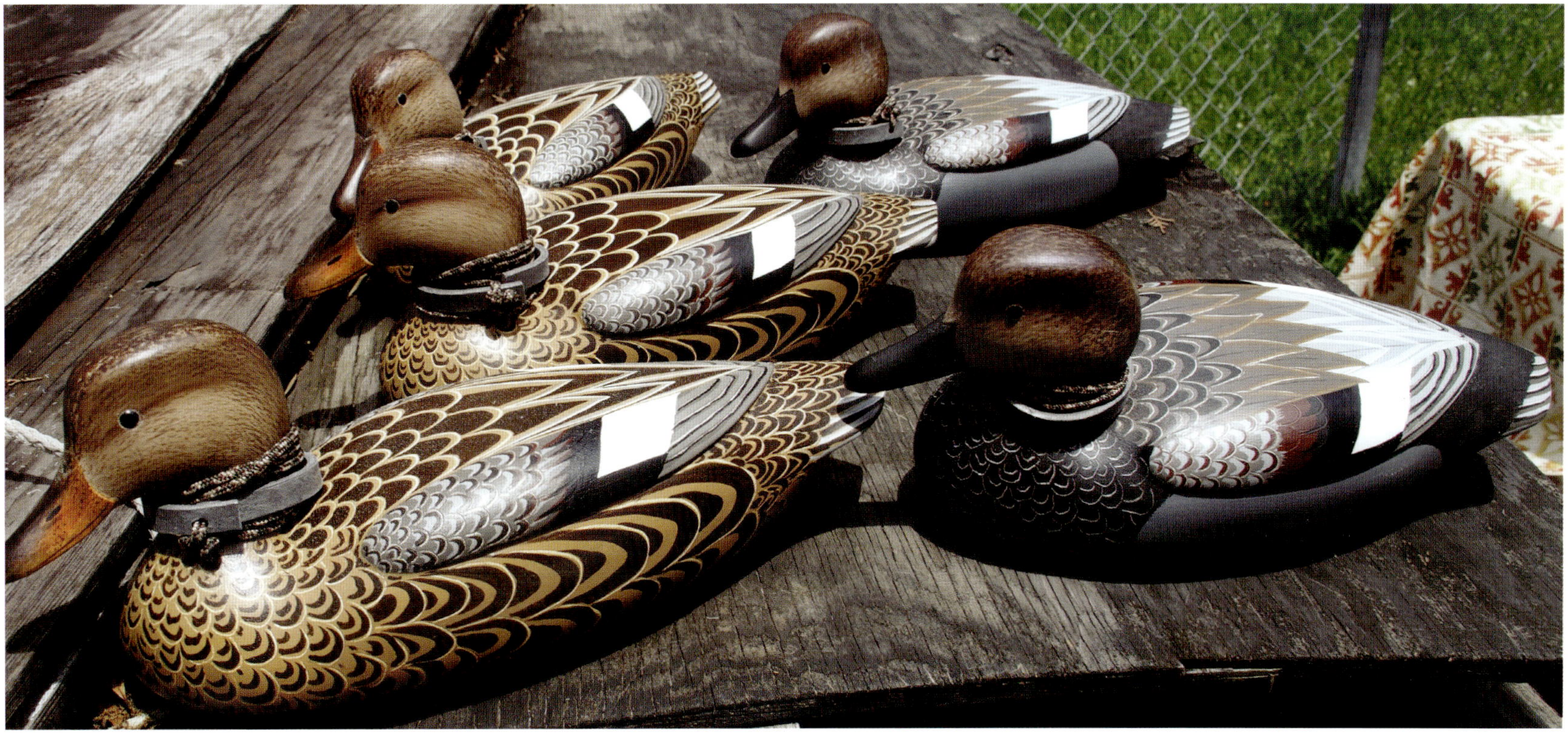

(8) Eric Hutchison's assorted hunting slicks

The era of contemporary hunting decoys, sometimes confusingly called "contemporary antiques," is unlikely to end soon. The growing demand for that style of decoys in Louisiana, the increasing number of skilled carvers and promising carving students in this state making that decoy style, and Louisiana's heritage and tradition combine to assure that result. Almost all of the contemporary masters teach decoy carving in some manner. Bill Hanemann, Cal Kingsmill, Eric Hutchison, the Danos brothers, and others regularly give lectures and carving exhibitions. Willie Badeaux, Carl Danos, and Mike Bonner hold formal classes on how to carve decoys in their workshops or at other locations as often as four days a week. Tan Brunet taught his sons Jett and Jude how to carve and both won national ribbons at the 2014 Louisiana Wildfowl Festival. One thing is certain, Louisiana's decoy carving tradition is in good hands.

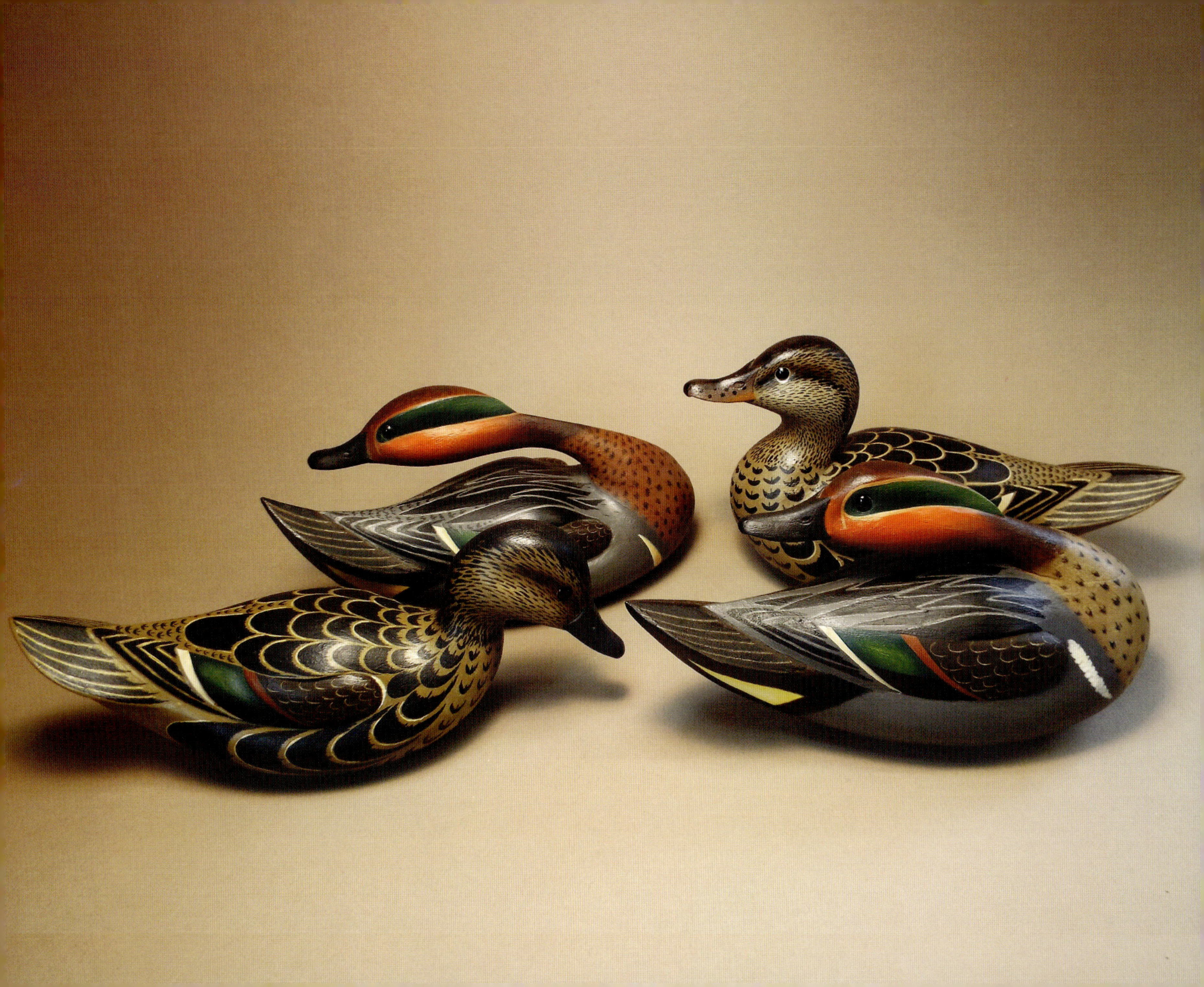

5 Collecting Contemporary Louisiana Decoys

Opposite page: Bill Hanemann's green-winged teal foursome

Contemporary Louisiana decoys, other than decoratives, can be hunted over, displayed, or both. To own a contemporary decorative decoy, however, is to own a fine art object that is an anatomically correct, wooden wildfowl sculpture—one that is more permanent, valuable, and more visually satisfying than a taxidermist's best specimen. The decision to collect slicks and decorative gunners is generally motivated by tradition, nostalgia, and a love of wildfowl hunting. Although contemporary decoys are aesthetically pleasing and properly classified as folk and/or fine art, few collect them for those reasons alone. Collectors and carvers find slicks and decorative gunners supremely attractive because of the association with hunting and outdoor adventures, past and future. Younger hunters want to hunt over wooden decoys rather than synthetics because they like using the same kind of decoys that were used by their forebears. Older hunters want to hunt over wooden decoys just like they used when they started hunting. Many hunters of all ages believe that wooden decoys float more realistically than synthetics and, hence, are better lures. Retired hunters, who now prefer the warmth of the hunting camp to the very cold duck blind, are drawn to a display of contemporary decoys because it evokes treasured memories of past hunts. One cannot exclude the "Rolex effect" as the reason some hunters collect and hunt over large rigs of contemporary decoys. Having fifty to a hundred slicks carved by a contemporary master, each costing $300 or more, floating around a duck blind does make a statement. In any case, well-done contemporary Louisiana decoys, whether on the pond or in a display case, have a soul that speaks to the collector.

Why collect contemporary Louisiana decoys?

There are a number of very good reasons to buy contemporary decoys. They are far less expensive and are much more readily available than genuine hunting decoys carved by one of Louisiana's old masters. There also is little risk of buying a counterfeit because the prospective purchaser can have the presumed carver confirm its authenticity.

Contemporary decoys provide a direct link to our state's unique culture and heritage. They are tangible evidence of why Louisiana is this country's "Sportsman's Paradise." Most importantly, almost all of the fine Louisiana contemporary carvers are still alive and creating decoys on a commission basis. This means, the collector can go to the carver's workshop and select the decoy's species, sex, and pose. The opportunity to meet and interact with the carver is invaluable. Hearing the carver's stories infuses the commissioned decoy with the carver's personality. Lastly, the collector can develop a meaningful friendship with a group of talented, interesting, and kind people.

I do not contend that contemporary hunting decoys are better than those carved by Louisiana's old masters. My thesis is that they are at least as well carved as the best of the old hunting decoys and they are generally better painted. This may result from the contemporary carvers having better tools and paint, but more likely it is due to the old masters having a different objective than the contemporary carvers. The old masters were content to produce inexpensive hunting tools that looked just enough like real ducks to lure them into shooting range. In contrast, contemporary carvers making slicks and decorative gunners want their decoys to look like real ducks and decorative carvers want to make a decoy that looks *exactly* like the real thing.

Some people prefer to own antiques while others prefer contemporary or modern objects. An increasing number of collectors want to own both; genuine Louisiana's old masters' decoys and good contemporary slicks and decorative gunners. The two vintage collectors proudly display their old hunting decoys and hunt over their contemporary ones. Some collectors want to display both vintages and hunt over synthetic decoys, not wanting to risk spoiling the appearance of their wooden decoys with errant pellets or weather-related damage.

How much can contemporary Louisiana decoys cost?

Contemporary hunting decoys of reasonable quality can be bought for $50-$200. Those carved by a contemporary master will cost $300 and up. Good quality decorative gunners carved by the contemporary masters will cost $450 and up. Competition grade decorative decoys sell for $5,000 and up. Large, complex wildlife sculptures command much higher prices. Please understand that these prices are only general guidelines and may differ from carver to carver depending on demand. I recommend against "haggling" with the carver over price, especially when commissioning a customized order. A carver who feels that he is being fairly compensated will invariably produce a better decoy than one who believes he is being "short changed."

What contemporary decoys should one collect?

Ultimately, this is a matter of personal taste. Collect what you like and can afford. For display, I find themed collections very interesting. Good examples are a male and a female of each species commonly hunted in Louisiana or different carvers' interpretations of the same duck, say all green-winged teal drakes. A pair of decorative gunners, one painted in winter plumage and the other in summer plumage would make a very interesting display. The most novel collection theme I've heard of (but have not seen) consists of a number of hunting decoys, each carved and painted by one of the great Louisiana contemporary masters, in the style of one the best old Louisiana masters. It is essential that such copies be permanently labeled as such and be signed by the carver that made them for the reasons set out in the chapter in this book on counterfeiting. One of my favorite displays consists of a pair of blue-winged teal carved by Reme Roussel, an old Louisiana master, and copies of that pair carved by Willie Badeaux, a featured contemporary master. The two pair are shown in photograph 1. Another favorite is a grouping of four green-winged teal by Bill Hanemann, which are shown on page 30.

How does one go about collecting contemporary decoys?

A good first step is to go to one or more of Louisiana's decoy shows or carving competitions and see not only what is on display but also what the carvers have for sale. The annual Louisiana Wildfowl Festival, sponsored by the Louisiana Wildfowl Carvers and Collectors Guild, is held in October in Mandeville, Louisiana, and is an excellent place to start as it is one of the largest decoy shows in the country. Other annual decoy shows are held in Houma, Larose, and Baton Rouge. These three shows feature a number of very fine contemporary Louisiana decoy carvers. The Houma and Baton Rouge shows also have a number of old hunting decoys on display and for sale. One can also see contemporary decoys being carved and displayed at the annual Sportsman's Show held in Gonzales. The Guild show in October tends to feature decorative style decoys while the others feature more hunting slicks and decorative hunting decoys.

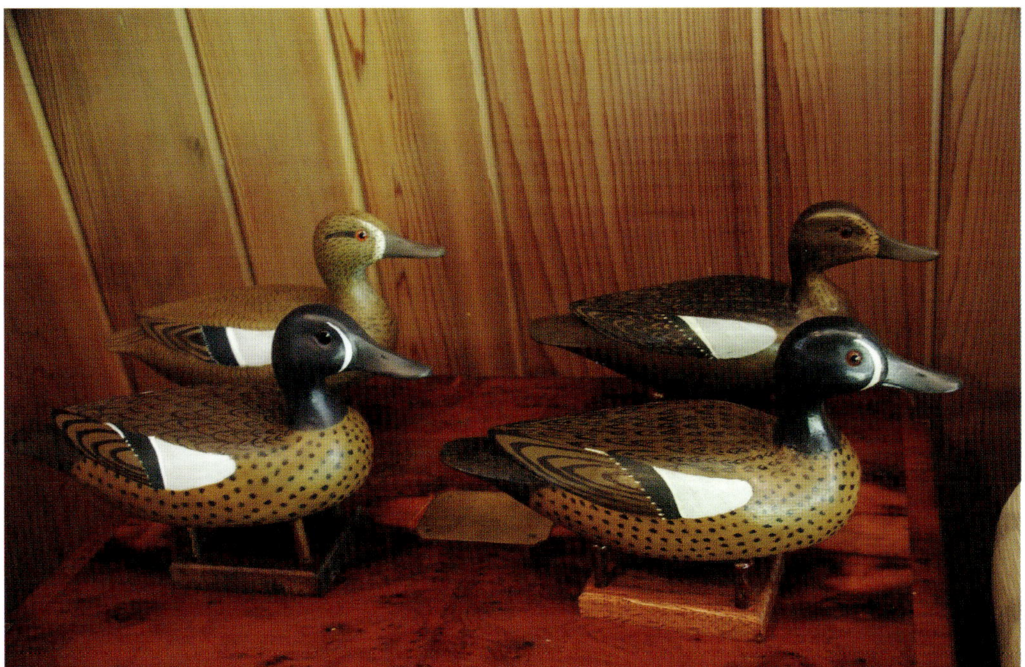

(1) Willie Badeaux's blue-winged teal pair following Reme Roussel's blue-winged teal pair

Ideally, the initial visit to a decoy show or an event where contemporary decoys are for sale should be an exploratory venture and not a buying trip. Look carefully at what is displayed and then closely examine every decoy that appeals to you. See what you like and try to meet the carver or carvers whose work you want to own. Rather than buying a ready-made decoy consider visiting the carver's shop at a later date when you will be better informed with the intent of commissioning a decoy that you want to own; one that will serve as the foundation of your collection. This advice is particularly appropriate if you intend to collect decorative decoys, which are much more expensive. Meet the carver, discuss your ideas and get his thoughts. Commission the decoy you want, but make sure that it is one that the carver wants to carve. The process is much like buying a custom made suit, which starts with selecting the fabric and then having it tailored to your specifications.

Are contemporary decoys a good investment?

That is a very difficult question to answer. How do you value the psychic reward of hunting over wooden slicks just like your father and grandfather did in years past or owning a great decorative decoy carved by one of Louisiana's world champions? The intrinsic value and excellence of Louisiana's contemporary carvers' decoys has been more than validated by Doug Miller, who, by all accounts, has the largest and very best collection of contemporary decorative decoys and wildfowl sculptures in this country. Miller was inspired to collect this art form by Dick Bonner, who was one of the carvers hired to make artwork for the Wildfowl World Museum in Monument, Colorado. Bonner also counseled Miller on whose wildfowl artwork to buy. The Miller collection was shown at a major exhibition sponsored by Ducks Unlimited in Memphis, Tennessee, in November 2014. The catalogue from that exhibition has photographs of fifteen decoys in the Miller

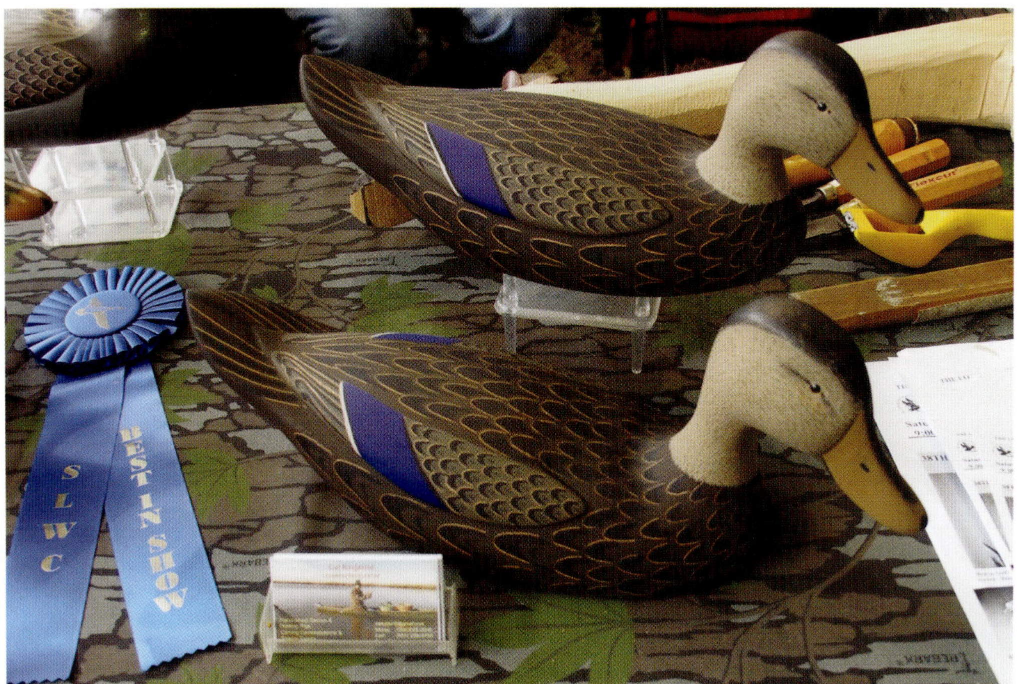

A pair of prize-winning Cal Kingsmill decoys on display at a decoy carving competition

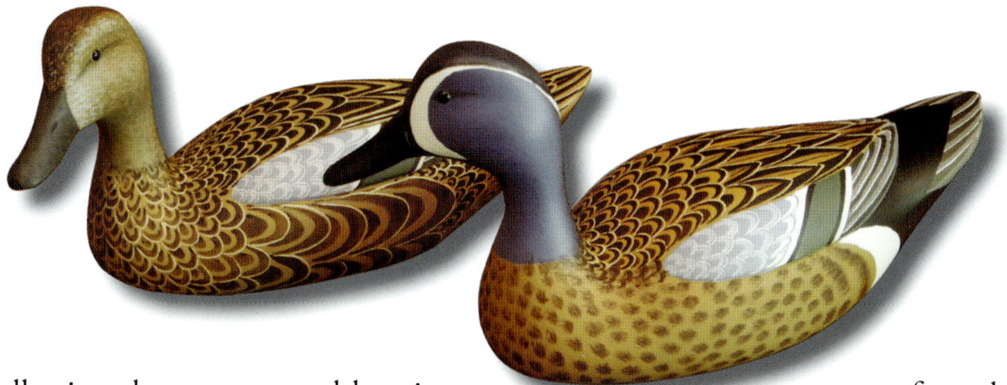

Left: A colorful pair of decoys carved by Eric Hutchison

collection that were carved by nine contemporary Louisiana carvers, Tan Brunet, Jett Brunet, Jude Brunet, Jimmie Vizier, Carl Danos, Ness Lefort, and Mike Bonner. That is certainly an impressive endorsement by such an important national collector.

For most serious collectors, investment value is largely irrelevant. Allan Kancher of New Orleans has been collecting Louisiana decorative decoys for over thirty years. His collection, now numbering in excess of 225 decoys, includes virtually all of the great contemporary Louisiana carvers as well as many of the out-of-state greats. From the outset he decided against commissioning a carver to make a decoy, fearing that he wouldn't like the finished product and would offend the carver if he rejected it. For this reason, he only bought ready-made decoys from established carvers that he liked. He has very good taste and sufficient knowledge to know if the decoy provides a good example of the carver's best work. He also had a good idea of what a fair price was for that decoy. If it was a well carved and painted decoy that he liked and it was fairly priced, he bought it. No consideration was given to what the decoy might be worth in the future. That is the same formula that was used by the collectors of good, old Louisiana hunting decoys, and it worked very well financially.

Allan recently decided to reduce the size of his collection and started selling some of his decoys. All of the sales have been for more than the collector's acquisition price, with decoys carved by Mike Frady, Jimmy Vizier, and Tan Brunet showing the largest increase. This is understandable as Frady and Vizier are deceased and Brunet is no longer carving.

What can be learned from this collector's experience?

Buy contemporary decoys because you like and want to own that art form or you want to own the work of one or more of the contemporary carvers. Over time, good contemporary decoys, particularly those by well-known contemporary carvers are likely, but not certain, to appreciate in value. Decorative decoys and decorative wildfowl sculptures are more problematic, especially the more expensive ones, because most were originally bought for a particular display location. Decorative pieces, especially the large, complex ones, are not thought to be as marketable as the contemporary hunting slicks and the decorative gunners.

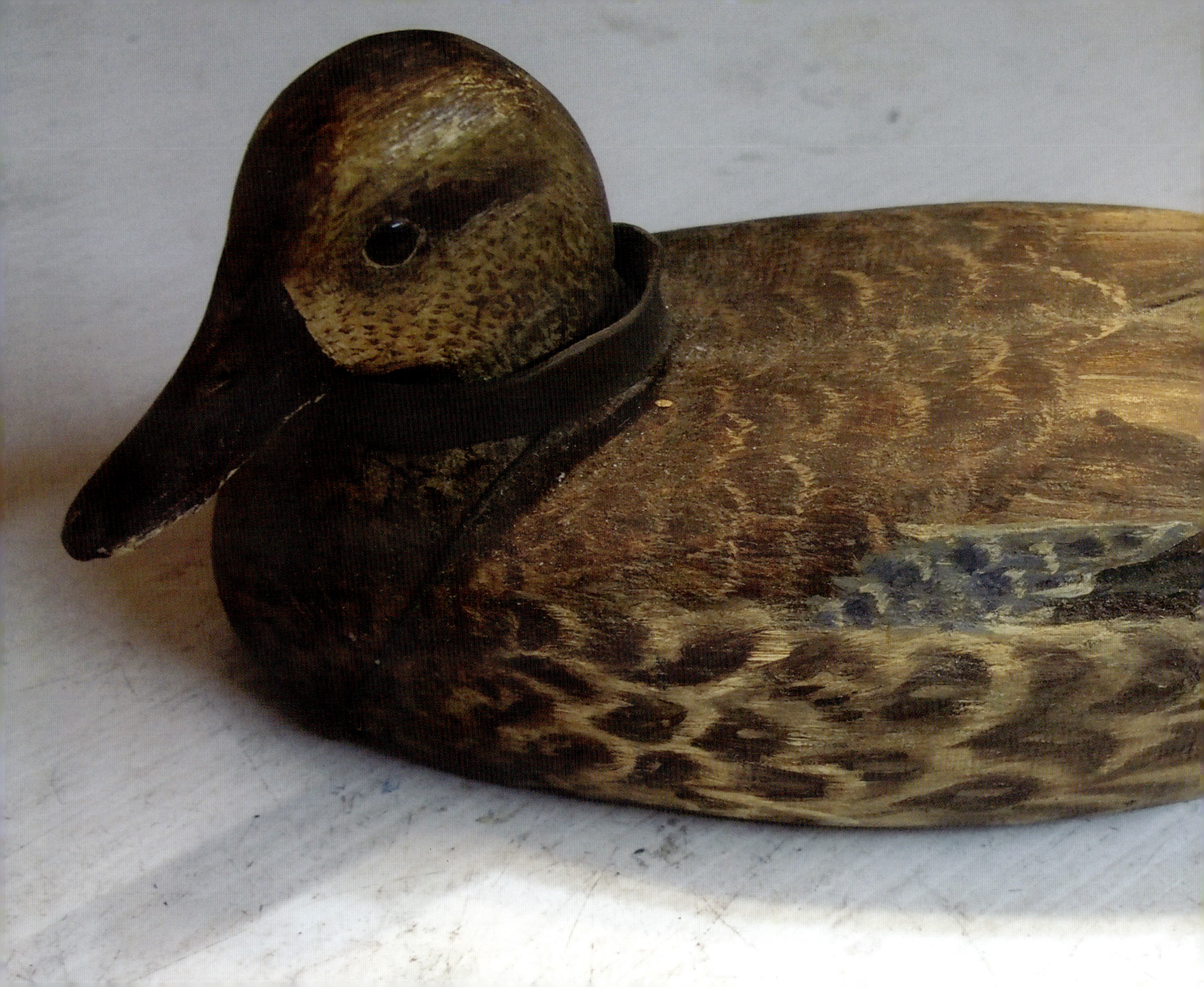

6 Mike Frady

The Transitional Link?

In the course of interviewing people for this book, contemporary carvers and collectors spoke often of Mike Frady (1912-1993) with respect and admiration for the man and his decoys. For about thirty years, he was head of the Commercial Arts Department at Delgado Junior College, mainly as an instructor in sign painting classes and teaching decoy carving after school hours. Frady's son, Wayne, describes his father as an educator, artist, boat builder, inventor, avid duck hunter, and a self-taught decoy carver. Frady taught Roy Legaux Sr. sign painting, and, after hours, decoy carving. Members of the Galatas family were among his decoy carving pupils, as were Dennis Treitler and Cal Kingsmill.

Besides making high-quality decoys, Frady specialized in building motorboat hulls, fourteen to eighteen feet long, as well as pirogues. The motorboats were made for Frady's own use and he named them *Greenwing I*, *Greenwing II*, and *Greenwing III*. He invented and got a patent on a bow-mounted spotlight that was very helpful when setting out and picking up decoys in the dark. He hunted ducks at Reggio, Shell Beach, and Lake Salvador, but his favorite hunting place was Lake Catherine, where he built a house trailer and used it as a hunting camp for fifty years. His son Wayne says his father was a "professional sportsman" and a "workaholic." (I didn't ask him to explain the seeming contradiction.)

Mike Frady started carving in his late twenties, and his early decoys bore a strong resemblance to Couret's Lifelike Lures."[1] Frady invented a wind-up device, powered by rubber bands, to hold and store the decoy's anchor line and weight. Knots were tied in the anchor line to mark the desired depths

Opposite page: (3) Mike Frady's green-winged teal hen

and fitted into the base of the decoy.[2]

Frady was a prolific carver, producing perhaps a thousand decoys or more during his carving career, which started around 1932 and continued until his death in 1993. He initially carved decoys to hunt over, but he also started selling the decoys he made, with the early ones going for three dollars each. Frady won numerous carving championships at the Louisiana Wildfowl Carvers and Collectors Guild Festivals, starting at the fourth one held in 1978. Thereafter, he was the perennial winner of the Senior Division. Over the years, he successfully competed against Jimmy Vizier, Tan Brunet, Willie Badeaux, and other contemporary master carvers. Certainly these honors, peer recognition, and, most of all, his beautifully carved decoys qualify Frady as a Louisiana contemporary master carver as well as an old master.

Frady is the transitional link between the old and the contemporary master carvers for a number of reasons. He started producing hunting slicks in the 1930s that closely resembled those carved by the old masters. Frady used patterns to "rough out" the decoy he was carving. His early decoys, especially those carved for his own hunting rig, were made of balsa wood because it was easier to carve and also because it made the blocks lighter and easier to carry to and from the duck blind. Later, he carved the decoys' head out of cypress because of its durability. Eventually, he only used cypress or tupelo gum to make the entire decoy

His early decoys also had minimal body carving but excellent painting, much like Mark Whipple and Reme Roussel's decoys. According to his son, Frady believed that painting was the most important part of decoy making. One of Frady's favorite sayings was that one "could take a mediocre carving and put a good paint job on it and you had a good

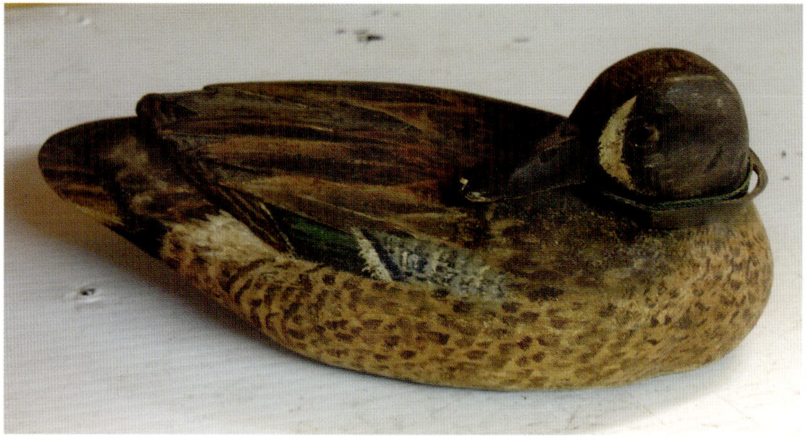

(1) Mike Frady's blue-winged teal drake

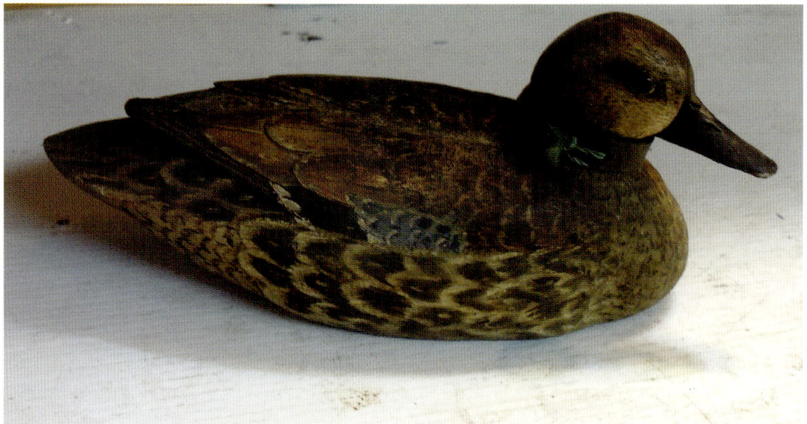

(2) Mike Frady's blue-winged teal hen

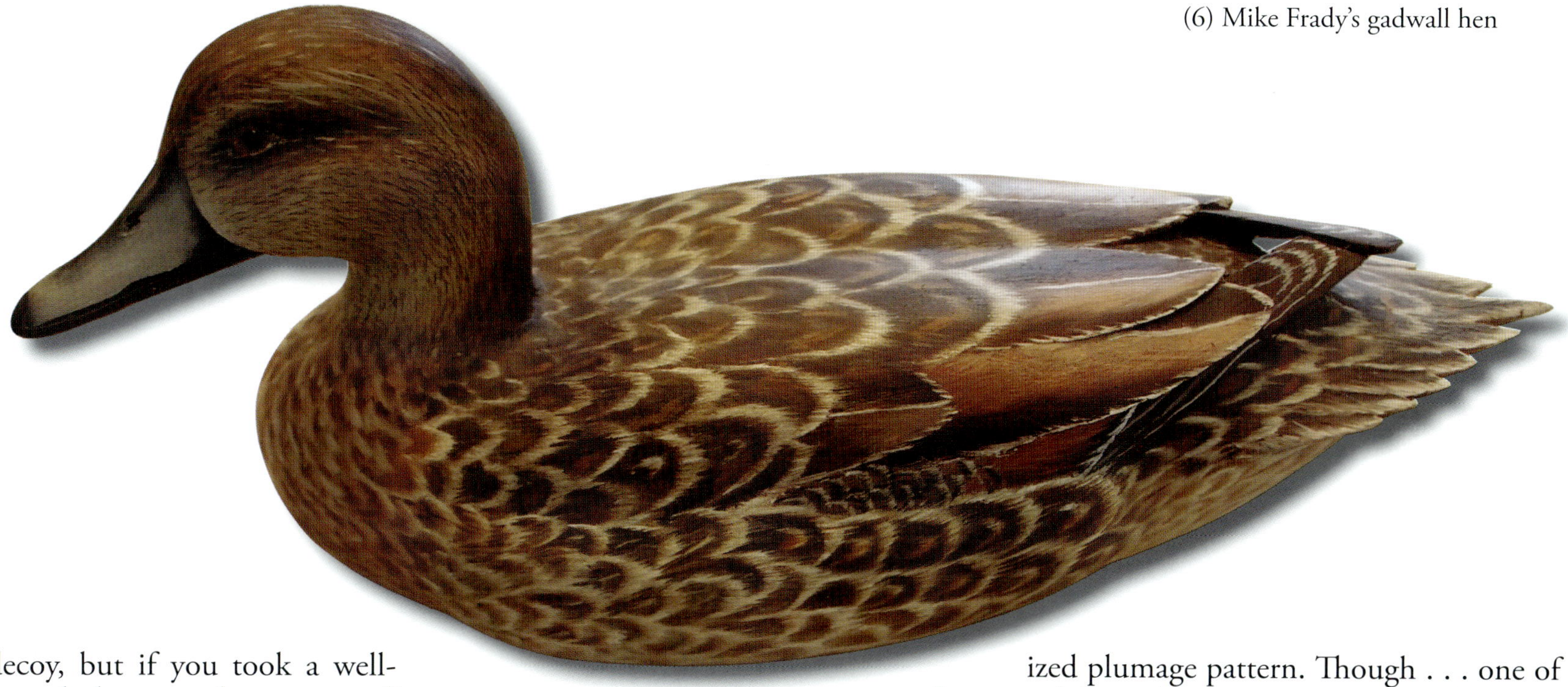

(6) Mike Frady's gadwall hen

decoy, but if you took a well-carved decoy and put a mediocre paint job on it, you had a mediocre decoy." Photographs 1, 2, and 3 show decoys from Frady's own hunting rig, which certainly are not "mediocre." In fact, they favorably compare with those carved by Lafrance, Vizier, and Comardelle.[3]

The Ward Foundation website says this about Mike Frady: He "carved species indigenous to the area like mallards, pintail, and teal. His decoys display a variety of head positions and attitudes. . . . Frady did only minor surface carving, he delineated the wing tips and detailed the bill. . . . What Frady lacked in surface carving he made up for with painting that combined dots with brushstrokes for a stylized plumage pattern. Though . . . one of Louisiana's lesser known . . . carvers, Mike Frady produced [a] quality stool that served area hunters well." I strongly suspect that the Ward regarded Frady as a "lesser known carver" because he didn't compete in the Ward or other national competitions. Frady is certainly not lesser known in Louisiana.

Photograph 4 shows a canvasback hen, photograph 5 shows a canvasback drake, and photograph 6 a very nice gadwall that Frady carved for LWCCG's competitions. Frady's canvasback looks very much like one carved by contemporary master Rock Zeringue many years later. Perhaps Frady's strongest tangible link to the contemporary masters is the resting black mallard shown in photograph 7. This

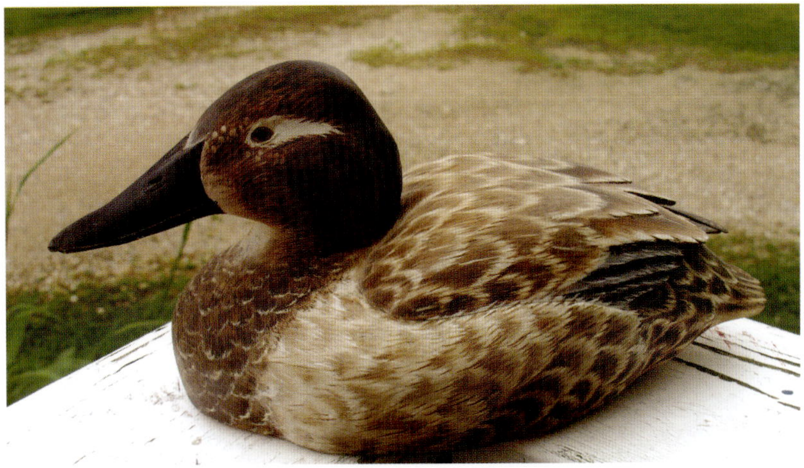

(4) Mike Frady's canvasback hen

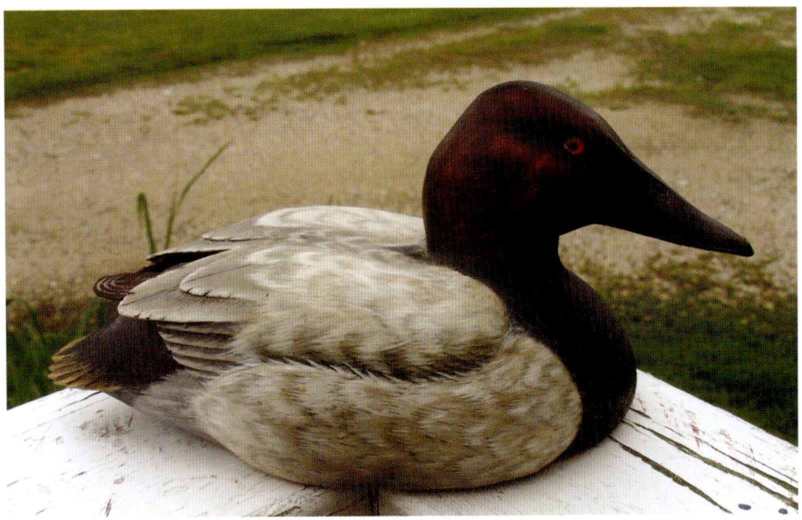

(5) Mike Frady's canvasback drake

decoy is thought to fall into the decorative category and was certainly intended for display and not to be hunted over.

Frady qualifies as both an old and a contemporary master, giving his decoys special value, especially since he is now deceased. The black mallard shown in photograph 7 sold several years ago at a Guyette & Deeter auction for $800 plus a buyer's premium. New Orleans collector Allan Kancher was a close friend of Mike Frady's and visited him weekly for years. During those visits, Kancher regularly bought Frady's decoys and now owns a large number that are very fine. Kancher regards his Frady decoys as more valuable than some in his collection that were carved by a number of Louisiana's world champions.

Endnotes

1. Frank, *Louisiana Duck Decoys*, 95-96.
2. See Ibid., 177 for a photograph of that device.
3. Mike Frady's status as one of Louisiana's best was confirmed by his inclusion in Brian Cheramie's definitive compilation of our states' great old decoy carvers, *Louisiana's Lures and Legends,* which includes a brief biography and several photographs at p.155.

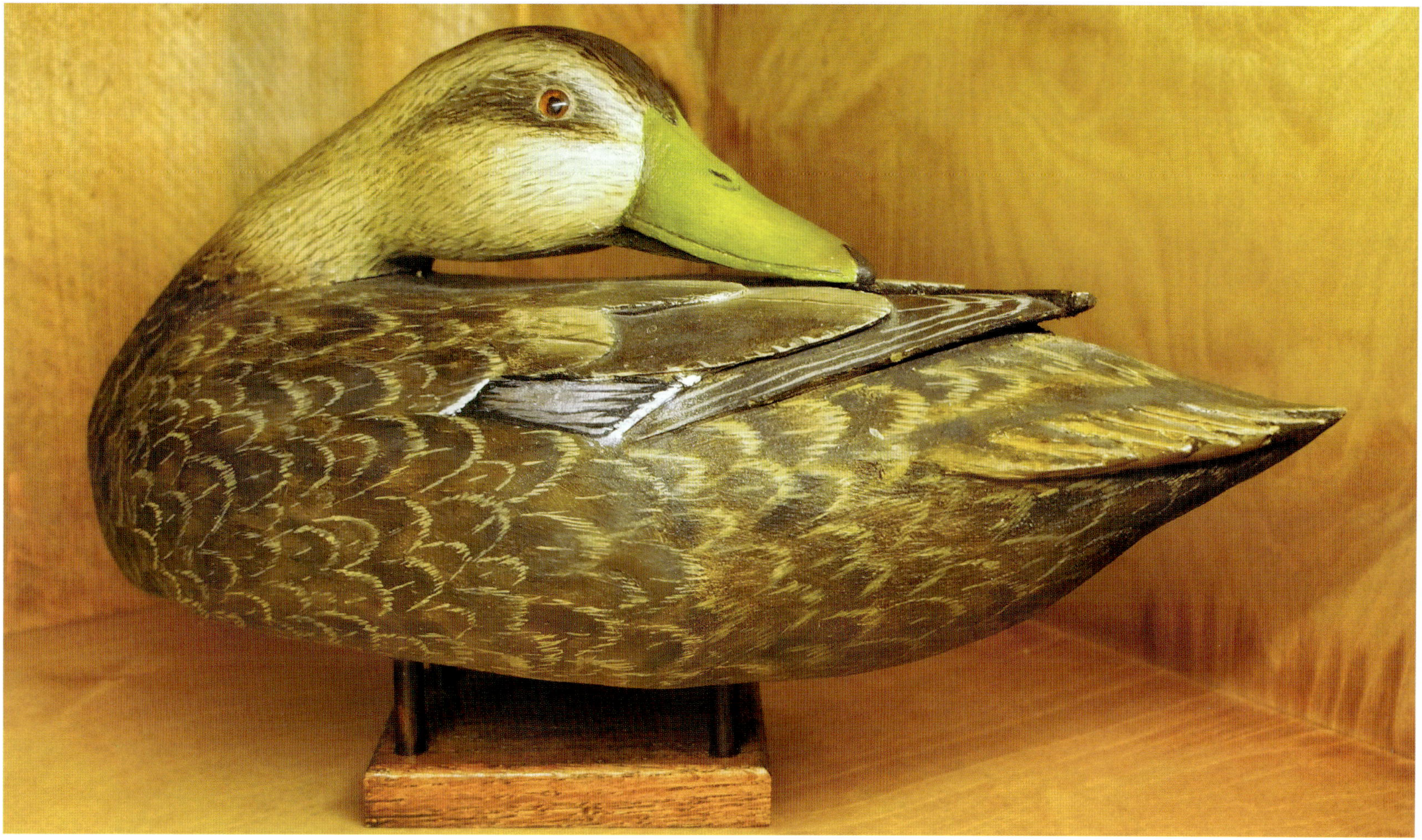

(7) Mike Frady's black mallard hen

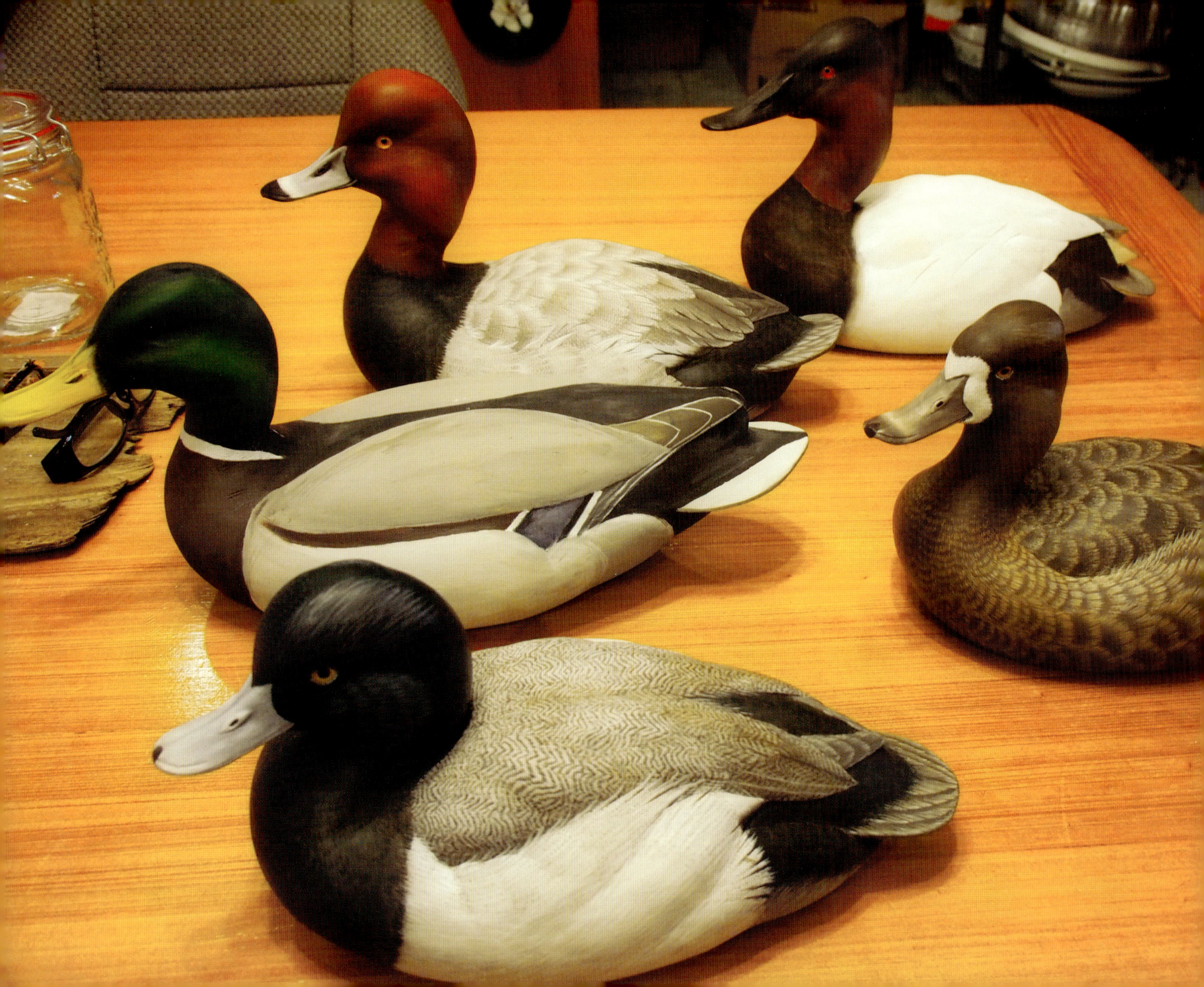

7 Willie and Gary Badeaux

Cajun Carving Masters

Opposite page: (5) Willie Badeaux's assorted hunting decoys

About thirty-five miles south of New Orleans, Bayou Gauche meanders into Bayou Des Allemands on one end and Lake Salvador on the other, making for some of the finest fishing and wildfowl hunting areas in Louisiana. It is a prime location for a decoy carver and home to two world-class carvers, Willie Badeaux and his son, Gary—both Ward carving contest prize winners and multiple Gulf South Carving champions. Willie and Gary live next door to each other on Badeaux Lane in the rural Bayou Gauche community near Des Allemands. The backyards of both of their homes end at the bank of Bayou Gauche, and the workshop where all their decoy carving is done is built over that waterway, as shown in photograph 1.

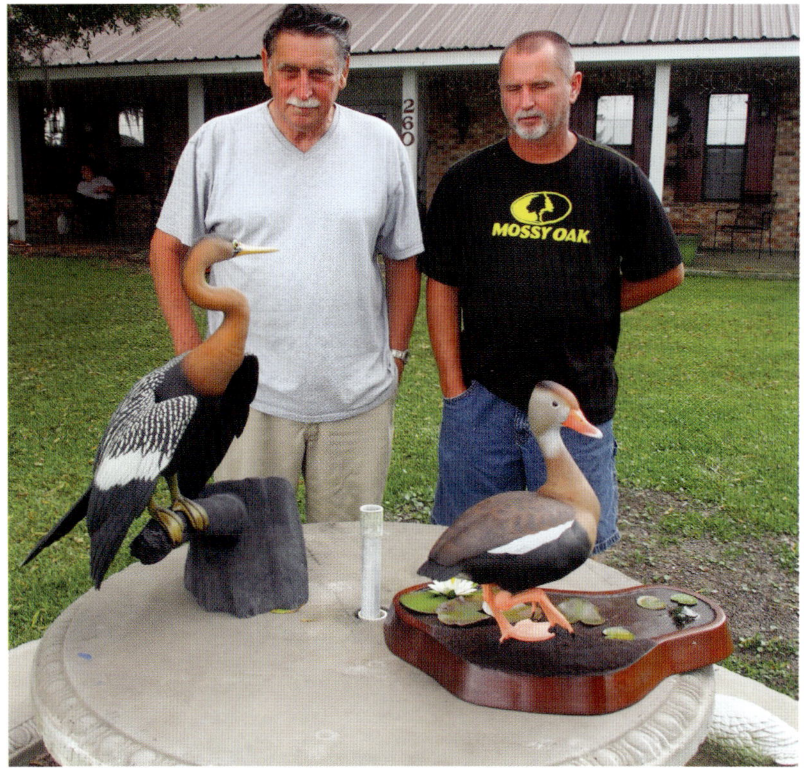

Willie (left) and Gary (right) Badeaux

I first met Willie Badeaux about forty years ago when I traveled to his home at 260 Badeaux Lane to ask him to carve a decorative wood duck drake for me. Willie was a tall man, well above six feet with a full head of thick black hair. We chatted for a few minutes about my request, and I left. Some weeks later, I returned and picked up my wood duck decoy, which was more beautiful and realistic than the real thing. It was an altogether wonderful experience.

In the spring of 2015, I made two more trips to visit Willie and his son and to do some research for this book. I looked forward to seeing my old acquaintance again. Wil-

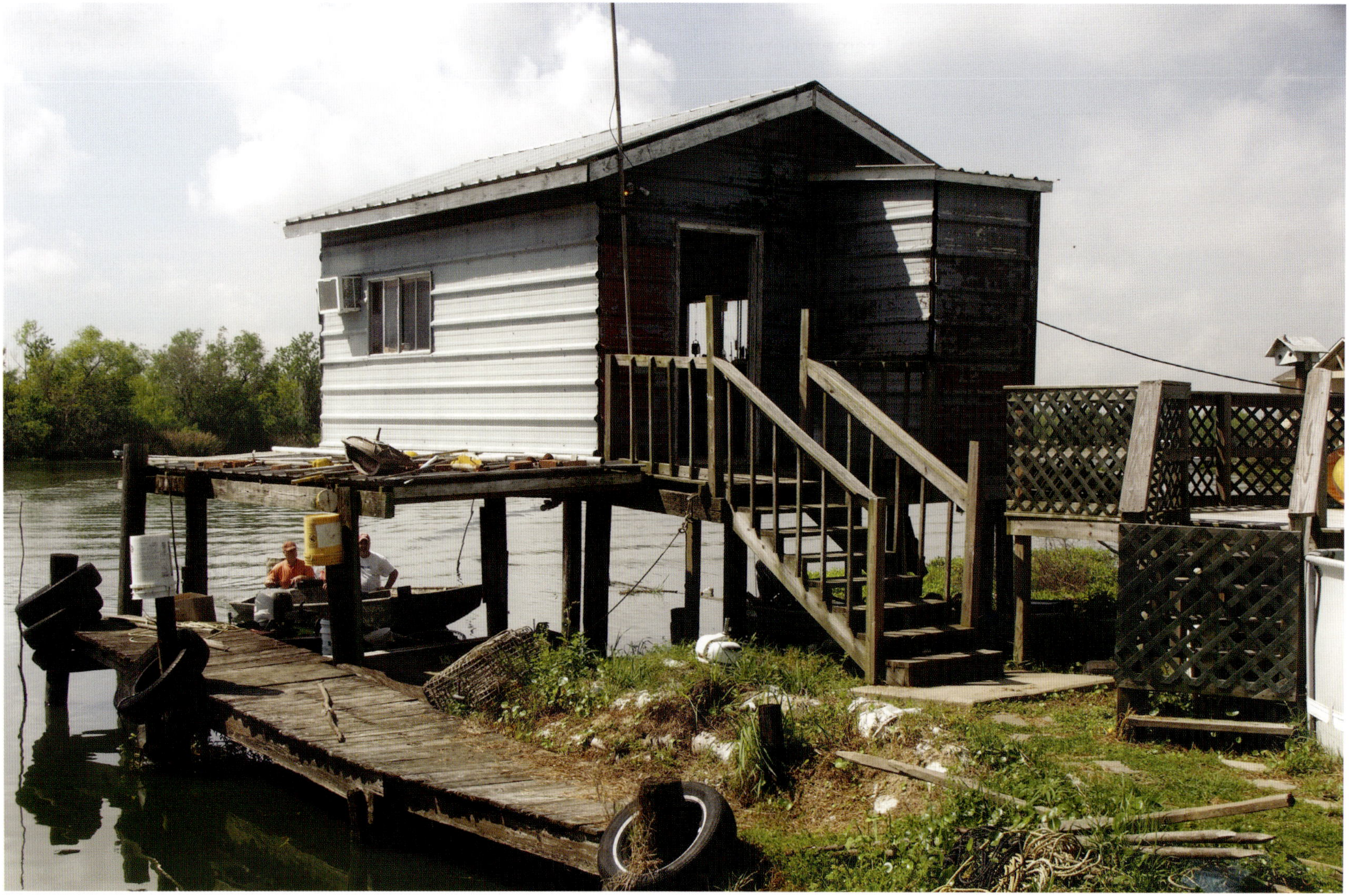

(1) Willie's carving shop

lie met me on arrival with a warm greeting and welcoming smile. He was less tall and less erect than I remembered and was now grey-haired, but then, so was I. During the course of those two trips, Willie and I were no longer acquaintances; we became friends, albeit aging ones. Willie is a kind and likeable person. It's hard to spend time with him and not become fast friends.

I had a mission on that spring visit. Besides interviewing him for this book, I wanted Willie to make an exact replica of a blue-winged teal drake, carved and painted by Reme Roussel, who had been Willie's decoy carving mentor. Willie was reluctant at first, but I explained it was needed for the book. I wanted to show how great contemporary carvers (and lesser ones too) can carve replicas of the old Louisiana masters' decoys for the decoy counterfeiting chapter. Willie agreed after I told him that I wanted him to sign his name on the bottom of that decoy and it would become a permanent addition to my collection. That decoy is shown in photograph 2.

Gary was working that day, so Willie, always the Cajun gentleman, suggested that we sit on his front porch and talk, which I readily agreed to do. Willie told me stories about the old days and his yearly visits to the national carving competitions with his close friends Jimmy Vizier and Tan Brunet. Each of this distinguished trio took a large number of decorative birds to these events and sold all they brought for good prices. I asked Willie why Louisiana decoy makers started carving decorative decoys. Willie said that some carvers liked competing to make the best decoy and to win the Best in Show purchase prizes. He explained that in the 1980s and 90s, the decorative style was very popular with collectors who were willing to pay high prices for competition-grade decoratives but that demand cooled off around 2000. I asked how that change affected what he was doing. He said that "decoratives take too much time to make" and there was "little demand" so he now concentrates on carving decorative gunners and hunting slicks that are in demand.

In due course, the conversation turned to Willie and even earlier days, starting with his birth on October 5, 1943. He was the third generation of his family to be born, raised, and live all of his life in the Bayou Gauche community. He quit school in

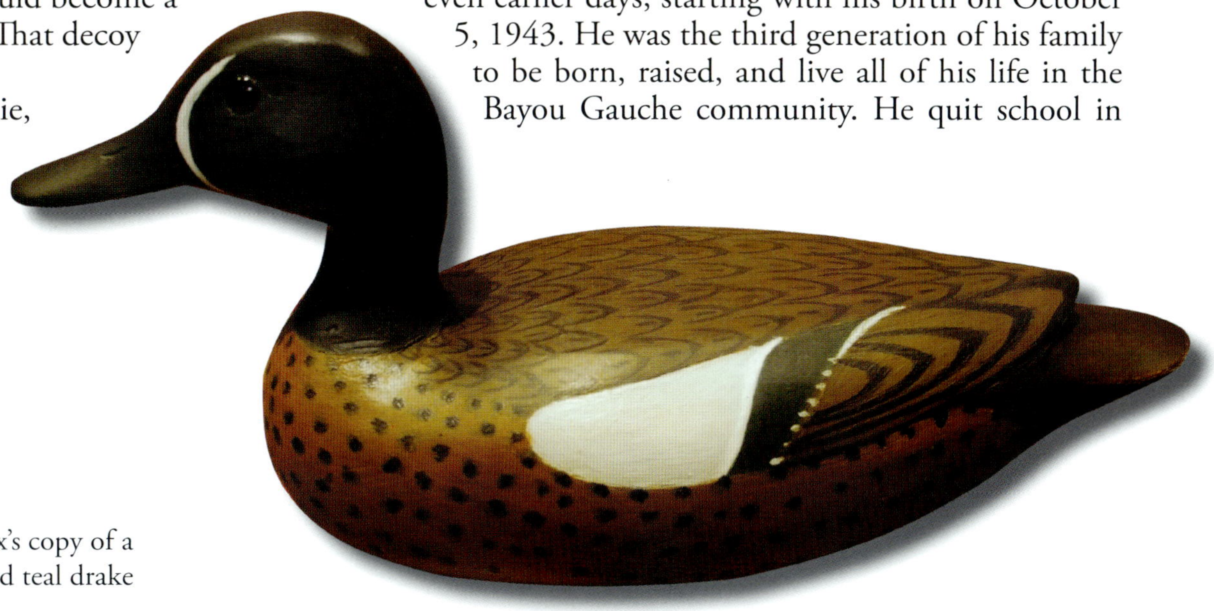

(2) Willie Badeaux's copy of a Reme Roussel blue-winged teal drake

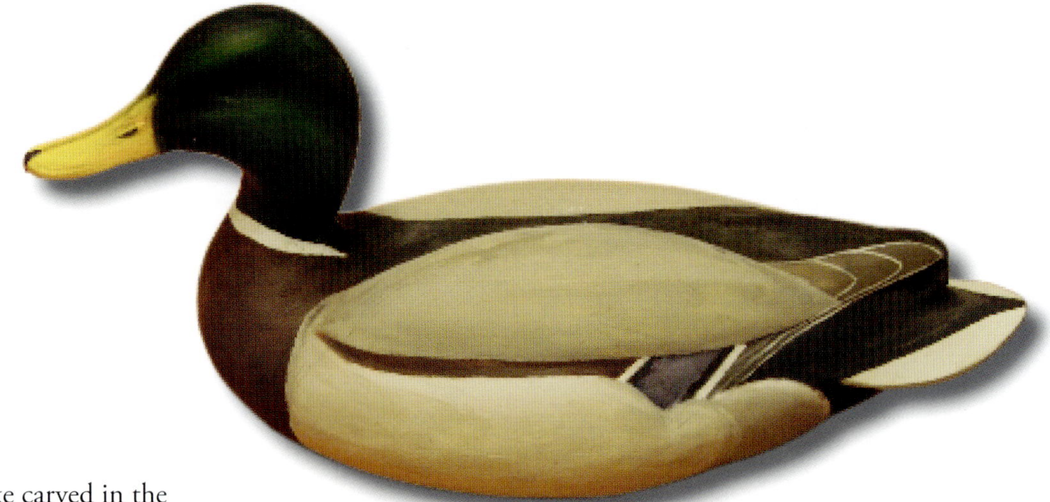

BELOW: (3) Reme Roussel's patterns
RIGHT: (3a) Willie Badeaux's mallard drake
BOTTOM RIGHT: (3b) Willie Badeaux's mallard drake carved in the style of Alcide Comardelle

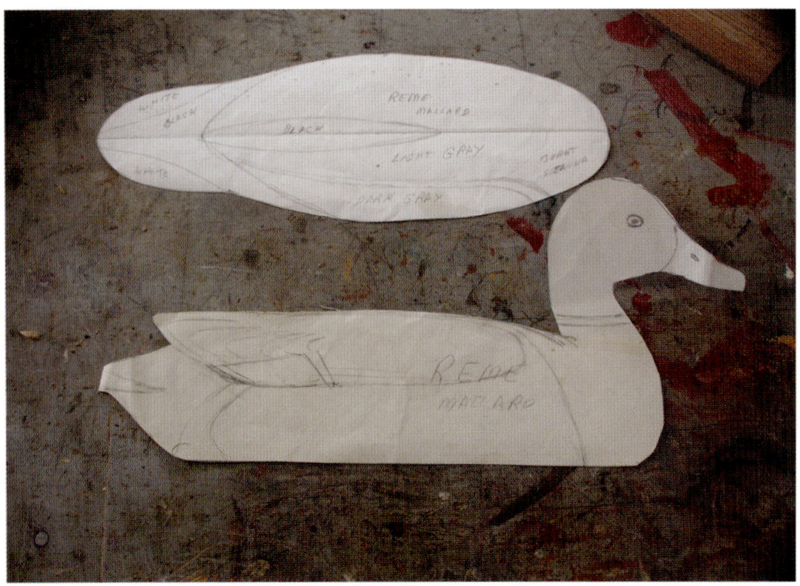

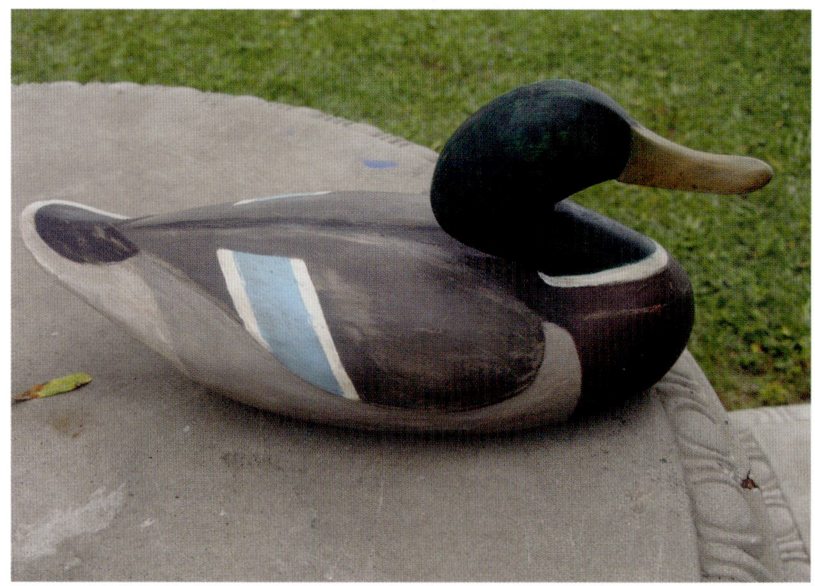

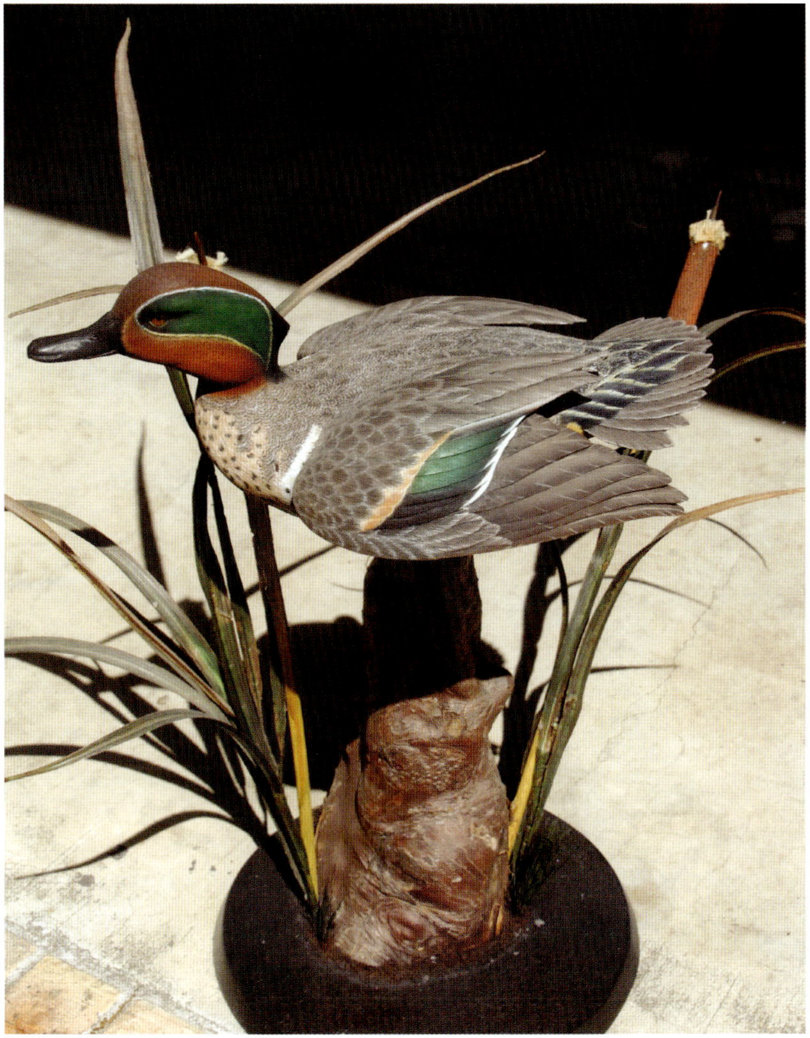

(4) Willie Badeaux's
green-winged teal sculpture

the eighth grade and soon started working as an industrial carpenter. Like his family for generations before him, Willie was an avid hunter. His grandfather carved his own decoy rig, and Willie starting carving decoys to hunt over when he was about seventeen.

Years ago, Willie's shotgun needed to be repaired so he took it to Reme Roussel (the nearest gunsmith) to have it fixed, not knowing at the time of old master Reme's decoy carving prowess. The two men became very good friends. Willie harvested cypress for Reme, and Reme gave Willie carving lessons as well as carving and painting patterns that he still has in his shop. Photograph 3 shows Roussel's pattern for a mallard drake. Photograph 3a shows a mallard drake decoy by Badeaux.

When discussing others influences, Willie told me that his wife's uncle was Alcide Comardelle, a Louisiana old master and lifelong Bayou Gauche resident until his death in 1955. Willie said that Alcide gave him very helpful carving advice and that he had gotten several of Alcide's decoys from family members after Alcide's death. Photograph 3b shows a mallard drake decoy by Willie in the style of Comardelle.

Willie was an apt pupil, and over time became one of Louisiana's very best and most versatile decoy carvers. He is an extraordinary decorative carver as the wildfowl sculpture shown in photograph 4 attests to. It is no surprise that he has won three Best in Show purchase awards at the LWCCG's annual Louisiana Wildfowl Festival and won multiple first place awards in various categories, including the best carved duck head in the 2014 contest. The blue-winged teal drake he carved for this book proves he can produce a great hunting slick, as well. He currently favors making decorative

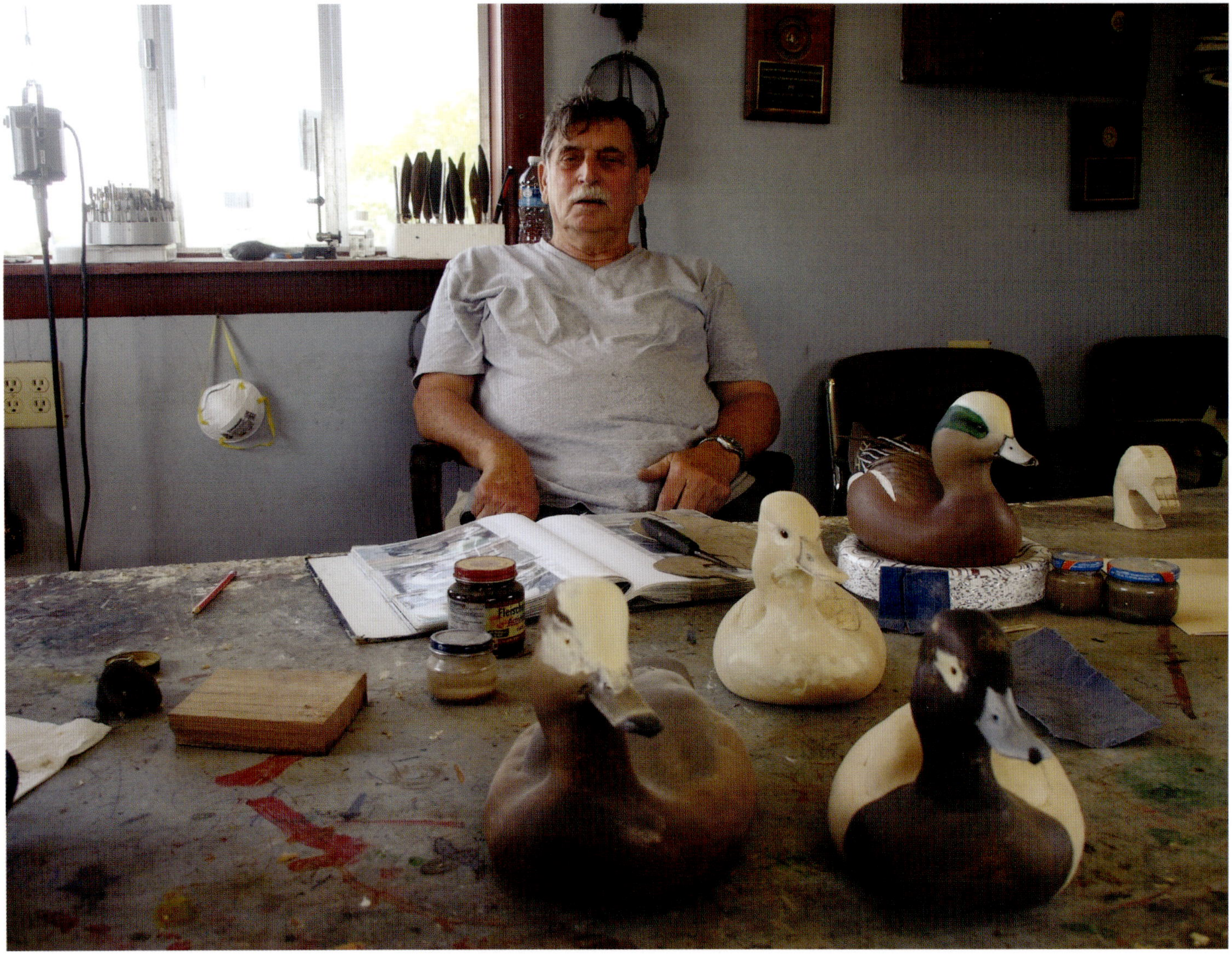

(6) "Professor" Willie Badeaux

gunners that are superbly carved and painted. Photograph 5 (pg. 42) shows a variety of Willie's recently completed decoys in this style.

Willie recognizes the unique place that decoy carving has in Louisiana's culture, and he is committed to preserving it. On Saturdays, his workshop is filled with aspiring decoy carvers who each pay $15 for a carving lesson from the master. Willie sits in his favorite workshop chair and presides over these sessions, teaching by example. Photograph 6 shows "Professor Willie" in teaching mode, ready to show his students how a decoy should be painted. Willie used to keep live ducks as models but stopped when alligators from the nearby bayou raided their pen. Now Willie, his son Gary, and Willie's students use illustrated wildlife books for their reference needs.

Willie makes his decoys out of cypress or tupelo gum. He lays a pattern on a block of wood and then cuts the head and body out separately using modern tools to make the rough and finish cuts. After they have had the final sanding, the head and body are glued together, and the decoy is ready for painting when the glue dries. Willie uses multiple coats of oil-based paint to get the color and feather delineation he wants. He is a perfectionist—if he thinks that the decoy is not just right, he puts it aside and starts all over again. He has shelves all around his shop lined with rejects.

While showing me around his workshop, Willie came across an unfinished, headless decoy body that had been carved by Reme Roussel, who gave it to Willie many years ago. I jokingly asked Willie if he thought he could carve a head that would do justice to the Roussel body and paint it as he saw fit, knowing that Willie likes challenges. The result is shown in photograph 7. What could be better, a decoy with a body carved by old master Roussel but completed and painted by contemporary master Badeaux?

Willie has a kind and unassuming disposition that complements his artistic skill and makes him one of my very favorite carvers. About two or three weeks after this visit, Willie called to say the Roussel teal drake copy was ready to be picked up and

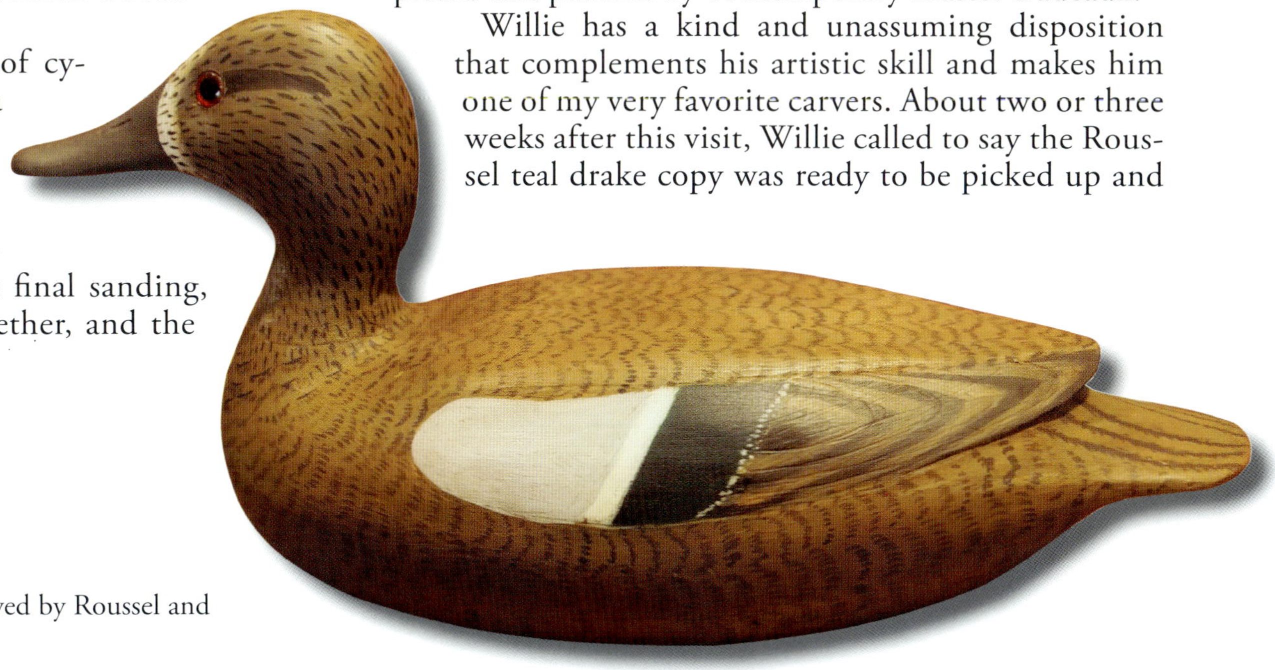

(7) Blue-winged teal hen with a body carved by Roussel and head and paint by Willie Badeaux

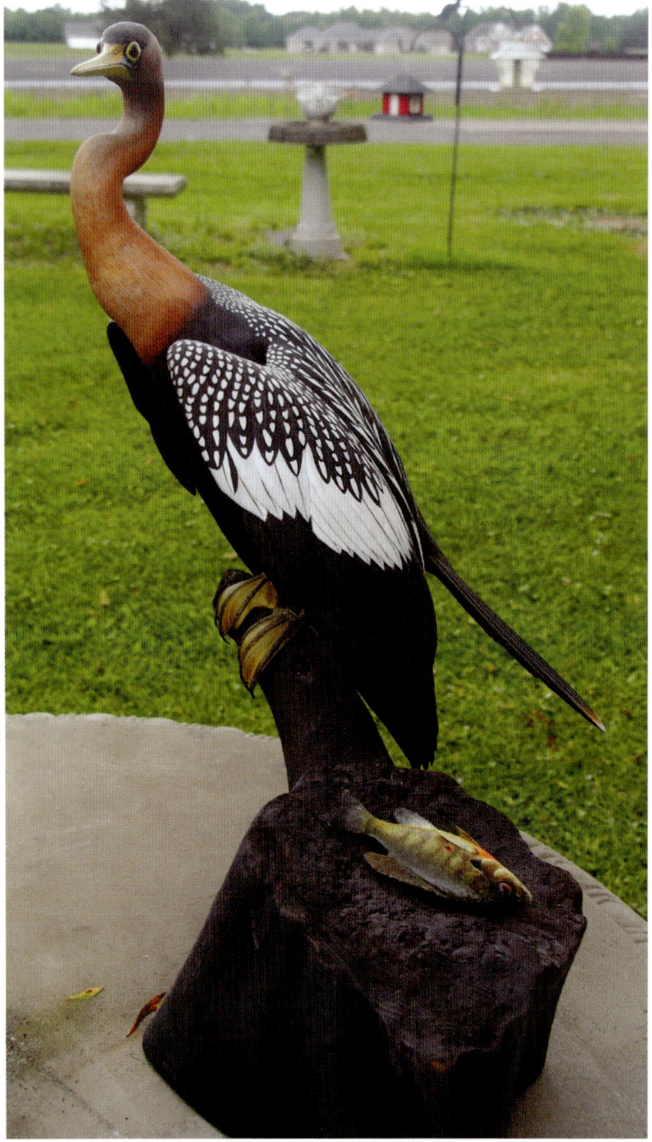

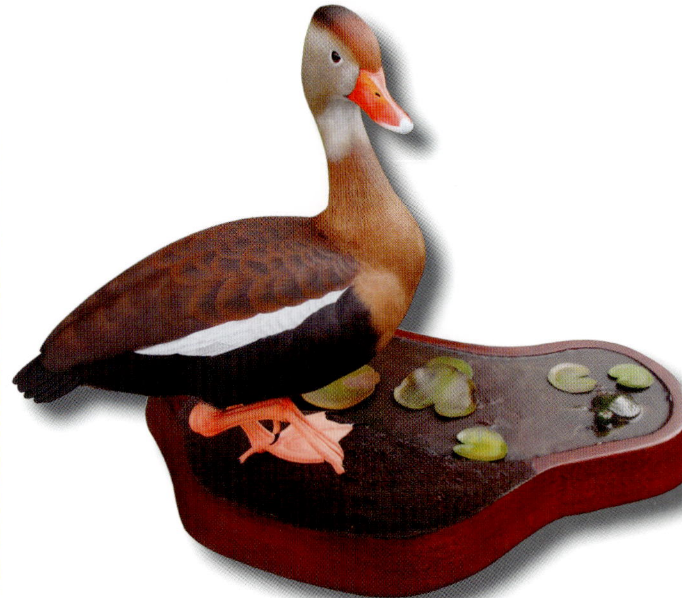

plans were made for me to come back to Bayou Gauche a few days later when Gary would be off work and I could pick up the "Roussel teal by W. Badeaux."

I arrived as planned and was welcomed by Willie and Gary. After introductions between Gary and I were completed, I learned that Gary was a self-employed fisherman, crabber, and airboat operator who had left school in the ninth grade. He is also an avid duck hunter. He got into decoy carving at an early age, inspired by his father's work as well as the wildlife he observed in the nearby marshes. He learned to carve watching his father and getting instructions from him. Gary admires the work of Jett Bru-

Left: (8) Gary Badeaux's anhinga
Above: (9) Gary Badeaux's fulvous tree duck

net, Russell Martin, and Mike Bonner—which helps explain why he likes decorative wildfowl carving. Gary's carving credentials were firmly established in 1977, when he won the A. Danner Frazer award for best teenage carver at the Ward World Carving Championship. After that prestigious achievement, Gary won numerous purchase prizes at the annual Gulf States Show.

Gary says he likes old-style decoys with high, turned heads. I asked to see and photograph some of his work. Gary apologized and said he had sold all of his recently carved duck decoys, but he had some decorative pieces that I could see. He first brought a wildfowl sculpture featuring a large Anhinga, a bird that I had never seen nor heard of. Gary explained that an Anhinga was an indigenous bird that is also called a "snake bird" because of its habit of swimming with only its head above water while pursuing fish, which it spears with its long, pointed beak and then swallows. It looked like some kind of prehistoric creature to me, but the rendering was very realistic. It is shown in photograph 8. Gary said he was inspired to carve the Anhinga because for some time he had watched one land on the bulkhead behind his home almost daily. The sculpture had finished second in a recent carving competition, and Gary was determined to repaint it and make it a winner. Gary also showed me a fulvous tree duck, aka "Mexican squealer," that he had recently carved. It is pictured in photograph 9. I was puzzled. Why would anyone carve two such obscure species? After thinking about it, I realized that it reflected a skilled carver's response to the carving competition judges' quest for something different.

Gary is a talented, relatively young carver, who does not technically fit into the older contemporary carver model for this book, but his past accomplishments coupled with his ever increasing skill, as evidenced by the exceptional canvasback drake seen in photograph 10, marks him for superstardom in the near future. It also makes him one of the standard bearers of the next generation of contemporary masters.

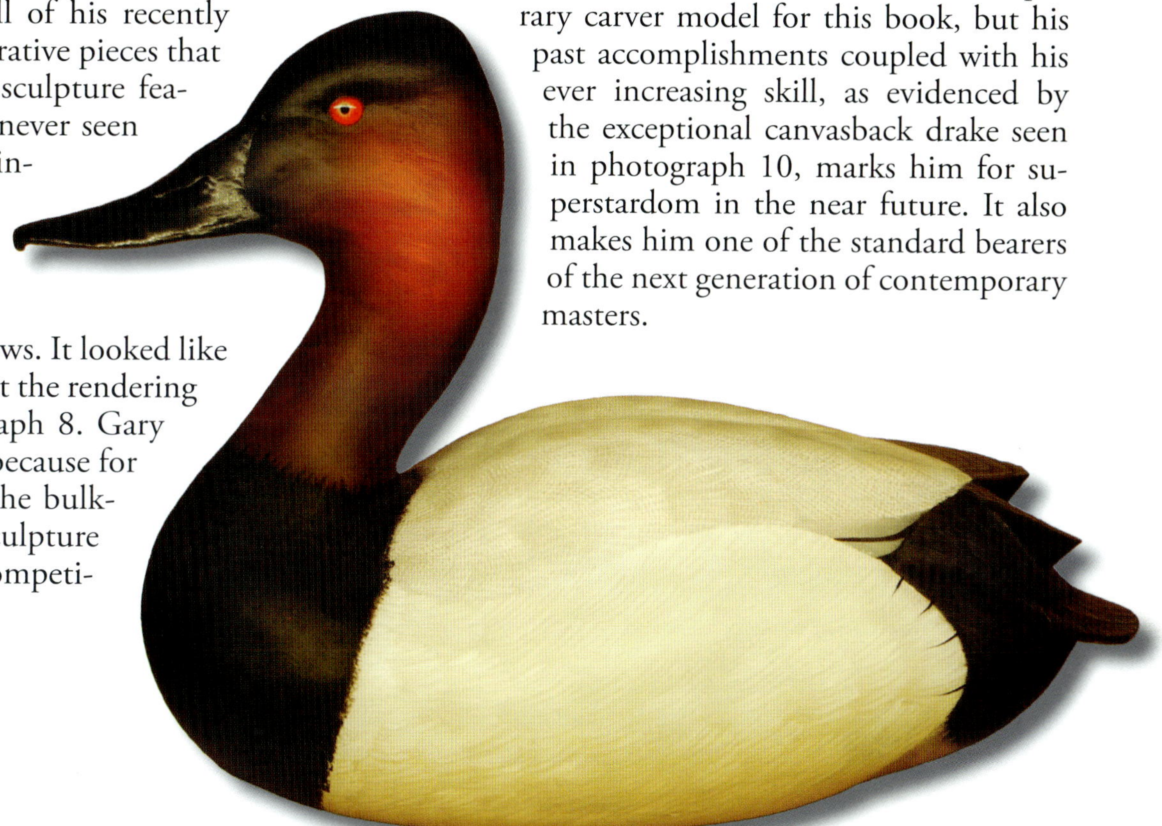

(10) Gary Badeaux's canvasback drake

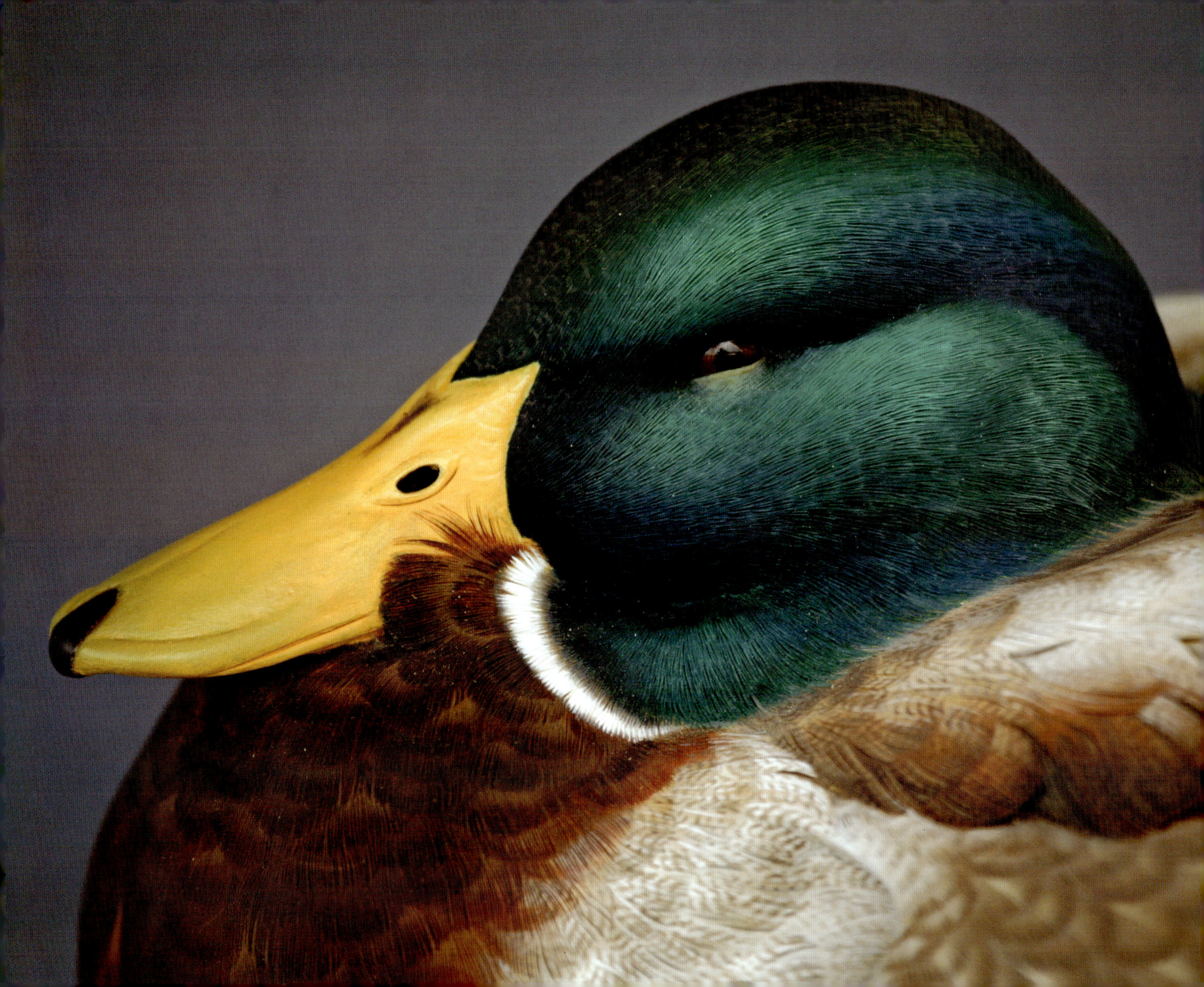

OPPOSITE PAGE: (5) Mike Bonner's mallard drake head

8 THE BONNERS

Master Decorative Carvers and Teachers

Is there an artistic gene that is transmitted from one generation to the next? If the Bonner family is any indication, the answer is "yes," absolutely. Born in 1937 and raised in Grand Rapids, Michigan, Dick Bonner, followed in his father's footsteps and became a skilled taxidermist and, on his own, gained widespread recognition as a world-class decorative decoy carver. In 1973, Dick sold his business, bought a sailboat, and decided to leave Michigan with his wife Joan and their youngest three sons and travel down the Mississippi River looking for adventure. The couple's eldest son, Mike, who was born in 1956, stayed behind with his grandparents in order to finish high school.

The Bonner sailboat and her intrepid crew stopped in New Orleans on January 7, 1973, primarily to have the boat repaired. While seeking out repair help, the family inadvertently wandered close to an urban battleground. That same day, Mark Essex, a deranged marksman, perched himself atop a downtown hotel across from city hall and engaged in a gun battle with most of the city's police force, including a large contingent of snipers stationed on top of a number of nearby buildings. As a result, the entire Central Business District of New Orleans was under lockdown. The Bonner family was detained until the gun battle was over and it was safe to move about. They were not put off by their harrowing brush with urban warfare, however, and in fact, they decided to remain in New Orleans.

In due course, Mike left Michigan and joined his parents. The family settled in Venetian Isles, located in the eastern part of the city between the Bayou Sauvage National Wildlife Preserve and the Rigolets, the wa-

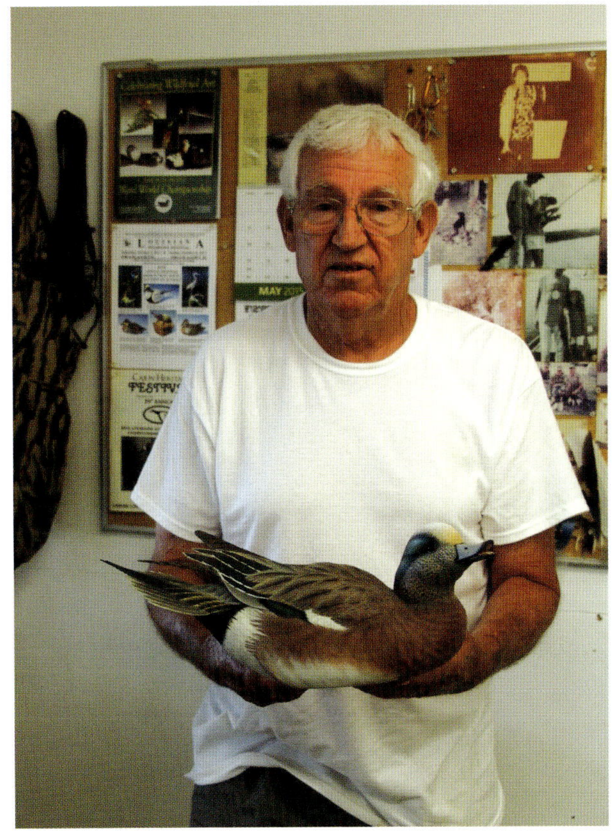

Dick Bonner

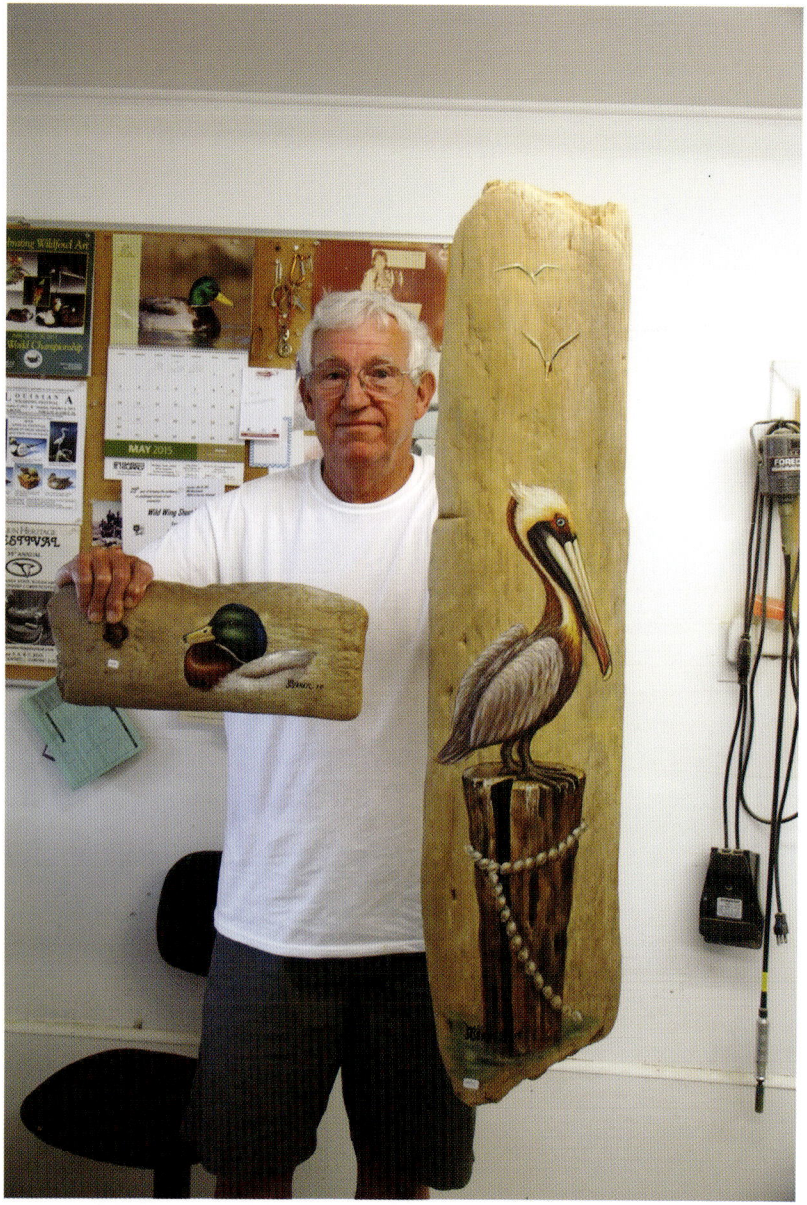

Left: (1) Dick Bonner holding wife's artwork

terway that connects Lake Pontchartrain and Lake Borne. The Bonners have a lovely home along a canal that provides easy access to the larger bodies of water nearby, the National Wildlife Preserve, and the surrounding marshes where wildfowl is seasonably abundant. Dick has even adopted an egret that he feeds several times a day with small fish he catches off the pier in front of his home. The Bonners absolutely love Louisiana.

Dick inherited his father's love of wildlife along with his belief in the importance of detail. He passed those traits onto his sons, Mike and Chris. Artistic talent was by no means limited to the paternal Bonner line. Dick's wife, Joan, is a wonderful working artist who specializes in painting wildlife scenes on drift wood that she then sells in Jackson Square in the heart of the French Quarter. Mrs. Bonner has been a fixture at that famed location for forty years and is rightly regarded as the doyenne of Jackson Square. Examples of her work being displayed by her husband are shown in photograph 1.

Dick and Mike are avid duck hunters, but unlike most of their Louisiana carving contemporaries, they did not develop their eye for wildfowl by watching ducks from a blind during hunting season. Dick started carving decoys when he was fourteen. He was self-taught and learned what wildfowl looked like by watching them in the spring as the ducks and geese flew north en route to their summer nesting grounds in Canada. He would stand in harvested grain fields and watch as the wildfowl landed to rest and feed on leftovers. Dick said the ducks were in their full mating plumage and were strikingly beautiful.

For years, the Bonners had an aviary on their property. As a youngster, Mike learned what ducks looked like by carefully studying live ones in the family's aviary and dead ones in his father's taxidermy shop. A quick glance at Dick's prize-winning decorative widgeon drake as shown in photograph 2 and Mike's prize-winning decorative mallard drake shown in photograph 3 proves that both men mastered "field training."

At age twenty-five, Dick entered his first prestigious carving competition, the 1963 U.S. National Decoy show in New York, and won second place in the Best of Show category. Mike attended his first decoy show at age two, but he waited until he was fourteen before he started carving. By age twenty-one, Mike was entering competitive events, having learned about decorative carving from his father and from his own efforts.

The Bonner men were hugely successful. Dick, Mike, and Chris have won over eighty Best in Show awards at national competitive events, including numerous first place awards at the Ward's World Championships. Most recently, Mike won the 2014 LWCCG's Charles Frank Decorative Decoy-Best in Gulf South Purchase Award. It is likely that award was almost as satisfying to Mike as when his youngest daughter, Chelsea, won the Best of Show in the Junior Division as well as the Danner Frazier Memorial award at the 2005 Ward World Championship. Four prize-winning generations of Bonners offer further proof of the artistic gene pool theory.

Mike's love of decoy carving is matched by his passion to teach others to carve. By all accounts, he is among the very best decorative decoy carving instructors in this coun-

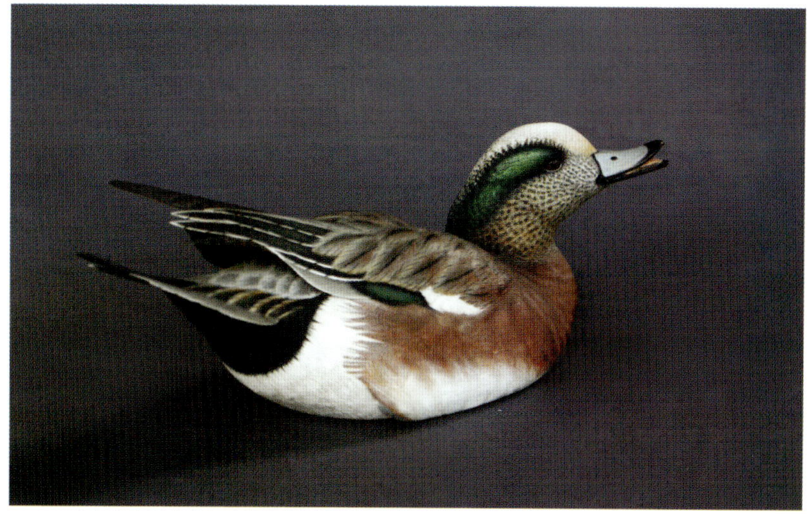

Above: (2) Dick Bonner's prize-winning widgeon drake

Below: (3) Dick Bonner's decorative mallard drake

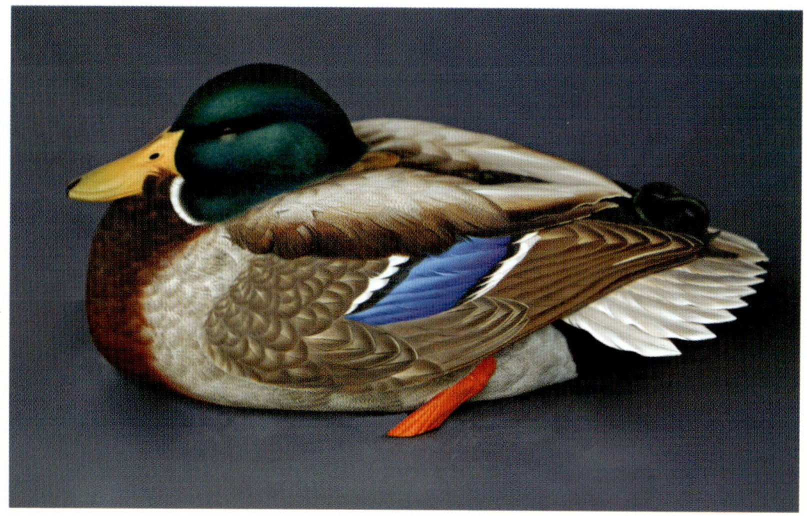

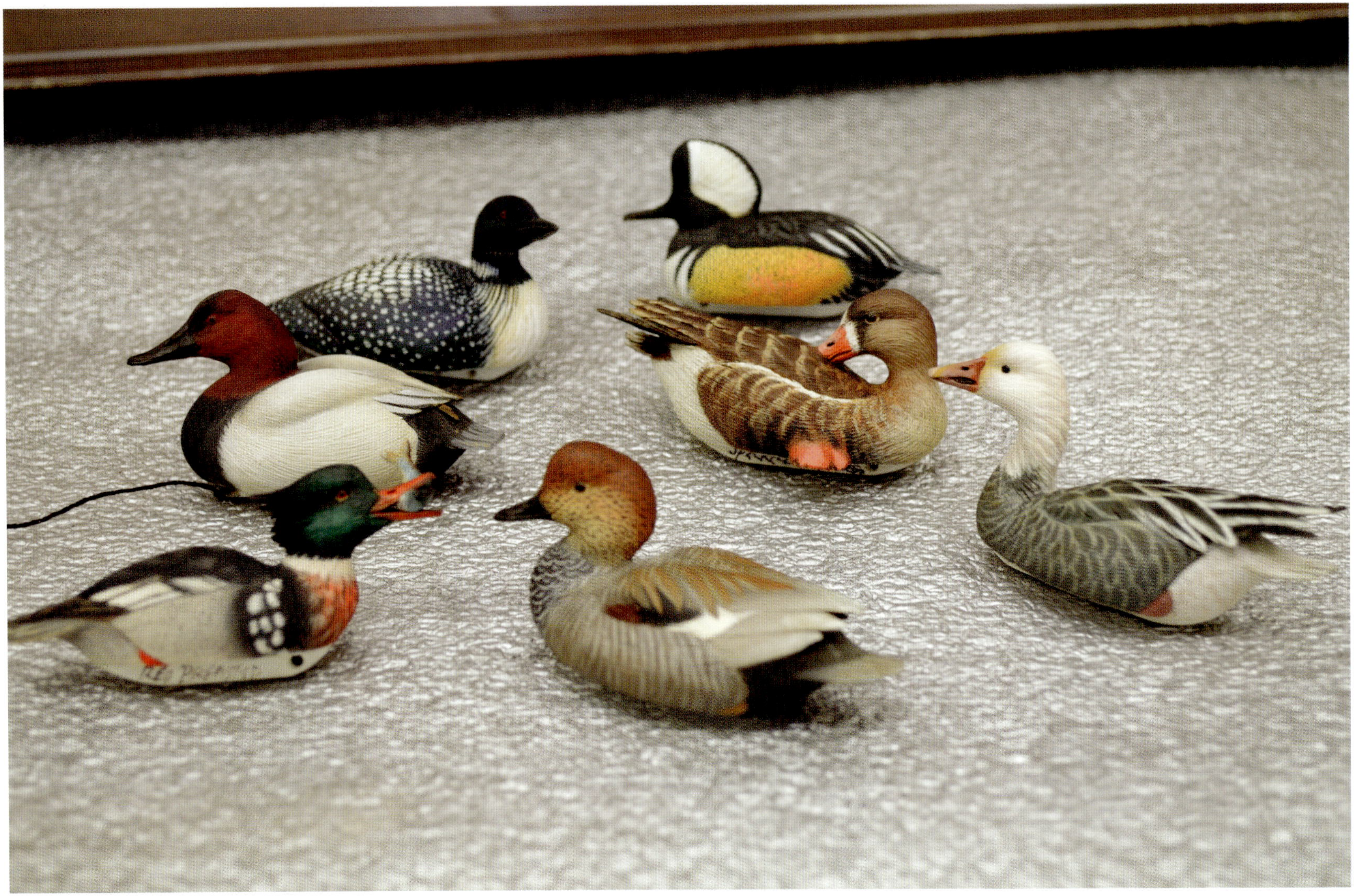

(4) Dick Bonner's assorted miniature decoys

try. Richard Reeves, a former pupil and fellow Louisiana resident is a three-time Ward World Best of Show champion. It is fair to say that Mike is prouder of his pupils' accomplishments than he is of his own. Over the years, Mike has significantly reduced the number of major decorative carving contests he enters because he doesn't want to compete against his carving students. He wants his pupils to win because that reflects favorably on his teaching skills and their victories are a source of great pride.

Dick and Mike are both very active. Mike teaches carving four days a week and carves two days. His decoratives are sturdier than other carvers' and have a lifetime guarantee. He will repair damage or replace a decoy if it can't be properly fixed. Dick likes carving and selling miniature decoys, which are a delight to look at and quite skillfully done as shown in photograph 4. Additionally, Dick carves a large decorative piece or two every year, mostly for longtime collectors of his work. Mike will take commissions to carve decorative decoys and decorative gunners as long as they are on his terms and timetable.

The Bonners have a significant presence in decorative carving circles nationwide. Dick inspired Doug Miller, a friend from Grand Rapids, to start collecting contemporary decoys starting in 1957 at age twenty-one. Miller went about acquiring the very best decorative decoys from all over the country by funding purchase prize awards at a number of major carving competitions. In 1973, Miller started hiring outstanding decorative carvers to make artworks for a wildlife museum in Colorado. Bonner was one of those chosen to participate. Since the 1970s, Miller has provided funding for the Life-Size Decorative Class winner at Ward World Championship Wildfowl Carving Competition. Over a forty-year period, Miller accumulated a collection of over three thousand works by the country's very best decorative carvers. The Miller collection was featured at a special showing in 2014 at the Ducks Unlimited National Headquarters in Memphis, Tennessee.

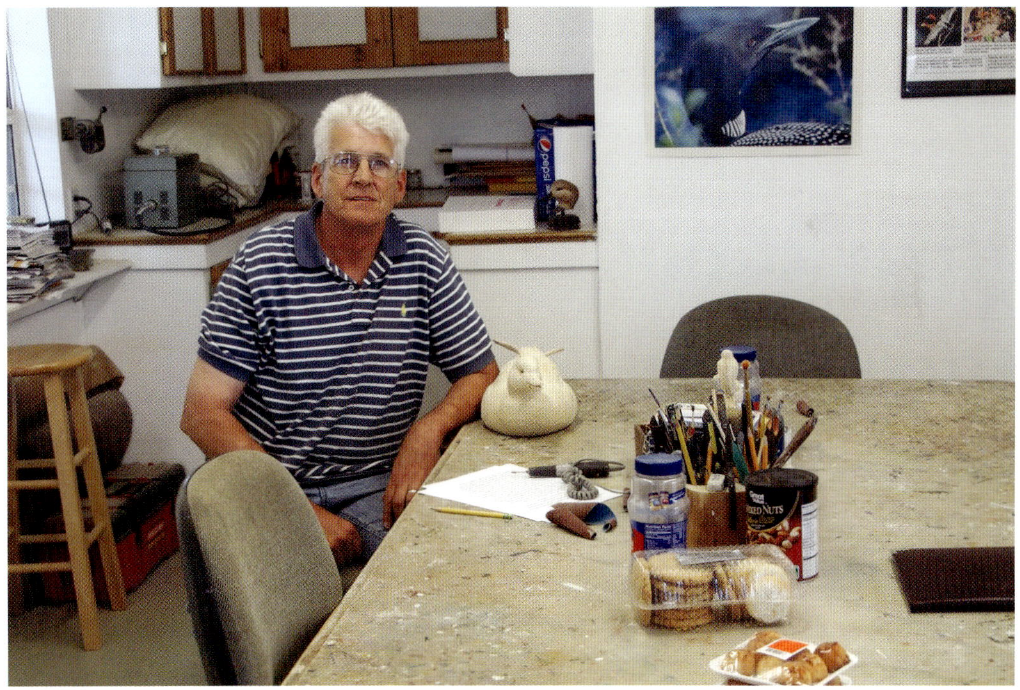

Right: Mike Bonner

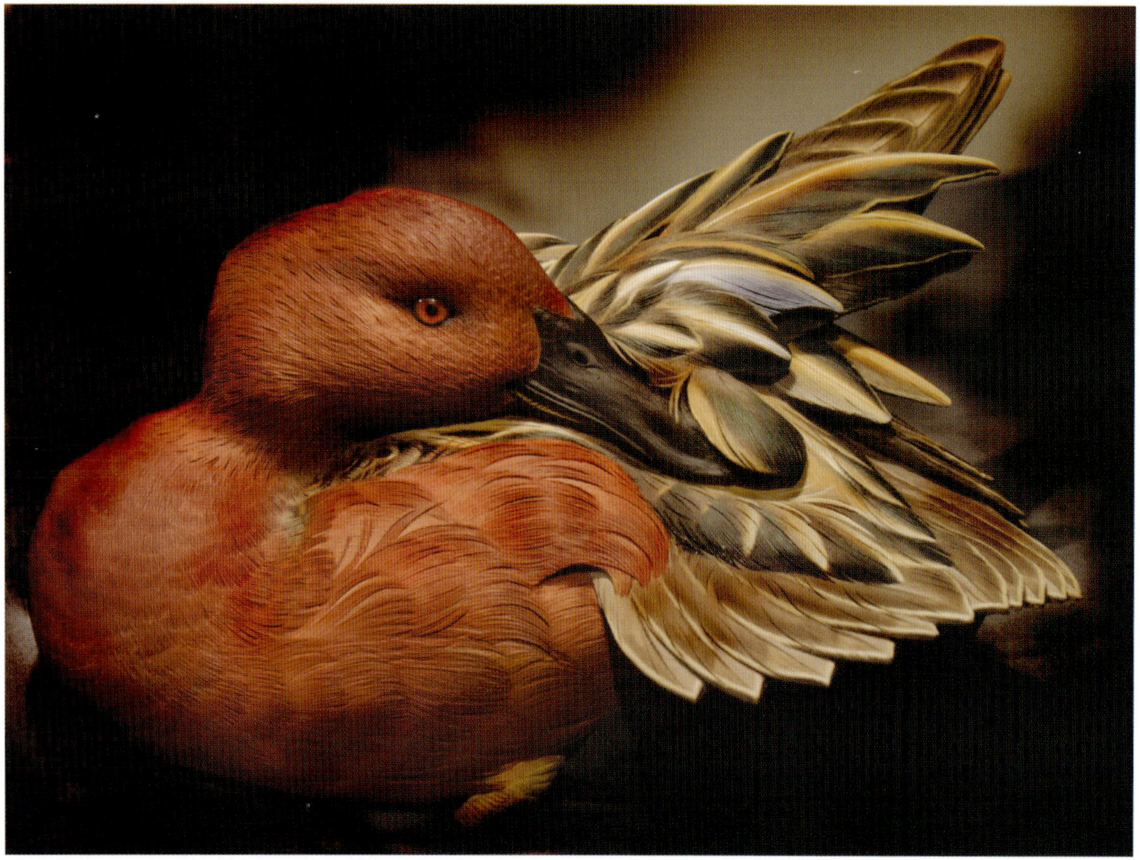

Mike Bonner's status as a world-class decorative carver was reaffirmed by having one of his decoratives included in the Miller collection. For further proof of Mike Bonner's incredible artistic ability, study the Mallard drake's head in photograph 5 (pg. 52), the pintail drake in photograph 6, the wood duck pair in photograph 7, and the cinnamon teal shown in photograph 8. They are some of Mike's very best carvings.

Carving decorative decoys, especially those intended to be entered in carving competitions, is very tedious and takes a great deal of time, patience, and intense concentration. Topflight decorative carvers infuse their decoys with a personal touch or attitude that often means the difference between winning and losing. Although an inanimate object, when a carver spends so much time and effort creating the decoy, it is understandable how and why they become so attached to it. No wonder Mike says he basically carves competitive decoratives for himself.

The story behind Dick Bonner's prize-winning widgeon provides a very good example of how a decorative carver feels about what he has created. After Dick's decoy won a Best of Show award, it was acquired by a col-

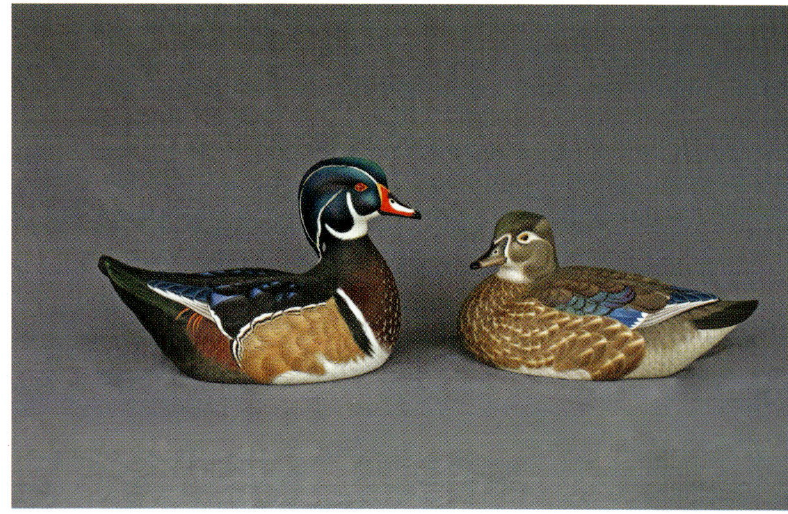

Above: (7) Mike Bonner's wood duck pair

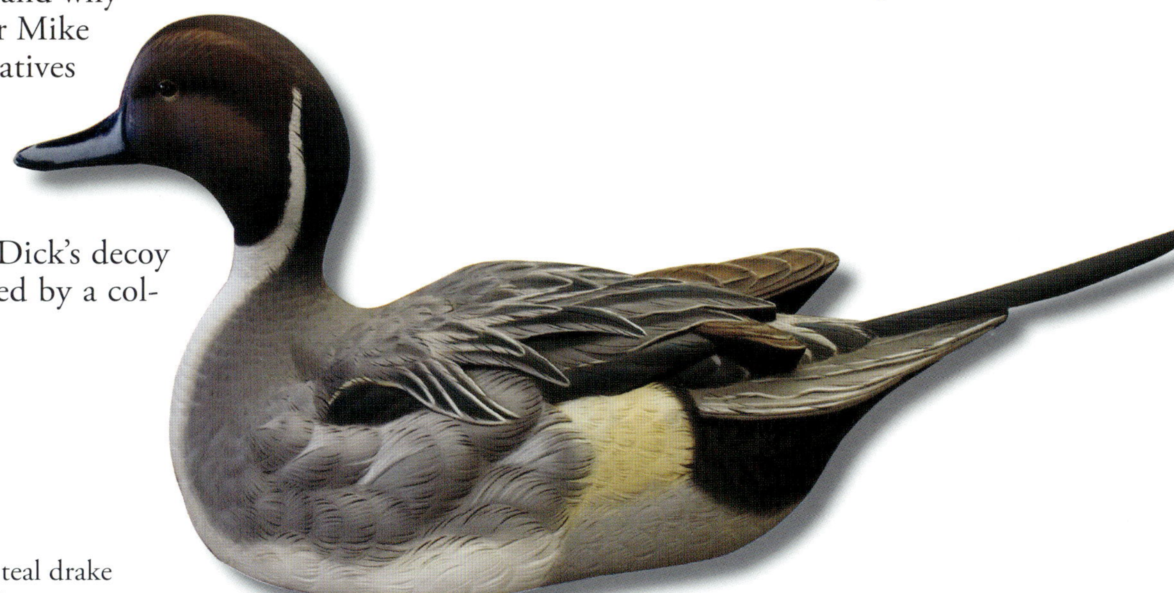

Opposite page: (8) Mike Bonner's cinnamon teal drake
Right: (6) Mike Bonner's pintail drake

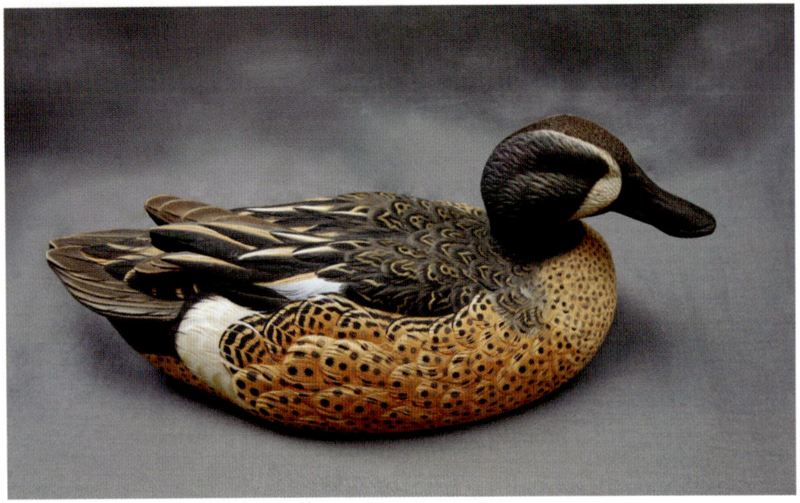

(9) Mike Bonner's blue-winged teal drake

Bonner family's profound love of and respect for nature in general and wildfowl in particular. During a discussion about duck hunting, I asked to see the decoys the Bonners hunt over. Mike brought in a pair of blue-winged teal and a mallard drake. The blue-winged teal drake is pictured in photograph 9, the hen in photograph 10, and the mallard drake in photograph 11. These are the most beautiful and lifelike hunting decoys that I have ever seen. I asked how anyone could hunt over such artwork. Dick replied "who else is more entitled to see the very best images of themselves than the ducks being hunted?

lector. Dick was thrilled and proud that his decoy had taken top honors but saddened that he no longer owned the prize widgeon. Many years later, the collector who bought Dick's widgeon died. When Dick learned of his passing, he contacted the collector's widow and bought the decoy back. Dick is overjoyed to be reunited with his cherished widgeon. Working decoys, old or contemporary, may be simple hunting tools but first-rate decorative decoys are works of fine art to be cherished and displayed.

I have great respect for Dick and Mike's artistry and even more for Mike's efforts to promote and perpetuate decoy carving in his adopted state as a carver and teacher—and as one of the leaders of the LCCWG in the aftermath of Hurricane Katrina. Most of all, I admire the

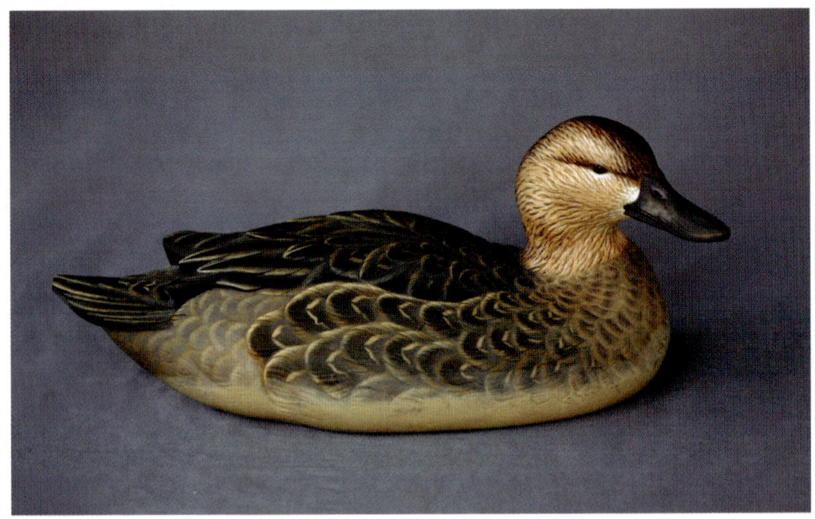

(10) Mike Bonner's blue-winged teal hen

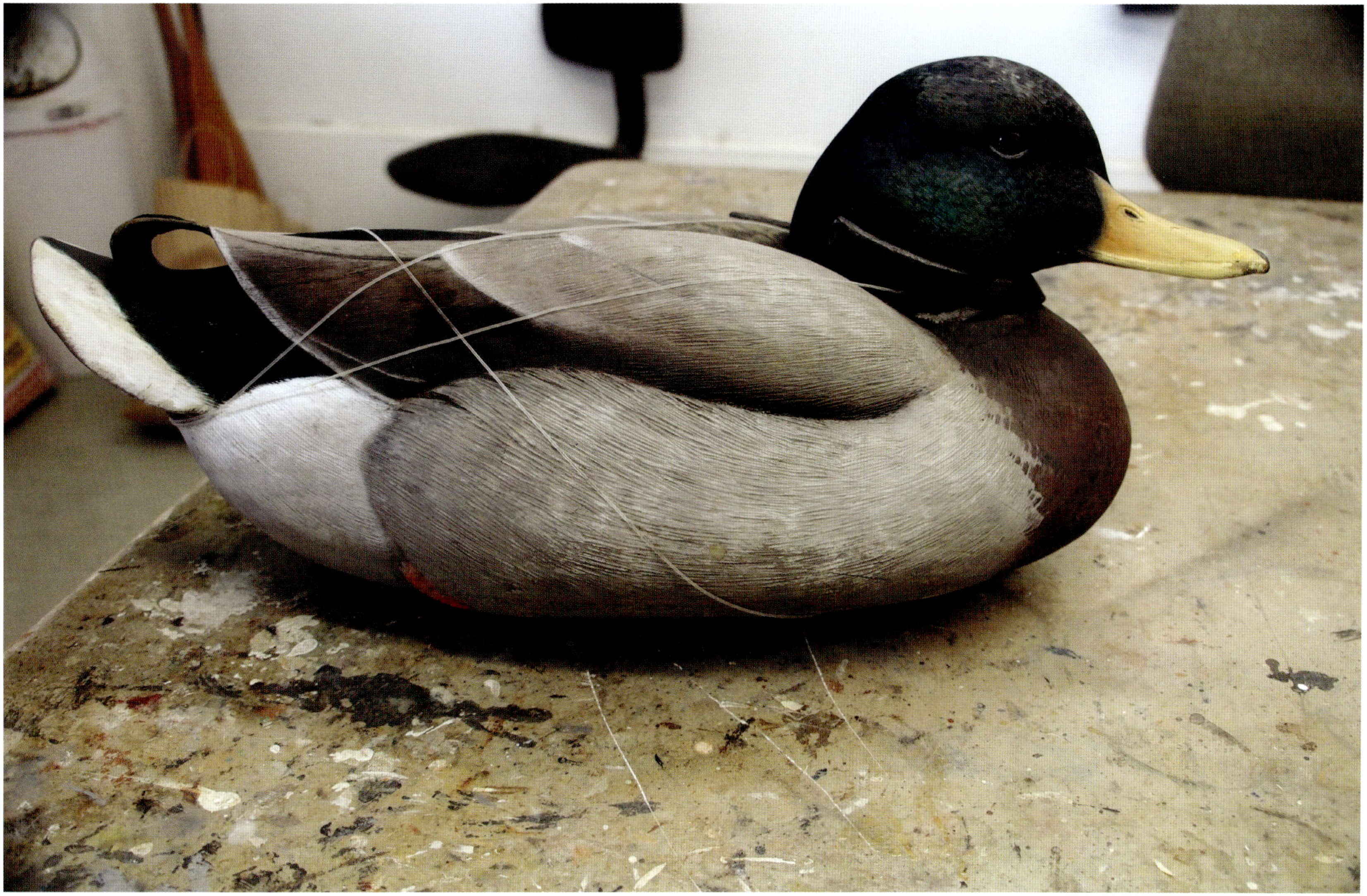

(11) Mike Bonner's mallard drake

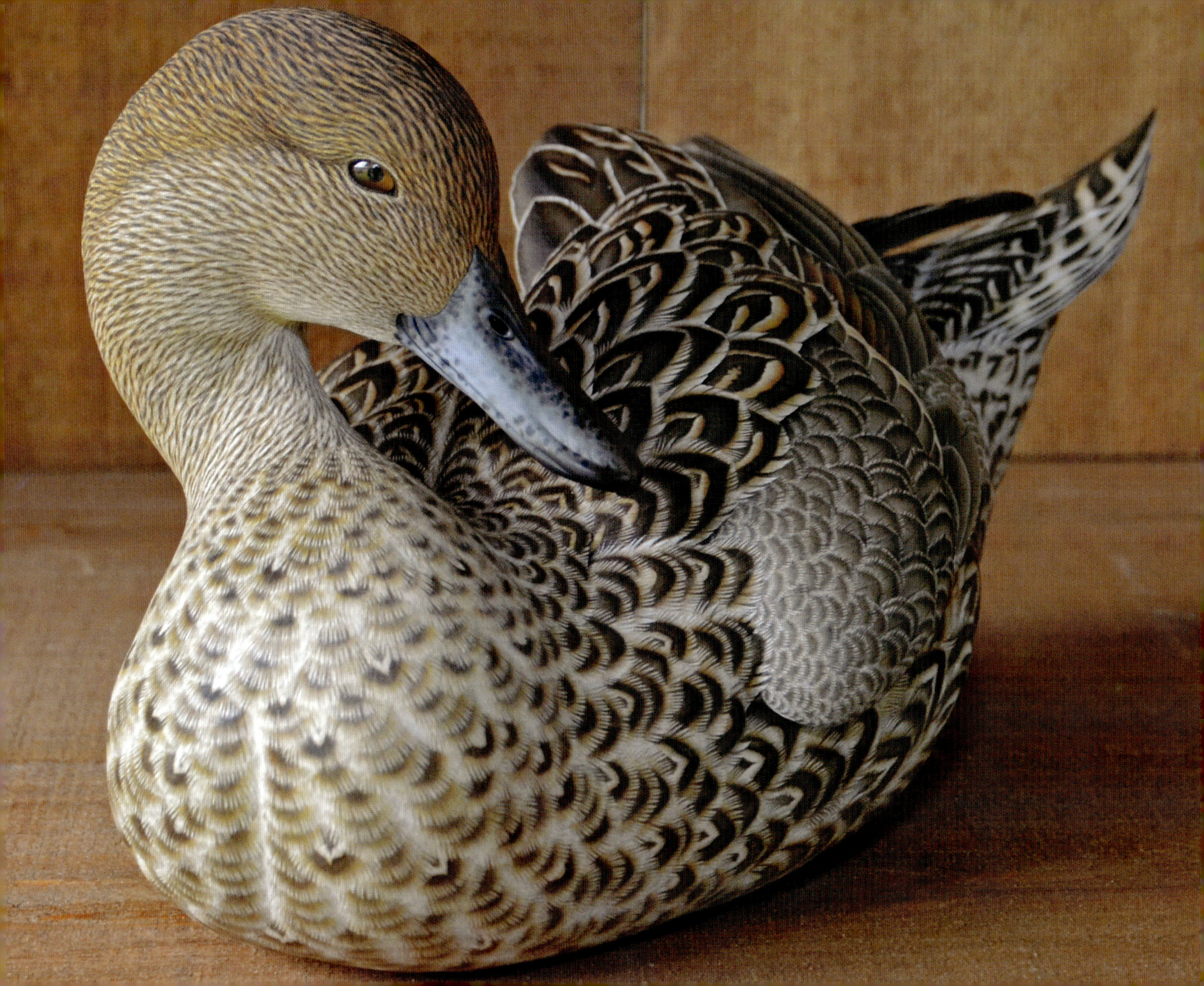

9 The Brunets

Cajun Carving Royalty

Opposite page: (10) Jett Brunet's decorative pintail hen

Galliano, Louisiana, is a small, rural village located on Bayou Lafourche, some seventy miles south of New Orleans. This bayou is a 106-mile aquatic route that large oil patch vessels, shrimp boats, and all manner of personal watercraft use to reach the Gulf of Mexico. The bayou also provides access to some of the best hunting and fishing grounds in the United States, which made it an ideal location for settlement by Acadians when they arrived in Louisiana in the eighteenth century. It is only in the last fifty years that English replaced French as the primary language in this area and more children graduated from high school than dropped out to go to work. As of 2010, Galliano was home to just under eight thousand people. The work of most of those who live there (ranging from multimillionaire oil patch vessel owners to minimum-wage shrimp peelers) is related in some way to the water or in jobs that supply equipment and services needed for waterborne work—especially the offshore oil and gas industry.

With the current worldwide surplus of fossil fuel, Galliano, like most coastal Louisiana towns, is mired in a recession. For some months, many boats, large and small, have been securely tied to the numerous docks that line Bayou Lafourche, which itself is clogged with water hyacinths (nature's testament to how few ships and boats are using the waterway these days). But things are not all dire in Galliano. Being out of work temporarily allows time to do important and enjoyable things like fishing, hunting, or getting ready for the next hunting season—the cultural callings of this area since before Louisiana became a state in 1812.

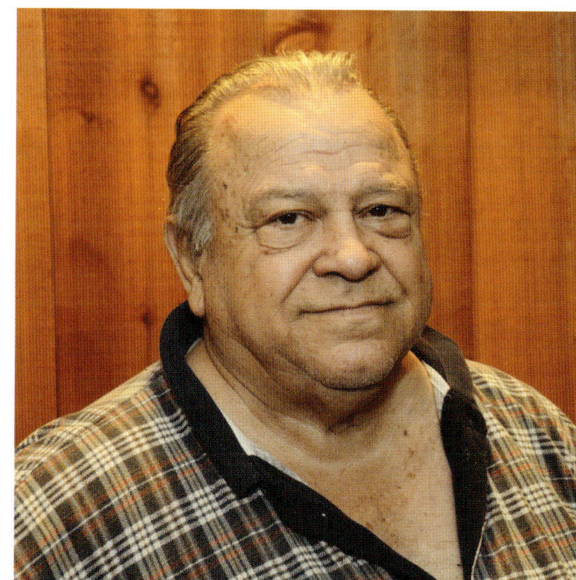

Tan Brunet

Galliano is home to Andrew "Tan" Brunet and his two sons, Jett and Jude—the most highly acclaimed and frequently honored decoy carving family of all time. Each of these three men has won the Ward World Championship[1] more than once. Tan won this prestigious award five times, starting in 1977, and again in 1978, 1981, 1982, and 1983. Winning the championship three years in a row is an unheard of accomplishment that no one has come close to before or since. Jett won in 1985 and 1987, and Jude followed in 1993 and 1995.[2]

All three Brunets are multitalented artists and each has different capabilities and interests. However, they all have shared experiences, influences, and heritage that have helped mold them. Put another way, they each have the same Bayou Lafourche roots, and it is helpful to examine those roots to see what role they played in what each has accomplished. In the process, reflect on the question of whether artistic greatness is an acquired or an inherited trait. In my view, the Brunets prove it is both.

Tan Brunet was born on October 20, 1938. His parents lived in Galliano, where the family owned and operated a lumberyard. Tan was the only one of his five siblings that graduated from a high school with twelve grades. Wildfowl hunting in the nearby marshes and shallow ponds was not a recreational activity for Tan and many other residents of the area; hunting, fishing, crabbing, trapping, and shrimping was a way of life for those who lived along Bayou Lafourche. In the early days, wildfowl was killed and seafood caught to provide food for the family to eat and produce some revenue if there was more than enough to provide for the family. In many ways, the lives of the Bayou Lafourche Cajuns were much like those of Maryland's watermen. But while some say the watermen became extinct by the 1940s, if not earlier, the Bayou Lafourche Cajuns' lives remain the same in many respects.

Well into the twentieth century, ducks and geese were abundant in southeast Louisiana, especially in the marshy areas and lakes on either side of Bayou Lafourche. However, the success of the hunt largely depended on properly setting out an adequate number of good working decoys—a tool as essential to wildfowl hunting as a shotgun, shell bucket, and duck call—which is why so many Cajuns became decoy carvers themselves. None are better, however, than the Brunets and their relatives in the Vizier family—decoy-carving patriarch, Beauregard Vizier (1850-1933), father of Clovis (Cadis) and Odde Vizier. All three carved good working decoys, especially Clovis (1887-1975), who was one of Louisiana's great old Masters.

The Brunets lived next door to the Odde Vizier family, and Odde's son Jimmy (1933-2011) became a close and lifelong friend of Tan's even though he was five years older. Jimmy was an exceptional decoy carver who, along with his father and uncle, made and sold decoys to hunt over. In the early days, the price of the elder Viziers' decoys was $2.50 each, so Tan decided it was more practical to let Clovis, Odee, and Jimmy teach him how to carve rather than buy their decoys. Since the Viziers were distantly related, there was no charge for the carving lessons. Tan started carving decoys when he was about sixteen, with Clovis being his major tutor in the early days as Jimmy was away working on boats offshore. Tan was understandably influenced by Clovis's distinctive carving style that featured raised wings, scribed feathers on the decoy's head and body, and etched tail feathers.

In 1951, Clovis entered a pair of mallards, presumably carved in this style, in a prestigious carving competition held in New York City and those mallards won second place in the decorative decoy category. Tan has a decoy in his personal collection that proves Louisiana-style decorative decoy carving was started by Clovis Vizier in Galliano, Louisiana. This decoy, shown in photograph 1, also demonstrates Tan's belief that good old decoys should be restored whenever possible in order to preserve the heritage. Someone gave Tan the Vizier-carved body but the decoy's head was missing, so Tan carved, painted, and attached a new one. The result is a great looking decoy; one that is fit to hunt over or put on display as Tan has done.

There is no question that Tan Brunet and his sons greatly improved on that style, winning nine World Championships between 1977 and 1995 as well as many divisional blue ribbons. The Brunets stopped competitive carving years ago, but Tan and Jett continued carving decorative wildfowl after they stopped competing. Jett is still actively carving, but Tan less so. Jude now prefers wildfowl painting, at which he excels.

Tan got married in 1957 at age twenty; his wife, Jan, was eighteen. The couple had three children, Jett and Jude and a daughter, Luz. Tan and his brother Elphege Brunet Jr., barely out of their teens, took over management of the family's lumberyard when their father retired so he could hunt and fish. Tan continued carving decoys as time permitted, and this work-carve regimen continued until 1977 when Tan and his brother had to close the lumberyard.

In 1973, Bill Hanemann introduced Tan to Dr. Harry Walsh, a founder and the driving force behind the Easton Waterfowl Fall Festival, and Walsh invited Tan to come to Easton and exhibit his decoys that fall. Tan had to decline the invitation for that year, but Walsh gave him a "rain check," and so in the fall of 1974, Tan made his "maiden voyage" to the Tidewater Inn, the East Coast's center of the decoy carving universe. Tan's initial visit to Easton and the decoys he exhibited left a very favorable impression but did not knock the decoy universe off its

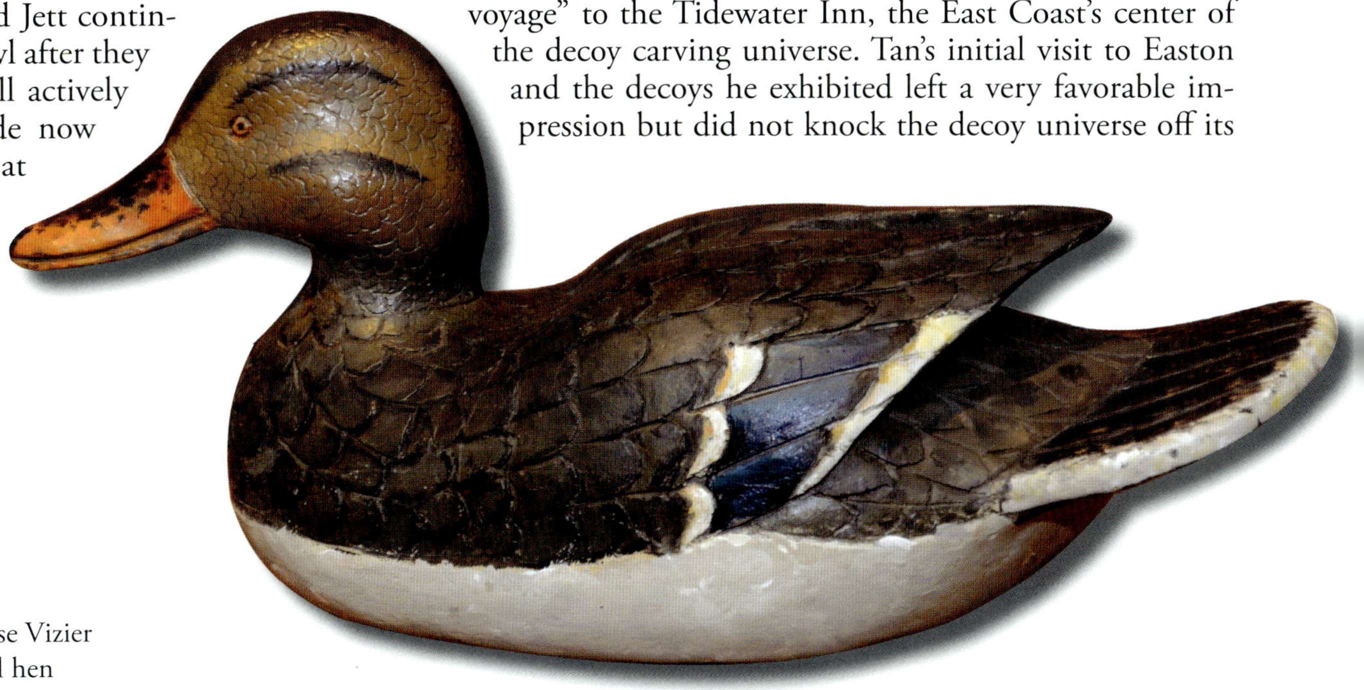

(1) Tan Brunet / Cadise Vizier
blue-winged teal hen

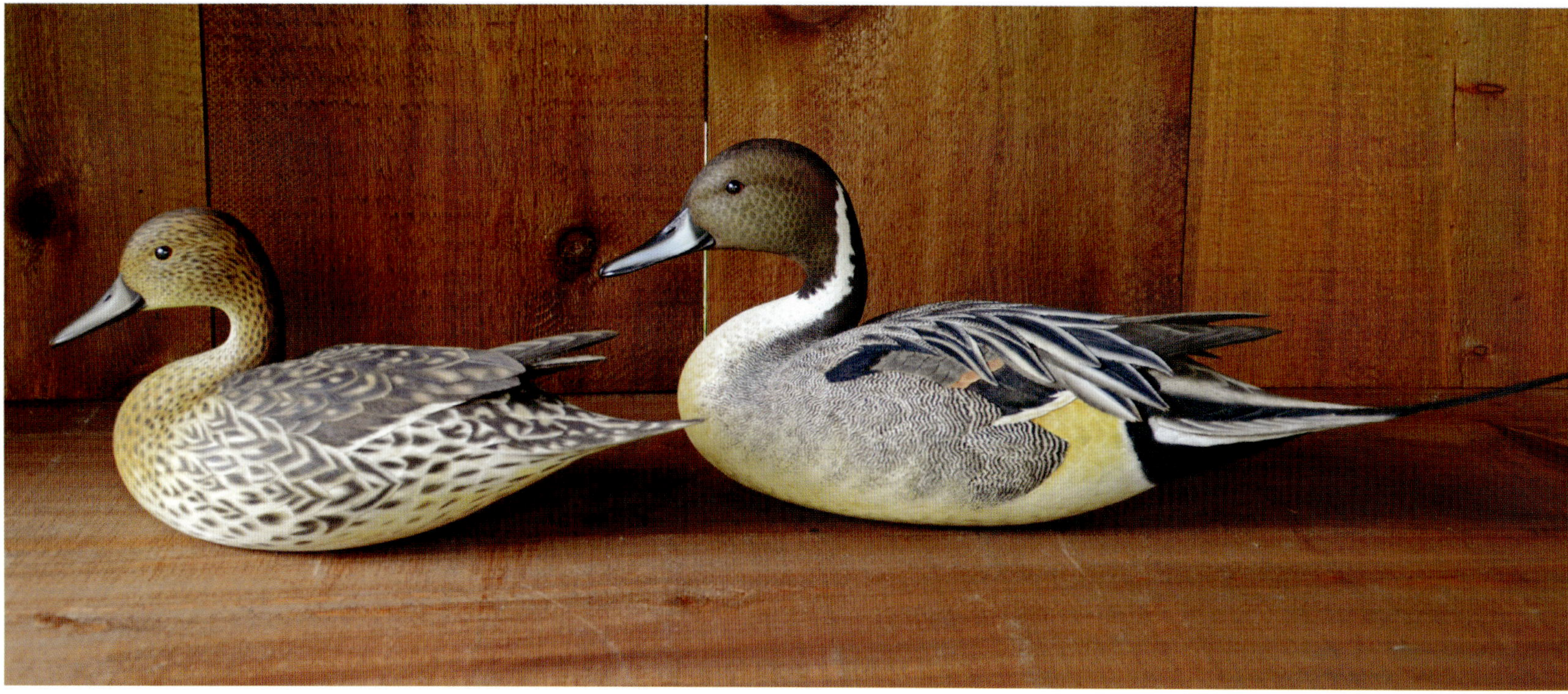

(2) Tan Brunet's decorative pintail pair

axis—that came a few years later. Photograph 2 shows a pair of pintails that Tan entered in the 1974 contest. They lost because they were not lifelike enough for the judges. What were they thinking?

Nonetheless, Tan's trips to the East Coast carving competitions and decoy shows from 1974 through 1976 convinced him that he could make a nice living carving, showing, competing with, and selling decoys. Tan also realized that he needed to carve something other than wooden hunting decoys, which by that time had been rendered virtually obsolete by synthetic ones. Tan wisely chose to make decoratives, the favored style at the East Coast competitions in the 1970s.

Tan carved his decoys out of blocks of cypress or tupelo gum, using only a hatchet to rough out the bird and a knife to do the finishing work. Unlike other carvers, Tan made his decoys out of a single piece of wood, which is a far more difficult undertaking. He also did not use patterns. In the early days, Tan used oil-based paint he got at the lumberyard. His models were wild ducks he kept in a pen near his home, what he saw while hunting, and what he saw in a book entitled *Game Bird Carving* by Bruce Burk. He was inspired by a pair of pintails he saw in the window at Sports Art, a New Orleans store that sold wildfowl paintings and decoys in the 1970s and 1980s. Those pintails were beautifully carved and exquisitely detailed with delineated feathering. They were so elaborately painted that they looked real. These pintails challenged Tan to make better ones, and he did.

Tan was innovative. He preferred carving his decoys so they looked serenely relaxed. He avoided carving decoys in unusual poses, like preeners or those with a raised wing, which he regarded as unnatural. He used three ice picks that he put in the flames coming from a burner on a gas stove in his kitchen; when the ice picks got red-hot, Tan sharpened and bent them into the shapes he wanted. Then he took a decoy ready for painting and burned the areas he wanted to different depths using the hot ice picks. After the decoy had been carved and the areas of the surface burned where desired, Tan applied artist grade oil paint to the raw wood but did not use a sealer. The application of paint to the burnt areas created a remarkably life-like appearance that is both beautiful and unique. Tan's sons use the same technique. It is so distinct and recognizable that it is referred to as the "Brunet soft finish."

Tan's most important contribution to decoy carving competitions was probably inventing a way to make his decoys self-righting so they would float in an upright position just like real ducks. Competition-grade decoys are placed in tanks or in ponds, and unless they float as naturally as real ducks they are disqualified, regardless of how well they are carved and painted. Ordinarily, carvers put keels on their decoys to make them self-righting but that detracts from the appearance of the decoy when it is not in the water. Removal of the keel leaves disfiguring holes in the bottom of the decoy. Tan solved the problem by drilling holes in the bottom of his competitive decoys, putting the amount of lead needed to obtain the desired buoyancy, and then filling the holes with wood and finishing the bottom to conceal the wooden plugs. Tan's self-righting buoyancy system works as long as one knows where to drill the holes and how much lead to put in them.

There is general agreement that Tan Brunet was the most competitive carver ever. He approached carving competitions like Vince Lombardi approached NFL championship games—"Winning isn't everything, it's the only thing." Tan was gracious the few times he lost, accepting without complaint that his decoy just wasn't good enough to win. Tan enjoyed the East Coast decoy carving contests so much that he became the "Pied Piper" of Bayou Lafourche, leading an intrepid band of Cajun carving colleagues in a car caravan to the Delmarva Peninsula and the Ward World Championships in Ocean City, Maryland, every spring, and to the decoy show in Easton, Maryland, every fall for a number of years. They regularly took home prizes, award ribbons, and "swag bags" filled with the bounty they got for selling all of the decoys they brought. Tan won numerous Best in Show ribbons but in 1977, he broke through and won his first Ward World Championship. He followed that up with World Championships in 1978, 1981, 1982, and 1983. By then, Tan was a legend. He was decoy carving's rock star. His sons said when Tan walked into any East Coast carving show venue, it was like "Elvis was in the house." He was also famous for his Cajun stories and jokes. He was immensely

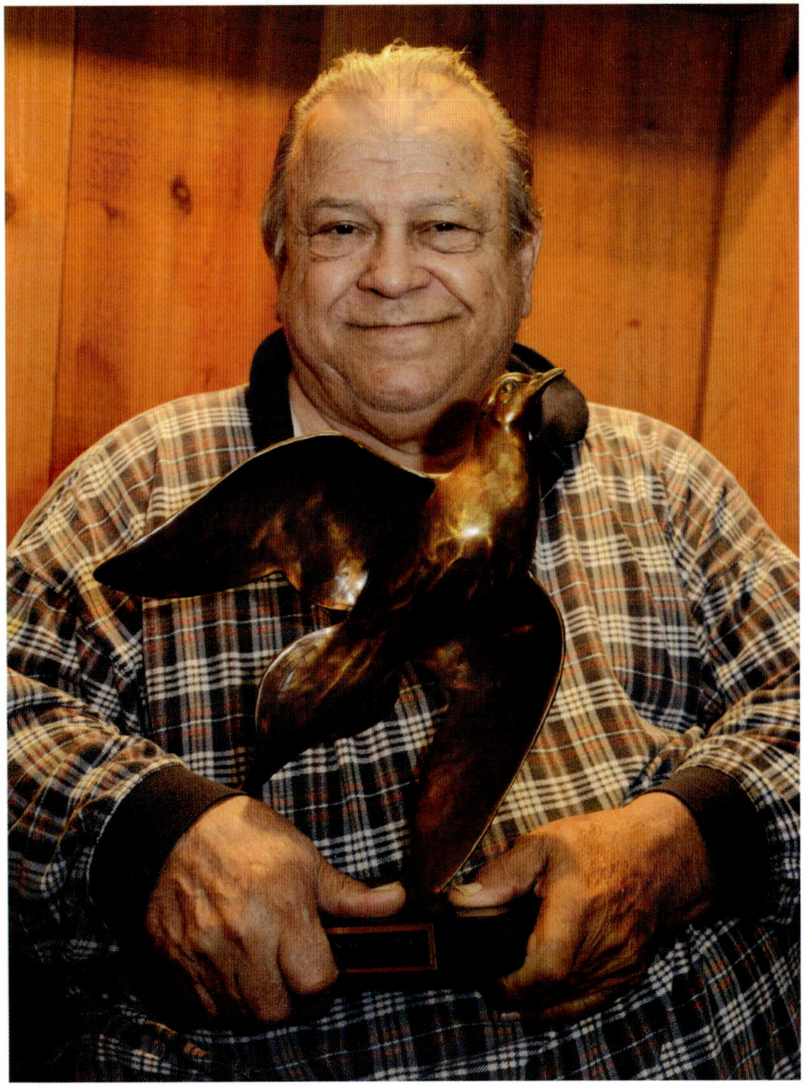

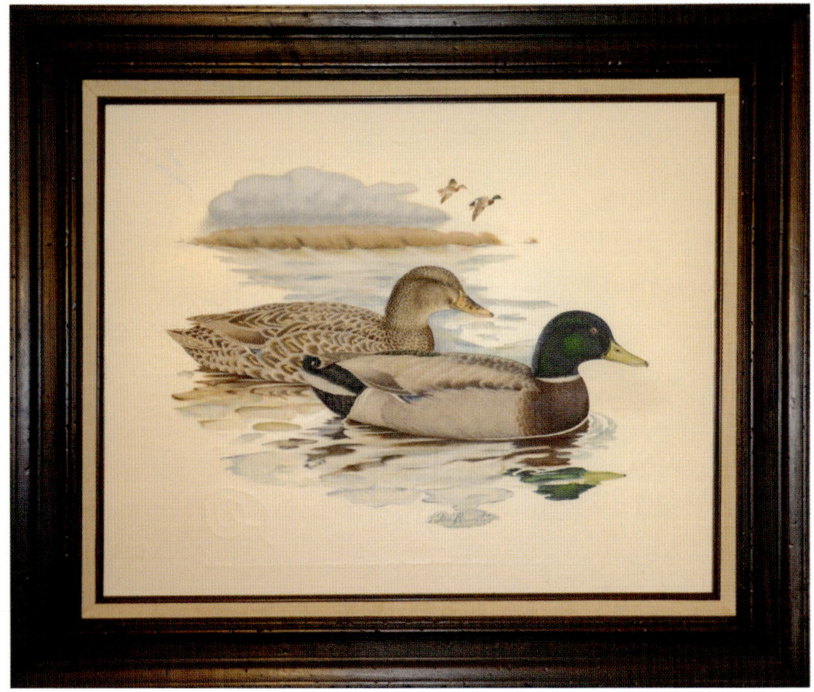

Above: (3) Tan Brunet holding Ward Lifetime Award
Right: (4) Tan Brunet's mallard painting

popular and thoroughly enjoyed being the center of attention for over thirty years.

Tan's nostalgic feelings for these East Coast decoy carving events were quite evident when he was telling me about the Tidewater Inn, a warm and congenial place in Easton, Maryland, where carving's most important people stayed during the winter show. Tan teared up when discussing the inn and the good times that he and his family had while staying there.

Tan's influence was paramount in promoting and protecting Louisiana's decoy carving heritage. He convinced his Cajun carving colleagues to compete in the LWCCG's annual Wildfowl Festivals. His status as a world-class artist and his role as the Festivals' artistic director and resident humorist enhanced the reputation of the Festivals, attracted excellent out-of-state carvers, and made them fun to attend. It is no exaggeration to say that Louisiana would not be home to more World Champions and more master carvers than any place else without Tan, his sons, and his carving colleagues.

Decoy carving is not Tan's only art form. He is a very talented and commercially successful sports art painter. Photograph 3 is Tan's favorite oil painting. One of my favorite Tan stories involves his flat art. Tan painted pictures of ducks in flight and then had about a thousand or so limited edition prints made. When ready, Tan put an ad in the local paper announcing that the prints were available for sale. These prints were very much in demand and sold out very quickly. When a particularly popular print was released, cousin Jimmy Vizier came over to Tan's shop early on and bought a hundred of them. Jimmy waited until Tan sold all of the remaining prints and then offered the ones he bought for sale at a higher price than Tan charged. Reportedly, Jimmy made more money than Tan did on this particular edition. As always, Tan took this in stride and in good humor.

Even after he retired from competitive carving in 1983, Tan continued making annual pilgrimages to the Maryland shows to see his sons compete and also to participate as a judge and resident humorist. Tan's status as a carving "living legend" was confirmed when the Ward Foundation formally bestowed that title on him in 2014; but that important and well deserved honor doesn't go far enough. There is no question that Tan is a world-class carver. He is also a world-class human being. Photograph 4 shows Tan tightly holding his Ward Living Legend award. Photographs 5, 6, and 7 show three of Tan's decoys that prove, in part, why he deserved all of the carving honors he received.

Tan, Jett, and Jude and their families are extremely close and live less than a half a mile from each other. The brothers are both very artistic but their artistic talents have taken different forms and they have different personalities, which makes discussing them individually a better choice. For example, Jett is focused and intensely competitive like his father. Jude is more laid back. He dislikes competitive decoy carving but loves to paint wildfowl like his father and he also likes carving objects other than decoys.

Jett and Jude insist that Tan is the best carver ever. Tan says his sons are better. Thankfully, I wasn't asked to judge a family carving competition. Tan stopped entering in the World's Pairs in 1983 after he won his fifth title because he did not want to compete against his sons. Jett stopped competing in the World's Pairs after winning his second title in 1987 because the purchase prize awarded the winner was significantly less than the price he received when he sold competition-grade decoys; but he continued to compete in the Ward Best of Show in the Open Class, where the winning decoy is recognized as the best decoy in the world and there is no purchase prize. For a time, Jude ably filled the competition void by winning the Ward World Pairs in 1993, only three years after he started carving decoys for competition. Jude won his second Ward World Pairs in 1995, but then retired from competitive decoy carving. In the eighteen years between Tan's first World Pairs prize and Jude's last, a Brunet won that prestigious award in competition with the world's best carvers an amazing 50 percent of the time.

Jett is an interesting, complex, and extraordinarily tal-

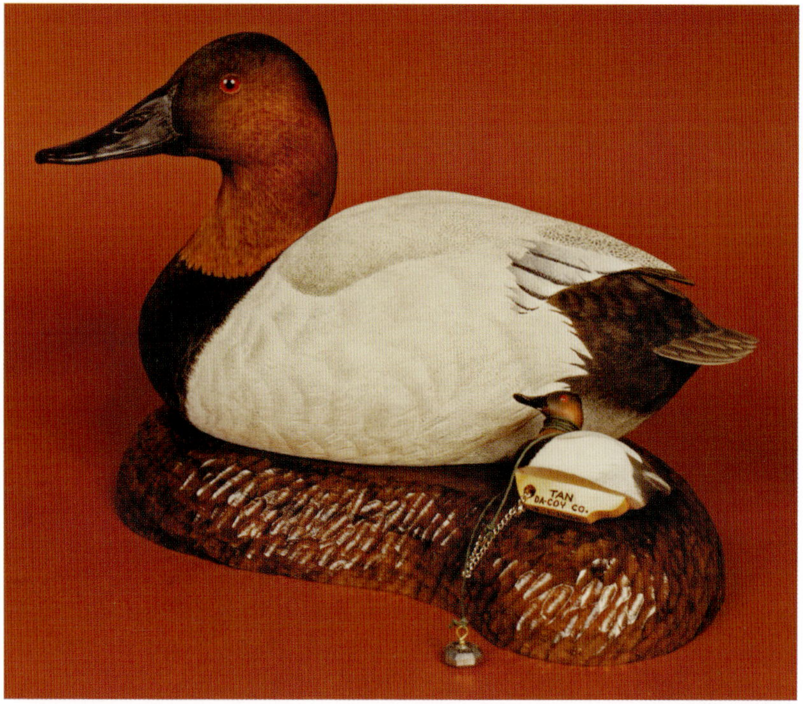

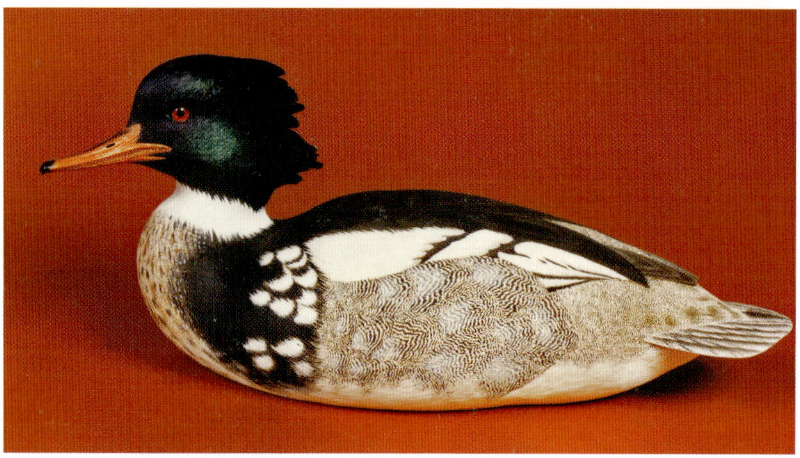

Top left: (5) Tan Brunet's canvasback drake
Bottom left: (6) Tan Brunet's merganser drake
Below: (7) Tan Brunet's canvasback hen

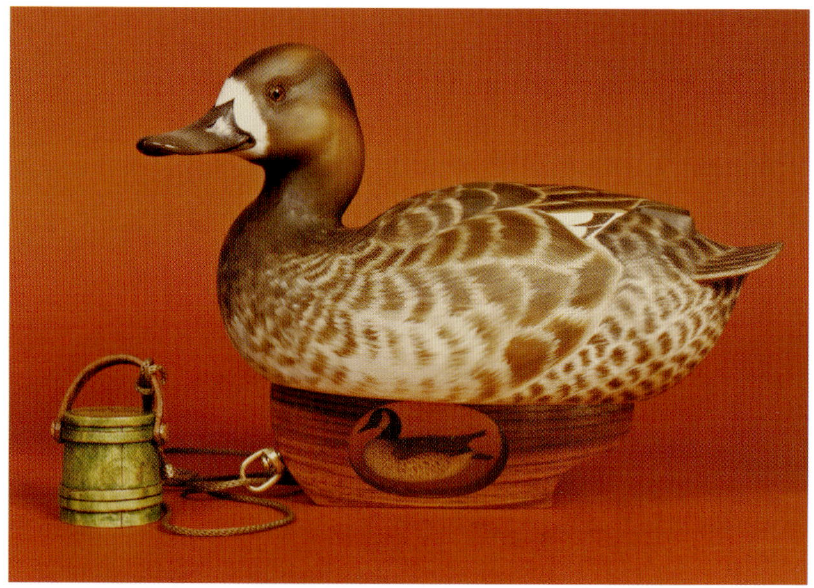

ented artist and decoy carver. He was born on November 8, 1963, and has lived in Galliano all of his life. Jett and his wife, Rhonda, have two children Amber and Jhett. Jett says he has three sides: an artist, an entrepreneur, and a "country boy."

Jett was a carving child prodigy who at age nine made his first decoy—a skill he learned watching his dad and Jimmy Vizier, who frequently carved with Tan. Jett won the Ward Foundation's Danner Frazier award twice, thereby making him the most outstanding teenage carver in the world on two occasions. In 1985, at age twenty-one, he became the youngest person to ever win the Ward World Championship, and in 1987 he won another Ward World Championship. In 1992, Jett carved a full-size bald eagle that was the featured piece of the Easton Wildfowl Festival. It was initially displayed in the lobby of the Tidewater Inn and now has a permanent home in the Champions Gallery at the Ward Wildfowl Museum.

Jett has won so many decoy carving championships that listing them all would take up much of this book, so only his most impressive accomplishments will be mentioned. Jett was a Best of Show winner in every carving level in the Ward World Championships: Novice, Intermediate, Open, and Master. He won eight Best of Show awards in the Decorative Floating Waterfowl category in the Open level at the championships, including a record five straight.

Photograph 8 shows the artistic evolution of a talented teenage carver into a Ward World Champion. Jett is famous for his intricate decorative decoys carved from a single block of cypress or, more frequently, tupelo gum and finished with artist grade oil-based paint. He likes relaxed poses for his decoys, like the green-winged teal shown in photograph 11, but on occasion Jett will carve decoys in more animated

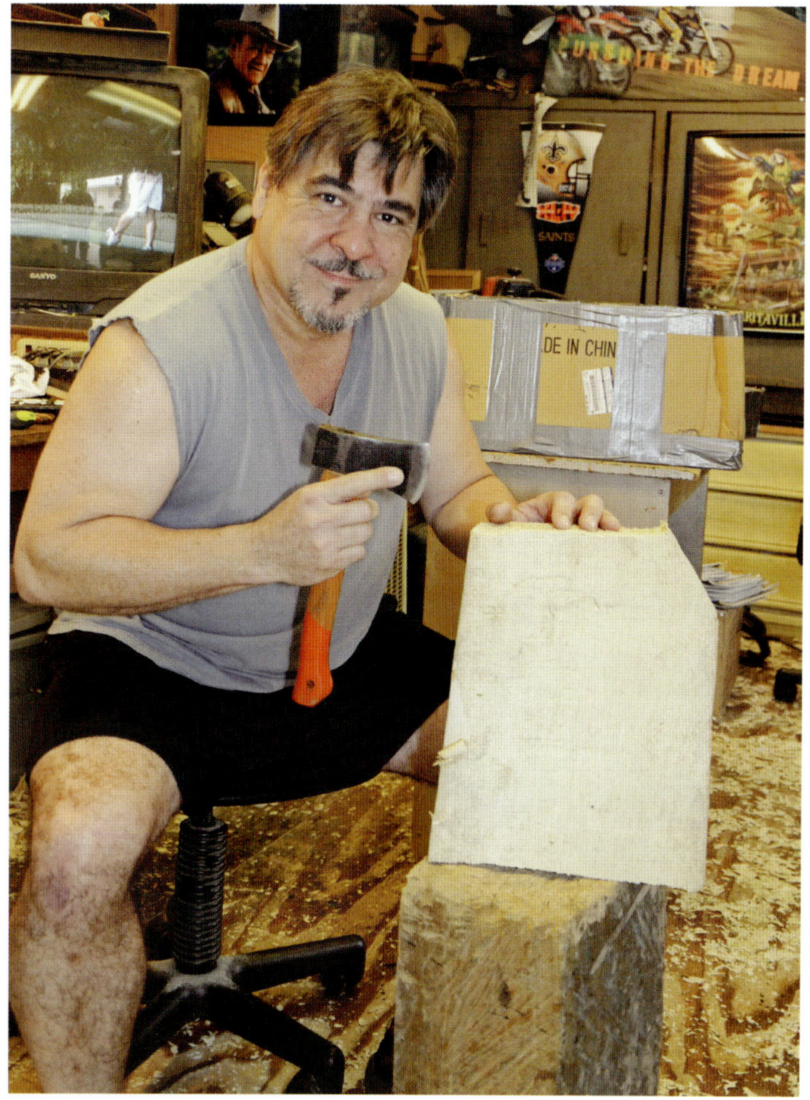

Jett Brunet

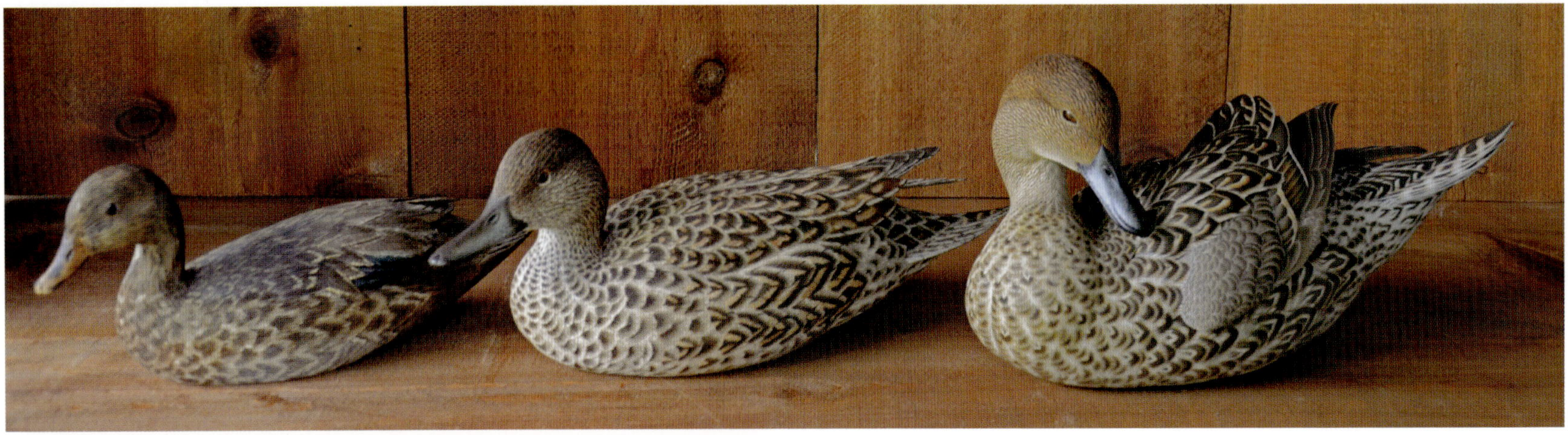

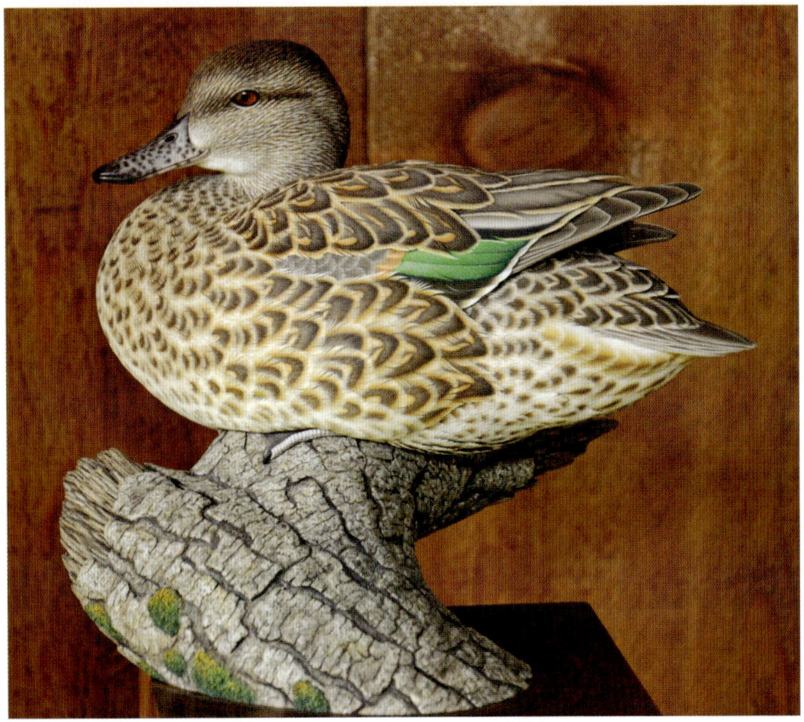

ABOVE: (8) Jett Brunet's pintail hen trio
LEFT: (11) Jett Brunet's decorative green-winged teal hen
BELOW: (9) Jett Brunet's decorative mallard drake

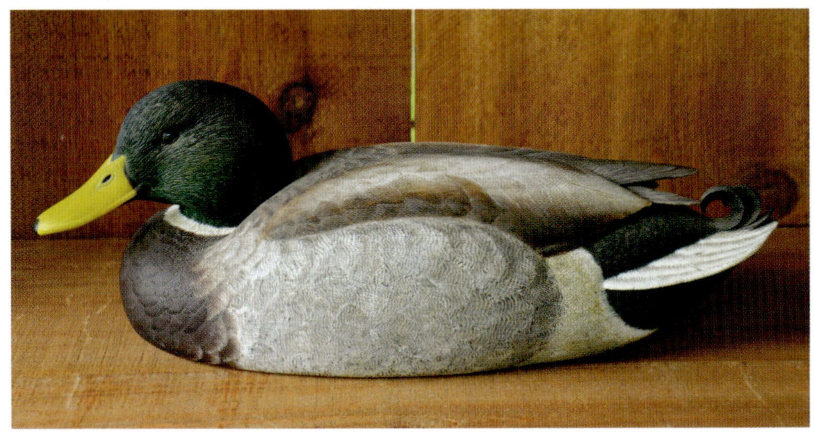

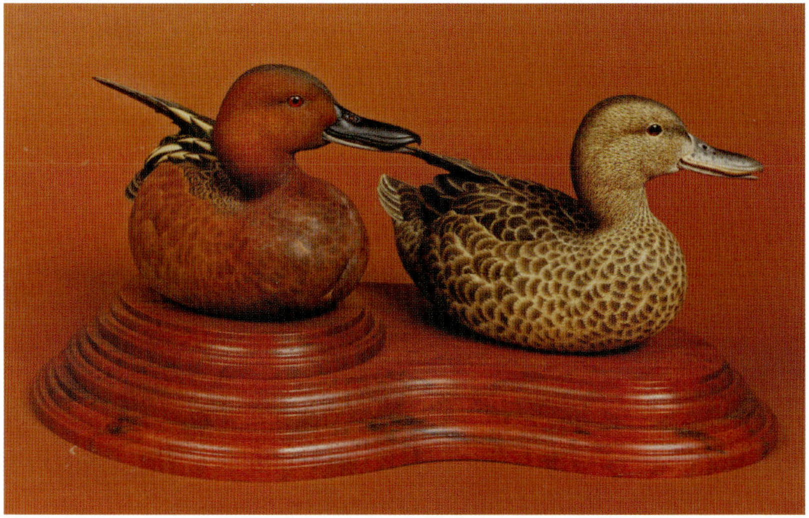

(13) Jett Brunet's cinnamon teal pair

poses. The mallard drake shown in photograph 9, the pintail hen seen in photograph 10 (pg. 62), and most of all, the green-winged teal hen shown in photograph 11 are examples of a world-class carver at his very best. Jett's canvasback decoy seen in photograph 12 and his pair of cinnamon teal seen in photograph 13 further cement his place as an incomparable artist.

In 1989, Jett won first, second, and third place Best in Show awards with a gadwall, pintail, and redhead at the Ward World Championships, a feat not accomplished before or since. Jett's green-winged teal hen, seen in photograph 11, has likely won more awards than any decorative decoy ever. After it won the Best in Show decorative at the 1993 Pacific Flyway Competition, a writer in the *Wildfowl Carving Competition '93* magazine wrote: "This most talented young Cajun dominates any class he enters. Like the 2,000 lb. gorilla . . . Brunet goes where he wants. He also wins where he goes."[3]

Likely as a result of Jett's overarching talent, at least in part, the Ward Foundation added an even higher competition level, the "Masters Class," limited to those carvers who had won at least one Ward carving competition in the Open Category. Jett entered and won the first Master's Class Best in Show competition. He also won the Ward Peoples' Choice prize for making the best decoy in competition with the winners of all divisions in that year's show.

Jett won fourteen consecutive Best of Show awards in Floating Waterfowl Competition at major carving shows throughout the country—and he did this twice. His 1985 World Championship ruddy ducks were exhibited at the Smithsonian Museum in 1987. Jett won thirty-eight of the last forty-one Best of Shows in Floating Waterfowl Competition. Not bad for a self-described "country boy." Jett stopped competitive decoy carving after having accomplished

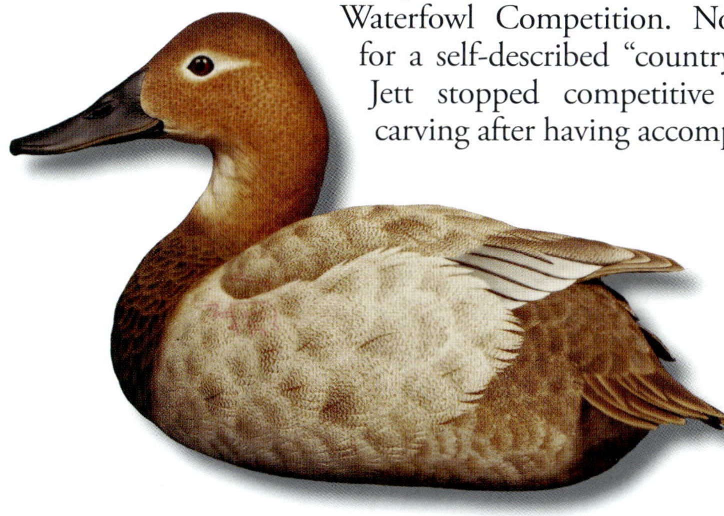

Right: (12) Jett Brunet's canvasback hen

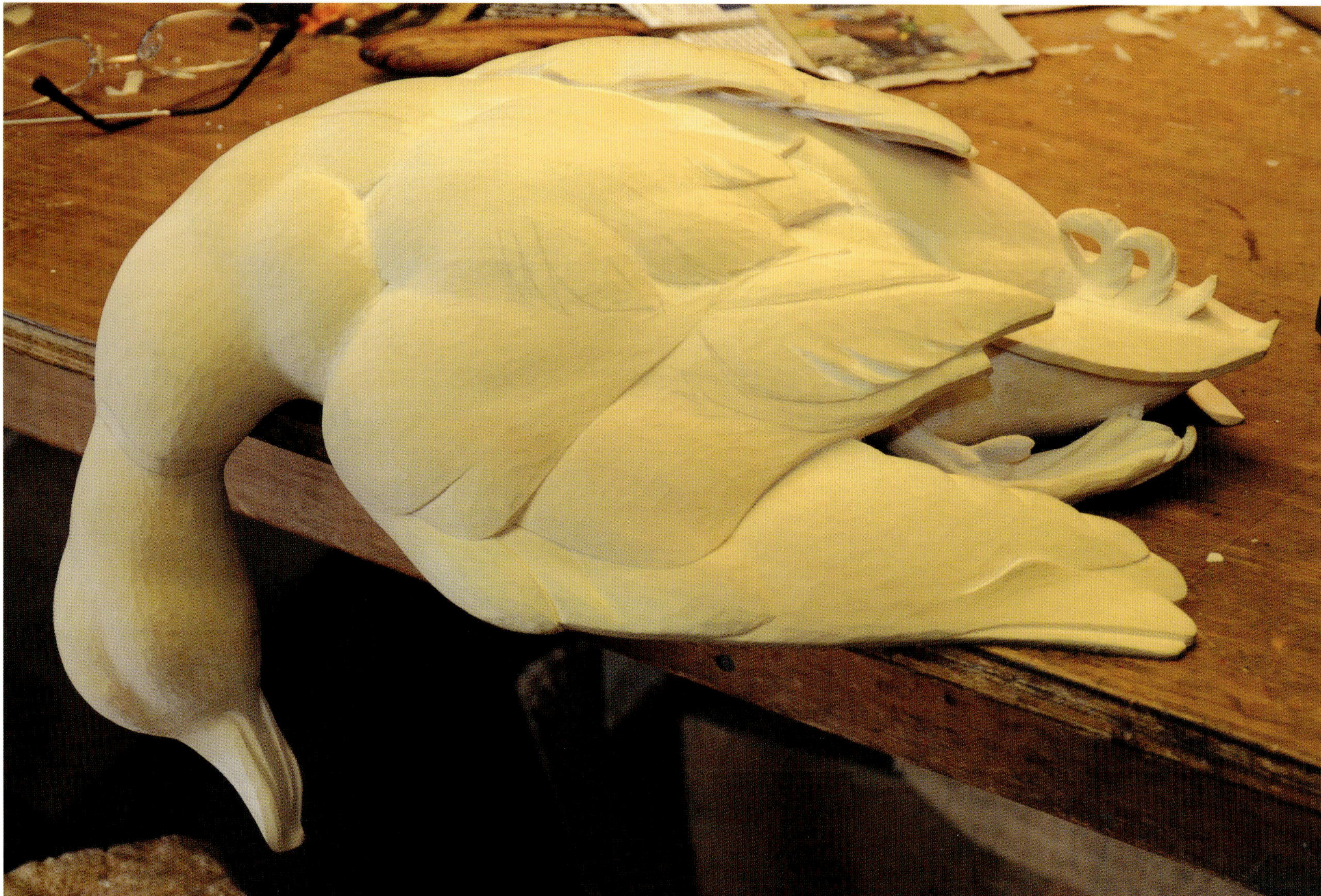

(14) Jett Brunet's interpretive mallard

every decoy carving goal he had set for himself and because "the relief of not losing became stronger than the joy of winning." Jett not only inherited his father's artistic gene, he also inherited his father's competitive nature (and then some). It is no surprise that Jett is working on an entry for the 2016 Ward Interpretative Wildfowl Sculpture category. It is seen in photograph 14.

Although the demand was great for Jett's decoys (as were the prices paid for them) a challenging opportunity came along that captured his entrepreneurial attention. Every year, Ducks Unlimited's selection committee chooses a "DU Decoy of the Year." The selected decoy is then copied and these exclusive copies are auctioned off at DU banquets around the country with the proceeds going to fund wildfowl conservation For the last seventeen years in a row, DU's selection committee has chosen a Jett Brunet carving as its "Decoy of the Year." To fill that commission, Jett carves a full-size decoy that is used to form a mold. The mold is then used to cast a poly resin decoy that Jett then paints. The painted poly resin decoy and the casting from which it was formed are sent to a factory in China that produces and paints the synthetic decoys using Jett's paint pattern and instructions. To assure the desired quality, Jett goes to China to oversee the painting. When finished, the poly resin decoys are shipped to Ducks Unlimited in the States to be distributed as the major prizes at DU functions. Jett's molded decoys are very attractive and remarkably detailed, as evidenced by the photograph of the mallard drake seen in photograph 15a, the pintail drake in photograph 15b, and

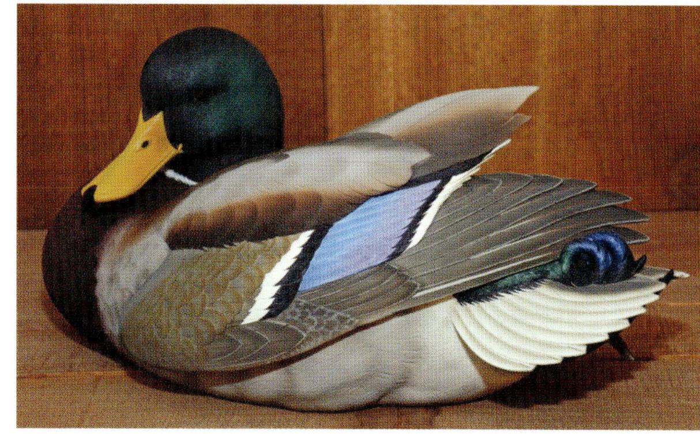

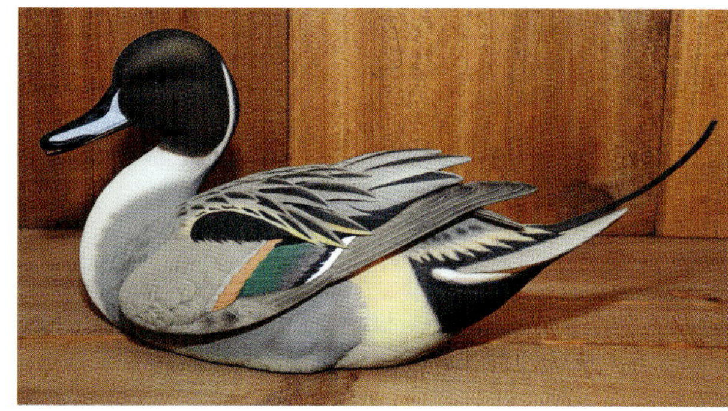

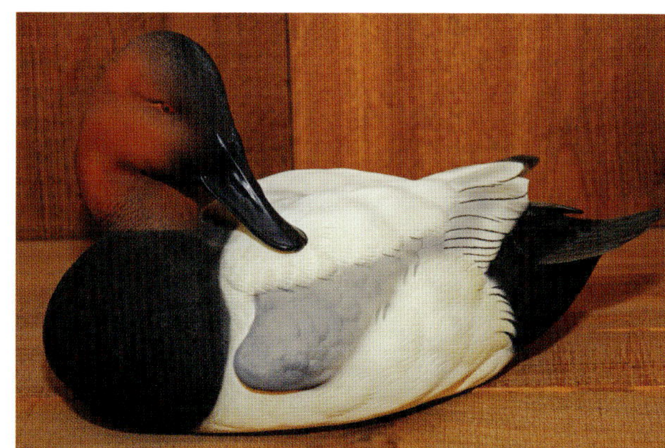

RIGHT: Jett Brunet's cast decoys, TOP TO BOTTOM: (15a) mallard drake, (15b) pintail drake, (15c) canvasback drake

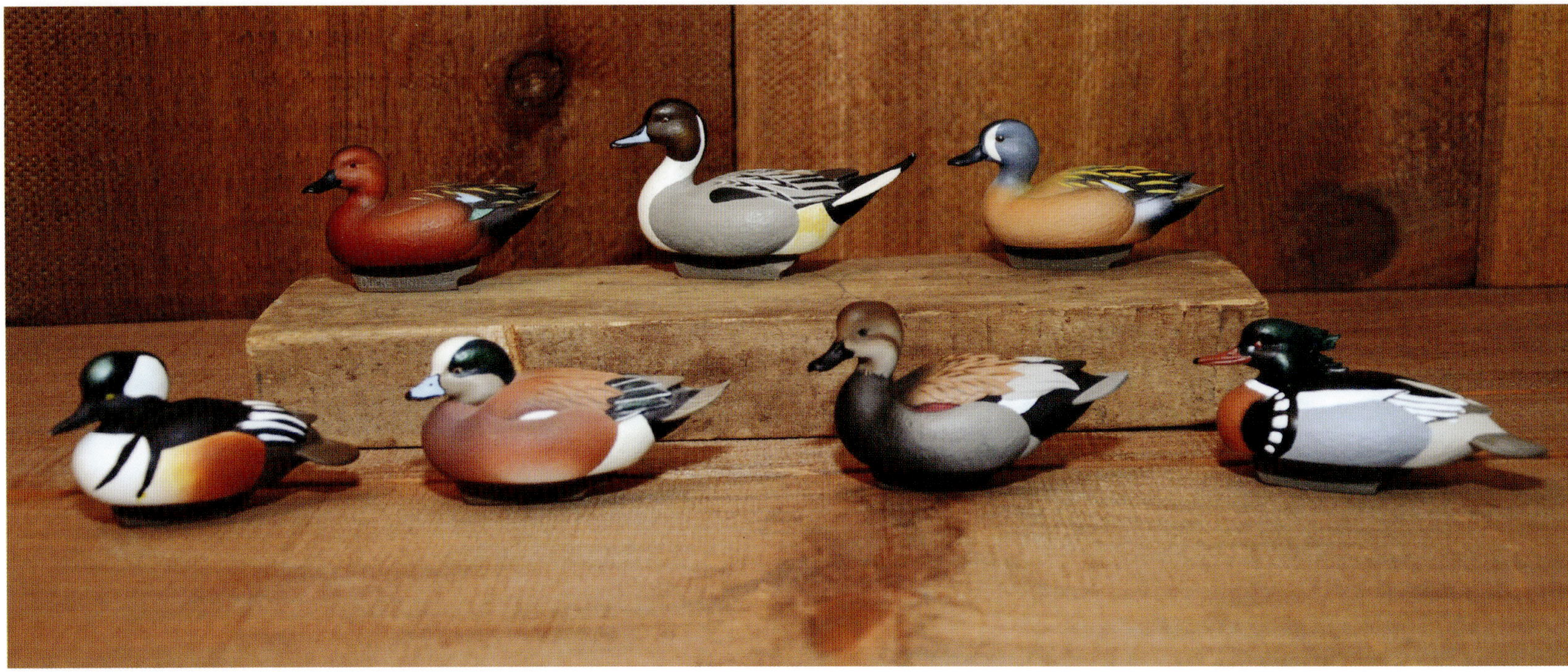

(15d) Jett Brunet's assorted miniatures

the canvasback drake seen in photograph 15c. These full-size decoys were so popular that DU's membership department commissioned Jett and an affiliated company to make a mold and paint a casting of a miniature decoy about two inches long that is also sent to China and reproduced. A collection of these miniatures is seen in photograph 15d. DU uses these miniatures as its annual gift to its members. Every year, the species of the decoy is changed. So far, over 1.2 million of Jett's full-size and miniature decoys have been produced and distributed to DU members.

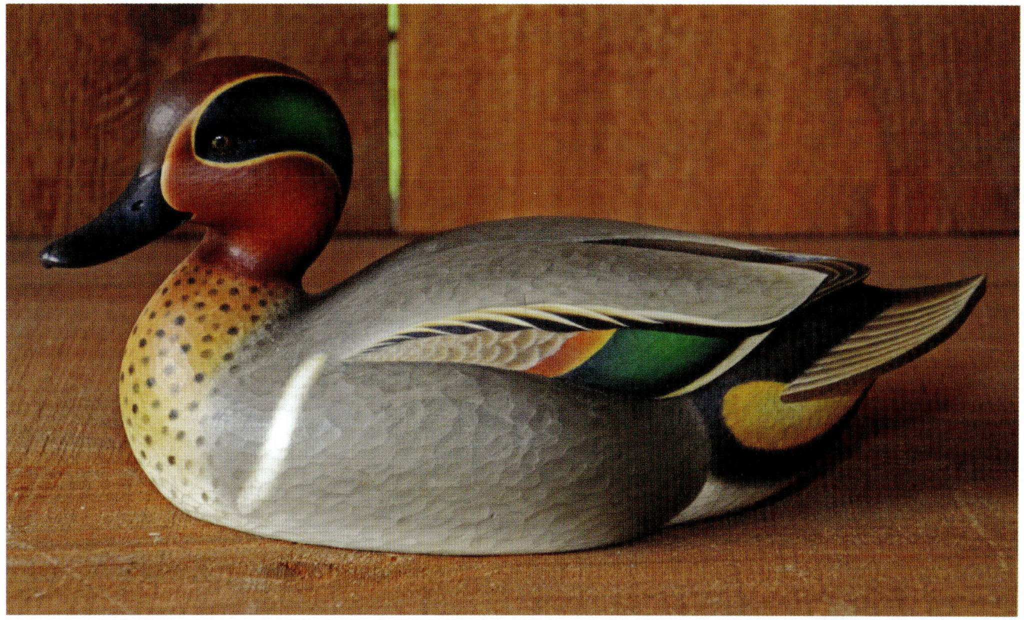

(16) Jett Brunet's
green-winged teal drake decorative gunner

Jett's arrangements with DU, when combined with the income realized from the sale of decoys he made and sold to others, have reportedly made Jett the most financially successful decoy carver ever. This success hasn't spoiled Jett or corrupted his great artistic talent. It has simply permitted him to come ever closer to achieving his dream of providing for his family and living life as a bayou-based country boy fishing and hunting in the marshes near Galliano. Jett's ambition is to carve old-style hunting decoys just like the green-winged teal drake shown in photograph 16. He recently made this decoy for fun and to counter the stress of carving exquisitely detailed decoratives. Jett also loves carving decorative wildfowl sculptures like the ones shown in photographs 17, 18, and 19 because they allow him complete artistic freedom.

Jude Brunet, Tan's youngest son, also a lifelong resident of Galliano, was born on May 14, 1969. After graduating from high school, Jude attended the Art Institute in Houston, Texas. He majored in commercial art, which may partly explain his preference for flat art. He first carved a decoy at age fourteen, which he learned to do by watching his father, brother Jett, and Jimmy Vizier. He started carving seriously in 1990 aided by tips from Jett. Jude was obviously a quick learner as he won the Ward Best in World Floating Decorative Life-Size Waterfowl Pair in 1993—only three years after he really started carving.

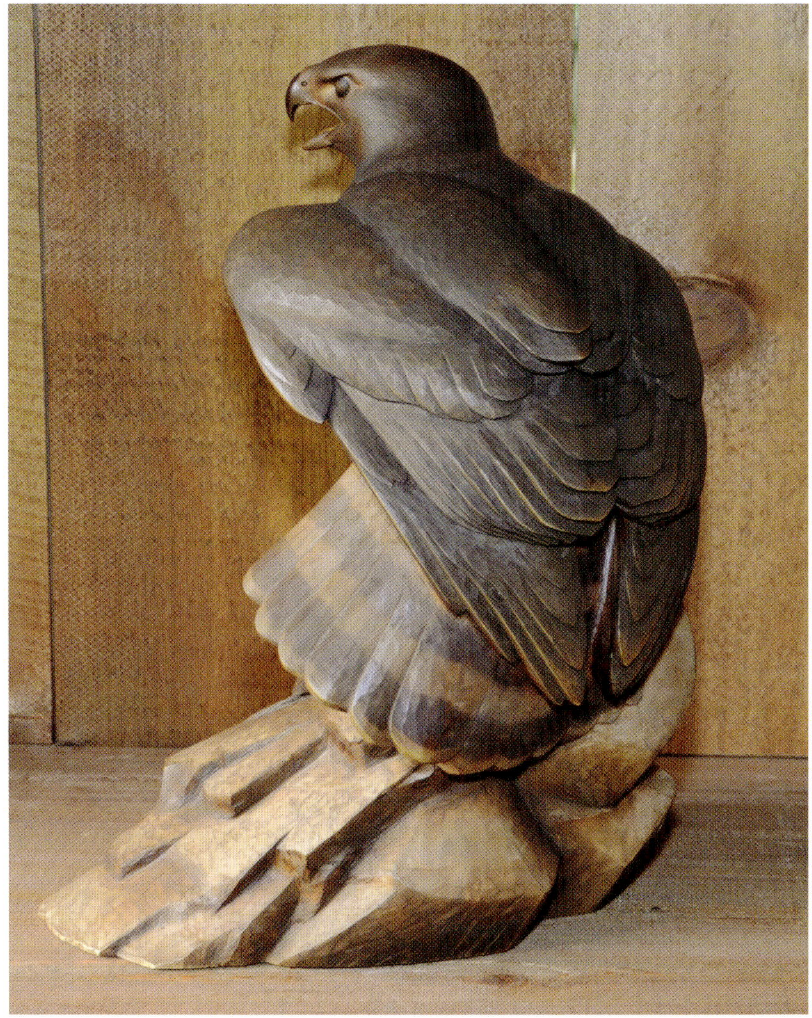

(17) Jett Brunet's interpretive hawk sculpture

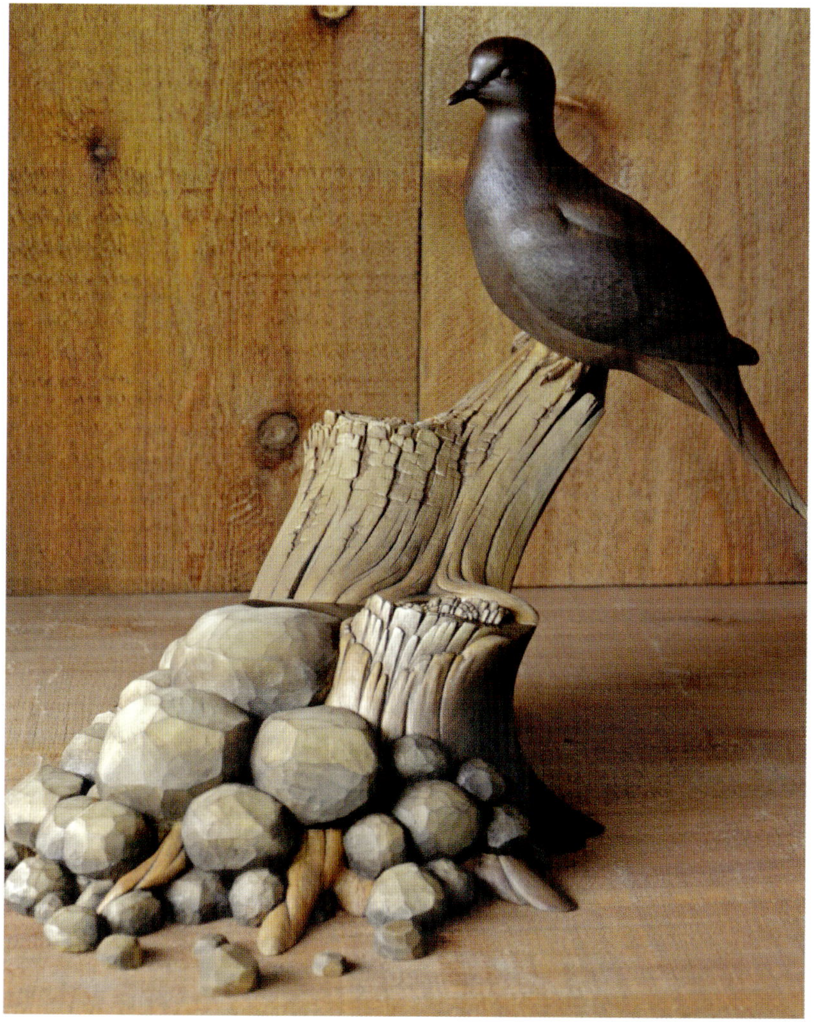

(18) Jett Brunet's interpretive dove sculpture

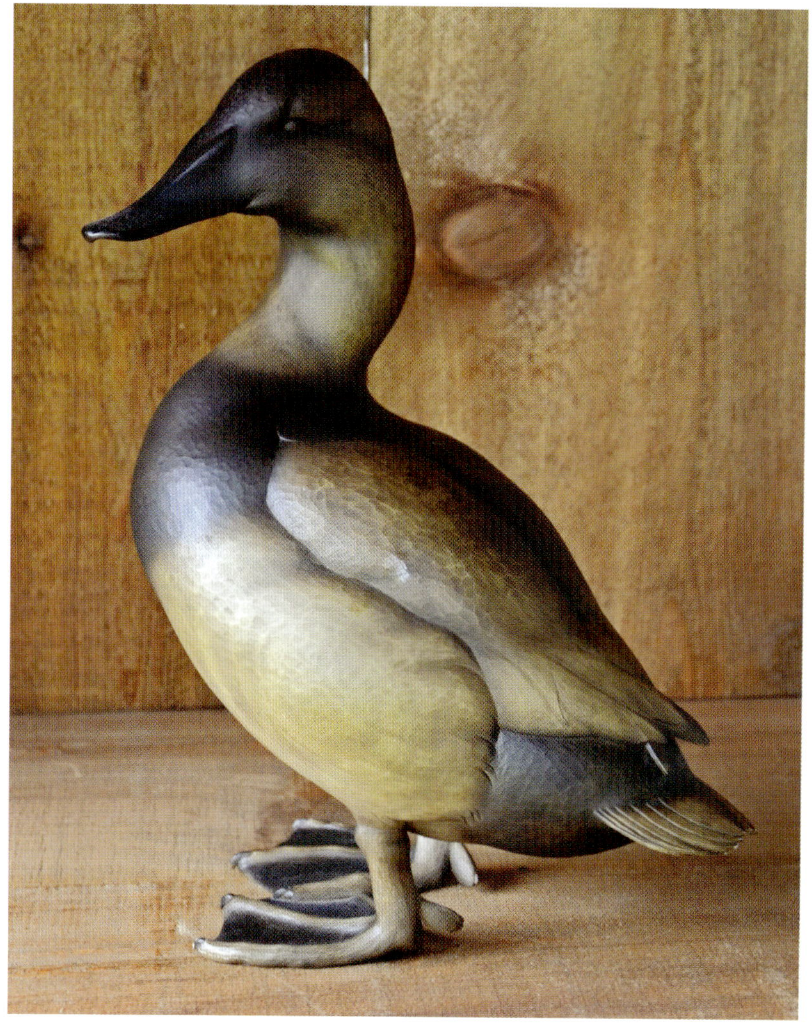

(19) Jett Brunet's standing canvasback drake

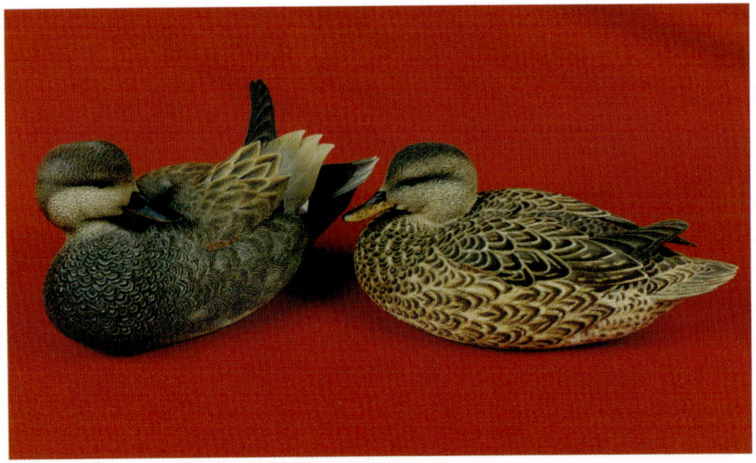

Top left: (20) Jude Brunet's gadwall pair
Bottom left: (21) Jude Brunet's Canada goose
Below: (22) Jude Brunet's redhead drake

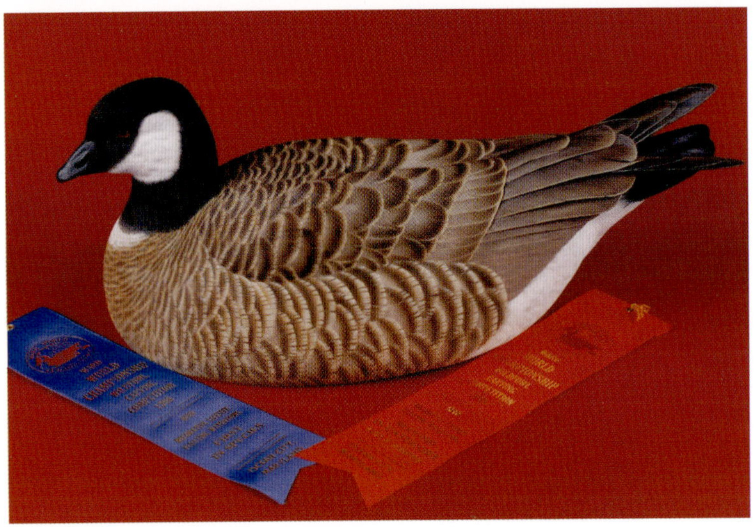

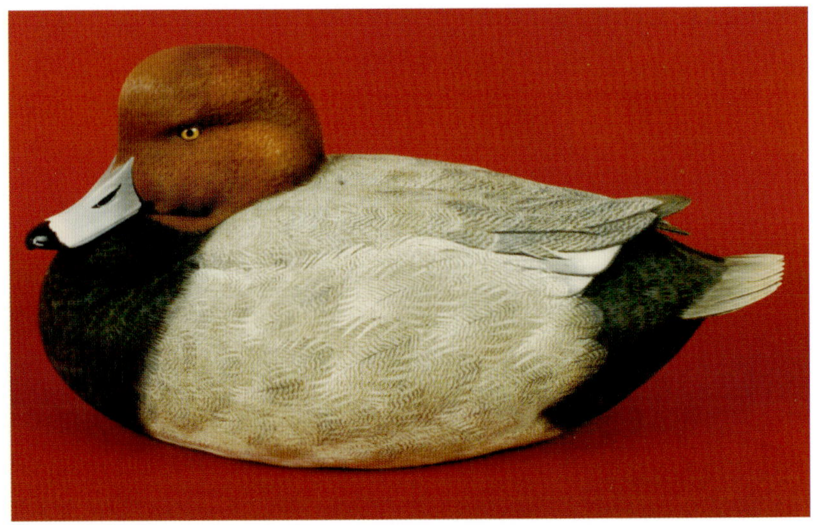

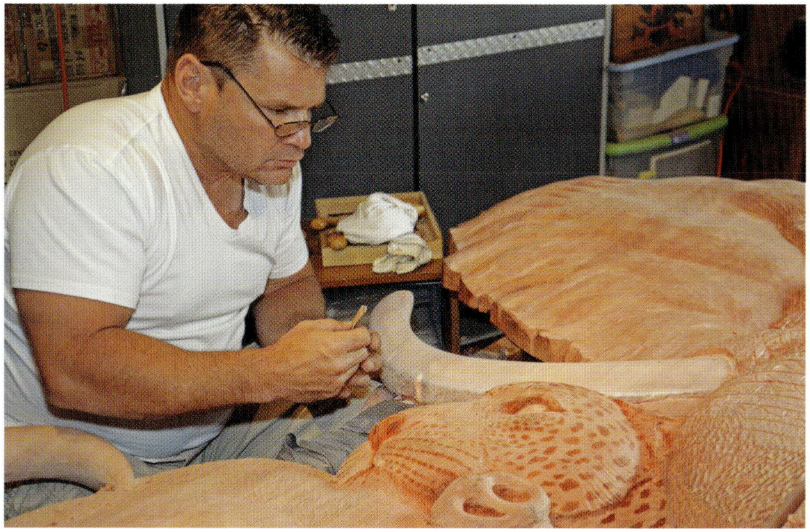

Left: Jude Brunet

Tan said that the most nervous he'd ever been was waiting for the results to be announced at the 1993 Ward Championship. He followed up by saying that the most relief he'd ever felt was hearing Jude had won his first championship. Jude followed his first win with a second Ward Best in World in 1995. Jude's two winning pairs are on display in the Ward Museum's Champions Gallery. Jude's pair of gadwalls shown in photograph 20, the prize-winning Canada goose seen in photograph 21, and the lovely redhead drake seen in photograph 22 offer further proof that Jude is a world-class carver. Despite his achievements, Jude never envisioned himself as a professional carver making and selling decoys for a living. He much prefers painting. This is not the result of any sibling rivalry, as there is none; nor is Jude intimidated in any way by his father, who is very supportive and proud of his younger son's achievements as a wildfowl painter. After all, Jude's painting of lesser scaup was selected for the 2000 Louisiana Duck Stamp. Jude insists that he doesn't miss carving competition at all and, in fact, hasn't carved a duck decoy in years, but he would consider carving one if presented with the right opportunity. He loves old hunting decoys, especially those carved by Curtis Roussel, Gaston Isadore, Clovis and Odee Vizier, and Jack Couret.

Jude is an incredibly versatile artist. Presently, he is doing bas-relief work on a pair of doors he was commissioned to make. The thing that makes this such a challenging assignment is that the doors are from a naturally felled giant sequoia tree. Each is eight feet tall, almost just as wide, over four inches thick, and weighs over two hundred pounds. The doors are destined for a home in Africa, and Jude's task is to manually carve images of Africa's five animal trophies out of these two giant slabs of red wood. He is shown working on that project in photograph 23.

In the course of our visit on a recent afternoon, Jude showed me another project he was working on—a life-size whistler swan, the largest of all swans. It was cut from the largest block of tupelo gum that the Brunets had ever seen. As photograph 24 shows, this goose is more than an arm full.

I found the Brunets to be warm and welcoming men once the ice was broken. As previously observed, the family is very close and mutually respectful. Jude said Jett "was the Michelangelo of decoy carvers," and his father quickly

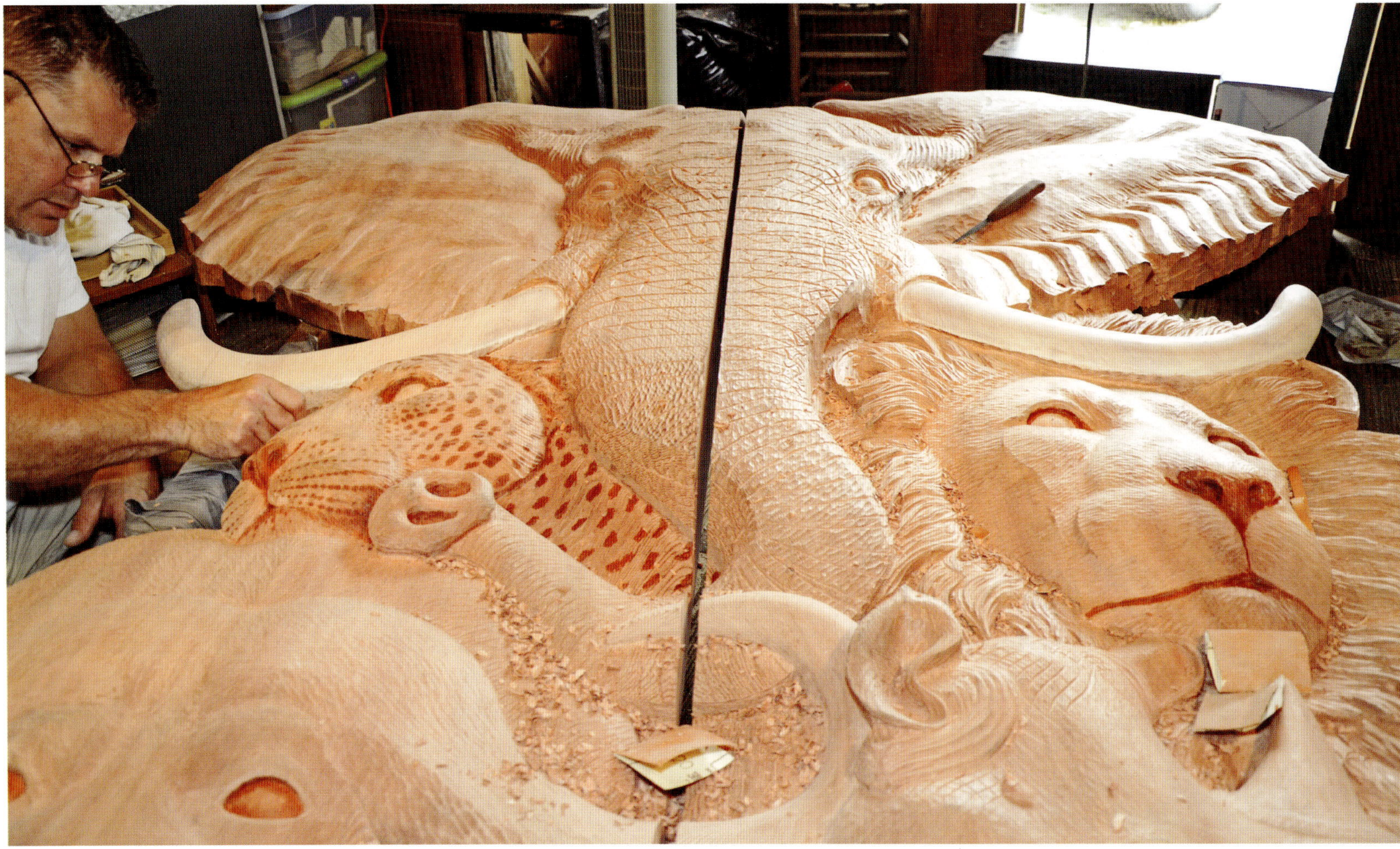

(23) Jude Brunet working on a bas relief sculpture

agreed. Jett said that Jude was the best all-around artist he ever knew, and Tan agreed with that assessment, too. Both boys said that Tan Brunet is and will always be the best decoy carver ever. All three are right. One of the best memories I have had while writing this book was when I shook Tan's hand and told him goodbye after our third meeting in less than two weeks. Tan said "Harvey come back anytime, you're now part of the family." It doesn't get any better than that.

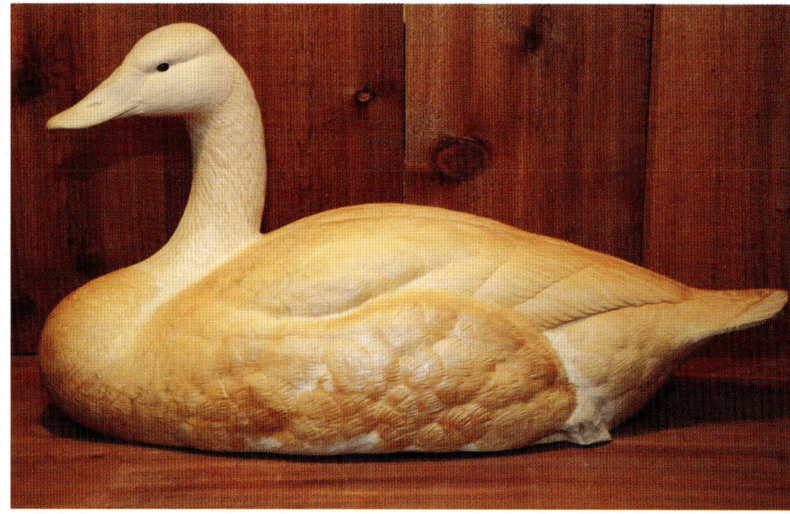

(24) Jude Brunet's goose, work in progress

Endnotes

1. Technically, the name of the top prize is "Floating Decorative Life-Size Waterfowl Pair: Best in World."

2. To enter and win a Ward World Championship in the "World Pair" category, one must either be an Open or Master class carver and his or her entry must be a pair of decoys of the species prescribed by the contest and those decoys must float properly when being judged. The winning pair chosen by the judges is that year's Ward World Champion.

The other competition category of special interest is floating waterfowl which is further divided into subcategories based on the species of duck such as mallards, pintail, gadwall, etc. Carvers enter a single decoy that competes against all others in the same species subcategory. Carvers in each class may enter a decoy in as many species subcategories as they choose. The winner of each species subcategory is given a "Best of Show" award for the best decoy of that species. For example, the Open class carver who produces the mallard judged best wins a "Best of Show" award for that subcategory. Then, the "Best of Show" Open Class winners in each subcategory compete against each other and first, second and third place "Best in Show" awards are selected by the judges.

3. International Wildfowl Carvers Association, *Wildfowl Carving Competition Magazine*, 1993, 87.

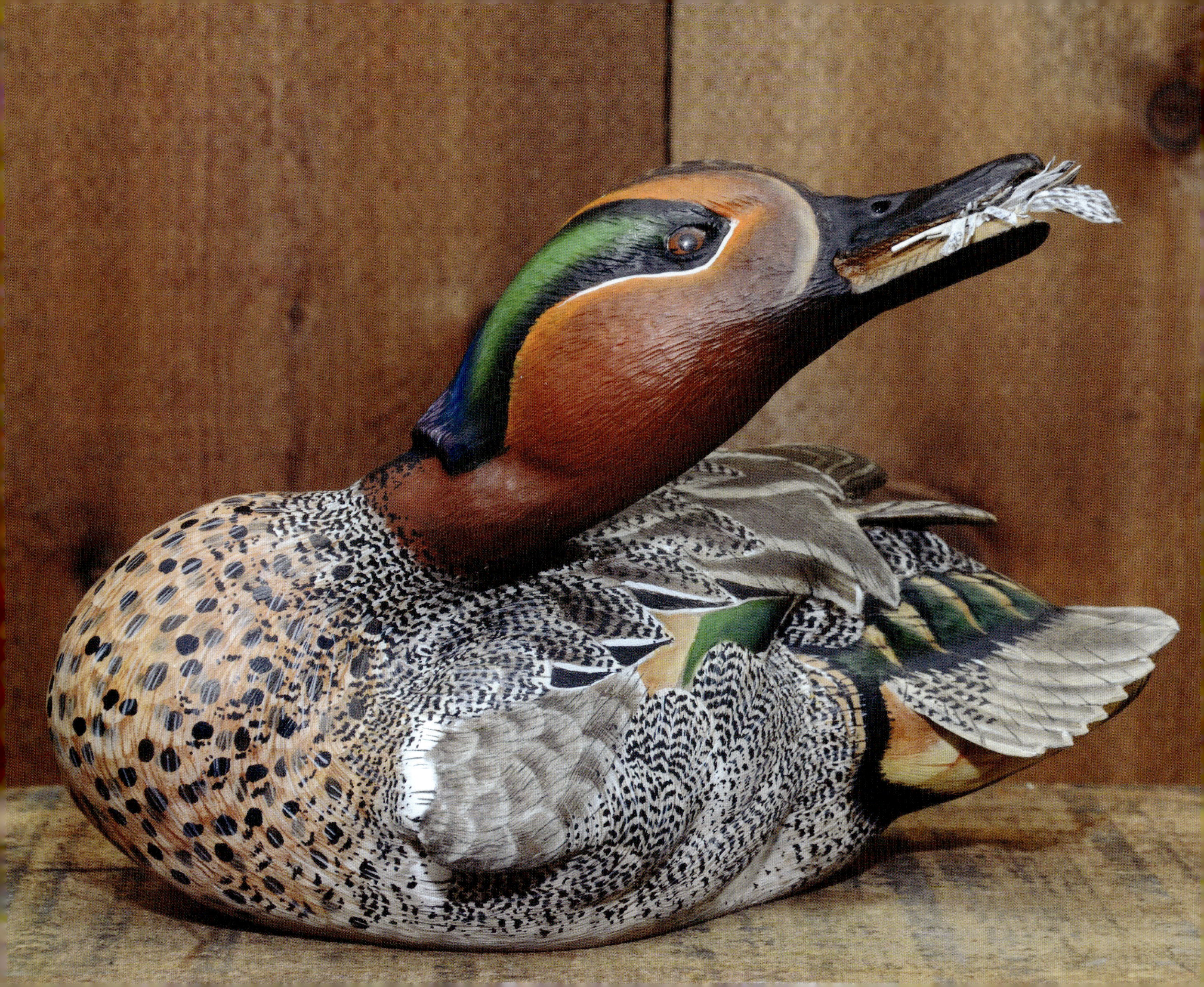

10 Carl and Reagan Danos

Larose Carving Legends

Opposite page: Carl Danos's preening green-winged teal drake

In the course of researching and writing this book, I happened to see decoys carved by the Danos brothers in several friends' collections. Those decoys were hauntingly beautiful, and I realized that this book would not be complete without a chapter on Carl and his younger brother Reagan, along with photographs of a number of their decoys. Another compelling reason for including Carl and Reagan is that both are World Champion Master Carvers, meaning that each has won at least one Best in Show award in the Ward Foundation's annual competition in the Professional Division. The Danos brothers together have won some three hundred carving competitions at the Ward and other venues. With a carving pedigree like that, I knew I had to have them in this book.

Over a period of several months, I visited the Danos brothers a number of times at their homes and workshops down Bayou Lafourche in Larose, Louisiana. Larose was home to Xavier Bourg (1901-1984), the town's shoemaker, bridge tender, and an excellent old master decoy carver. Early on, I learned that Bourg influenced the Danos brothers' carving, as did Clovis Vizier, another old master who lived about eleven miles further down the bayou in nearby Galliano. Carl so admired these two men that he carved replicas of their decoys for his personal collection, as shown in photographs 1 and 2. Photograph 3 shows two fine Bourg teal and is included to show the similarity between the styles of

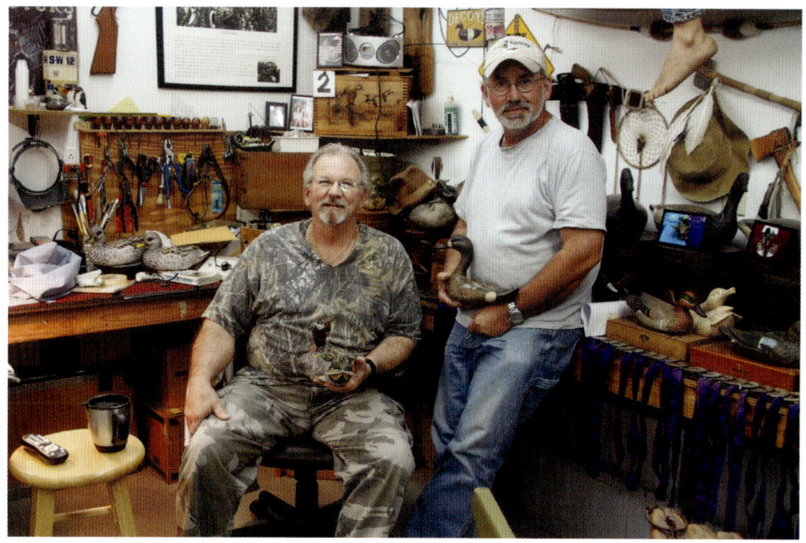

Carl (left) and Reagan (right) Danos

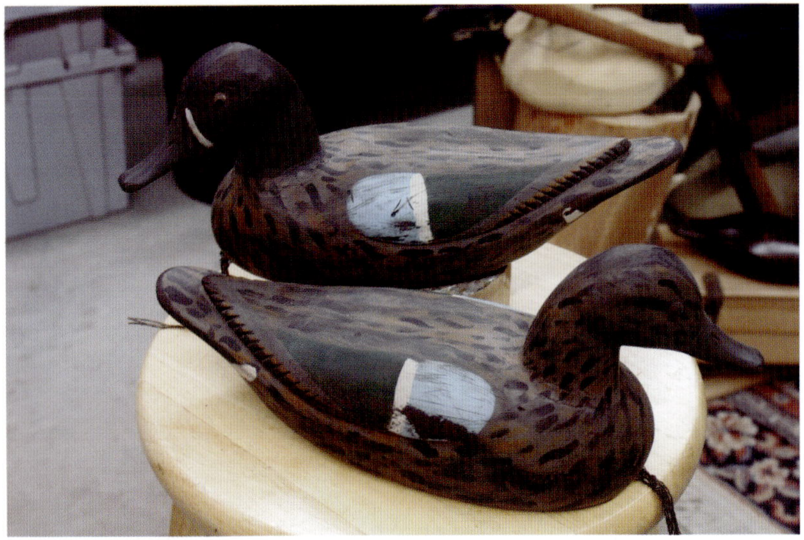

(1) Carl Danos's copy of Xavier Bourg blue-winged teal pair

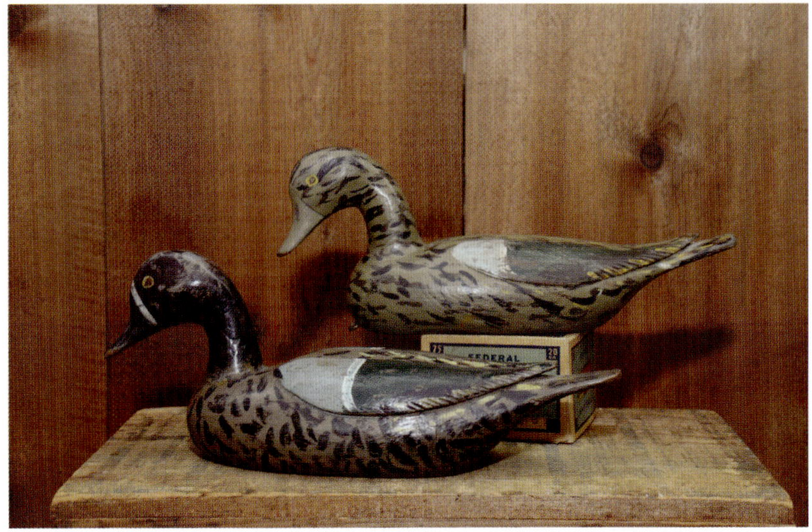

(3) Xavier Bourg blue-winged teal pair

Bourg and Carl Danos when carving hunting slicks. Ultimately, it is unfair to compare the old masters' hunting decoys with the Danos brothers' decorative decoys. Although the former have ultimately been recognized as folk art, they are still simple hunting tools from an earlier time. In contrast, the latter are works of fine art enabled by better tools, paint, and, frankly, more artistic talent. There can be little debate that the Danos brothers' decoy carving artistry does far more than just preserve the old masters' legacy.

Although there is a ten-year difference in age between them, Carl and Reagan are extremely close. Reagan likes it when he is referred to as "Carl's brother." It happens so often that he frequently responds, "I am Carl's twin brother," jokingly explaining away the ten-year age difference by saying their mother had a difficult pregnancy. The brothers live next door to each other and share a passion for decoy carving that is grounded in how and where they grew up. Both their grandfather and their father were avid duck hunters. For these two men, duck hunting was not a sport; it was a means of obtaining food to eat. Having the same needs and interests as their elders, the Danos boys learned to carve decoys at an early age, not to sell, but to use to gather food for the family's dinner table.

Although Carl and Reagan have their own carving shops a short distance apart, they frequently carve together. Their shared mantra is "make every decoy better than the last one." This sets the bar very high, considering that every decoy they make seems as good as it gets. Carl says that he and

Reagan have a "synergistic carving relationship" that makes both of them better artists. While interviewed separately and asked what carver's work they like and most admire, Carl unhesitatingly said Reagan, and Reagan said Carl with equal quickness.

When the brothers started carving professionally in their early twenties each was drawn to decoratives for three reasons. First, both enjoyed the challenge of trying to be the very best at carving competitions at the state and national levels. Second, these carving competitions awarded significant cash prizes for the winning carvers, and similar or even higher prices were being paid by collectors attending the competitions. Third, the demand for wooden hunting decoys was almost nonexistent because of the popularity of synthetic decoys that were much cheaper, lighter, more durable, essentially maintenance free, and perceived by most duck hunters as being as effective at luring ducks as wooden ones.

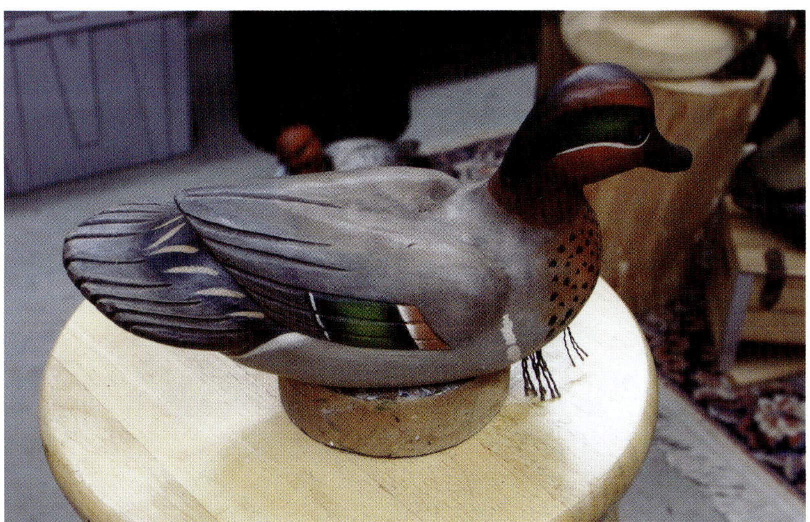

As previously mentioned, the popularity of decoratives peaked in the 1990s when prices rose to $50,000 or more for a single decoy—and even more for wooden wildlife sculptures. Over time, collectors willing to pay those prices became fewer and farther between. Carvers (including the Danos brothers) started making decorative gunners that were less elaborately carved than decoratives and much more ornately painted than old-style hunting slicks. Decorative gunners took far less time to complete than the decoratives and sold at prices that collectors were willing to pay.

Although the Danos brothers enjoyed competitive carving contests, they entered different categories in order to avoid directly competing against each other. That there is no sibling rivalry between the Danos brothers is surprising given the story that Reagan told me about how their father dealt with his decoy carving progeny. He said his father would often come into his carving shop, close the door, and ask: "Reagan, why do you waste your time trying to carve decoys when your brother's decoys are so much better than yours." This would certainly have been demoralizing if Reagan had not known that shortly after leaving, his father would walk into his brother's carving shop and ask Carl: "Why do you keep carving when Reagan's decoys are so much better?" The brothers soon realized that their father's "encouragement" was intended to make each of his sons the best that they could be. It worked.

LEFT: (2) Copy of Cadise Vizier green-winged teal drake

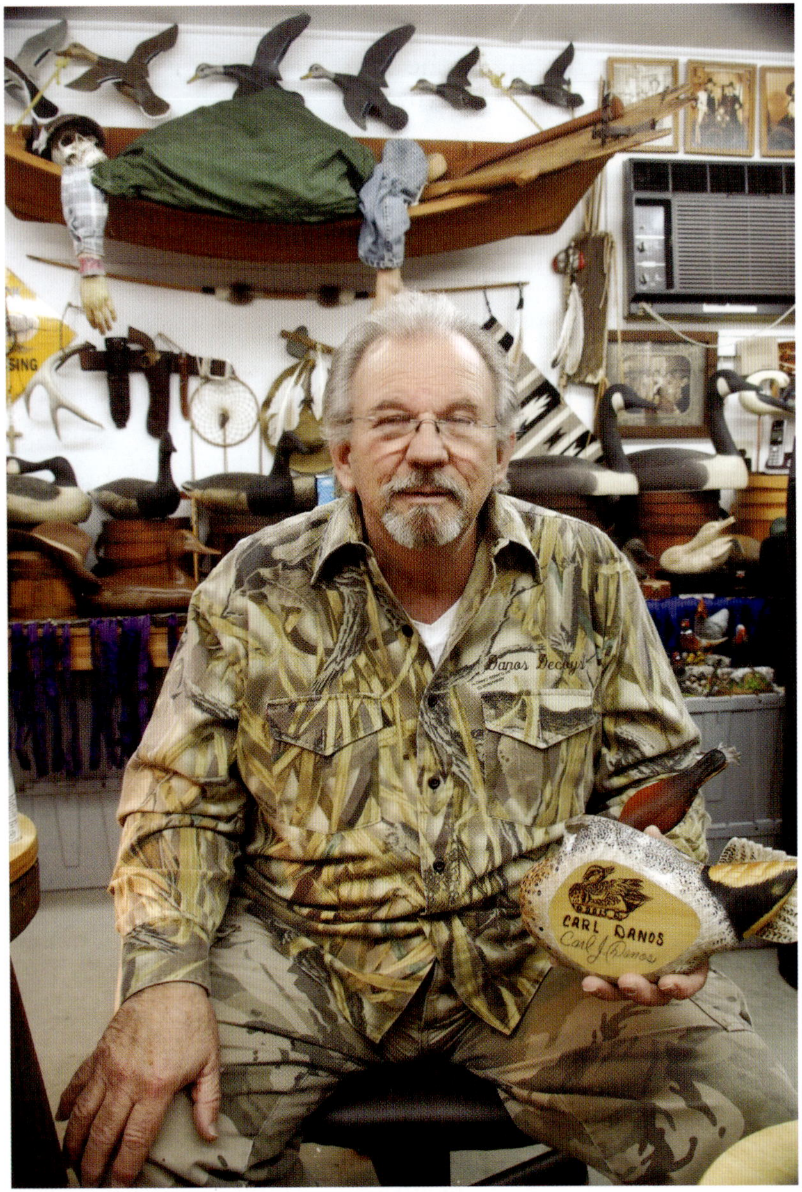

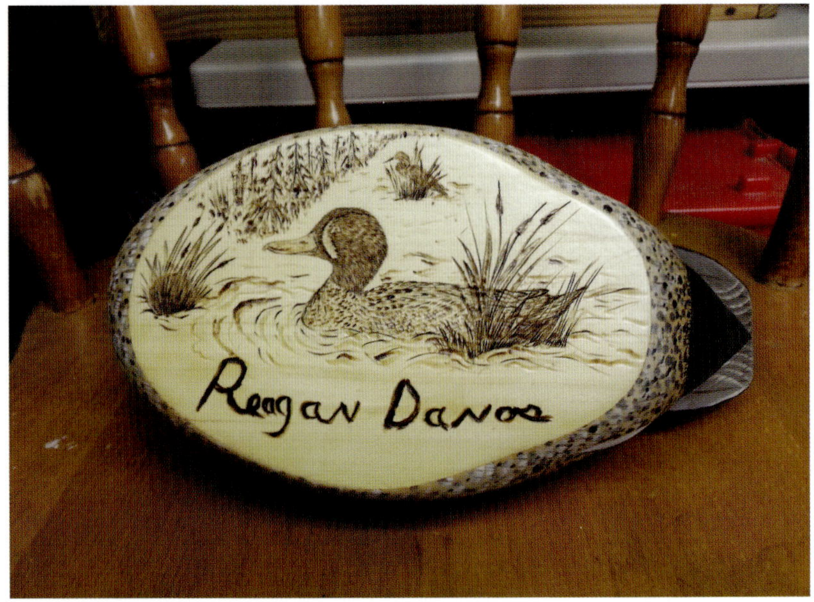

Left: (4) Carl Danos holding inscribed decoy bottom
Above: (5) Reagan Danos's inscribed decoy bottom

Carl and Reagan share another artistic innovation. Each uses a burning tool to sign, date, and remarque the bottom of every decoy they carve, as shown in photographs 4 and 5. Carl adds the letter "D" in memory of his teenage grandson and carving buddy.

The Danos brothers have warm and welcoming personalities. Besides their shared passion for wildfowl carving and the need to preserve it, Carl and Reagan are equally intent on giving back by teaching their craft to others. For years, they travelled from Texas to the East Coast, teaching decoy carving seminars and giving carving demonstrations.

Although very similar in their personalities, carving, and painting styles, both men and their decoys deserve to be discussed separately as there are some significant differences.

Carl is a self-taught carver with an eighth-grade education. Born on October 20, 1948, he has lived in Larose all of his life—his Cajun ancestors have lived in that area for generations. Carl is married with grown children. He and his lovely wife, Gail, have a nice home situated less than a hundred yards from Bayou Lafourche—in the very heart of Charlie Frank's "tilted triangle," where the greatest concentration of Louisiana's decoy carvers live or lived. Carl is one of the kindest, most determined, modest, and deeply religious men that I have ever met. He is also one of the most intelligent.

For over thirty years, Carl worked in a grocery store in Golden Meadow, starting as a butcher's helper and ending up as manager of the meat department. Years before he started carving professionally, Carl became a taxidermist and worked in that vocation for five years. Carl credits his wife for persuading him to become a taxidermist as a supplemental vocation. She enrolled Carl in the taxidermy course, bought his course materials, and encouraged him to pursue that vocation because she realized that working fifty or more hours a week wasn't enough to keep her "workaholic" husband occupied. Carl's work as a taxidermist significantly enhanced his ability as a decoy maker—thus proving, once again, that behind every good man, there is an even better woman.

Over forty years ago, Carl transitioned from making working decoys to carving exquisite decorative decoys. Early on, he won first and second place awards at the 1979 Wildfowl Carvers and Collectors' Guild show. Since then, he has won multiple carving awards at major decoy competitions locally and nationally, including the Ward and the fall show in Easton, Maryland, on the Delmarva Peninsula. He has earned more than two hundred Best in Show awards; and, amazingly, he still has all of the winners, which he keeps in storage.

Gail was also responsible, at least in part, for Carl's becoming a decorative decoy carver. It seems there was a wildlife show in nearby Galliano, and Carl had Gail take some of his taxidermy specimens to display there. Gail did as requested and on the way out the exhibition hall, she passed by the table of John Viola, a skilled decoy carver from New Orleans. Gail noticed a duck just like one that she brought to the show for Carl. Right in front of it was a small but easily readable sign that said "Do not touch." Gail could not resist a quick touch and was mortified when Mr. Viola saw her and asked "if she could read." Gail was speechless when she realized the duck that looked so lifelike was actually made of wood. When she regained her composure, she called Carl and told him to come to the show immediately to see this wooden replica, indistinguishable from the real thing. He did, and thus began his career as a decorative decoy carver..

Carl carves in all three contemporary styles. He uses tupelo gum to make his decoys because he says "it is like carving a bar of soap." He prefers to use acrylic paint because it is water-soluble, has no toxic fumes, and doesn't fade. Carl's incomparable artistry is confirmed by the decorative pair of redhead and the pair of gadwalls shown in photographs 6 and 7. These decoys are exquisitely detailed and beautifully painted. Many carvers avoid making gadwall decoys because they are difficult to paint properly, but Carl embraces that challenge and enjoys carving that species. Carl graciously says that his ability to produce beautiful wildfowl fine art is a "gift

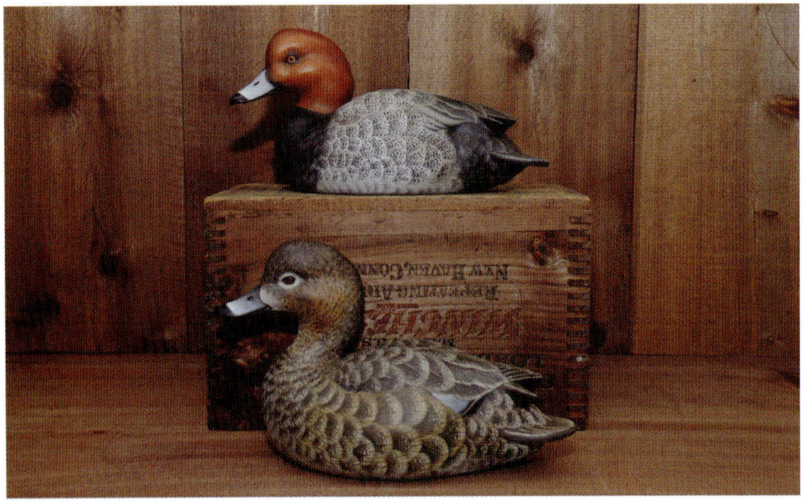

Above: (6) Redhead pair

Below: (7) Gadwall pair

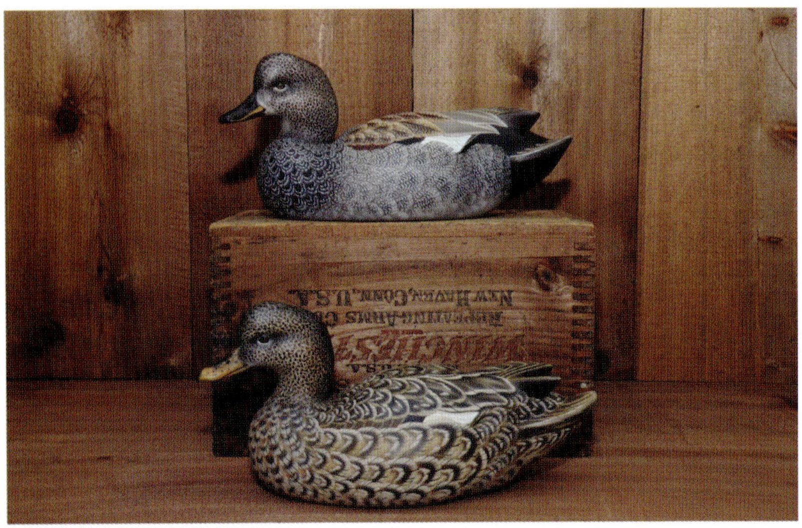

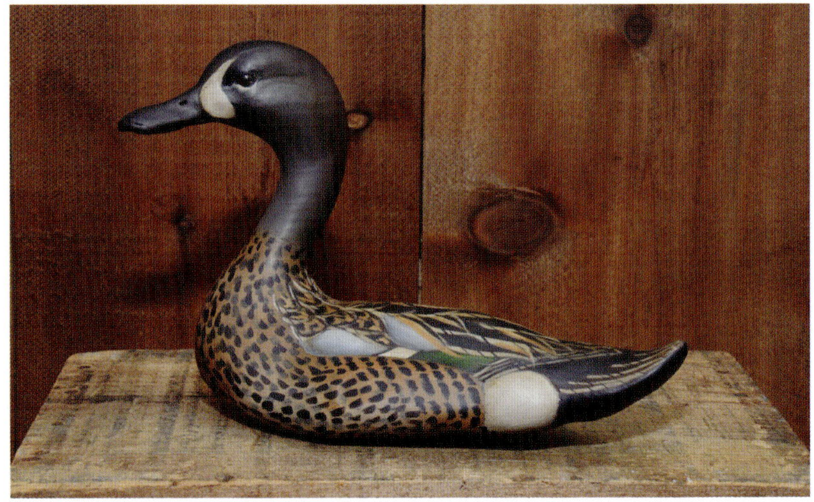

Above: (8) Blue-winged teal drake (sentinel pose)

Below: (10) Mallard drake and friend (English caller)

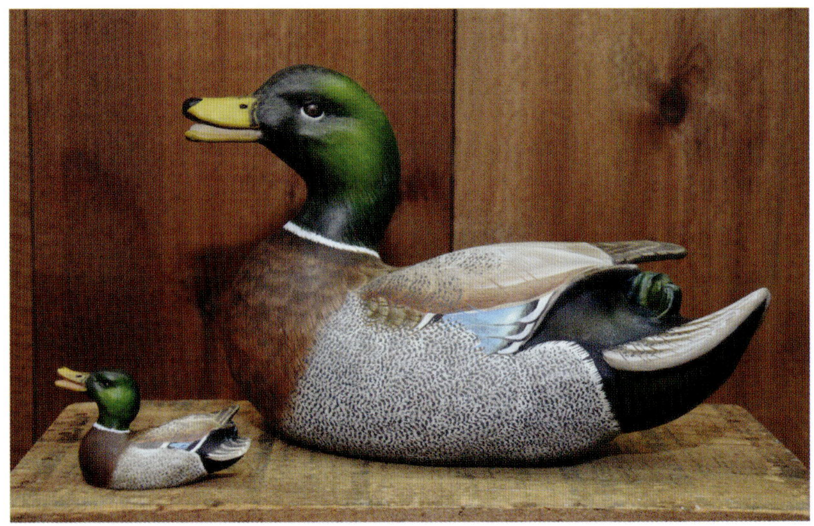

from God," one that he shares with brother, Reagan.

When the decorative decoy era was coming to an end and demand for that style began waning, Carl started carving more gunners and decorative gunners like the blue-winged teal with the elongated neck in the sentinel goose pose, shown in photograph 8. Carl's widegeon drake in photograph 9 is particularly interesting and colorful. Perhaps the most unique decoy that Carl carves is an English Caller. I'd never seen nor even heard of an English Caller until Carl showed me one that he had just finished for a Louisiana Supreme Court justice, and it was an eye opener. An English Caller was a domesticated mallard that was about 25 percent smaller than a wild mallard but not as tame and well trained as the mallards that march daily, on command, into the wading pool in the lobby of the Peabody Hotel in Memphis, Tennessee. The English Callers were live decoys that were used, very effectively, to attract wild ducks until they were outlawed by the Federal Migratory Game Bird Act of 1918. Carl's English Caller decoy along with a friend is shown in photograph 10.

It is difficult for Carl to part with his decoys because he invests so much of himself in their creation. Carl is almost evangelically passionate about decoy carving. For years, he has taught decoy carving four times a week—twice in Larose and twice in Houma, a sixty-mile round trip. He is a major force in the Larose decoy carving community, especially the annual "Cocktail Carving Contest," where carvers from the area donate decoys that are auctioned off at high prices with the money going to charitable causes. Carl is affectionately called the "Godfather," and his decoys always command high prices at these auctions.

On my visits to Carl's workshop, I spent a great deal of time carefully looking at the decoys he has on display. One day I asked Carl: "How does a collector know which of these magnificent works of art to buy?" He quietly told me, "buy the one that makes you smile" because "a smile means that you are happy" and it is likely that the chosen decoy will always evoke good memories. Carl Danos makes me smile even more than his decoys. His passion for decoy carving, teaching others, and zest for life is contagious.

There is an even more compelling back-story to the man who has carved the incredible decoys shown in the photographs that accompany this chapter and many others—Carl Danos is almost completely blind. That he is able to create these beautiful works of art is a miraculous achievement—a testament to his indomitable spirit and his boundless religious faith. As an infant, Carl developed an eye infection that

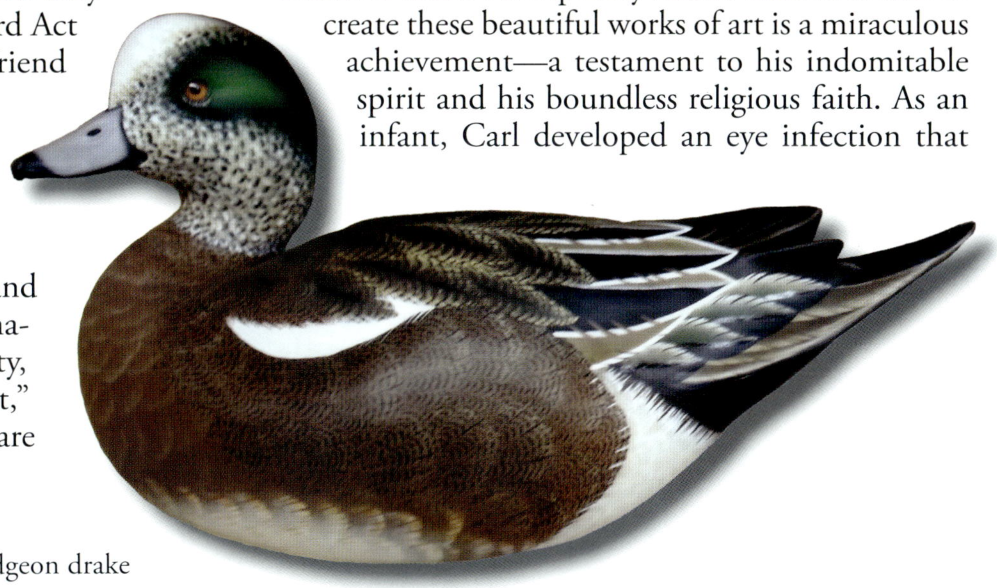

RIGHT: (9) Carl Danos's widgeon drake

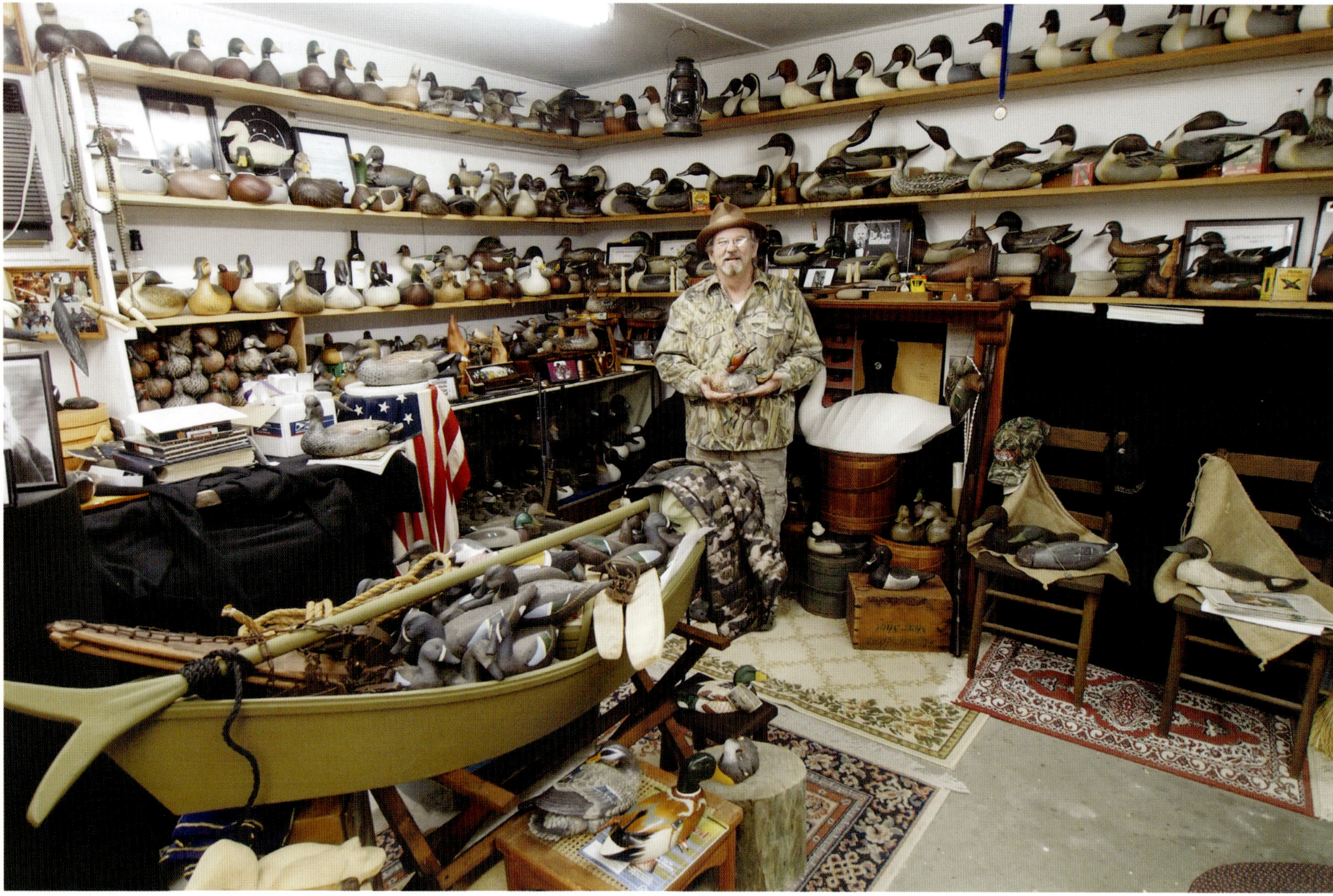

(11) Carl Danos in his workshop

scarred the pupil in his left eye, causing him to be legally blind in that eye. Then, about eight years ago, the optic nerve in his right eye ruptured, leaving him totally blind in that eye. Carl was able to drive and continue carving decoys because of some medically inexplicable minor improvement in his left eye. Unfortunately, that changed for the worse in the fall of 2015 when the optic nerve in his left eye also ruptured, leaving Carl virtually sightless. As if the loss of sight were not enough for any human being, Carl also lost his beloved teenage grandson, Dylan, to cystic fibrosis, and his mother had a stroke during the same time period.

These events understandably devastated Carl, but he never complained and his faith never wavered. He fervently prayed to be able to carve again, and his prayers were answered. The combination of his religious devotion and personal determination coupled with encouragement from his family, especially his wife Gail, caused Carl to return to his workshop, which he tediously cleaned and rearranged without any assistance. When he finished, his workshop looked as seen in photograph 11. That achievement (no small accomplishment for a fully sighted man) gave Carl the confidence he needed to try and start carving again, even though he had no depth perception and his vision was "like looking through visqueen."

At first, Carl had Reagan rough cut his decoys with a band saw and help with his painting, but Carl's perseverance paid off. In a matter of months, he was able to carve and paint his decoys without assistance just as well as ever. The preening green-winged teal drake at the front of this chapter on page 84 is a decorative masterpiece and a miraculous accomplishment for a blind carver. Seeing that decoy makes me smile and feel happy almost as much as spending time with Carl. He is truly one of God's great and inspiring people.

Reagan Danos was born January 13, 1958. He lives with his high-school-sweetheart wife Robin, in Larose, Louisiana, next door to his "twin brother" and sister-in-law. The couple has two grown children. Reagan and Carl have the same deep-seated roots in the small Cajun community where they live, which explains why they are so close and have so much in common. Both men are genuinely warm and welcoming and are equally passionate about decoy carving at the highest level. Both see decoy carving as a link to the past and how they were raised. Both do whatever they can to keep this art form alive and flourishing because it is an essential part of their culture and heritage.

Reagan graduated from South Lafourche High School where he concentrated in Distributive Education, an after school program that offered hands-on training in industrial operations. Reagan worked in a hardware and feed store as part of the program. After graduation, he worked for an oil field service company that disposed of drilling fluids for twenty-four years until he was recently laid off. For years, Reagan served his employer as field site manager and was responsible for orchestrating the removal, storage, and transportation of oil field waste from offshore drilling sites to various disposal sites.

As a youngster, Reagan was a fervent duck hunter. He was inspired to carve hunting decoys by his father and uncles. Around 1980, when Reagan was in his early twenties, his interest in hunting waned as he became serious about carving decoys to sell. Since then, Reagan likes to sit in a blind and observe ducks and geese in the wild. Early on, he wanted to carve decoratives for the same reasons that motivated his older brother. He liked competing to be the best

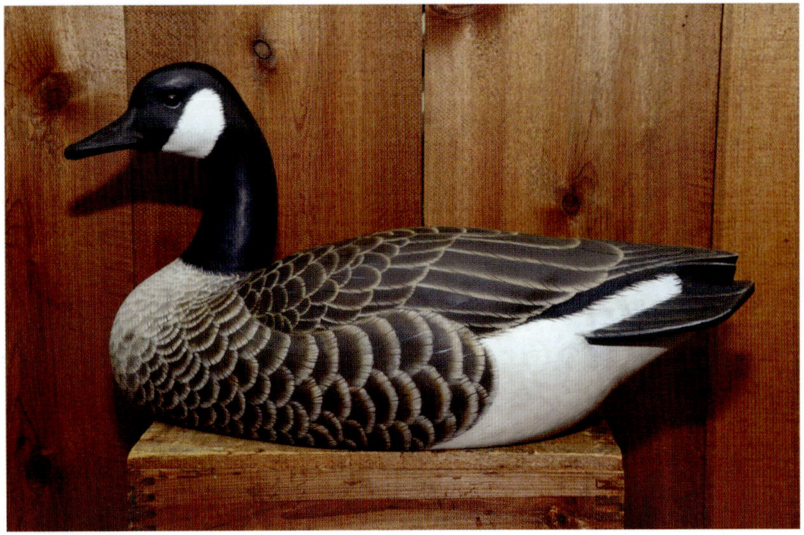

(12) Reagan Danos's Canada goose

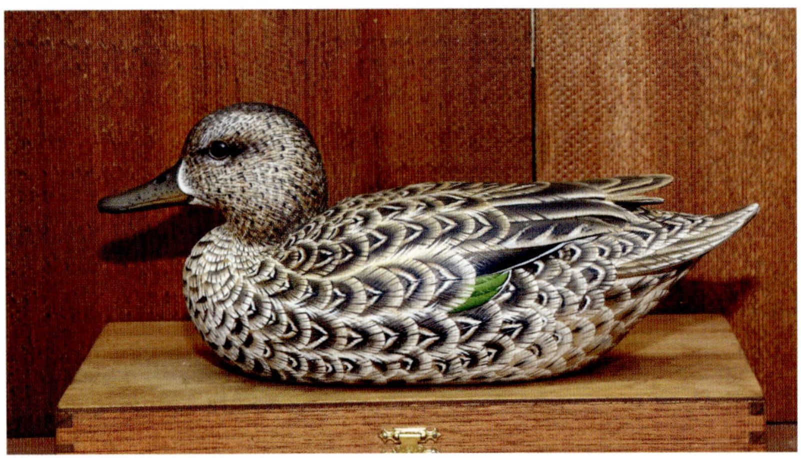

(13) Reagan Danos's prize-winning green-winged teal hen

and earning substantial prize money when he succeeded. A picture of Reagan's decorative Canada goose decoy is shown in photograph 12.

Over his career, Reagan has won approximately one hundred awards in such prestigious events as the Ward Foundation annual competition in Ocean City, Maryland. In the 1990s, he won a first and a third place award in the annual Ward Shooting Rig Division, which requires three decoys, including two of the same species. Reagan submitted a rig of three hunting decoys, as this division expects, but a number of competing carvers entered rigs consisting of three decorative decoys. The only thing that Reagan's hunting decoys and his competitors' decorative decoys had in common was that they all floated. Esthetically, it was like a buzzard competing against a swan in a wildfowl beauty contest. Reagan didn't complain; it just made winning that much sweeter. In 2014, Reagan's green-winged teal hen took Best in Show honors in the Master Carver Division in that year's Ward Foundation carving competition. That very special decorative decoy is shown in photograph 13.

Reagan carves decorative decoys, decorative gunners, and shore birds. He normally uses tupelo gum to make his decoys because it is easier to carve. Occasionally, he uses cypress, which he thinks makes better hunting decoys. He also uses sinker cypress when carving a piece that will have a natural finish. He uses acrylic paint for the same reasons as his brother.

Although Jimmy Vizier and Tan Brunet were major carving influences for him, Reagan reserves his highest admiration and respect for his brother's decoy making skills. Reagan regards Carl's return to high-quality decoy carving after his recent visual set back as nothing short of an inspiring miracle.

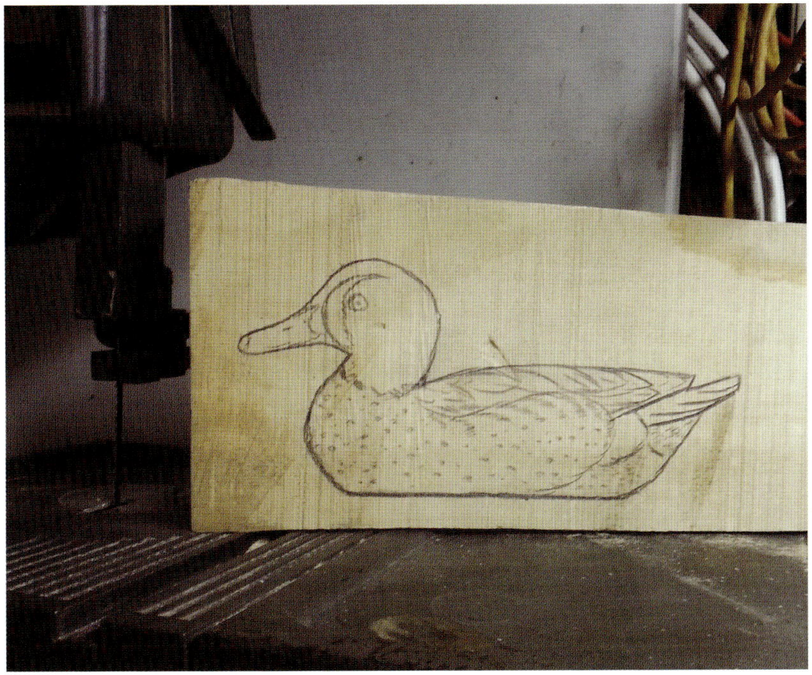

(14) Step one in creating a blue-winged teal:
pattern drawn on cyprus block

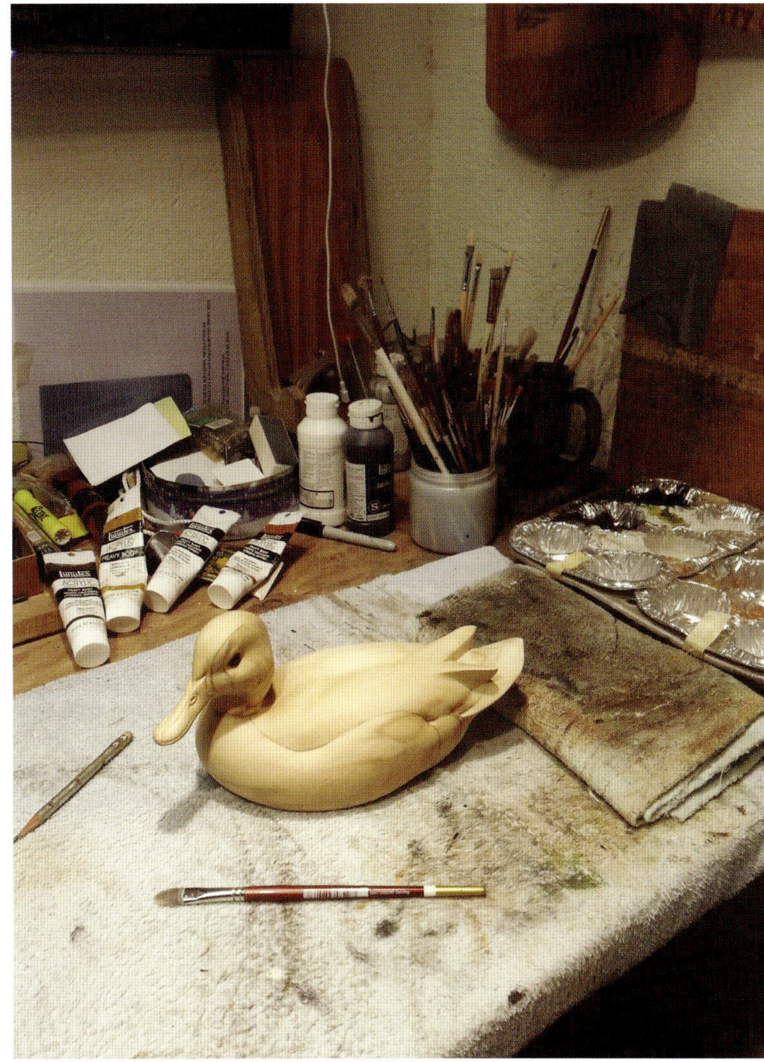

(15) Decoy carved out and awaiting painting

Reagan is a superb carver and painter. His best decorative decoys are as good as any other carver's, as his Best in Show green-winged teal decoy demonstrates. Reagan provides a step-by-step graphic illustration of what a talented wildfowl artist does to convert a block of wood into an award-winning decoy in photographs 14, 15, 16, 17, and 18. The final product—his blue-winged teal drake decorative gunner—shown in photograph 19 is an excellent example of that award-winning carving style.

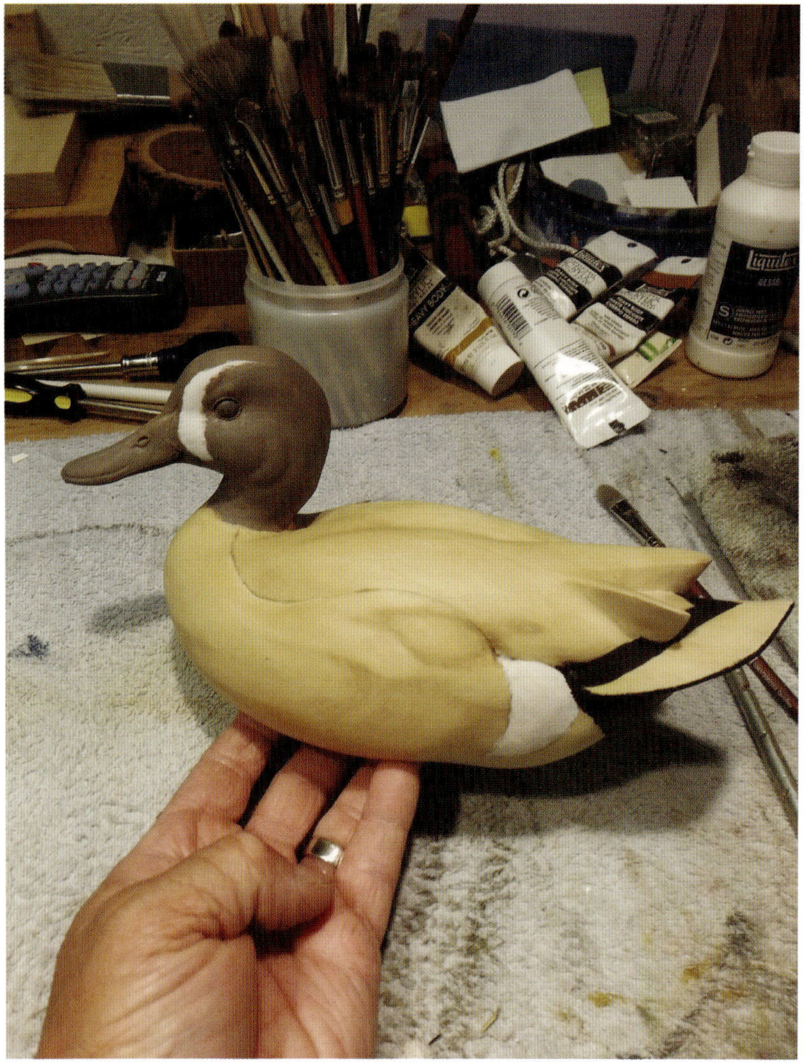

(16) Blue-winged teal head and tail feathers painted

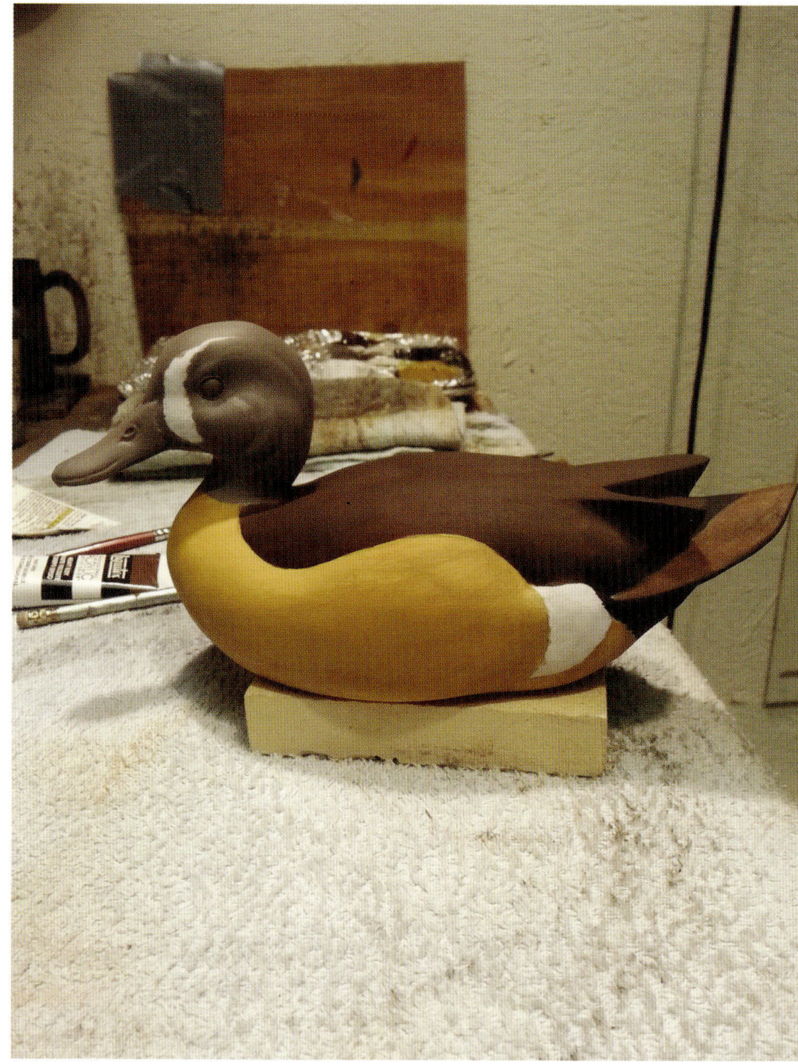

(17) First body paint coat

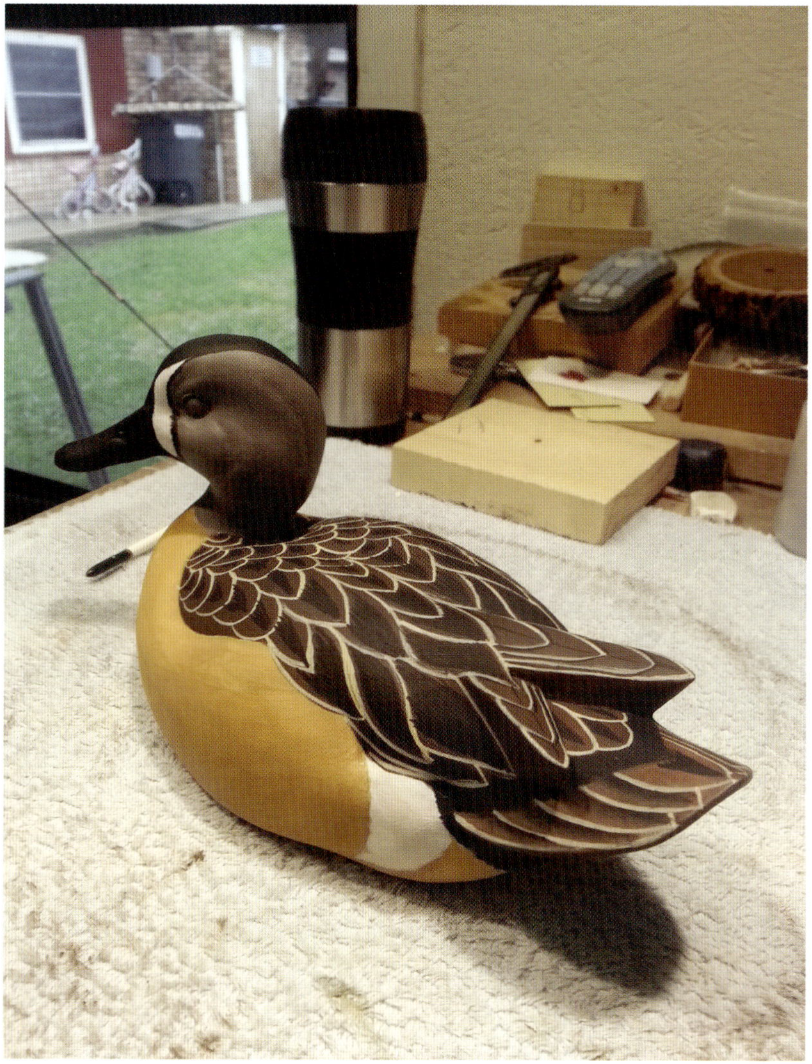

(18) Second body paint coat

Early on, I said that there were some differences between Reagan and Carl. It is not in their carving and painting skills, which are equal in all respects. It is not in their interpersonal skills; both are kind, capable, intelligent, and caring human beings. They both make you smile when you're in their company. So what are the differences? Well, Carl likes to carve green-winged teal best and Reagan likes to carve blue-winged teal. Additionally, Reagan has a separate building where he paints his decoys, and Carl carves and paints his decoys in the same workshop. It doesn't really matter because the Danos brothers frequently work together, and they are always pushing each other to be the best each can be.

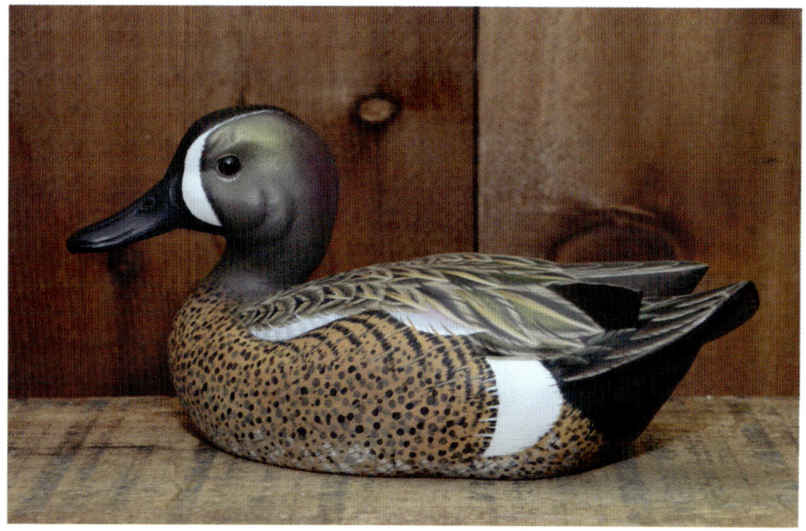

(19) Reagan Danos's blue-winged teal drake: final product

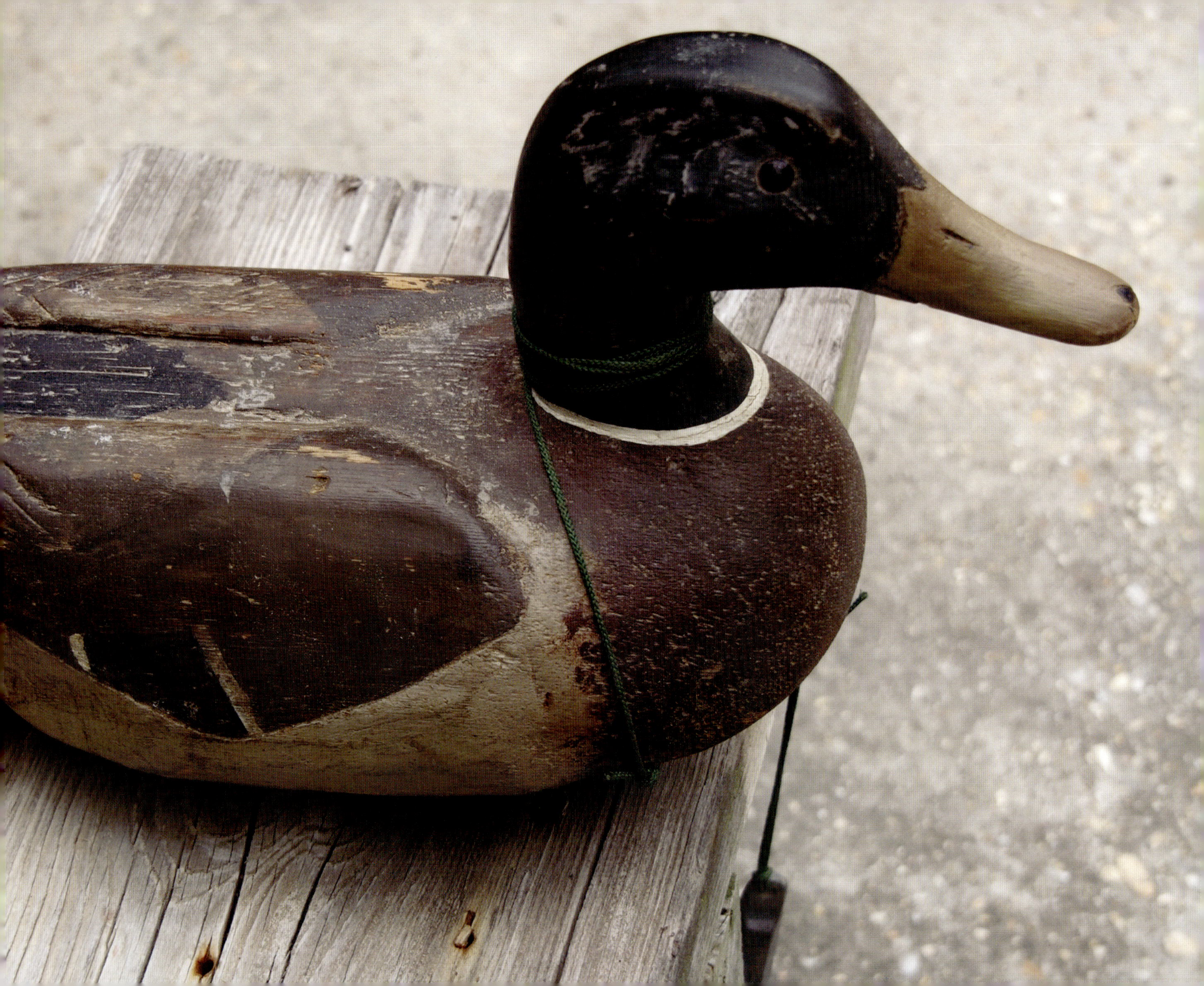

Opposite page: Ronnie Flynn's mallard drake decoy

11 Ronnie Flynn

Decoy Carving Family Man

Early in this project, Bill Hanemann urged me to go meet Ronnie Flynn, suggesting that not only was he a very fine carver, he was also "one of a kind." Bill said "if war ever broke out, Ronnie Flynn was the one man that [he'd] want in his foxhole." With a mixture of curiosity and trepidation, and with Bill's assistance, I made arrangements to visit Ronnie in May 2015. It was quite an experience.

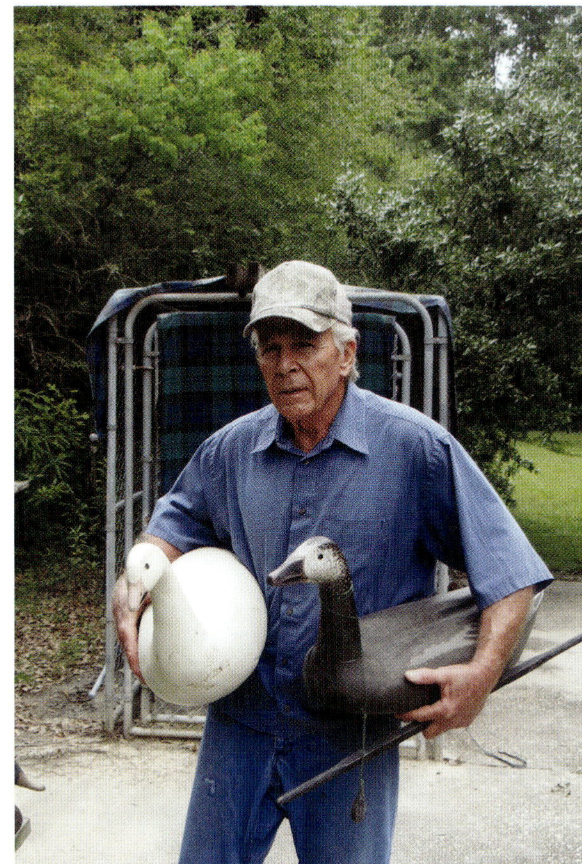

Ronnie lives in a remote part of St. Tammany Parish on a secluded, park-like property complete with a pond filled with ducks and geese, pens for various animal (including turkeys), several storage buildings, and a lovely home, elevated to protect against flooding. Ronnie came out of his home and down the steps to welcome me as I was getting out of my car. As he approached, I noticed he was about five foot ten, obviously very fit, and appeared much younger than seventy-two. I could tell he was studying me intensely with his piercing blue eyes. Apparently he decided that I didn't pose any threat that he couldn't handle because he invited me to come visit inside the house.

Despite the invite, I felt like an intruder about to enter Ronnie's private domain. I walked into a large room and was immediately surrounded by a number of very large stuffed animals, including mountain lions, black bears, and other creatures. A tall stack of antler racks leaned against one wall and numerous pelts covered the other walls in the few spaces where there weren't photographs showing Ronnie and his son Ben with trophy kills from big game hunts over the years. I thought I'd walked into a regional branch of the Museum of Natural History. Ronnie was clearly different.

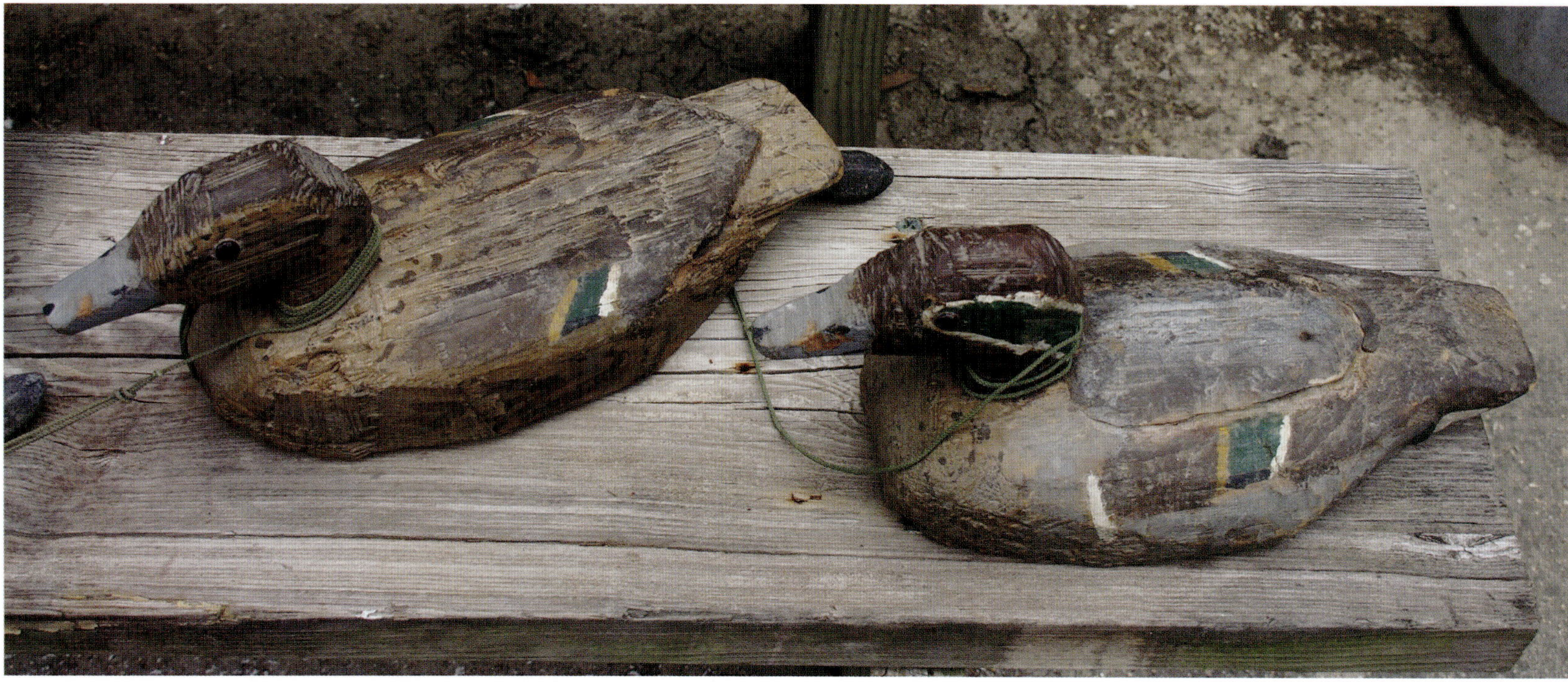

(1) Ronnie Flynn's primitive mallard pair

As I stared at this wildlife trophy room in wonderment, Ronnie quietly told me that his wife, Elaine, had decorated this part of the Flynn residence. Then I thought to myself, how could any man be lucky enough to marry a woman who wanted her home to look like a plush hunting lodge, complete with all of the trophy animals that her spouse had killed?

Ronnie led me over to a comfortable pair of chairs and we sat down. He told me that he "loved and lived to hunt." That was clear in the way his home was furnished. He said big game hunting in North and South America was his passion and that the only meat that he ever eats comes from game that he has killed.

The talk then turned to duck hunting and decoys. Ronnie said that when he was about five years old, his father gave him a .410 shotgun with the stock cut down and took him on his first duck hunt. Ronnie was hooked, and by age seven he was carving decoys to hunt over. Photograph 1 shows a pair of the first decoys Ronnie ever carved. Ronnie said he was entirely self-taught and didn't copy anyone else's style because he "wanted to make his own mistakes." While

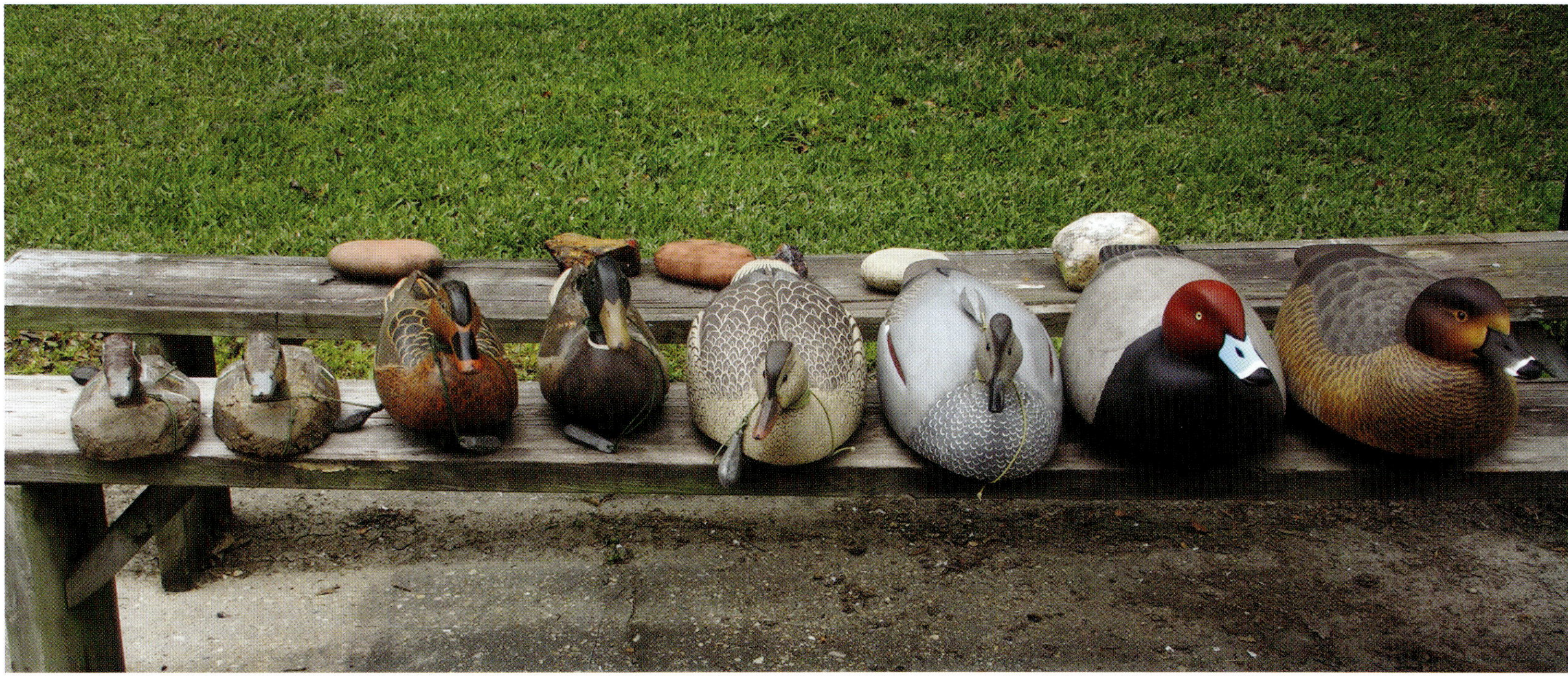

(2) Ronnie Flynn's decoys showing increasing skill

still in his teens, Ronnie carved decoys to hunt over about every two years. Photograph 2 shows a group of decoys Ronnie carved during that period. The two decoys on the left end of the lineup were the first ones he carved, and the ones on the right end he carved later. Ronnie was carving teal decoys when he was eight years old, mallards when he was twelve, and grey ducks when he was sixteen. When he was fifteen, Ronnie made some blue goose "stick up" decoys that he still uses today. He was truly a child prodigy. Photograph 3 shows Ronnie holding up one of his blue goose decoys. Most recently, Ronnie carved redhead decoys that are shown in photograph 4.

Ronnie loved duck hunting with his father, who fortuitously played a role in his son becoming a professional decoy carver and collector. One day, Ronnie's father brought home some DuraDuck Decoys, which were made of thick rubber. After a few hunts over the rubber decoys Ronnie became dissatisfied and, from then on, he would only hunt ducks with wooden decoys he had carved himself. He shrewdly started collecting old wooden hunting decoys when peo-

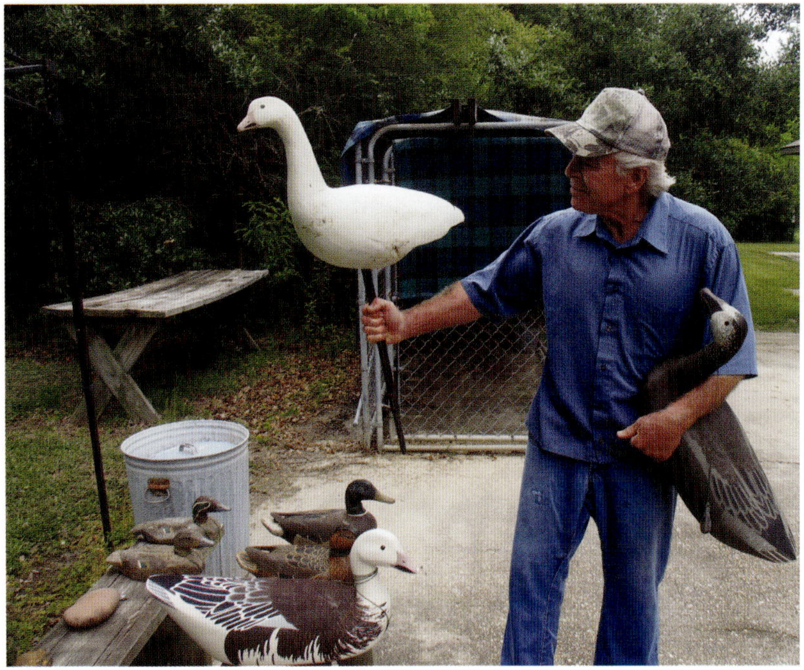

(3) Flynn holding a goose decoy

ple, en masse, started buying rubber and plastic decoys and throwing away their wooden ones.

In January 1964, Ronnie married Elaine, his high school sweetheart, and in December 1964, the couple had their first child—a son, Ben—who inherited his father's love of hunting, decoy carving, and his .410 gauge shotgun. In the early days of the marriage, making decoys was a joint venture. Ronnie carved and assembled the decoys; Elaine sanded and primed them; then Ronnie did the painting. The decoys the couple produced were "working birds" made for Ronnie and his son to hunt over. As Ben grew older, he started helping his parents. Making decoys became a family affair for the Flynns. In later years, the Flynn family of carvers added a new member when Elaine taught a granddaughter how to carve and paint decoys.

In 1964, Ronnie went hunting with Shaun Viguerie, a well-known New Orleans sportsman, and a longtime friend and hunting companion. Shaun liked Ronnie's decoys and commissioned him to make two or three dozen at a cost of $15 to 20 each, kickstarting Ronnie's career as a professional decoy carver. Ronnie was never into competitive carving—with one exception. In 1967, he mailed a pair of grey ducks to a decoy collector's guild show and won first and second place. That was the only competition Ronnie ever entered.

In the years that followed, Ronnie worked as a guide and caretaker at several of the area's private hunting clubs. He also did some construction work, but carving decoys was always his primary focus. Ronnie was commissioned to carve dec-

(4) Ronnie Flynn's redhead drake and hen

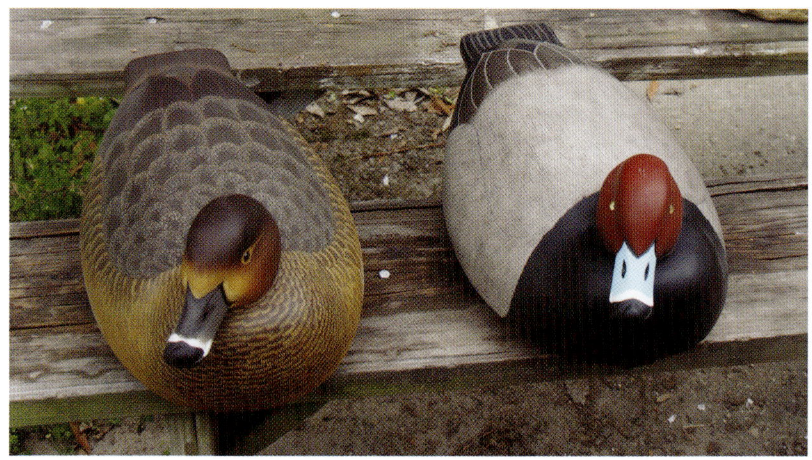

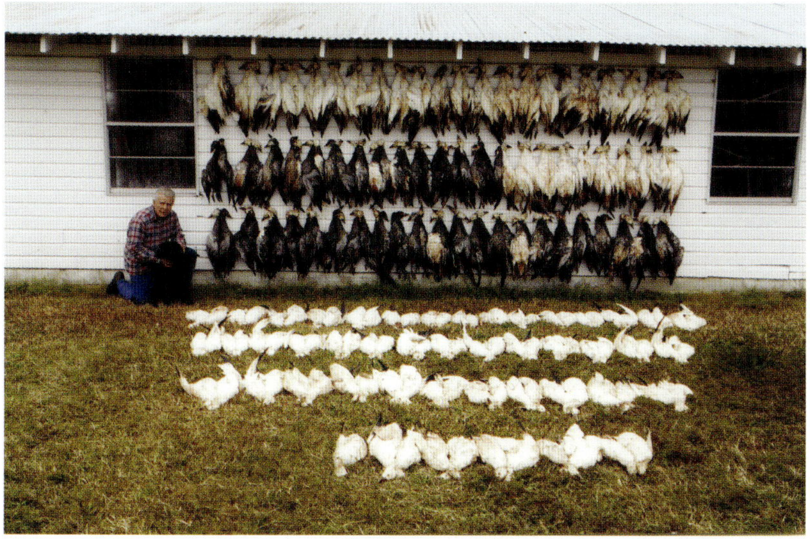

(5) Flynn and son: conservation hunt results

oratives, which were very popular at the time, but he didn't like carving them because he believes that "a decoy is no good unless you hunt over it"; it has to be "useful." In Ronnie's view, a decoy is a hunting tool. It is not a mantelpiece display item. He feels that decoratives have no history and do not talk to you like hunting decoys do. For these reasons, he doesn't regard decoratives as true decoys. With Ronnie, function trumps form. He makes working decoys that work.

Ronnie believes he makes the very best hunting decoys based on the only meaningful measurement—how many wildfowl the decoys bring within gunning range. Photograph 5 is proof that Ronnie's decoys work. Ronnie and his son killed over two hundred geese on one of Louisiana's conservation hunting dates, when there is no bag limit and hunter's shotguns are not required to be plugged. It is part of the federal government's programs to control the number of geese when there is an overpopulation and threat of disease. Although, the number of geese killed on this hunt is well above normal limits, it was entirely legal on the date and at the place where Ronnie and Ben made this hunt.

Ronnie is a very practical decoy carver. For example, he prefers hunting with slicks because too much carving on the decoy makes it hard to clean the mud off. Over the years his painting style has become more ornate. He prefers oversized decoys, especially when carving mallards and pintails, because he finds them to be more effective. His decoys have hollow bodies to make them lighter. They also have a keel to wind the line and weight around. He doesn't like wrapping the line and lead weight around the decoy's neck because it scars the decoy. Ronnie uses tupelo gum and clear western red cedar to make his decoys. He uses a pattern and cuts out the decoys with a band saw.

It is no surprise that Ronnie believes that old master Domingo Campo carved the best hunting decoys because they were oversized and very sturdy. He has some decoys that came from Reme Roussel's own hunting rig, which he treasures. He also has a number of Clovis Vizier's decoys that he likes very much but regards as "too small" to hunt over.

Tragedy struck the Flynn family is 2011 when Ronnie's beloved wife and carving partner Elaine died after forty-seven years of marriage. Ronnie was so devastated by Elaine's death that he lost the desire to carve decoys and stopped taking commissions. Recently he was motivated enough to carve some decoys to hunt over with his son. If and when he starts accepting commissions, I have reserved a place at the head of the line.

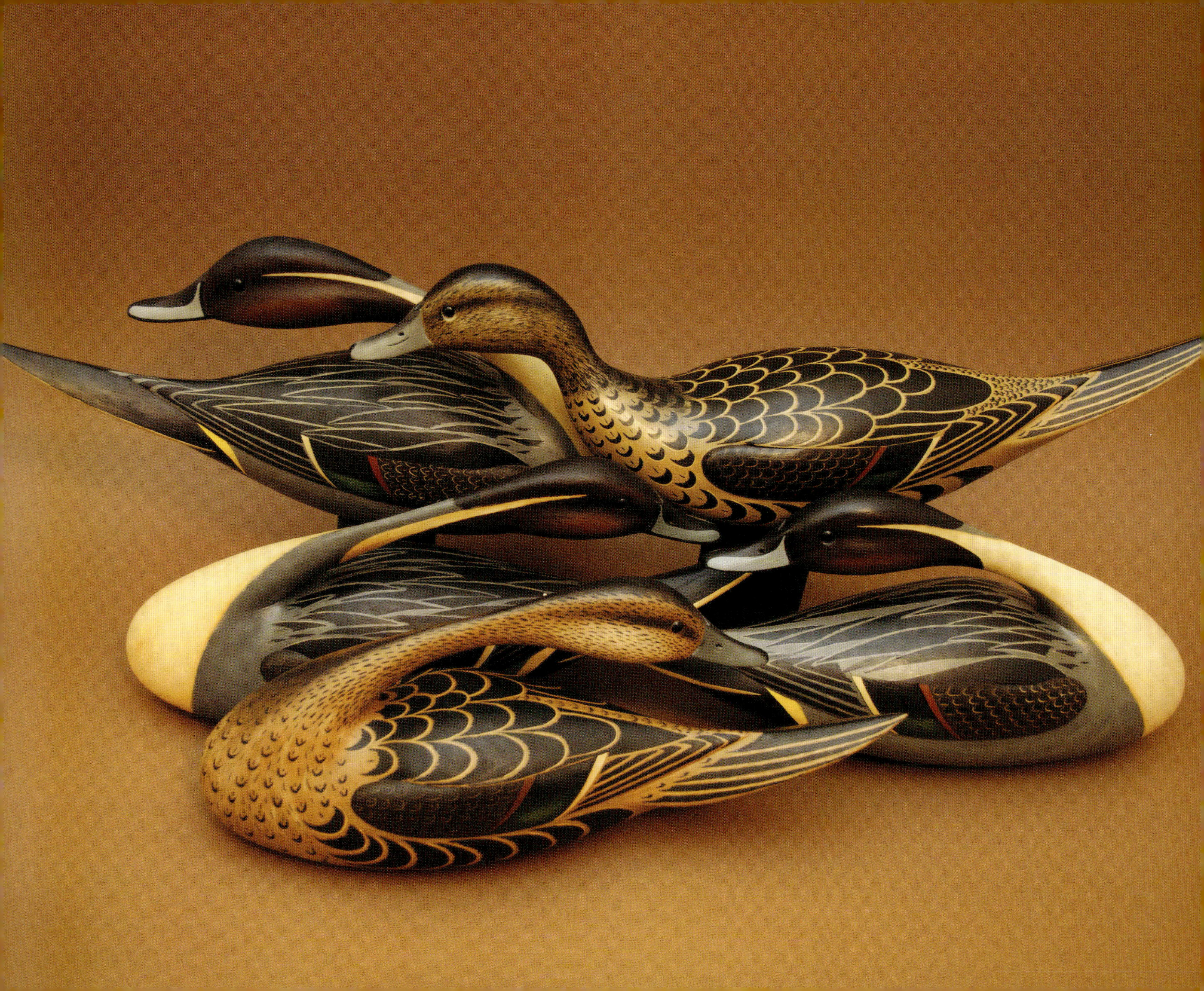

Opposite page: Bill Hanemann's pintail decoys

12 Bill Hanemann

Master Fine Art Carver

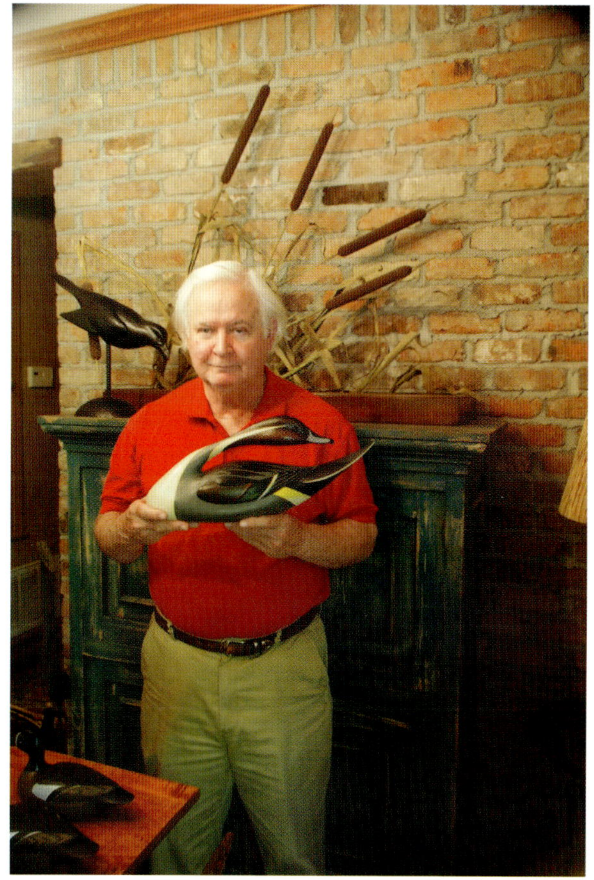

The lack of any reference to decoys, wildfowl, or even nature in the title of this chapter is purely intentional, as those words do not begin to define William "Bill" Hanemann's artistic versatility. To call Bill Hanemann a decoy carver is to call Michelangelo a painter. Bill is a master decorative carver but his talent is not limited to carving decoys. In the interest of full disclosure, I have known Bill for nearly forty years and have very high regard for his carving and painting skill but even higher respect for him as a person. His incomparable artistic talent is matched by his knowledge of decoys, his integrity, and his modesty. Over the years, Bill has made a number of decoys for me. He has also restored and/or repainted others. He has appraised my old hunting decoy collection and advised me on authentication matters. He inspired and encouraged me to write this book. For years, I called him Billy. For even longer, I have called him my friend.

Bill was born in 1947 in New Orleans. At an early age he was exposed to George Viavant's exquisite wildfowl paintings that later inspired his three-dimensional wildfowl *trompe l'oeil* (fool the eye) carving style as shown in photograph 1. As a teenager, he regularly visited his uncle, Jimmie Hanemann. At the time, Jimmie was Louisiana's premier wildfowl collector, ultimately amassing over three thousand decoys, many made by Louisiana old master carvers. Young Bill spent countless hours in the cavernous building that housed his uncle's decoy collection and learned all about them from his uncle. Hanemann's interest in hunting decoys, particularly those carved by Louisiana's old masters, was contagious.

Bill "caught the bug" and was so inspired that he started carving minia-

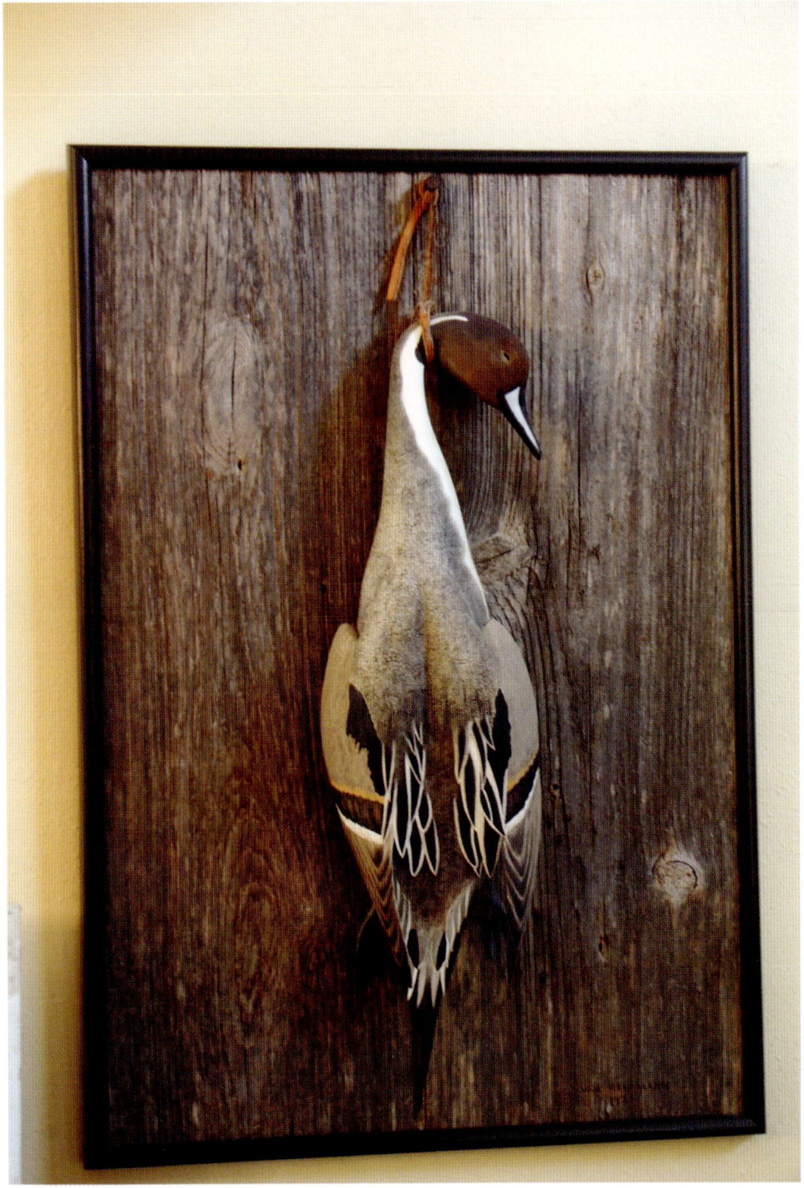

ture decoys at age sixteen. Bill's high school industrial arts classes helped improve his carving skills to the point that he was able to sell his miniature decoys for $7.50 each. Demand for Bill's miniatures was high enough to allow him to carve decoys rather than bag groceries in a supermarket after school. He became a self-taught professional decoy carver as a teenager and continued carving while in college at Southeastern Louisiana University, selling decoys to earn spending money. Bill graduated from college with a degree in business administration, but, fortunately, he decided to keep his "day job" carving decoys.

Shortly after completing his undergraduate studies, Bill met Charlie Frank Jr., who offered him what amounted to a post graduate course in all aspects of hunting decoy carving in Louisiana. The year was 1970, and Bill was twenty-three years old and a newlywed. For the better part of two or three years, Bill and Charlie spent nearly every weekend traveling all over an area generally south of New Orleans, bounded by Lake Pontchartrain on the north, the Mississippi River on the east, Bayou Lafourche on the west, and the Gulf of Mexico on the south. The purpose of each trip was to meet carvers and acquire decoys for Charlie's collection. Stories about the pair's quest reminds one of the adventures of Don Quixote and his faithful sidekick, Sancho Panza. Charlie's first book, *Louisiana Duck Decoys*, chronicles and offers photographic evidence of the intrepid twosome's forays in and around some of the most isolated places in this country. Seeing the old Louisiana masters carve, assemble, and paint their decoys up close gave Bill an understanding of and an

(1) Bill Hanemann's hanging pintail drake in "fool the eye" style

appreciation for the uniqueness of virtually every old Louisiana carver's decoys. Clearly, Charlie got some very good decoys at favorable prices, but Bill learned things from his in-person contact with many of the old masters that later proved to be vital to him as a decoy carver, restorer, painter, and authenticator. His relationship with Charlie and his involvement in the Louisiana Wildfowl Carvers and Collectors Guild from its founding days to date also gave Bill opportunities to meet Louisiana's biggest decoy collectors. Many of these collectors became his friends and best clients.

Bill names his Uncle Jimmie, Charlie Frank, and Robyn Hardy (a very fine New Orleans radiologist), now all deceased, as the three people who most influenced his career. I was puzzled about Dr. Hardy's role until Bill explained that the doctor taught him a new way to look at things using a Socratic approach. Bill learned that when viewing an object, do it up close, and carefully observe the object's smallest detail. Bill has used Hardy's approach on everything he carves, restores, or appraises.

Bill's carving is not limited to decoys. He makes furniture, carves mantles, and restores carousel animals. He has carved a number of objects for the Catholic Church in New Orleans, including croziers (staffs) for two archbishops. In the 1970s, Bill carved a trio of large, three-dimensional still life sculptures that he named *Days End*, *Cabin Wall*, and *Workbench*. *Cabin Wall* is shown in photograph 2. *Workbench* is shown in photograph 3. In an article appearing in the tenth anniversary issue of *Hunting and Fishing Collectibles Magazine* Erin Greenwald, an

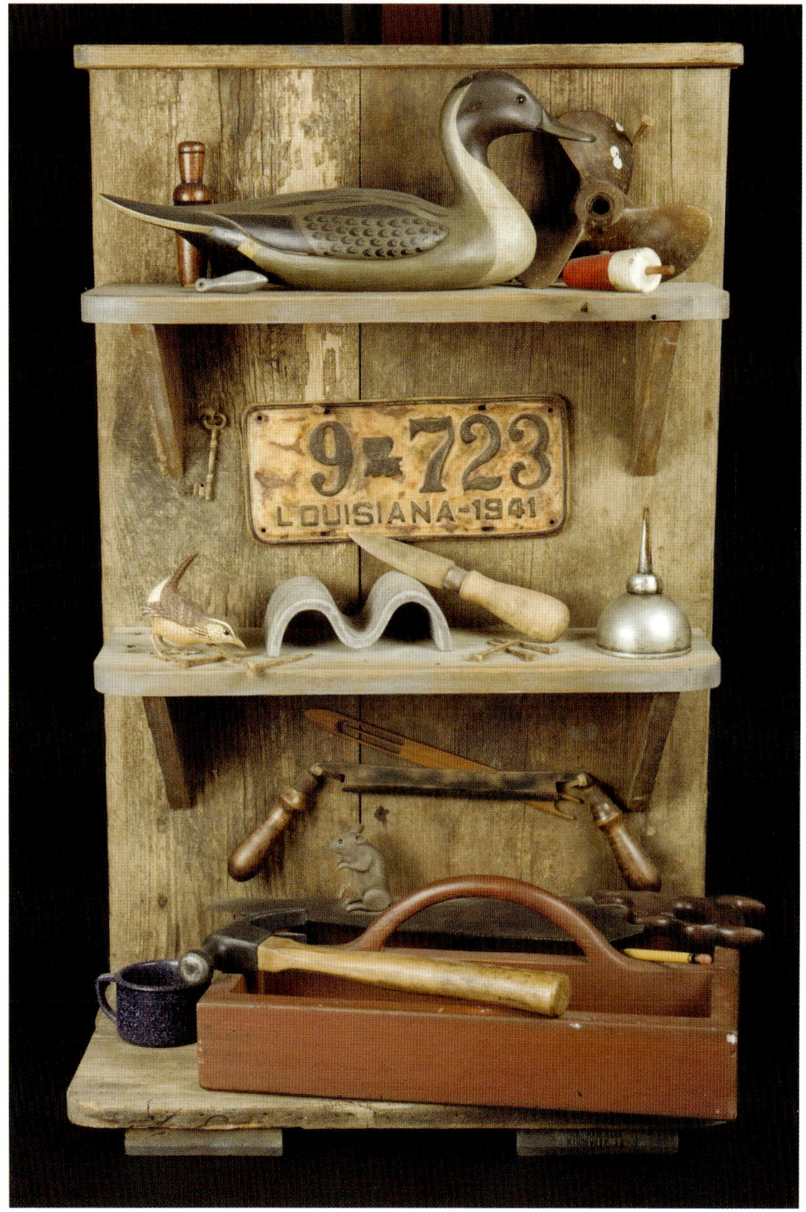

(2) Bill Hanemann's *Trapper's Cabin Wall* (all items made of wood)

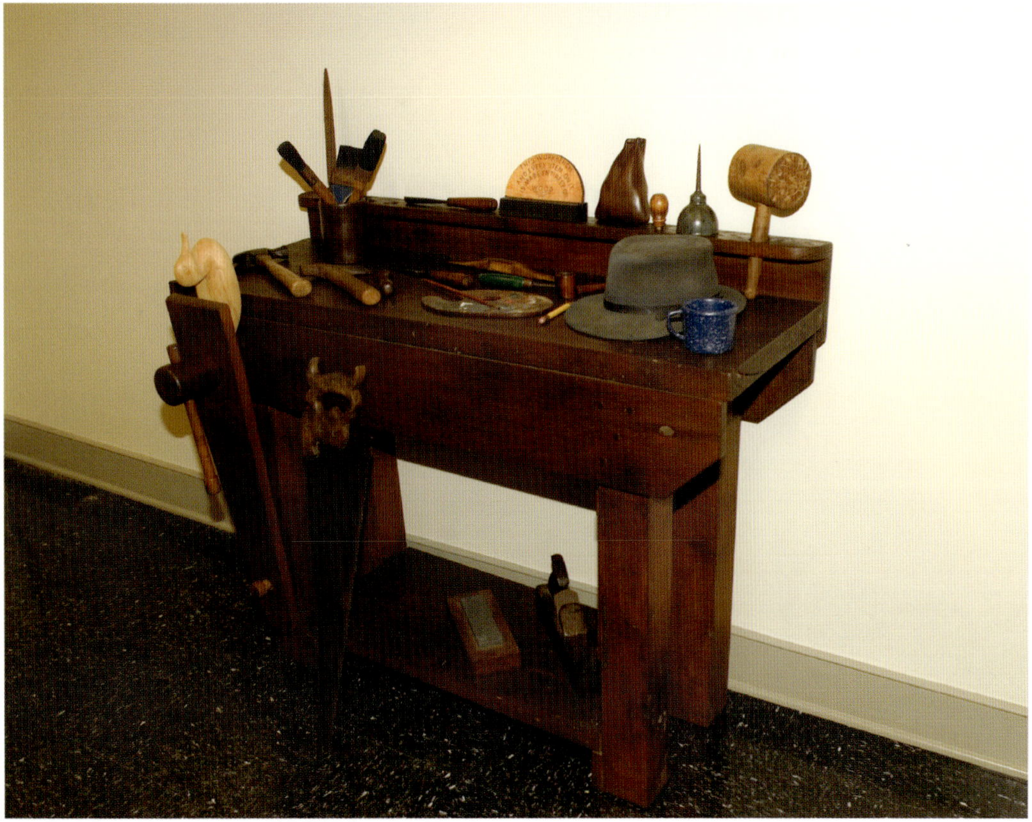

(3) Bill Hanemann's *Carver's Work Bench*
(all items wood carved)

editor and writer for The Historic New Orleans Collection, describes *Workbench* as "a large still life of a carver's workspace . . . [that] included more than thirty individually carved and painted objects—carving and texturing implements, a brimmed grey hat, well-worn saws, knives and brushes; an enameled cup filled with coffee. . . . [The three named still life sculptures] are filled with nostalgia. Through their creation, Hanemann paid homage to simpler times and generations."[1]

Hanemann's decorative sculptures were tedious to carve and each took six months or so to finish. This left relatively little time for him to complete the decoys he was commissioned to make. By the end of the 1980s, the exquisitely detailed decorative still life sculptures took their toll. They "burned him out," just as making decoratives had done to so many decorative decoy carvers.

Bill has an entrepreneurial as well as a creative side. For instance, he devised a way to mass produce decoys using a duplicating lathe that roughed out a number of decoys at one time. Bill would then do the finish carving and painting. Unfortunately, this enterprise wasn't a commercial success as only about two hundred decoys were sold. In a later venture, Bill and a partner produced and sold decoys made of resin using a cold cast bronze technique. Bill made the bronze model and the rubber mold, and his partner and crew produced the resin decoys. This venture did well and had several major retail customers, including Orvis. Unfortunately, the resin decoy business literally "flamed out" when the factory burned down.

Nonetheless, Bill was resilient and the increasing demand for old Louisiana hunting decoys created new opportunities for him, a contemporary carver, as odd as that seems. Virtually every serious collector of old Louisiana decoys regards Bill as the ultimate authority on the topic. When one of their newly collected decoys needs any restoration or repainting they invariably have Bill do it. The collectors know that Bill knows how their decoy was originally carved and painted. They also know that Bill would use the original masters' carving and painting techniques when doing the needed work. Bill's earlier travels with Charlie Frank paid off.

But Bill has too much talent to just do repair work, even complicated jobs like replacing a decoy's missing head or tail. Soon Bill was being asked to carve a mate for one of the collector's old decoys when the collector was unable to obtain a real one. To make an exact replica of an old Louisiana master's decoy, sometimes called a "contemporary antique," is in some respects a harder assignment than that facing a contemporary decoy carver, who is tasked to make a particular wildfowl species. To make the copied old decoy look authentic, Bill typically had to use the same primitive tools and paint that the old master would have used, but he also had to carve just like the old master would have done. The preening mallard shown in photograph 4 is a good example of Hanemann's skill as a renovator. Originally, this decoy was a gunner with an erect head, but the head was missing, so Bill replaced it with a head and elongated neck in a preening pose.

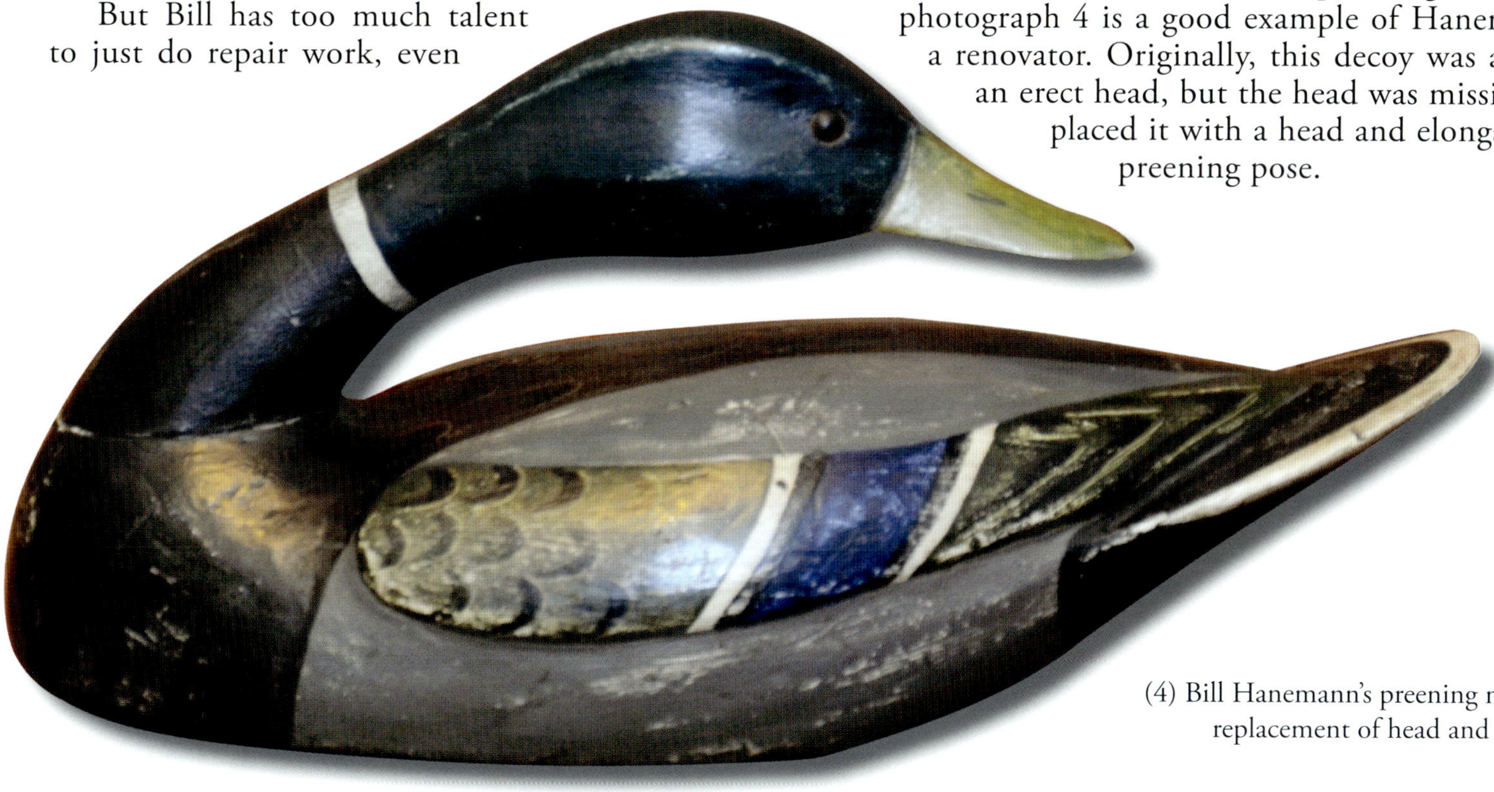

(4) Bill Hanemann's preening mallard drake, replacement of head and neck

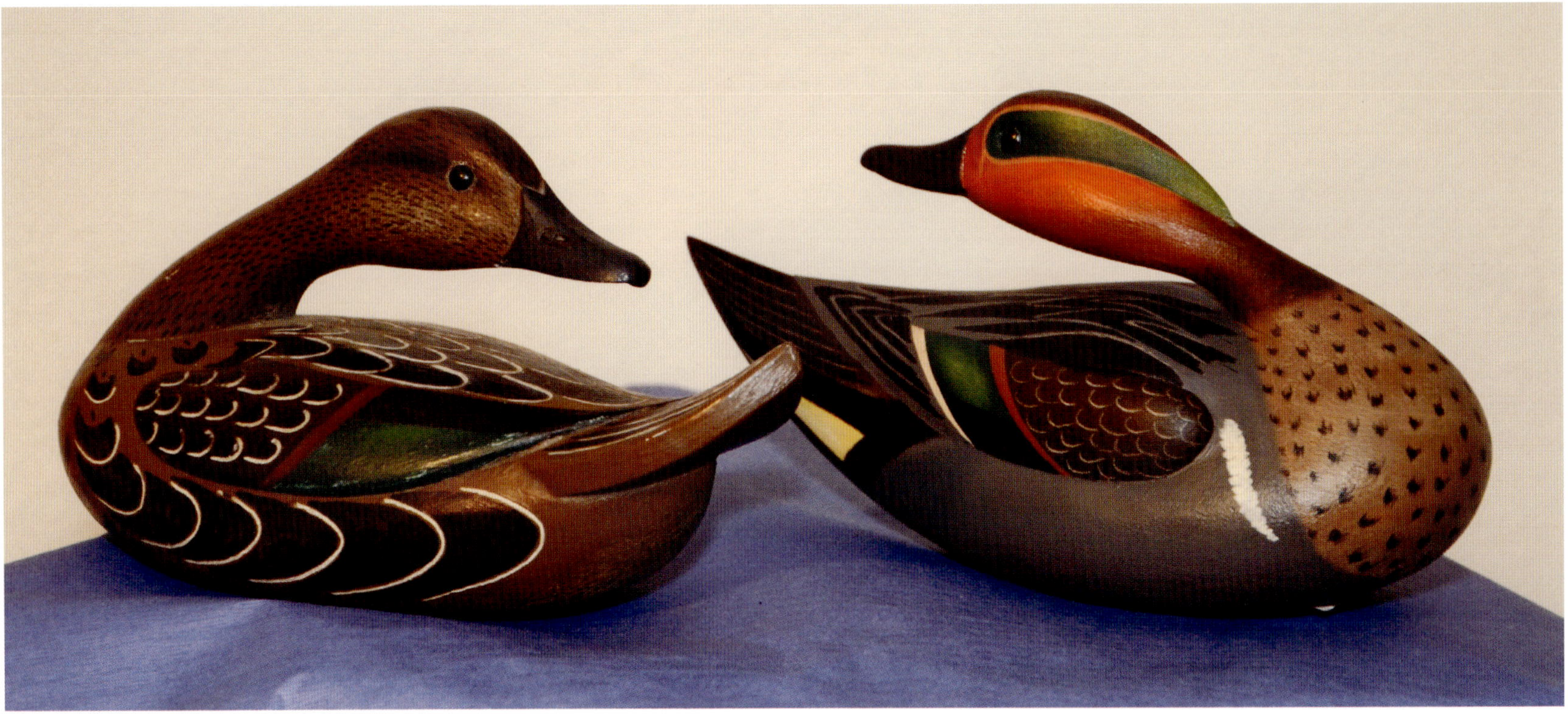

ABOVE: (5) Bill Hanemann's 1980s green-winged teal hen (LEFT) vs. 2016 green-winged teal drake (RIGHT)

OPPOSITE PAGE: (6) Bill Hanemann's green-winged teal pair

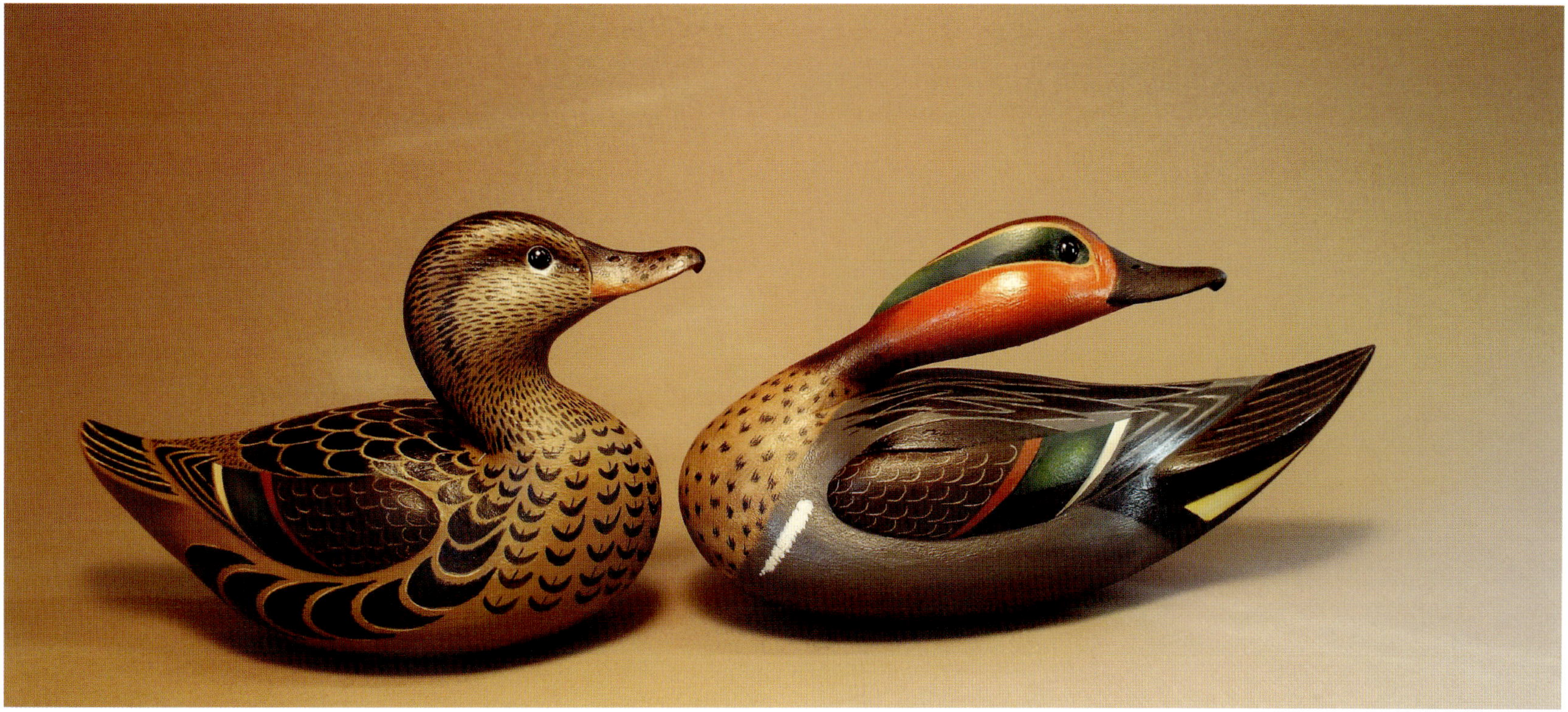

Bill grew so proficient that he was being commissioned to carve replicas in the style of virtually all of the old carvers. In recent years, Bill has taken steps to combat counterfeiting by making very subtle carving variations and branding the contemporary antiques he was commissioned to make in an effort to prevent the decoy from being sold as one carved by one of the old masters.

Bill's well-deserved reputation as the most knowledgeable expert on old Louisiana decoys gave rise to non-carving assignments. He was, and still is, frequently called upon to authenticate old decoys. He continues to appraise decoys and decoy collections, and, on occasion, helps curate museums' decoy shows.

All along, Bill has continued to carve decoys in his own unique and improving style as evidenced by comparing the photograph of a green-winged teal Bill carved in the 1980s with the photograph of a pair of green-winged teal Bill carved in 2015. Those photos are numbered 5 and 6.

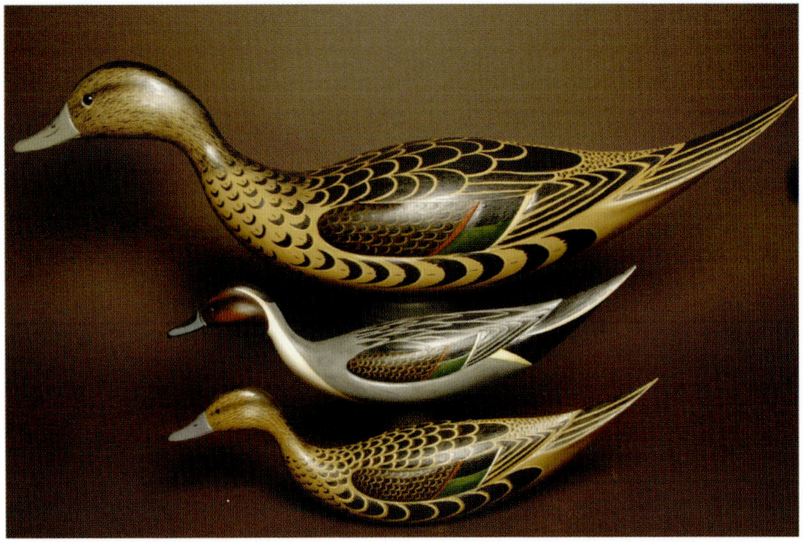

Top left: (7) Bill Hanemann's different size pintails
Bottom left: (8) Bill Hanemann's preening pintail drake
Below: (9) Bill Hanemann's pintail drake with egg

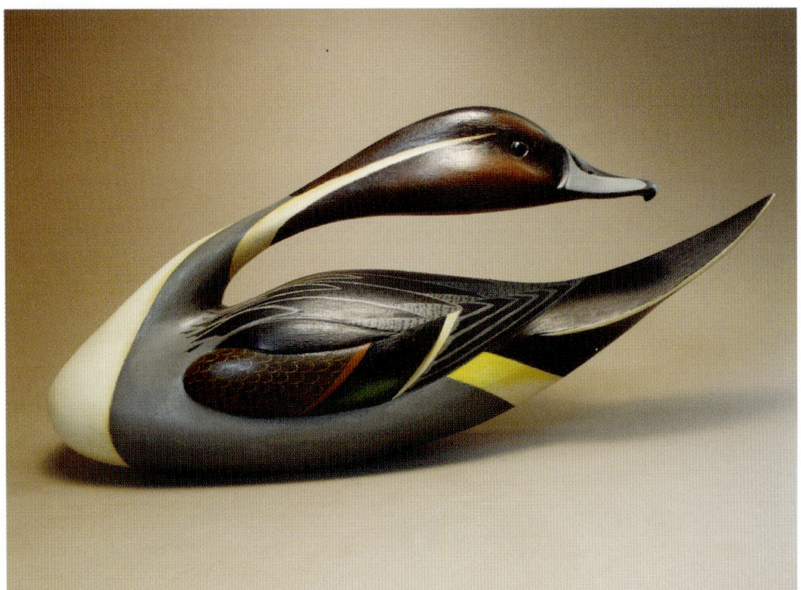

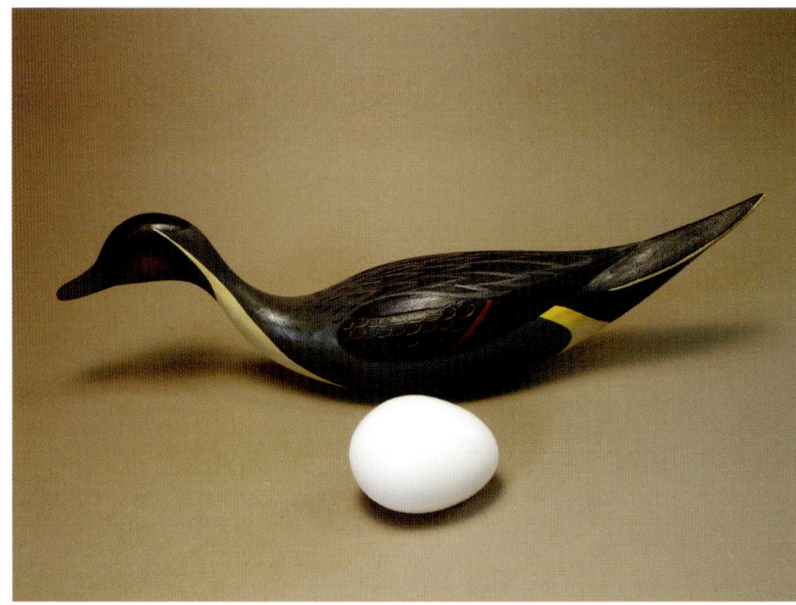

In recent years, Bill has lived in a tranquil, wooded home near the Louisiana-Mississippi border. He works in a modern, well-equipped studio built after Hurricane Katrina. His preference is to carve and paint decoys in his own style in which he incorporates aspects of the old masters' work that he admires. Photographs of a preening pintail drake, canvasback drake, a group of different size pintails, and a lovely miniature pintail that he recently carved show the work of an artist at his very best as photographs 7, 8, 9, and 10 illustrate. These later decoys have a graceful elegance that can be described as Hanemann's with faint suggestions of Vidacovich's carving and Joefrau's painting.

Bill has just started carving a very large still life for himself titled *A Self Portrait.* It will ultimately incorporate various carved objects that tell his life story. The first one completed is a sculpture of Bill's right hand and is shown in photograph 11. I am confident that when finished it will be his finest masterpiece.

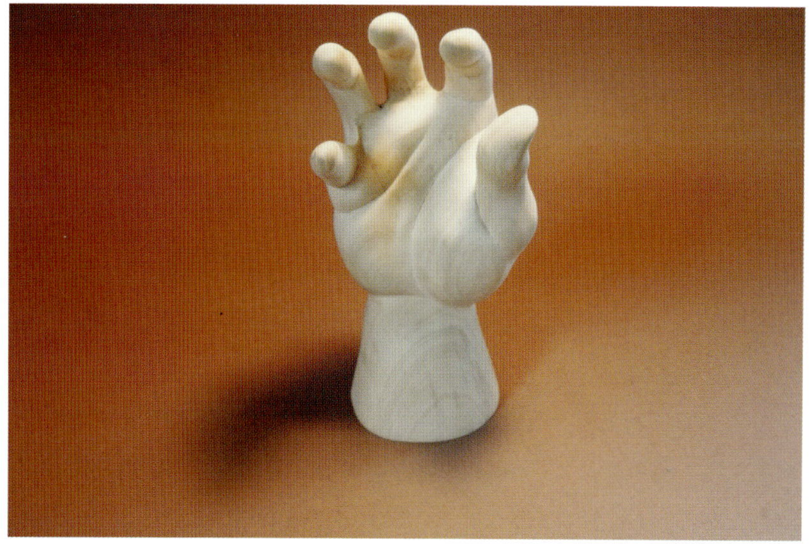

ABOVE: (11) Bill Hanemann's carver's hand, step one in *Self Portrait*

ENDNOTES

1. Erin Greenwald, "Louisiana's William Hanemann," *Hunting and Fishing Collectibles Magazine*, 10, no. 6 (November-December 2010).

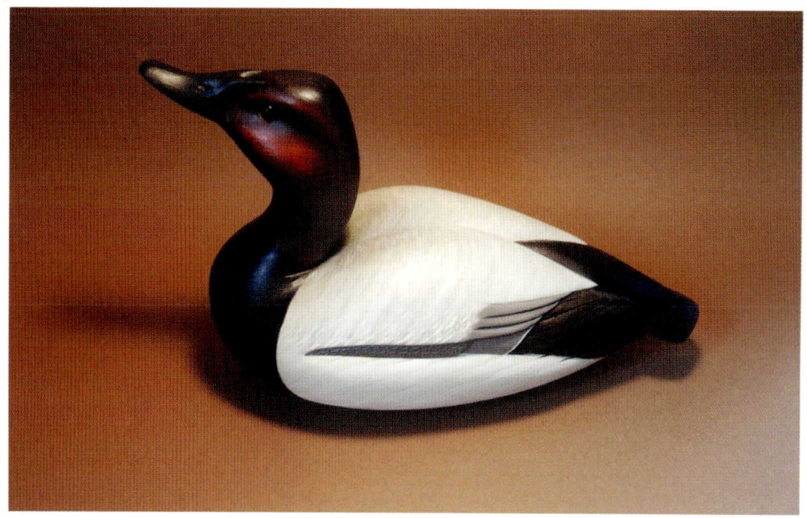

RIGHT: (10) Bill Hanemann's canvasback drake

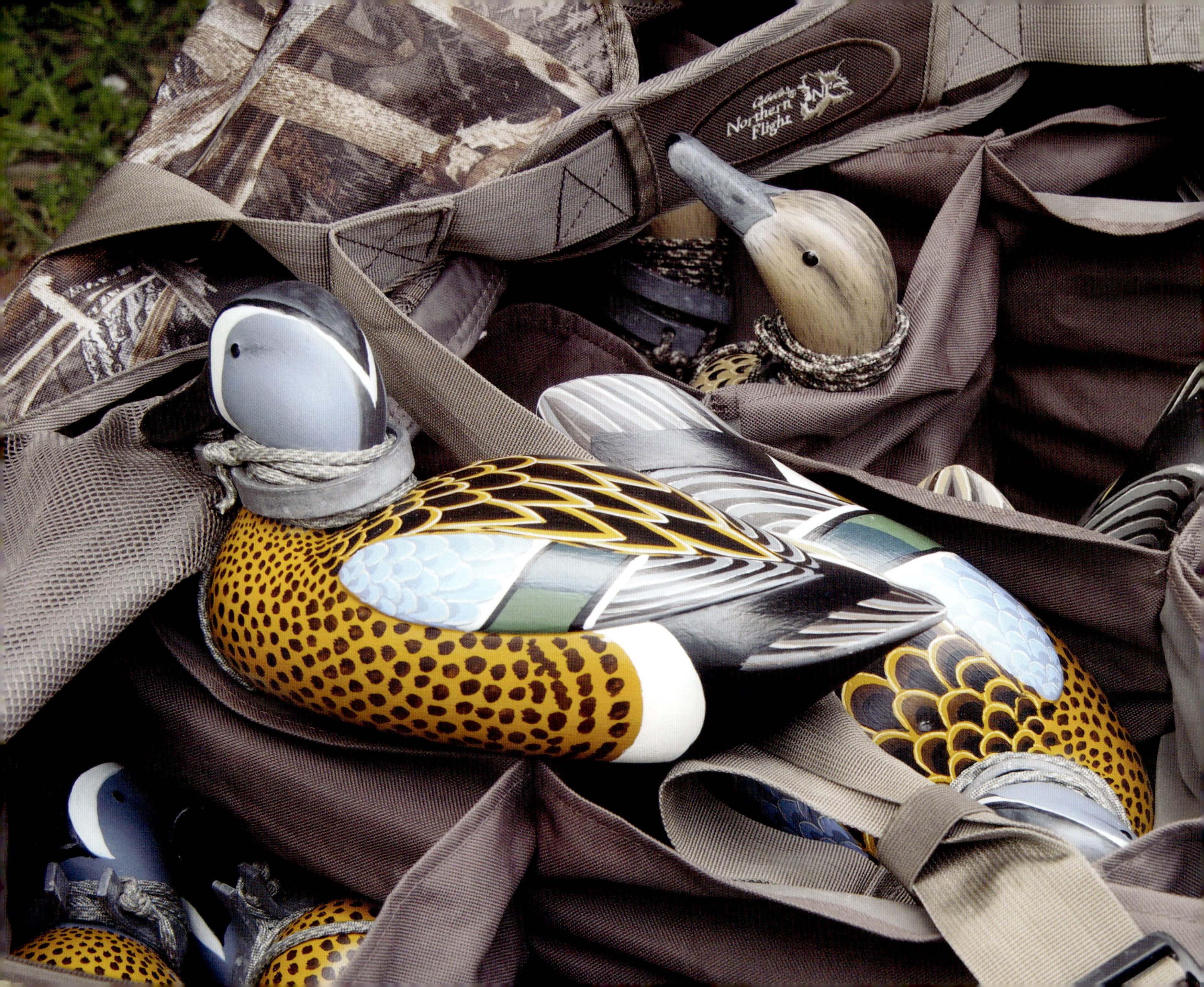
Northern Flight

13 Eric Hutchison

Creole Carving Master

Opposite page: (6) Hutchison's bag of hunting decoys

Eric Hutchison is one of the most intelligent and sensitive men I have ever met, despite being reserved and modest to a fault. He is also one of Louisiana's very best and most versatile contemporary decoy carvers, with a compelling back-story.

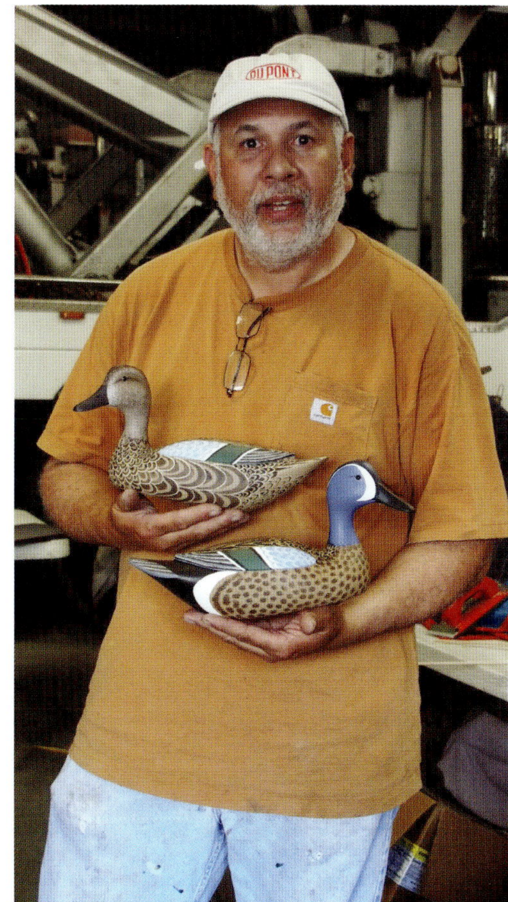

Eric was born on September 14, 1957, in New Orleans. He has lived all his life in the city's Seventh Ward. He learned about decoy carving from his father and uncle, as well as fellow Seventh Ward resident and legendary carver, Mitchell Lafrance. "Mr. Mitchell's" portrait has a place of honor in Eric's home, now partially restored after being ravaged in 2005 by Hurricane Katrina and the flooding that followed. Photograph 3 shows that portrait. August and Jules Frederick were other artistic influences for Eric. Since little is known of August Frederick's decoys, photograph 4 shows a pair of his pintails that bears some similarity to Eric's hunting decoys.

Eric's father, Charles, and his uncle Rudy were master decoy carvers who specialized in making large, lifelike wildfowl sculptures for which they won numerous Best in Show awards in the early years of the Louisiana Wildfowl Carvers and Collectors Guild's carving competitions. Photograph 1 is a large hawk with its prey, and 2 is an osprey with its prey. The elder Hutchisons produced large, realistic works, and these are two of their very best. Eric helped create these pieces; he describes them as "making thoughts and dreams a reality."

The elder Hutchisons were avid duck hunters, and they started taking Eric with them at a very early age. With that background and with those carving masters as mentors, it is no surprise that Eric started carving decoys

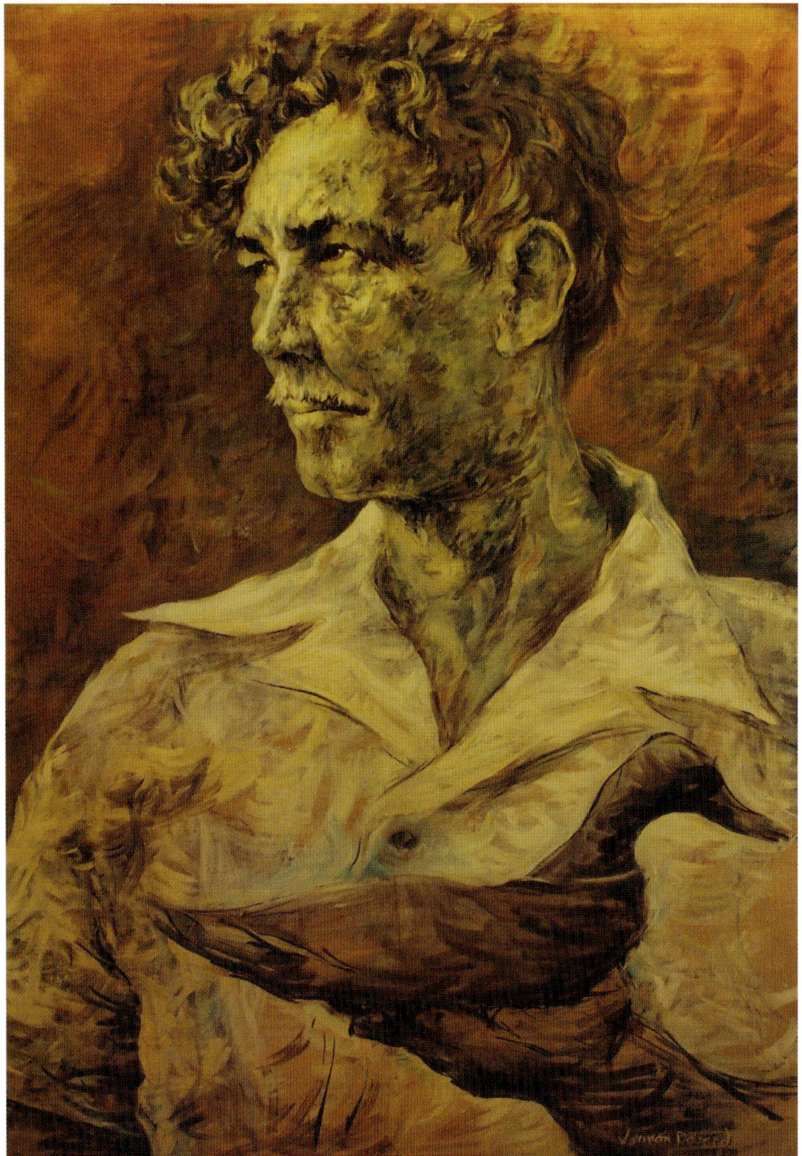

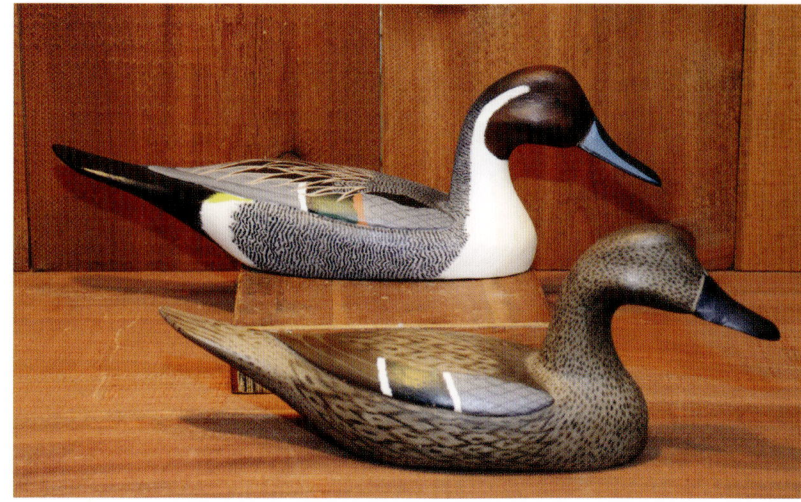

(4) August Frederick's pintail pair, circa 1974

when he was about ten years old. At age fifteen Eric was carving decorative decoys that he called "mantelpiece birds" and selling them for as much as $300 each. He regularly won Best of Show awards at the annual LWCCG carving festivals in the teenage division.

Very early in his carving career, Eric became a true perfectionist. He said that his smallest mistakes drove him crazy and his few errors stymied him. He carved not only duck decoys but also birds of prey and songbirds. Today, Eric carves anything from old-style hunting decoys to super realistic

Left: (3) Painting of Mr. Mitchell Lafrance
Right: (1) Eric Hutchison's hawk and prey
Far right: (2) Eric Hutchison's osprey and fish

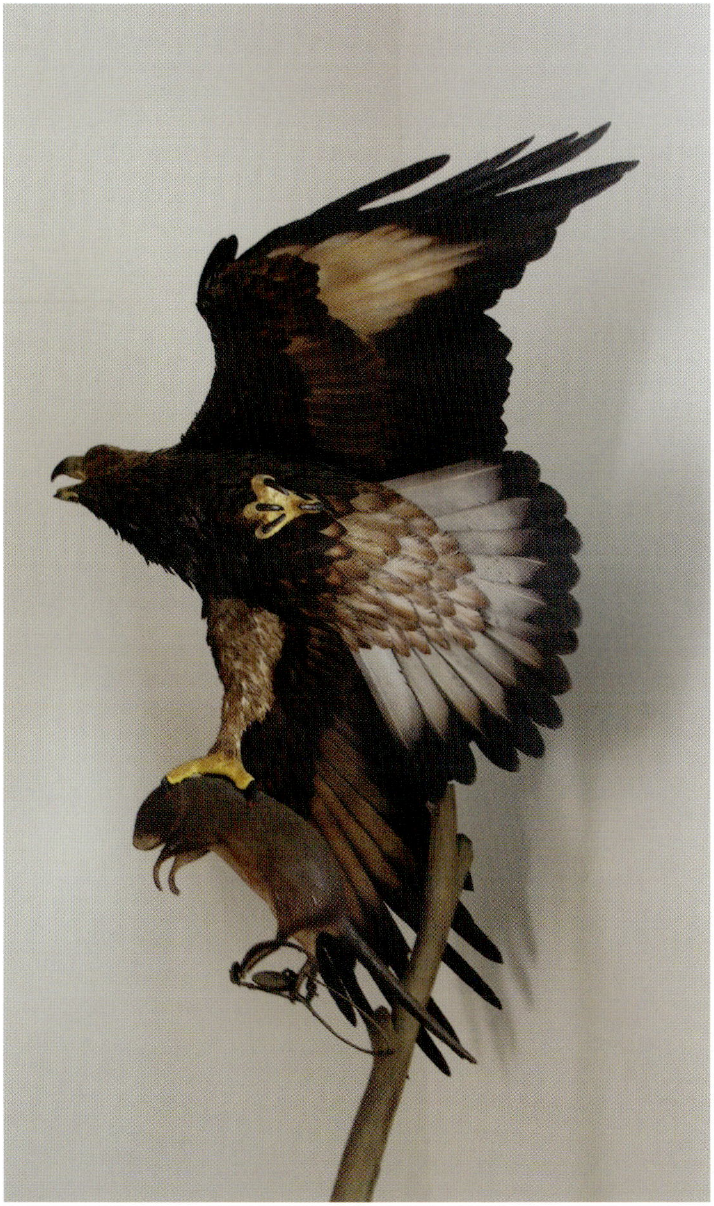

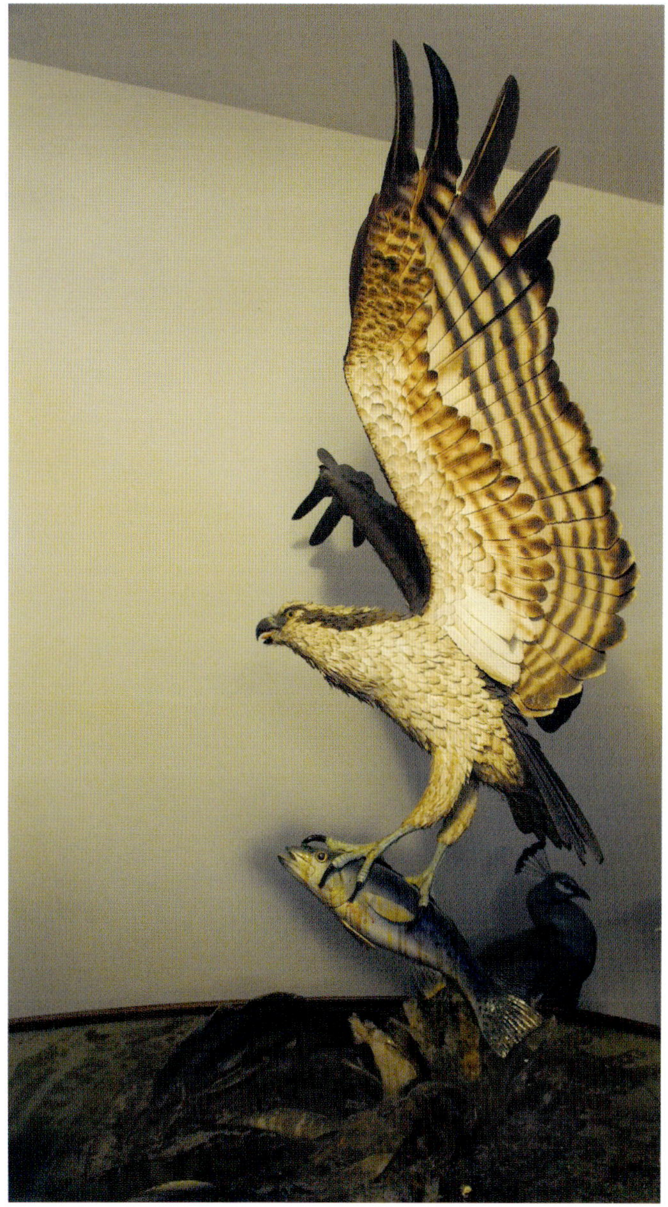

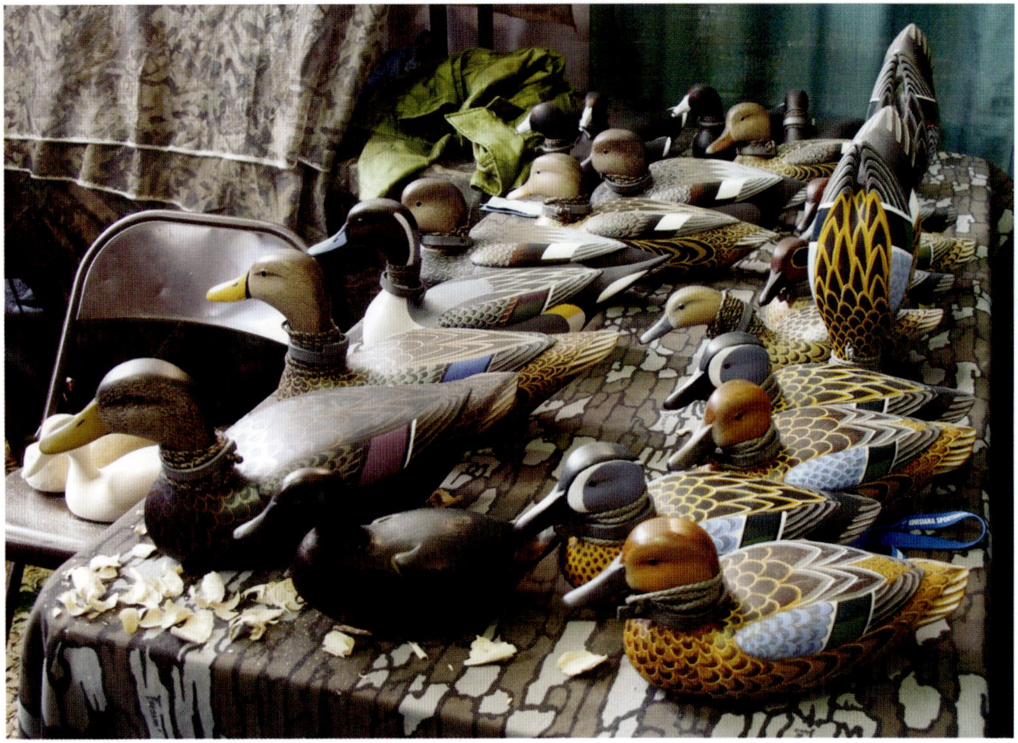

(5) Exhibition of Hutchison's decoys at the 2015 Louisiana Sportsman's Show

decorative pieces. Photograph 5 shows a display of his decoys taken at the 2015 Sportsmen's Show in Gonzales, Louisiana. Photograph 6 (pg. 114) shows a number of hunting slicks from Eric's personal rig. He finds competitive carving events too confining, effectively hampering his creativity. His decoys, even his hunting slicks, tend to be more brightly painted than most carvers'. The pair of blue-winged teal shown in photograph 7 is a very good example. Eric says "hunting decoys are made to attract ducks and decorative decoys are made to attract people."

Eric and Cal Kingsmill are neighbors, close friends, hunting partners, and decoy carving companions. Both men share a common goal to do everything they can to promote and preserve decoy carving in Louisiana. They recognize the unique and invaluable role that decoy carving plays in this state's culture. For years, Eric visited schools in New Orleans and put on decoy carving exhibitions and gave instructions in hopes of getting young people involved. More recently, he and Cal joined forces and put on carving exhibitions at large events like the Duck, Duck, Goose Day at the BREC Blue Bonnet Swampland and Nature Center in Baton Rouge and the Louisiana Sportsmen's Show and Festival in Gonzales. Eric was honored for his work at last year's Blue Bonnet Swamp and Nature Center show. In explaining why he participated in these carving exhibitions (which he and Cal do without being compensated), Eric says decoy carving is "carrying on a tradition" and that such activities are necessary "to keep the heritage alive." There is something else that motivates Eric to do these things. When he was seventeen, Mr. Mitchell, then ninety-seven and near death, summoned Eric to his bedside and whispered to him, "You have a unique talent, you must pass it on"—a challenging assignment but one that Eric has successfully completed many times over.

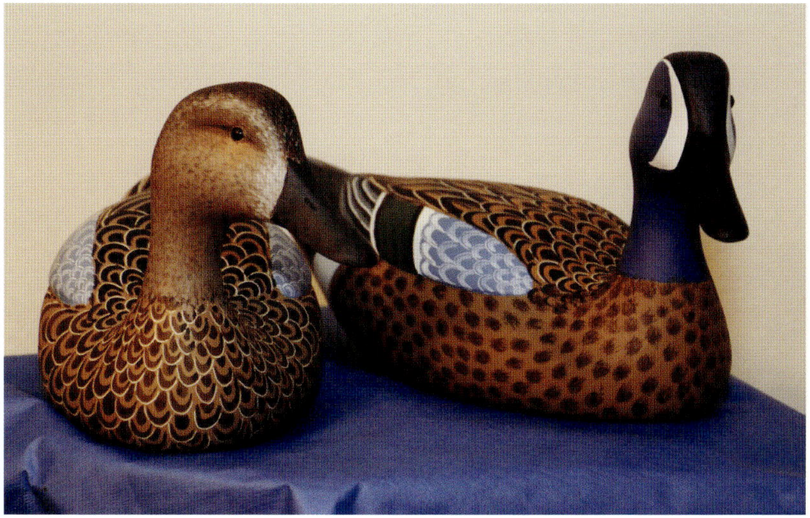

(7) Eric Hutchison's colorful blue-winged decoy pair

That Eric is able to carve such excellent decoys, especially decorative masterpieces, is truly remarkable. At age two, he suffered a fractured skull and at age five, he suffered another skull fracture. As a result, it is thought that his brain was damaged. Additionally, at a young age, he was diagnosed with dyslexia, a neurological disorder that makes it very difficult to read, concentrate, and stay on task. School was very difficult for him, both academically and socially. It took Eric much longer to complete his assignments and his grades were subpar. Eric was embarrassed by his performance and felt rejected by his classmates. Nonetheless, he was determined to overcome these disabilities and succeed. He graduated from high school and enrolled in the University of New Orleans, majoring in engineering and architecture. He made it through three or four semesters, but ultimately his reading difficulties and inability to remain focused caused him to drop out and become a full time professional decoy carver. In the years that followed, Eric married his college sweetheart, raised two college-educated children, and earned a nice living as a decoy carver. During the slow times, Eric periodically worked with his brother, a painting contractor, but he never stopped carving.

Eric's carving career paralleled what happened during the contemporary era. As a young man, he loved carving competitive decoratives. Carving decoratives is time consuming, and it requires a great deal of patience and intense concentration. For anyone with dyslexia, carving a decoy would be a very difficult task; carving a prize-winning decorative would be virtually impossible. Obviously, Eric is not an "ordinary person." He is a winner, and his accomplishments should inspire others to overcome their disabilities and succeed in their chosen vocations as he has done.

As Eric has gotten older, he prefers to carve simpler pieces, like traditional hunting slicks, because that style allows him more artistic freedom. Photograph 7 shows a pair of blue-winged teal that Eric finished in April 2015. Mr. Mitchell's influence is evident in the carving and in the scratch painting, but the bold color scheme is solely a product of Eric's artistic imagination.

As mentioned above, Hurricane Katrina and the flooding that followed substantially damaged Eric's home as well as the homes of close family members. He has been repairing those structures since August 2005, but he still found time to carve some decoys and put on numerous carving demonstrations. He has also continued hunting ducks and greatly enjoys shooting over decoys that he made.

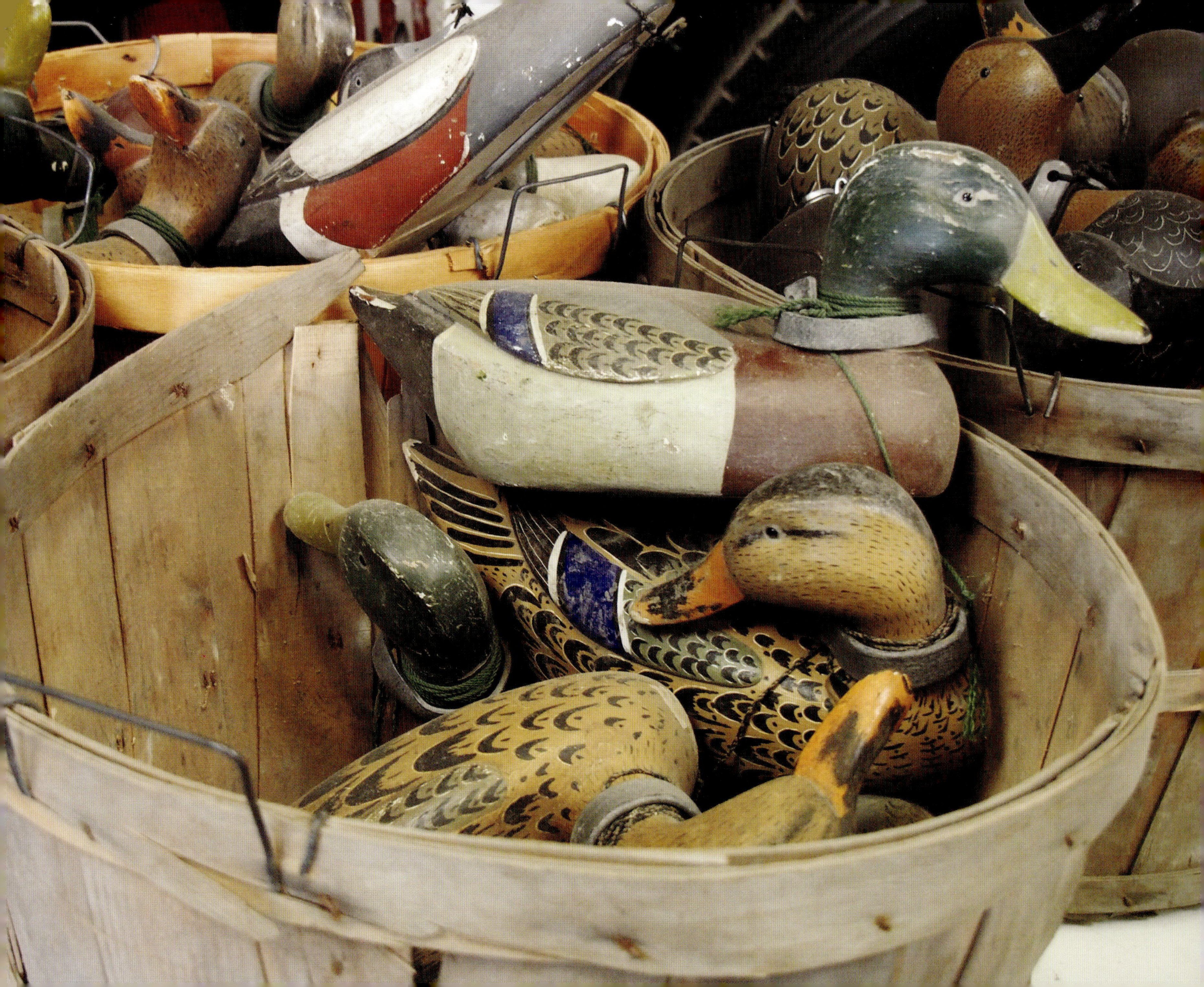

OPPOSITE PAGE: (7) Cal Kingsmill assorted hunting slicks

14 Cal Kingsmill

Decoy Carving Rembrandt

Cal Kingsmill is a reserved but friendly man—one of seeming contradictions. He left junior high in the seventh grade, and, after working various jobs, entered trade school at Delgado Community College, majoring in welding and mechanics. His father owned and operated a filling station on Duel Street as well as a towing company specializing in large vehicles. It was located in a very big garage, inside a fenced lot, at 1732 Benefit Street in the St. Roch area of New Orleans alongside an I-610 overpass.

Cal's courses at Delgado were good choices since he wanted to go into business with his father, but sometimes fate intervenes and modifies one's vocational plans. That happened to Cal. He was drafted and served in the Vietnam War. When he got out, Cal enrolled in Delgado's fine arts program, which he successfully completed with the help of the G.I. Bill. It is hard to imagine that one could excel in mechanics and also the applied arts but that is exactly what this incredibly versatile and multitalented man did.

Cal's artistic side is built on a foundation almost as solid as his father's businesses, which were the underpinnings of his vocational side. Young Cal's favorite pastime was duck hunting with his Dad and brother in the marshes of eastern New Orleans. The trio hunted over decoys produced by the Lafrance, Joefrau, and Frederick combine. It turns out that the Lafrance team lived very near and were customers of Cal's

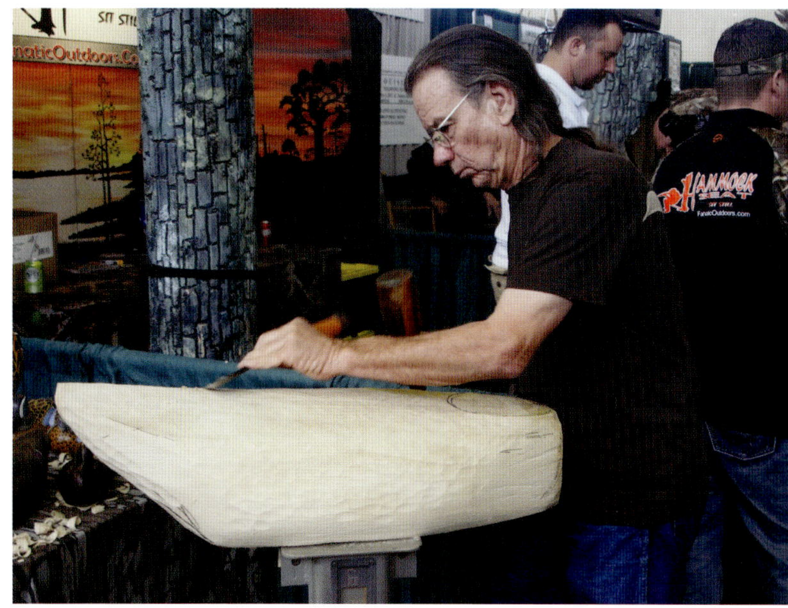

Cal Kingsmill carving a swan at the 2015 Louisiana Sportman's Show

father's gas station. Over time, Mr. Kingsmill and the old masters became close friends, and these all-star carvers traded decoys they made for Mr. Kingsmill's gasoline, tires, and such. Cal learned how to carve and paint by studying these decoys. Charles and Rudy Hutchison, who were also Cal's neighbors, frequent hunting partners, and two of the state's greatest decorative carvers, gave Cal carving and painting help.

When the Kingsmills read Charlie Frank's *Louisiana Duck Decoys* they realized that the Lafrance team's decoys had become too valuable to hunt over, and they were retired to be prominently displayed at Cal's home. For a time, Cal and family hunted over plastic decoys but found them to be unsatisfactory. Cal had started carving hunting decoys about 1974, and his decoys quickly proved to be far more effective in luring ducks into shooting range than the store-bought plastic ones. In a short time, Cal's decoys matched, if not exceeded, the Lafrance team's blocks in effectiveness.

In the May/June 2000 edition of *Decoy Magazine*, Charlie Frank wrote an article entitled "Cal Kingsmill, Creating Louisiana decoys in the Image of the Legends."[1] The first paragraph of that article reads:

> Cal Kingsmill carves a classic style of Louisiana decoy, fashioning cypress root or tupelo gum with a knife and sandpaper, just as the legendary Cajun Carvers—Mitchell Lafrance (1882-1979), Charles Joefrau (1913-1983), and George Frederick, Jr. (1907-1977)—did before him. True to their traditions, a bandsaw is the only power tool he uses. And although each of his carvings is made in the image of these bayou legends, Cal is meticulous in designing each decoy as his own.

Several names are used to describe Kingsmill's hunting decoys. One is "old New Orleans style." Another is "contem-

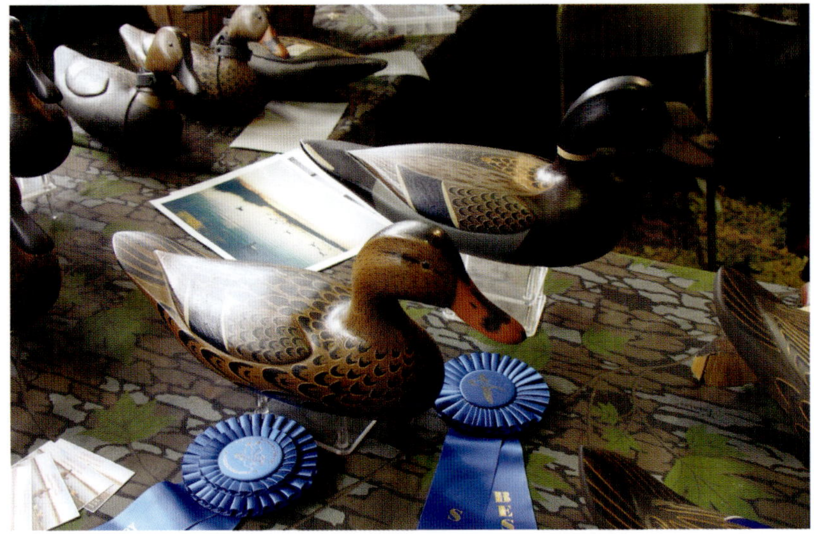

ABOVE: (1) Cal Kingsmill's mallard pair
BELOW: (2) Cal Kingsmill's black mallard pair

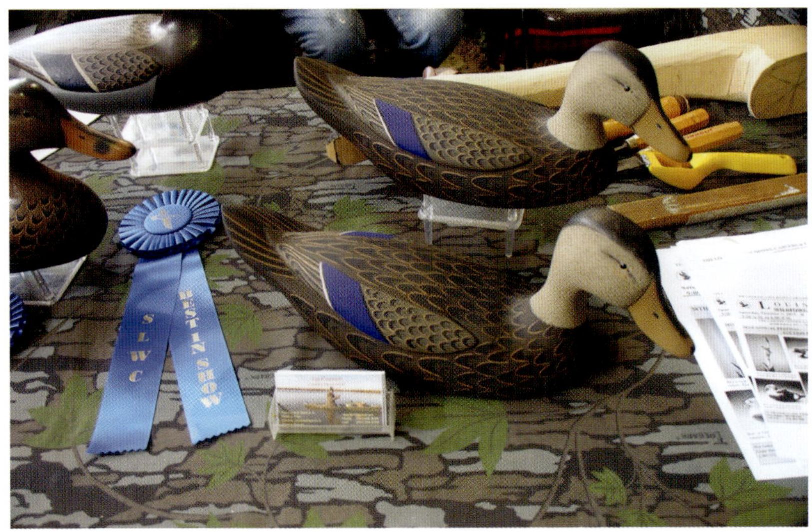

porary antique decoys." Cal is the very best at carving and, especially, painting "contemporary antiques," so much so that he won first place in that category at the LWCCG's 2014 Louisiana Wildfowl Festival. Photograph 1 and 2 show some of Cal's prize-winning decoys.

Cal's carving and painting style is deeply rooted in the old master carvers' decoys, especially the Lafrance group and the Hutchison brothers, Charles and Rudy. Cal's home has bookshelves in the main rooms that are lined with these masters' decoys as well as several by Eric Hutchison and a few of his own. The old masters' decoys remind Cal of great duck hunts in the past with good friends and also inspire him to continue carving decoys and preserving Louisiana's heritage and tradition.

Cal carves two types of decoys: "better" and "best." On both types, the wings are undercut, and that is the only carving on his decoys. Cal intends for both types to be hunted over. For that reason, he came up with an innovation to make a stronger head/body joint to reduce the chance of breakage. Before the head is glued to the body, Cal drills a hole in the head and another in the body. Then he inserts a small dowel in the two holes and joins the head and the body together.

There are a few basic differences between Cal's "better" and "best" decoys. The better type is Cal's basic hunting decoy. In that type the head is almost always erect and in the gunner position—that is, looking straight ahead. The bill may also be a bit thicker to reduce the chance of breakage. Cal's best type decoy is the equivalent of other carvers' decorative gunners. In that type, the decoy's head is often in different positions or poses. It may be turned, preening, resting, or sleeping. The body is usually more stylized. For example, the body of his best style pintail drake will have a more elongated and upturned tail than his better pintail drake. Photograph

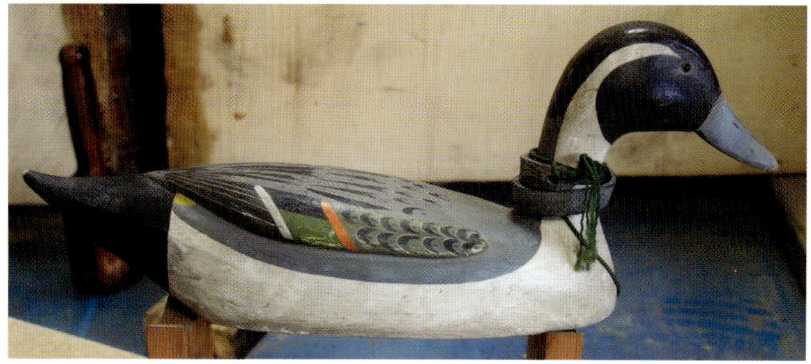

ABOVE: (3) Cal Kingsmill's pintail hunting decoy
BELOW: (4) Cal Kingsmill's pintail pair, better grade

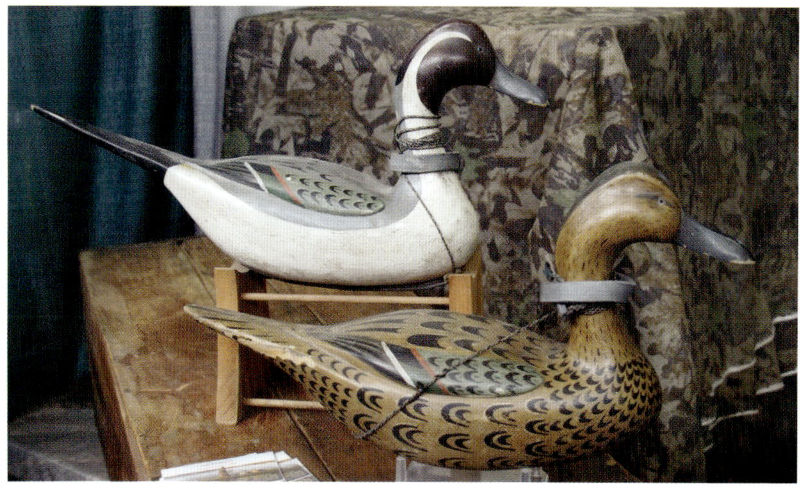

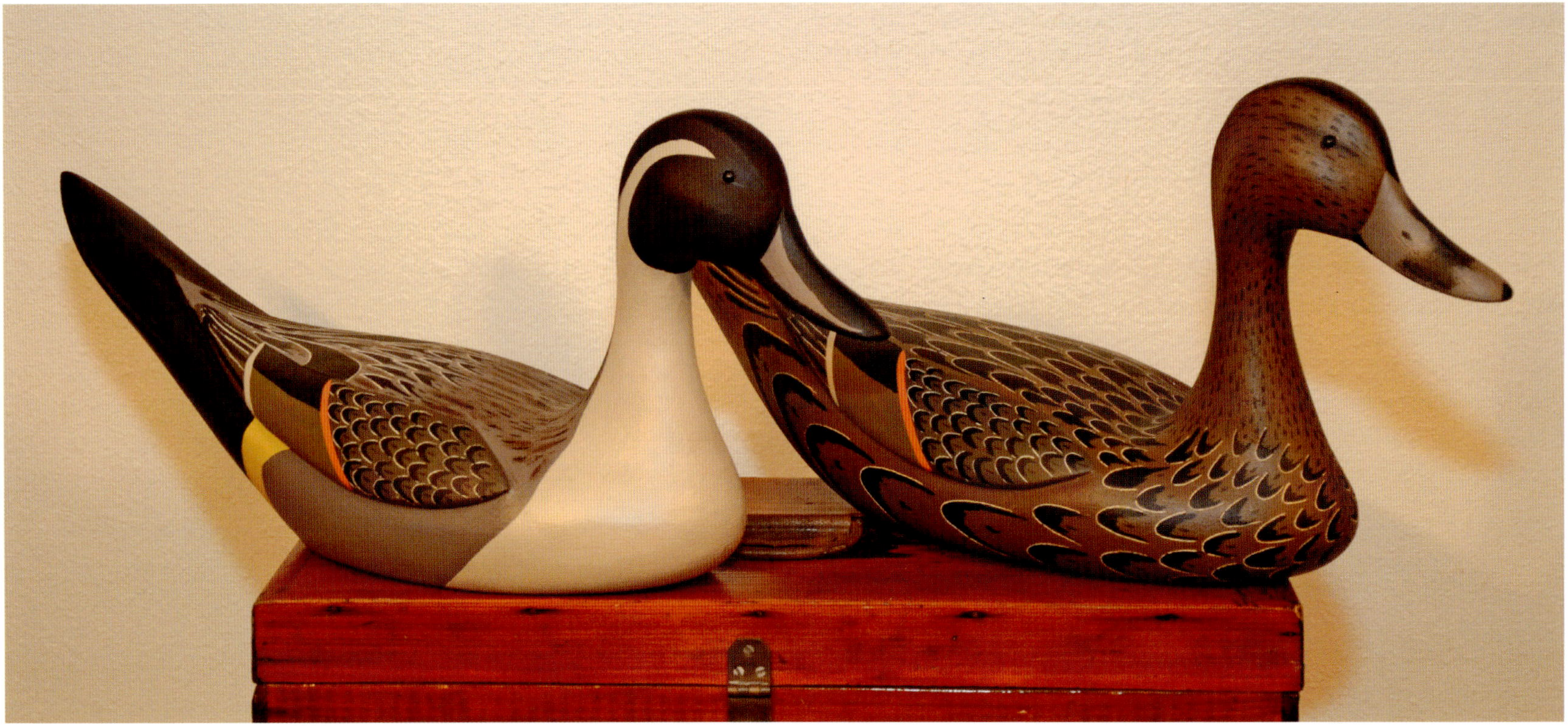

(5) Cal Kingsmill's pintail pair, best grade

3 shows a good pintail drake and photograph 4 shows a better pair, and photograph 5 shows the best grade. Photograph 6 shows all three grades together.

The most significant difference between Cal's better and best type decoys is how they are painted. It should be noted that Cal is generally regarded as the best hunting decoy painter of all of the contemporary carvers. In an article entitled "'An Endangered Species:' Cal Kingsmill's decoys" published in the August 2010 issue of *New Orleans Magazine*, author George Gurtner referred to Cal as "the Rembrandt of waterfowl decoy carvers."[2] High and well-deserved praise. Cal's better decoys are painted in an improved version of the Lafrance group's scratch painting. His best type decoys are more ornately painted. Cal has taken the Lafrance group's pattern to a new level. The same paint concepts are used in both types of Kingsmill's decoys but they are not painted the same way. In an article by Morgan Packard, entitled "The Call of the Hunt," Cal's painting technique was described as follows:

> Once the bird is sculpted, Kingsmill seals it with three coats of lacquer-sealer, then it is hand sanded and prepared with two coats of artist's gesso (a pasty mixture of white paint and glue). Next, he mixes his basecoat using Ronan Superfine Japan Colors . . . the same paint used on old Carousel horses. . . . At this point, years of training and practice in an old-time technique called scratch painting, which utilizes wet paint and the handle of a paint brush, lets him create the lifelike feathers along the body of the decoy. [3]

No wonder Cal's finished decoys look so great.

A mutual friend told me that Cal's mechanical skills match his decoy carving artistry. Cal is a prolific carver while still working full time at the towing company. The filling station has closed, but nearly fifty years later, Kingsmill Auto Service and Towing Company is still going strong. It is jointly run by Cal, his wife, his son, and his brother Bob. The large garage building that houses the towing company's vehicles and equipment also serves as Cal's decoy carving workshop. Photograph 7 shows Cal working on decoys inside the garage with some of the towing company's very large tow trucks in the background. Cal and his wife live just across the street from the garage and adjacent storage facilities. This makes it very convenient for Cal to work on decoys in his shop,

Below: (6) Pintail drakes-good, better, and best

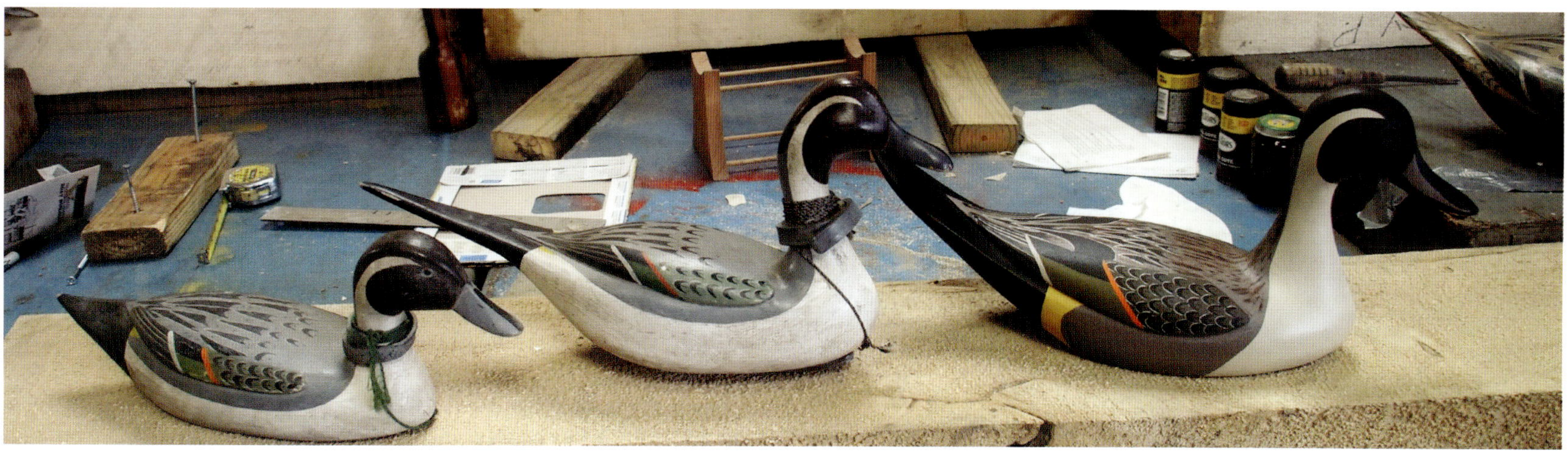

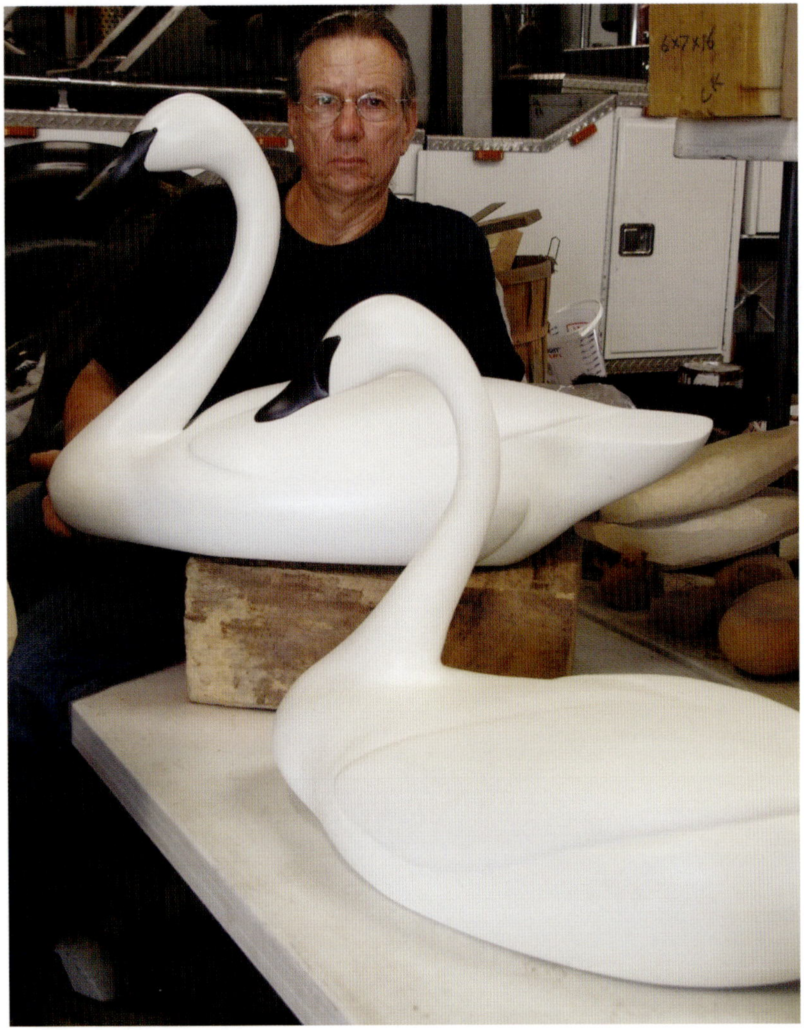

(8) Cal Kingsmill and decorative swan decoys

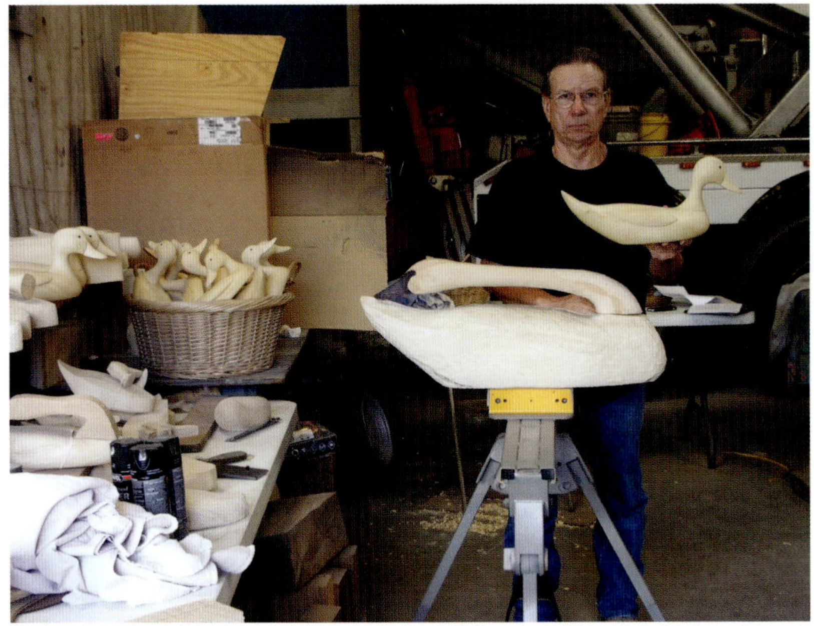

(7) Kingsmill in shop carving a goose decoy

day or night. When he is not doing work related to the service and towing company, Cal can be found carving decoys mostly for hunting, but he also carves beautiful swans, as photograph 8 shows. His preference for hunting decoys is best illustrated by photograph 9, which shows Cal's work in progress.

Cal no longer teaches decoy carving, but he recognizes that wildfowl carving has been an essential part of Louisiana's cultural history and it must be preserved and protected. That was Charlie Frank's mission, and now Cal Kingsmill has assumed a lead role. He does this by selflessly giving

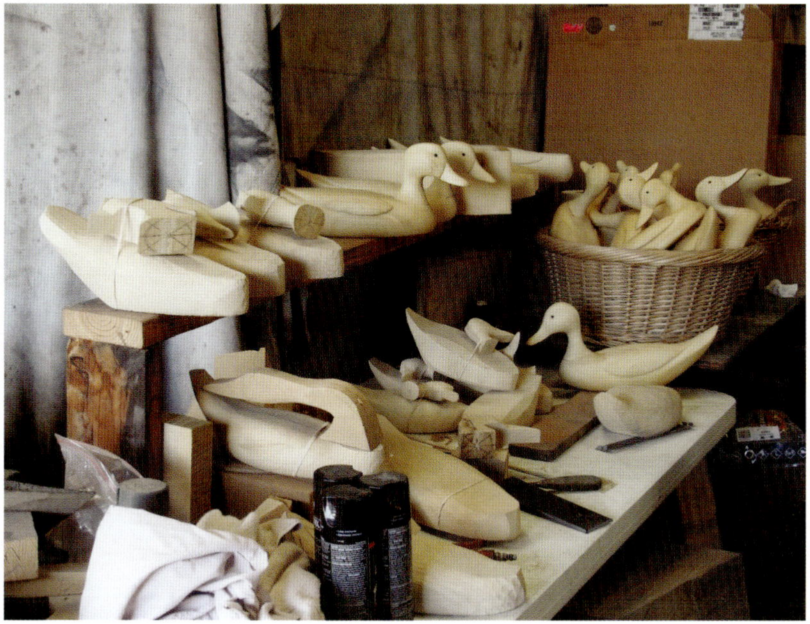

(9) Hunting decoys in progress

countless decoy carving exhibitions throughout the state, frequently accompanied by Eric Hutchison, a fellow carver, hunting partner, and longtime friend. A picture of both men taken at Cal's workshop is seen in photograph 10.

Cal Kingsmill is a great carver, despite his protests to the contrary, and an even better painter. No one produces a better hunting slick. Cal has been very active in the LWCCG as a board member, competitor, and staunch advocate. Largely because of Cal's efforts, along with a number of his fellow carvers, decoy carving in Louisiana in the post-Hurricane Katrina era is as good as or better than it has ever been.

Endnotes

1. Charles Frank Jr., "Cal Kingsmill, Creating Louisiana decoys in the Image of the Legends," *Decoy Magazine*, May/June 2000, 36.

2. George Gurtner, "'An Endangered Species:' Cal Kingsmill's decoys," *New Orleans Magazine*, August 2010, 54.

3. Morgan Packard, "The Call of the Hunt," myNew Orleans.com, Dec. 2006.

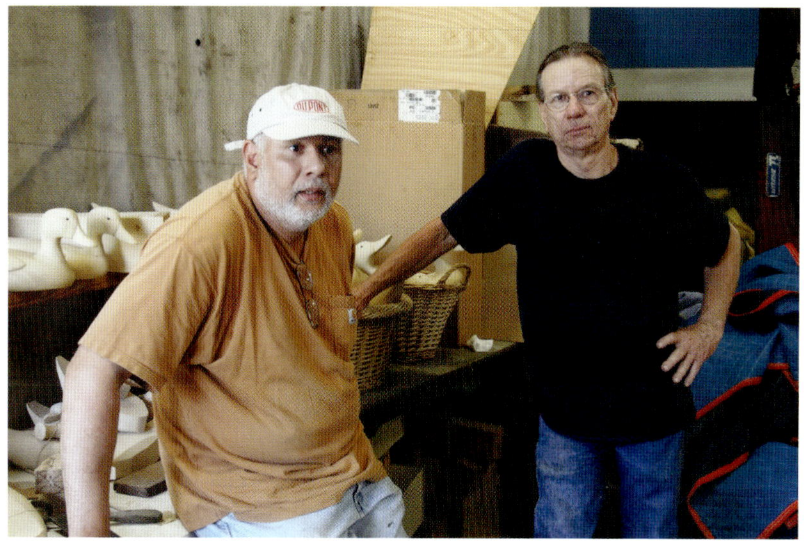

(10) Cal Kingsmill and best pal Eric Hutchison

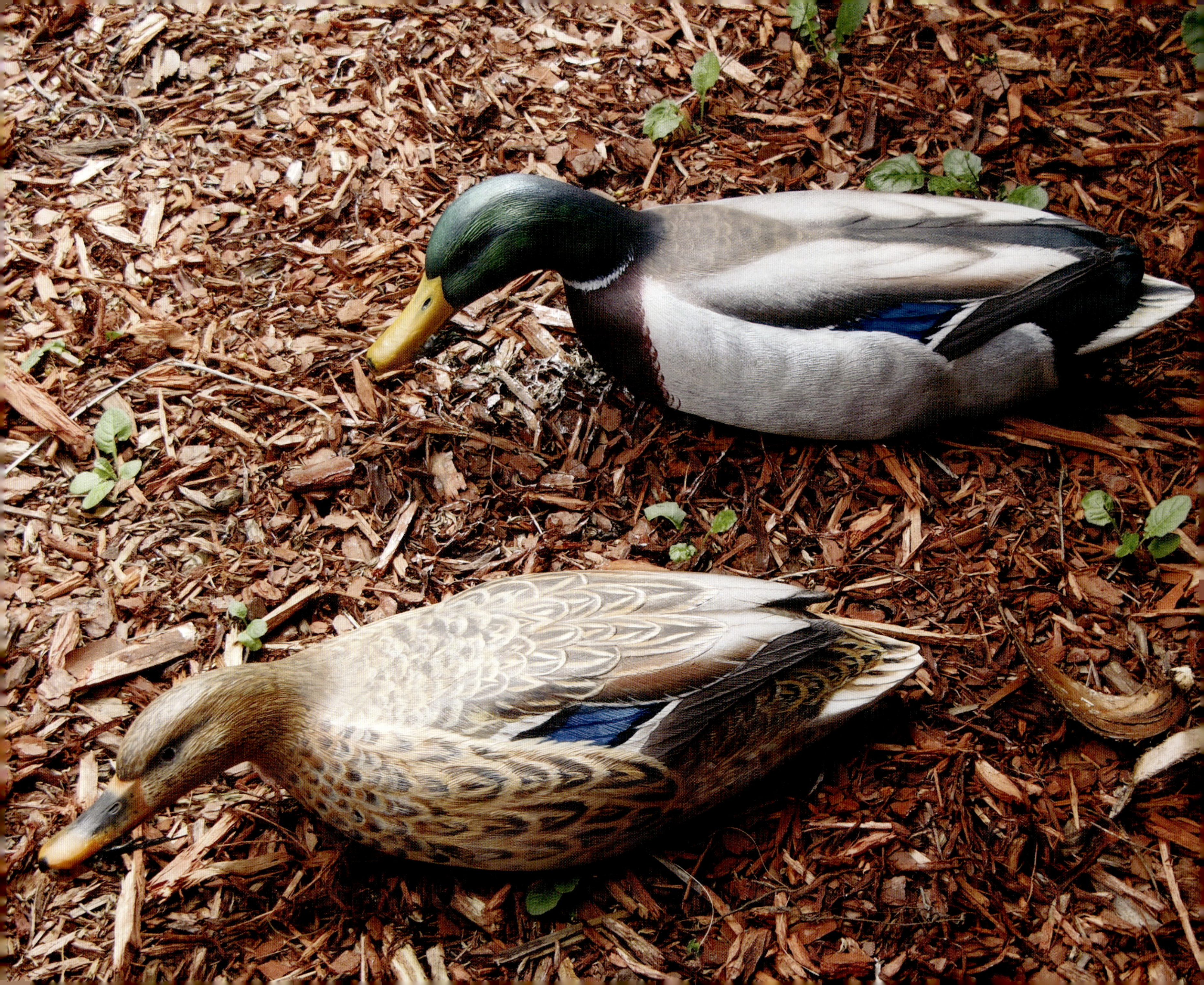

15 Roy Legaux Sr.

Frady's Decoy Carving Disciple

Opposite page: (5) Roy Legaux's mallard pair feeding

Roy Legaux Sr. is one of Louisiana's best contemporary decoy carvers and the head of one of the state's most talented decoy carving families. He is also one of the nicest and most interesting people that I have ever met. He is a decoy carving maverick. Roy was born in New Orleans on November 5, 1939. His father was an avid duck hunter who carved his own decoys. He delighted in taking his sons, Roy and older brother Ralph, hunting in the marshes on the eastern fringe of the city. By age seventeen, Roy was carving his own decoys to hunt over. It is fair to say that Roy was a better decoy carver than he was a student. He dropped out of school in the ninth grade and, a short time later, he enrolled in Delgado Community College, majoring in industrial arts. Legaux's professor was the legendary Mike Frady, longtime chairman of Delgado's industrial arts department. Up to this time, Legaux was a self-taught decoy carver. With Professor Frady, he got a "twofer": sign painting instruction during school hours and personalized decoy carving lessons when class was over.

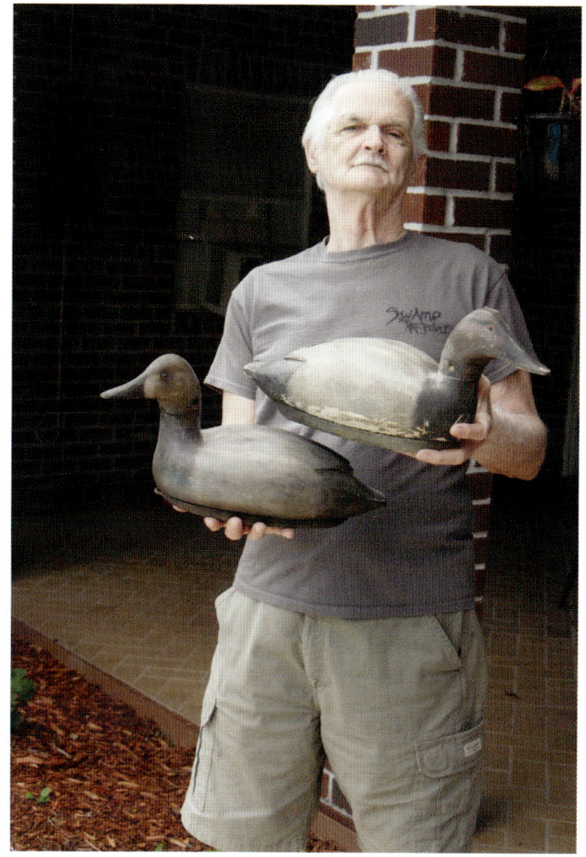

Roy was a good industrial arts student and a better decoy carving pupil. He benefitted greatly from Frady's tutelage and became a versatile and multitalented artist. In the late 1960s, Charlie Frank fortuitously discovered Roy and his decoy carving skills when he happened upon him coming out of the marsh after a duck hunt with his decoys in hand. Charlie was so impressed that he bought seven of Roy's decoys for $100 and talked Roy into becoming a professional decoy carver. A year or so later, Roy began carving decoys and also painting waterfowl—selling everything he produced.

To say that Roy quickly matured as a decoy carver is a great understate-

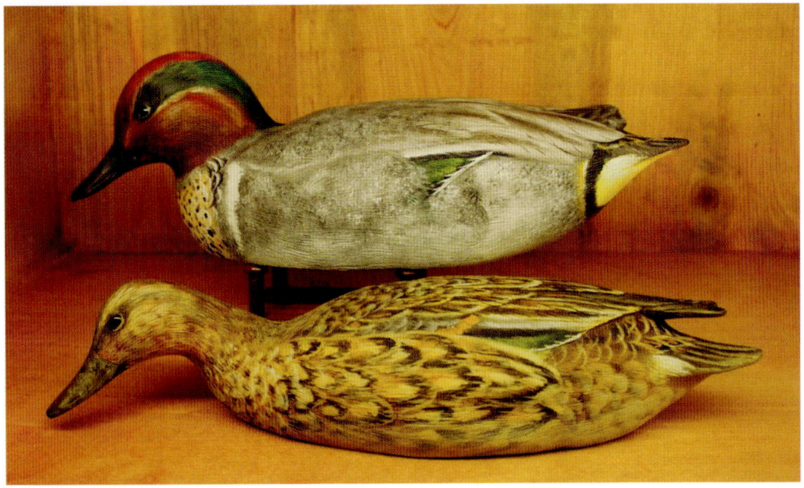

(1) Roy Legaux's pair of green-winged teal

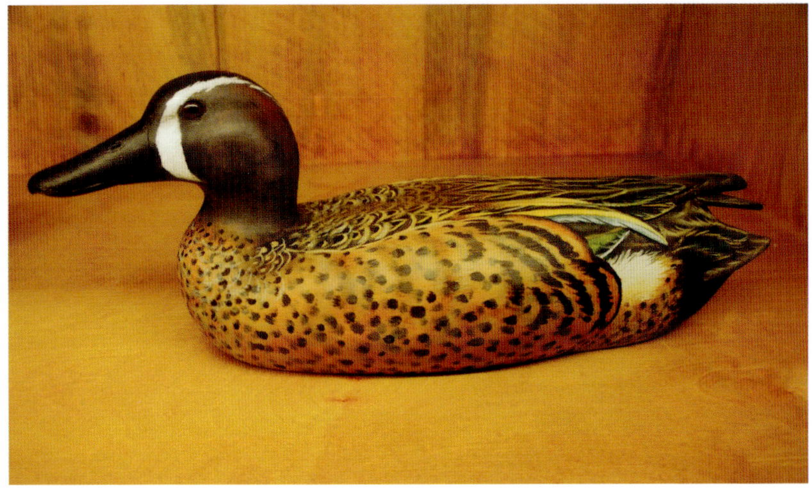

(2) Roy Legaux's blue-winged teal drake

ment. He was the first Louisiana decoy carver to win a Best in Show award at the Ward World Championship; it was in the Novice Class in 1974. Roy followed that up with a third place finish the following year in the Professional Class at the Ward. Such progress was the equivalent of going from batboy to World Series starter in one season. Over the years, Roy has won many carving competitions at the state level and at the East Coast shows where he still competes. He was one of the original founders of the Louisiana Wildlife Carvers and Collector's Guild, and he has won many awards at the Guild's annual carving competitions.

Roy has the distinction of being one of the two Louisiana carvers included in Loy S. Harrell Jr.'s book *Decoys, Sixty Living and Outstanding North American Carvers* published in 2007. Sadly, Jimmy Vizier, the other Louisiana carver listed in Harrell's book, died in 2010

Roy also taught decoy carving—initially in his home and later at several community colleges. Interestingly, Charlie Frank was one of his early pupils. Some other established carvers were critical of Roy for teaching future competitors. Roy's response to his fellow carvers was that competition would make them better, and more important, it would assure continuation of Louisiana's priceless tradition of decoy carving and its rightful place in the state's cultural heritage. Roy was certainly right about that.

One of Louisiana's first world-class contemporary decorative carvers, Roy enjoyed the economic rewards when that carving style reached its zenith. Collectors were paying as much as $18,000 for his sculptured pieces in the 1980s. When the decorative bubble burst in the 1990s, Roy, like most other professional decorative carvers in Louisiana, turned to other carving styles in order to earn a living. It was about that time that Roy moved from Louisiana and took a job as a billboard foreman in Arkansas, where he lived and worked until 1998. During this period Roy continued carving and selling decoys but on a much smaller scale. He wasn't able to enter carving competitions, and he had little, if any, carving visibility in Louisiana. That changed soon after he returned home in 1998 and established a residence in Reggio in St. Bernard Parish. He was thrilled to be reunited with his two sons, Roy Jr. and Jason Legaux, with whom he could hunt and teach how to carve and paint decoys. Under Roy's tutelage, Jason became a very good decoy carver and painter.

Then, just when Roy was regaining his rightful place in Louisiana's decoy carving world, tragedy struck. In 2005, Hurricane Katrina completely destroyed the Legaux family home and almost all of their possessions. After recovering from Katrina, the Legaux family moved to Braithwaite in Plaquemines Parish, and Roy resumed carving. Then, seven years to the day, tragedy struck again when Hurricane Isaac roared ashore and completely destroyed the Legaux home and swept away all of the family's possessions for a second time. After these two losses, the Legaux clan regrouped and relocated in Meraux in St. Bernard Parish, where Roy now lives. Today, Roy is producing some of the best decoys and other forms of artwork in his long career. It is said that if you can overcome adversity, the experience will make you stronger. That is certainly true of the Legaux family.

Roy is a fine carver and an even better painter. He has his own unique painting method. If Cal Kingsmill is the Rembrandt of contemporary carvers, then Legaux is the Van Gogh. Roy likes carving slick decoys. He also paints decoys with a textured finish that he feels more closely resembles feathers. He achieves this texturing by grinding the feather detail into the wood before he paints the decoy.

Roy's view is that you can make an effective decoy with a good paint job even if the carving is mediocre. His mantra is "spend far more time on the painting than the carving"

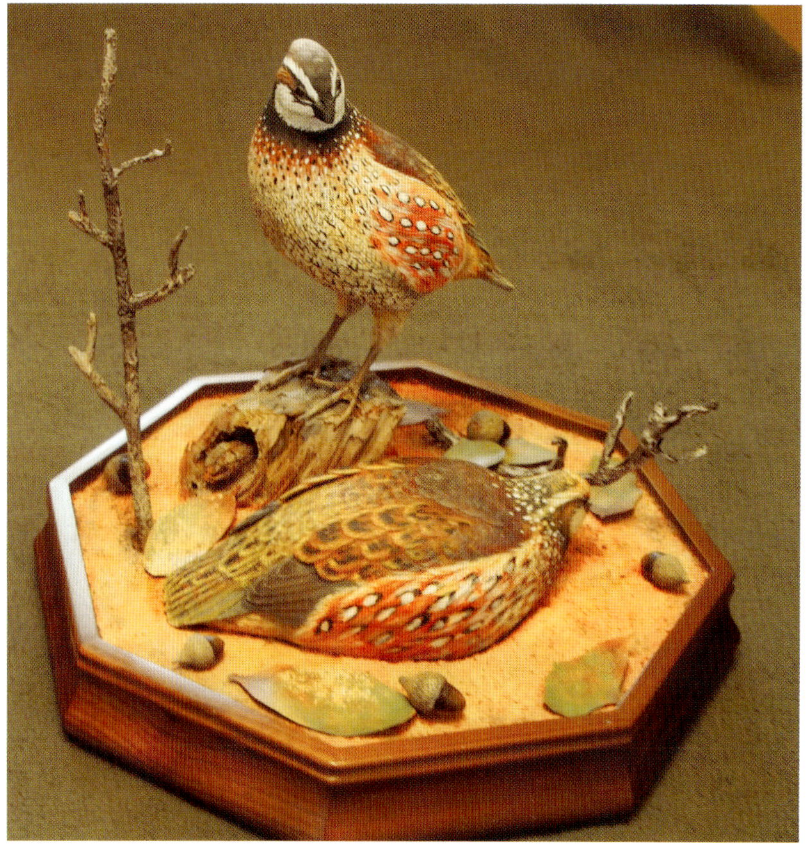

(3) Roy Legaux sculpture featuring pair of quail

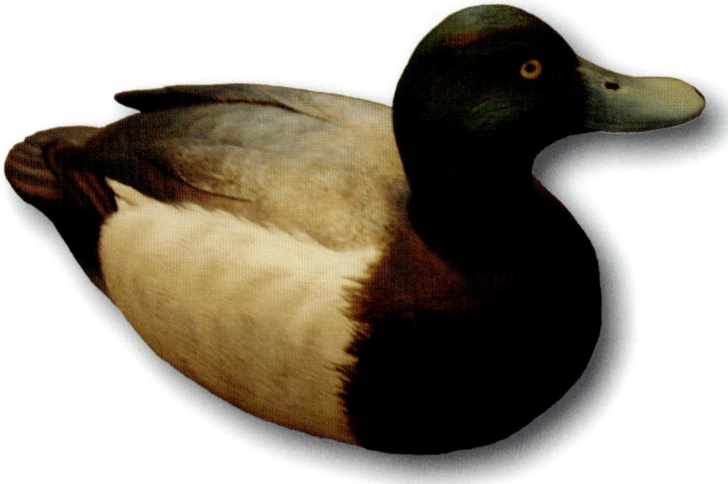

(8) Scaup, also known as a *dos gris*

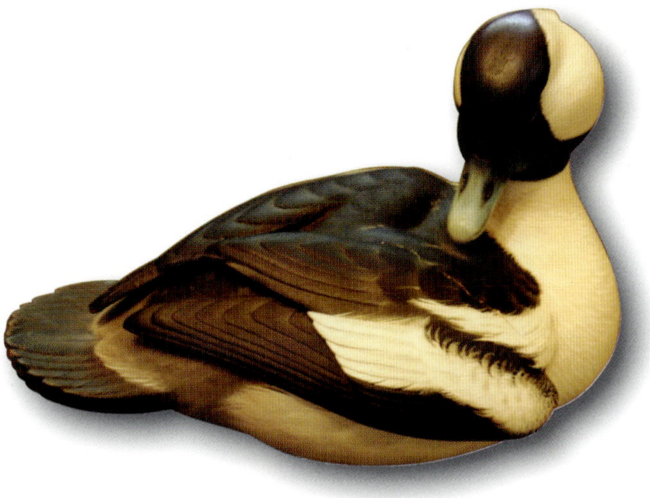

(6) Preening bufflehead

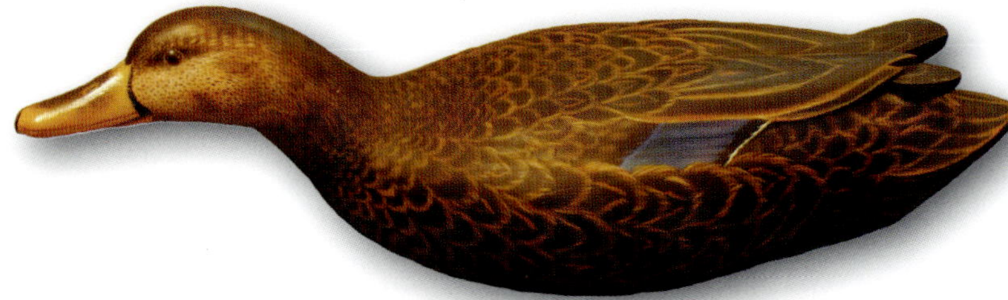

(7) Black mallard chasing minnows

and "make sure that the decoy looks the way it is supposed to look before starting to paint it." It must be anatomically correct for the decoy's species and sex. He feels that if the painting is realistic, it will appeal to the collector's eye as well as the real duck's. Photograph 1 shows a pair of Roy's recently carved green-winged teal, and photograph 2 shows an even more recent blue-winged teal drake. These three decoys are beautifully carved. Even more striking is the textured paint job and how realistic it makes the feathers look.

Roy doesn't just carve duck decoys. He also carves decorative quail, as seen in photograph 3. He has also carved some of the finest wildfowl sculptures, as photograph 4 confirms. His carving isn't limited to "mantel birds." Study the pair of mallards shown in photograph 5, look at the detail this carver achieves, and then realize that these are hunting decoys. Perhaps the most amazing thing is that Roy did all of the photographed art work after hurricanes took his home and virtually all of his belongings not once, but twice, in a seven-year span.

Roy carves decoys in all three contemporary styles. A decorative duck is seen in photograph 6. Photograph 7 shows a decorative gunning black mallard, and photograph 8 shows a scaup that some may classify as a decorative gunner. Roy is not just a world-class wood carver, he is a capable taxidermist and a wonderful wildlife painter and illustrator.

Roy does the "difficult immediately, the impossible takes a bit longer." He insists that now he only carves "money birds." When asked to explain, he said he only wants to carve what his clients want to collect. That is certainly understandable for a carver nearing his seventy-sixth birthday. If you don't find something you want to buy, Roy will carve exactly what you want, and it will be available in less than a week, unless you order a decorative, which will take a bit longer. Roy is a people-person and decoy carving is his life. He truly enjoys company. Visiting with Roy and listening to his stories is interesting and informative. It makes owning his artwork, whether it be decorative sculptures, hunting decoys, song birds, or paintings very special.

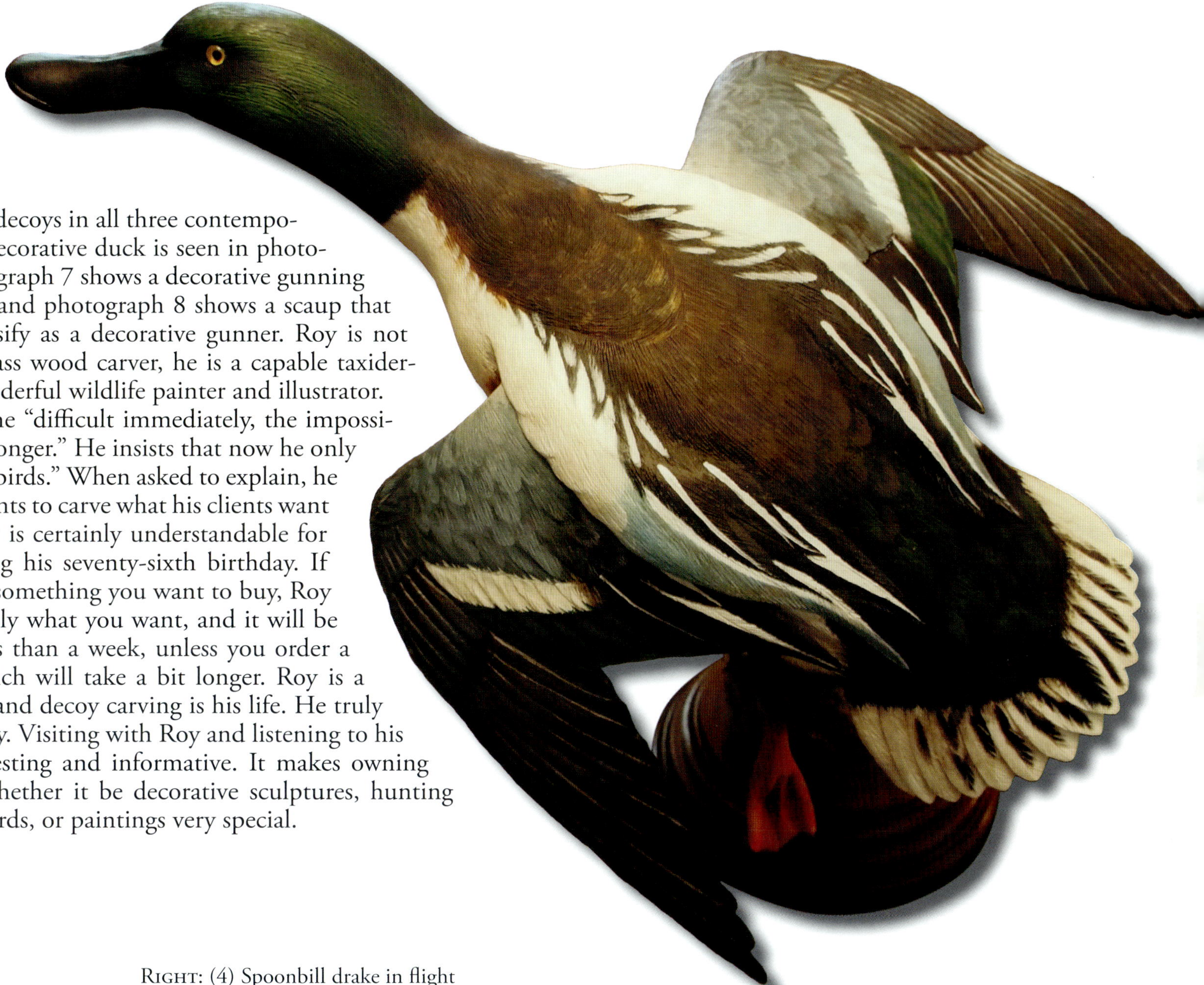

RIGHT: (4) Spoonbill drake in flight

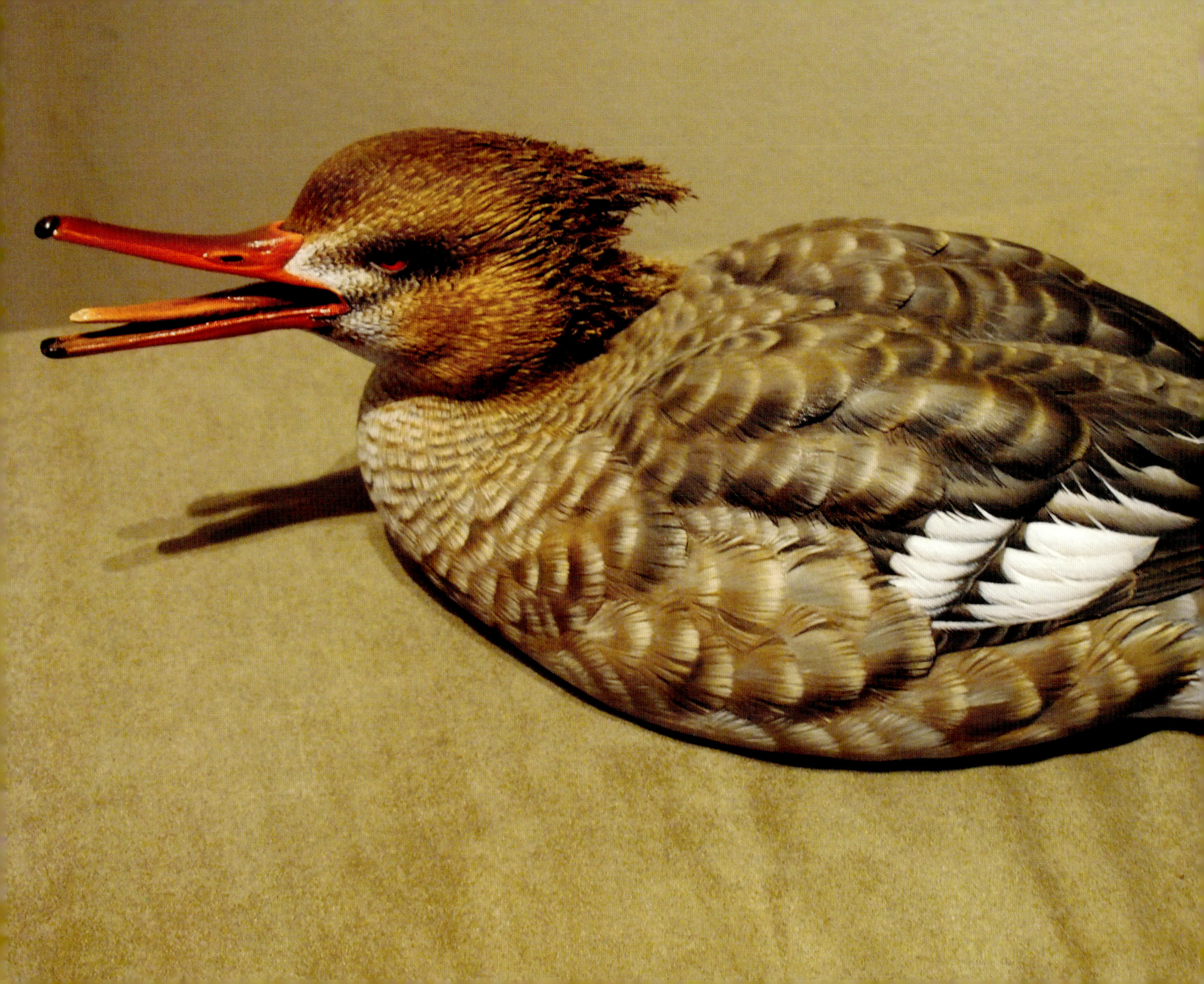

Opposite page: Richard Reeves's merganser hen

16 Richard Reeves

Ward World Decorative Champion

Richard Reeves is a retired New Orleans Police Department major as well as a retired lawyer. He is also the immediate past president of the LWCCG who led the post-Katrina renaissance of the Guild and the revival of the annual Louisiana Wildfowl Festival. He is a three-time Ward Best of Show World Champion carver, including most recently in 2015. Despite these impressive achievements, Richard remains a cordial, modest, soft-spoken gentleman, who is seen in his shop (right), working on a small kingfisher.

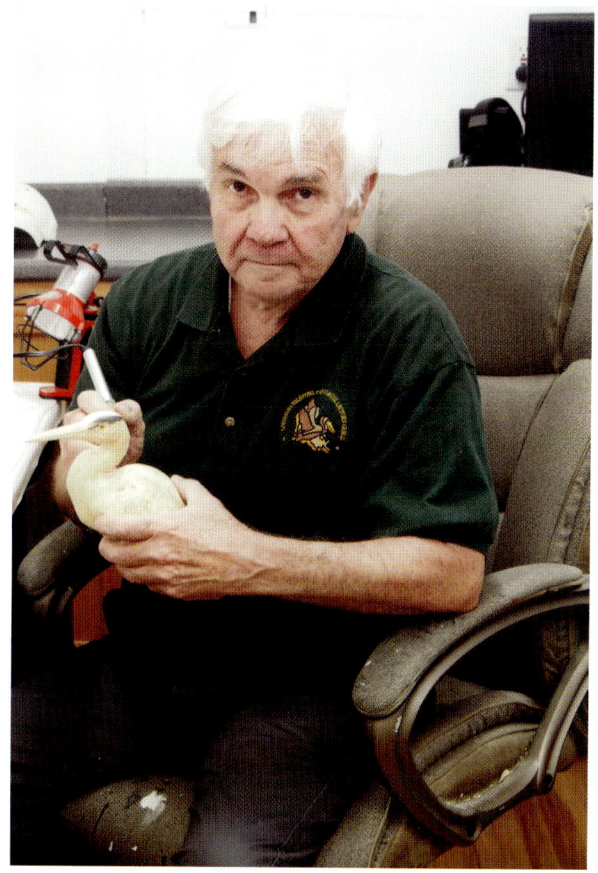

Richard was born in 1944 and grew up in St. Bernard Parish, an area filled with great places to hunt wildfowl. But unlike the other carvers featured in this book, Richard was not a hunter. He didn't even start watching wildfowl until well after he started carving decoys. His work as a ranking officer in the New Orleans Police Department's Internal Affairs section was quite stressful. To relieve that stress, Richard would carve crude objects out of pieces of pine using a penknife. In the late 1970s, a friend gave Richard an instruction book on decoy carving. This gift, coupled with his innate ability, led Richard to take up decoy carving as a self-taught hobby in the early 1980s. By 1984, Richard's carving had improved to the point that he won Best of Show in the Novice Division of the LWCCG's Gulf South Championship. Richard started taking carving lessons from Mike Bonner, and by 1990 he became a professional decoy carver. Early on, he won Best of Show awards in six different states, including Michigan, Ohio, Texas, and Maryland, where many of the country's best decorative carvers live. At the time, Richard was working full time as a police officer, which makes his accomplishments even more impressive.

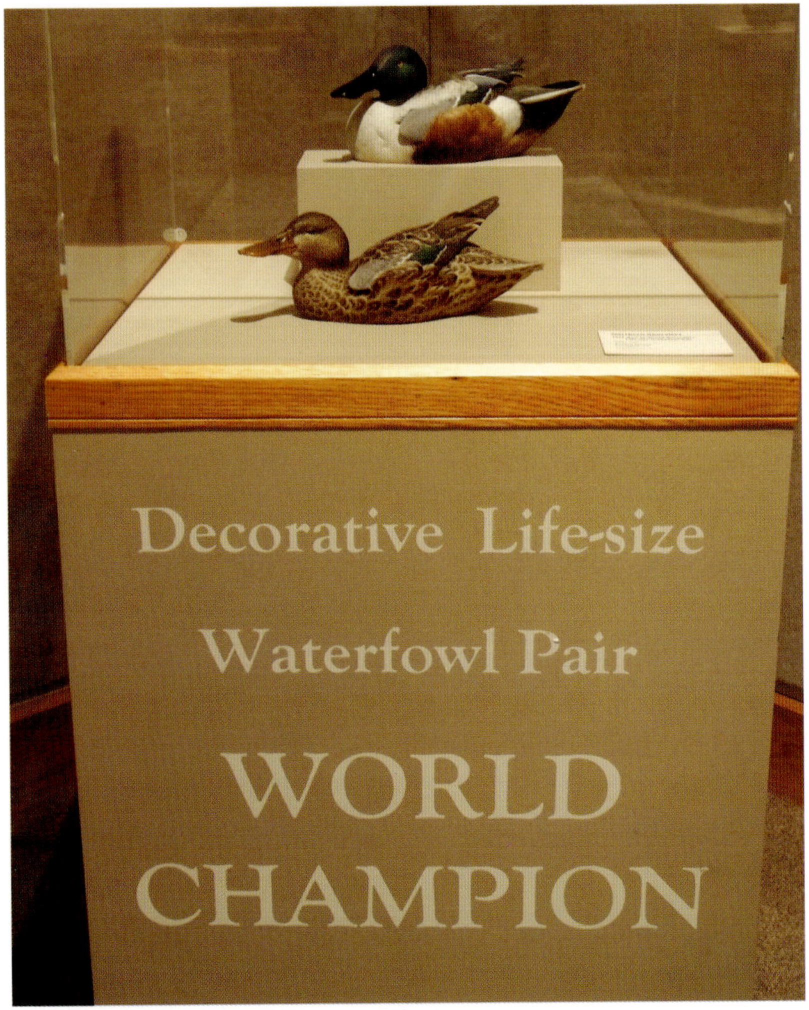

(1) 2015 Ward World Champion decorative spoonbill pair

Richard retired from the police force in June 1997 and began carving full time. In 2001, just eleven years after becoming a professional decoy carver, Richard won the first of his three Ward World Wildfowl Carving Championships with a pair of mallards. From there he went on to win other major awards, including:

2004, Ward Best of Show award in the Masters Division with a pintail hen
2007, Ward World Carving Championship with a pair of red breasted mergansers
2008, Best of Show in the Masters Division of the Ward competition with a mallard drake
2009, Best of Show winner in the Masters Class with a pintail hen
2015, Ward World Carving Championship with a pair of spoonbills, which are seen in photograph 1

During this incredible run, Richard also won the North American Decoy Carving Championship three times and other decoys of his placed second and third.

I first visited Richard and his lovely wife at their home north of Covington in late March 2015, shortly after he won the 2015 Ward World Championship. As is customary, the winner of that award must leave the decoy pair to be displayed for a year in the Ward Museum. Not getting to see the 2015 award-winning decoy was disappointing, but the Reeves's gracious hospitality more than made up for it. In addition, I was treated to viewing and photographing the decoys that won the 2001, 2004, and 2007 Ward Championships. Those decoys are shown in photographs 2, 3, and 4. Moreover, some months later I saw Richard's 2015

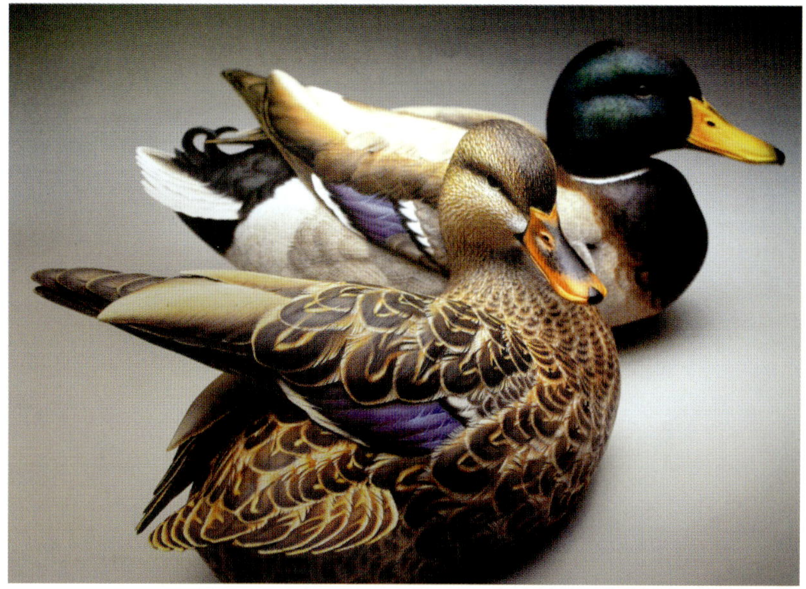

Right: (2) Ward World Champion, decorative mallard pair
Bottom left: (3) Ward World Champion, mallard hen and duckling
Bottom right: (4) Ward World Champion, merganser pair

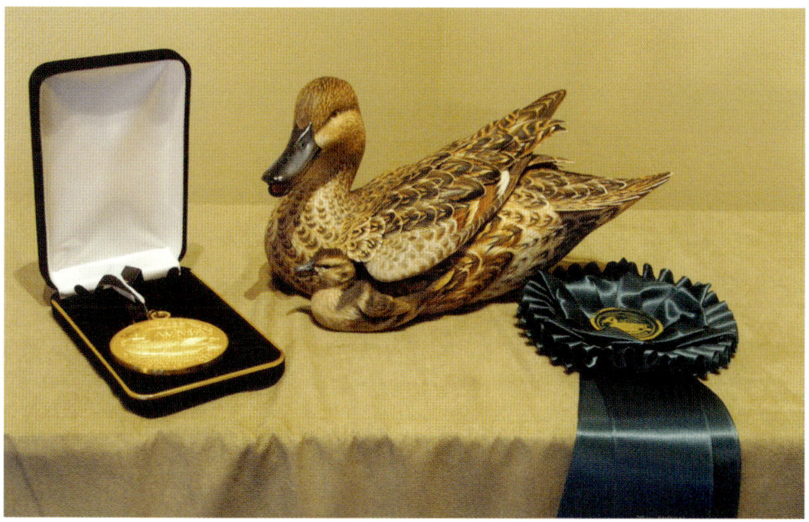

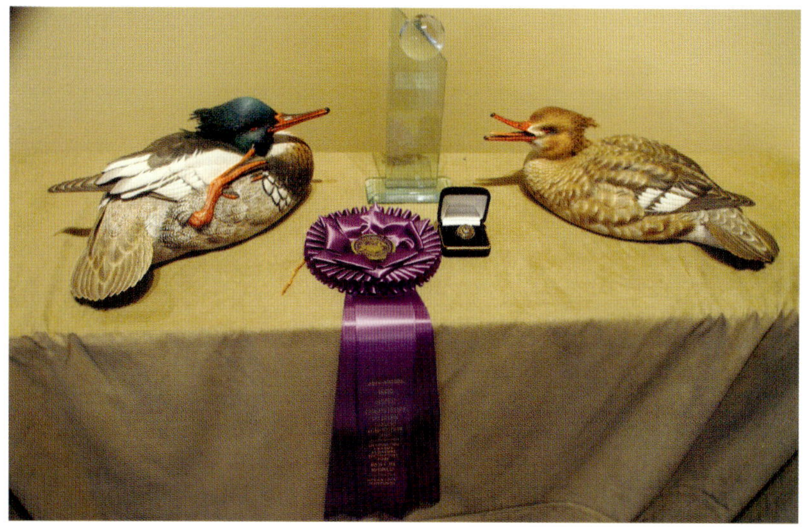

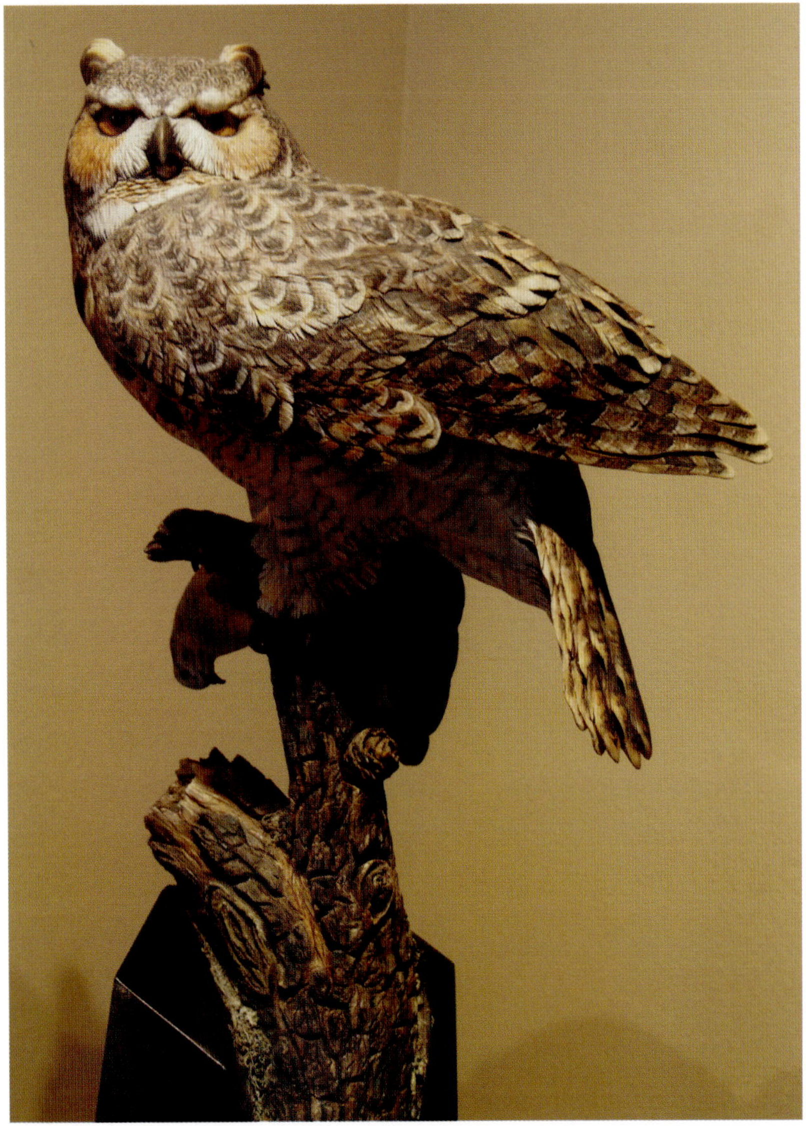

(5) Richard Reeves sculpture featuring great owl

prize-winning mergansers at the Ward Wildfowl Museum

I also got an introduction to competitive decorative decoy carving at the world-class level. Richard believes that the decorative decoy period began with the first Ward World Carving Competition in 1971. In his view, in the early days it was the competition to be the best that motivated carvers to make decorative decoys. Over time, sizeable carving contest purchase awards and the greatly increased prices collectors were willing to pay for topflight decoratives became more important incentives for the carvers.

Interestingly, the Ward Foundation, sponsor of the annual world champion carving competitions as well as the very nice wildfowl museum in Salisbury, Maryland, has a different view of the origin of the decorative decoy. According to the Foundation's website, starting in the 1950s, carvers turned to making decoratives because rubber and plastic decoys caused hunters to stop buying wooden ones. Based on the research done for this book, including the interviews with the carvers, Richard's explanation is more persuasive, though synthetic decoys certainly decreased demand for hunting slicks in Louisiana.

In talking to Richard, he said that most of his decoratives were commissioned by collectors, although some he carved for competition. He acknowledged that in recent years demand for decoratives is down and the number of decoratives for sale is also down, primarily because so many carvers stopped carving true decoratives and are now only carving decorative gunners and hunting slicks. Those styles are easier to carve, take far less time, and are in greater demand because they are much less expensive. For example, Richard's decoratives start at $3,500 and go up from there, while decorative gunners by good contemporary carvers can be bought for around $500, and hunting slicks cost even less.

Richard said that his decoratives are guaranteed for life. If any of his decoys are damaged, he will do the repair work at no charge. This commitment is not only very generous, it is also very valuable to the buyer since decoratives are very fragile.

Our discussion then turned to how long it takes Richard to carve a decorative decoy for competition. He first explained that the objective of decorative decoy carving is to produce an exact replica of the real thing—one that is anatomically correct in all respects. When completed, the decorative decoy must look just like the real thing, whether viewed from across the room or when examining one of the decoy's feathers under magnification. Richard said that carving decoratives is very demanding and tedious. As an example, he said getting the decoy's eyes in the right place is crucially important. If the eyes are not perfectly symmetrical the decoy is not acceptable. For these reasons, Richard prefers working on more than one decoy at a time, occasionally stopping work on a particular carving for a week at a time. Richard said it is not unusual for him to take a year or more to produce a competitive-grade decorative decoy. He said that if he was able to work eight hours a day, seven days a week on just one decoy, he could finish it in less time. Then, he quickly added that would be an unpleasant, if not impossible, task and one that he would not willingly undertake.

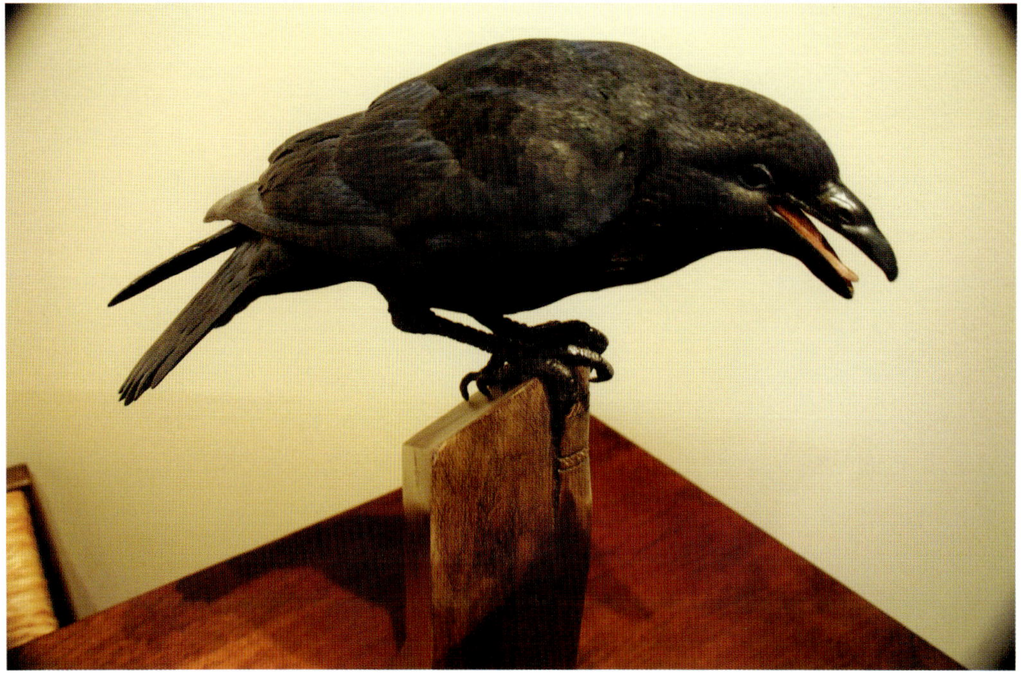

(6) Richard Reeves sculpture featuring decorative crow

Richard then talked about competitive carving and carving tournaments. Despite his accomplishments, he strives to get better, and he welcomes criticism of his work by other carvers he respects. His personal collection includes decoys carved by Jimmy Vizier, Jett Brunet, Cal Kingsmill, Mike Bonner, and Weldon Bordelon, all from Louisiana. In the early days of his carving career Rich-

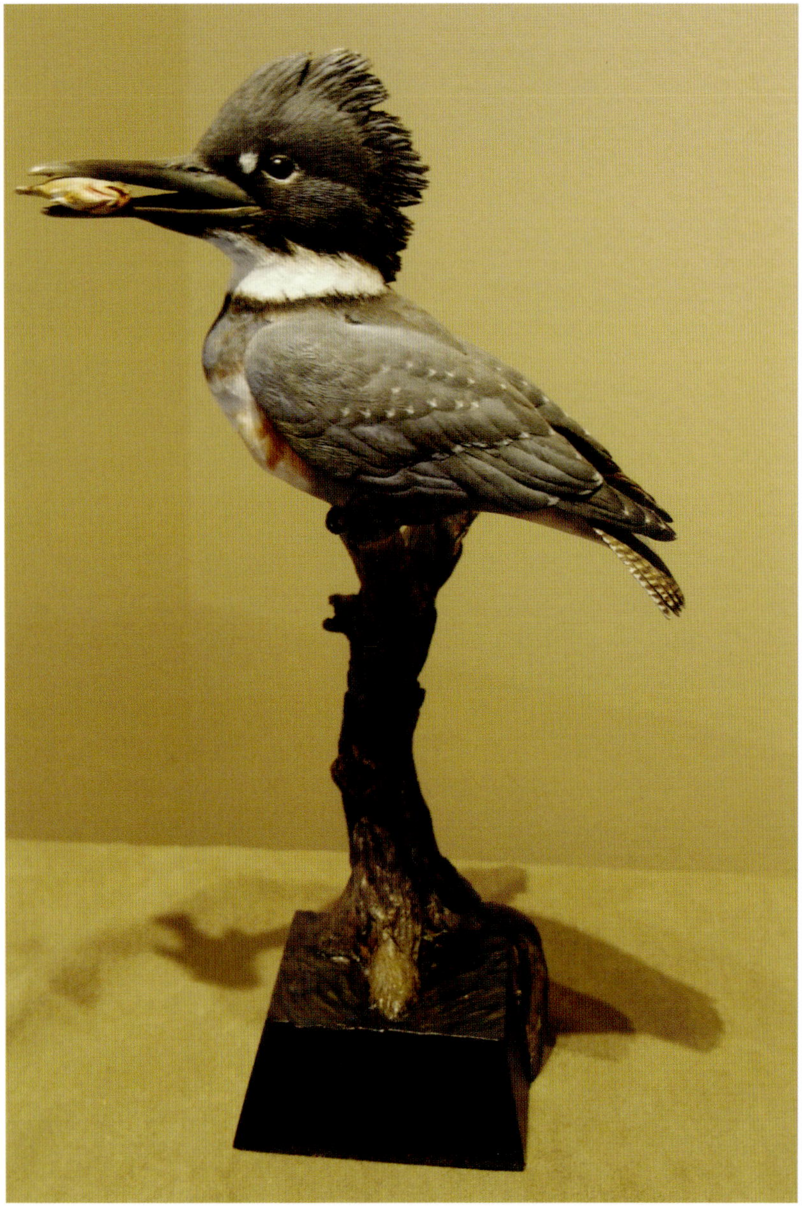

ard traveled to decoy shows and competitions around the country in order to learn things to improve his carving and painting, a practice he still follows even when he has entered the competition.

I asked how he felt about winning a carving competition that has a purchase prize, meaning the winner gets the money, but the purchaser becomes the owner of the decoy. Richard replied, "I am happy that someone thought enough of my decoy to buy it but sad to lose a piece that I spent so much time working on."

Then I asked how the judges decide who carved the Best of Show decoy when all of the world-class carvers in that competition category are carving an exact replica of the same species of wildfowl. Richard's answer was straightforward: "the winner is the carver who best captures the posture and mannerisms of the designated wildfowl, whose carving is the most artistic, lifelike, and difficult, and who makes the fewest mistakes."

Finally, we discussed if winning the 2015 Best in World award for the third time, along with his many other awards, had affected his attitude about future competitions. Richard explained that he "was honored and very happy that the judges liked my decoys but I have lost some competitiveness." Now, "in its place, my incentive is to improve my carving skills." Spoken like a true champion.

Richard doesn't just carve decorative duck decoys. His story would not be complete without viewing his incredible owl, raven, and kingfisher, shown in photographs 5, 6,

(7) Richard Reeves sculpture featuring decorative kingfisher

and 7. Occasionally, he will carve a decorative gunner like the one shown in photograph 8 if requested to do so.[1]

Perhaps Richard's most important and long lasting achievement is his role in reviving decoy carving in post-Katrina Louisiana. In August 2005, Hurricane Katrina devastated the Gulf Coast, destroying Richard's home as well as the homes and workshops, tools, and equipment of countless decoy carvers who lived in the area, causing them to move elsewhere. It shut down the LWCCG and brought it to the edge of extinction at a time when the number of decoy carvers nationwide was in decline. Richard led the LWCCG's long and difficult recovery. After a three-year hiatus, Richard and a few stalwarts helped the carvers to return, reunite, and reinstitute the annual Wildfowl Carving show. Today, the LWCCG has the second largest membership in the country, and it is still growing. The LWCCG's annual decoy carving competition distributes more prize money than any other competition. Richard Reeves deserves a lifetime achievement award for his efforts in rescuing decoy carving in Louisiana, which is such an important part of this state's heritage and tradition.

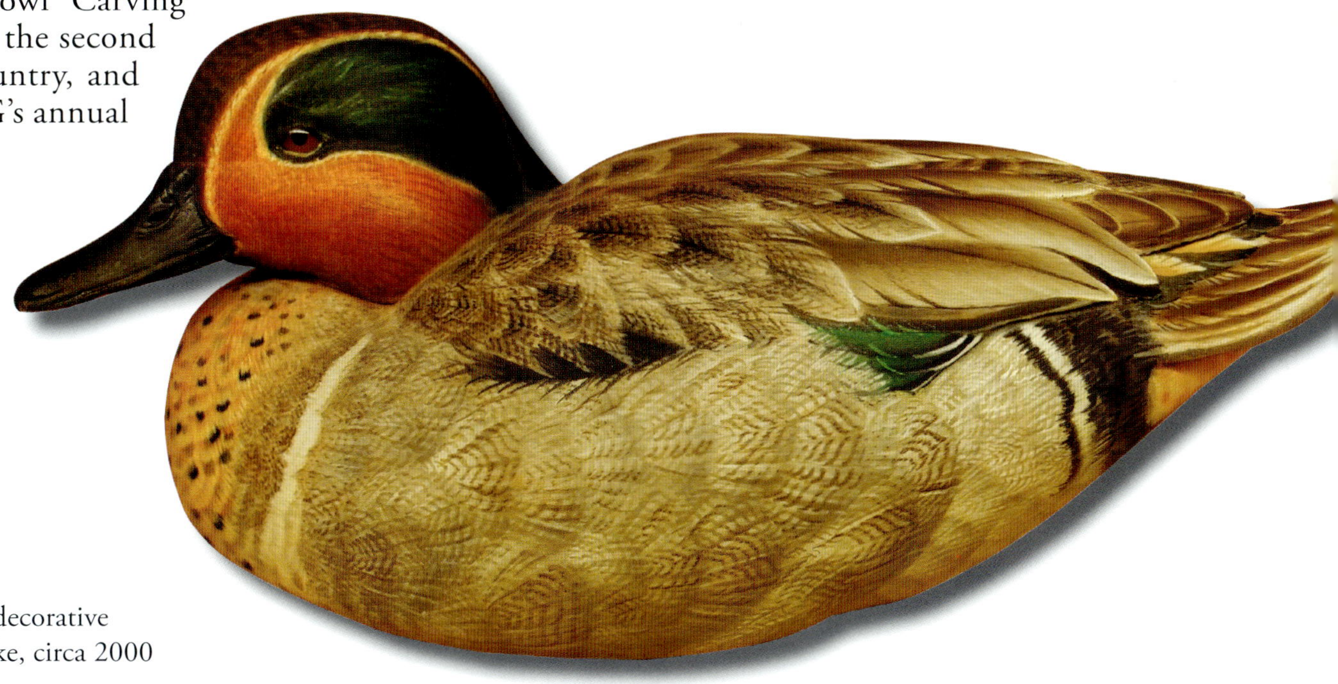

Right: (8) Richard Reeves's decorative gunner green-winged teal drake, circa 2000

Endnotes

1. The reader is urged to visit Richard's website, www. carvingsbyrichardreeves.com for contact information and more photographs.

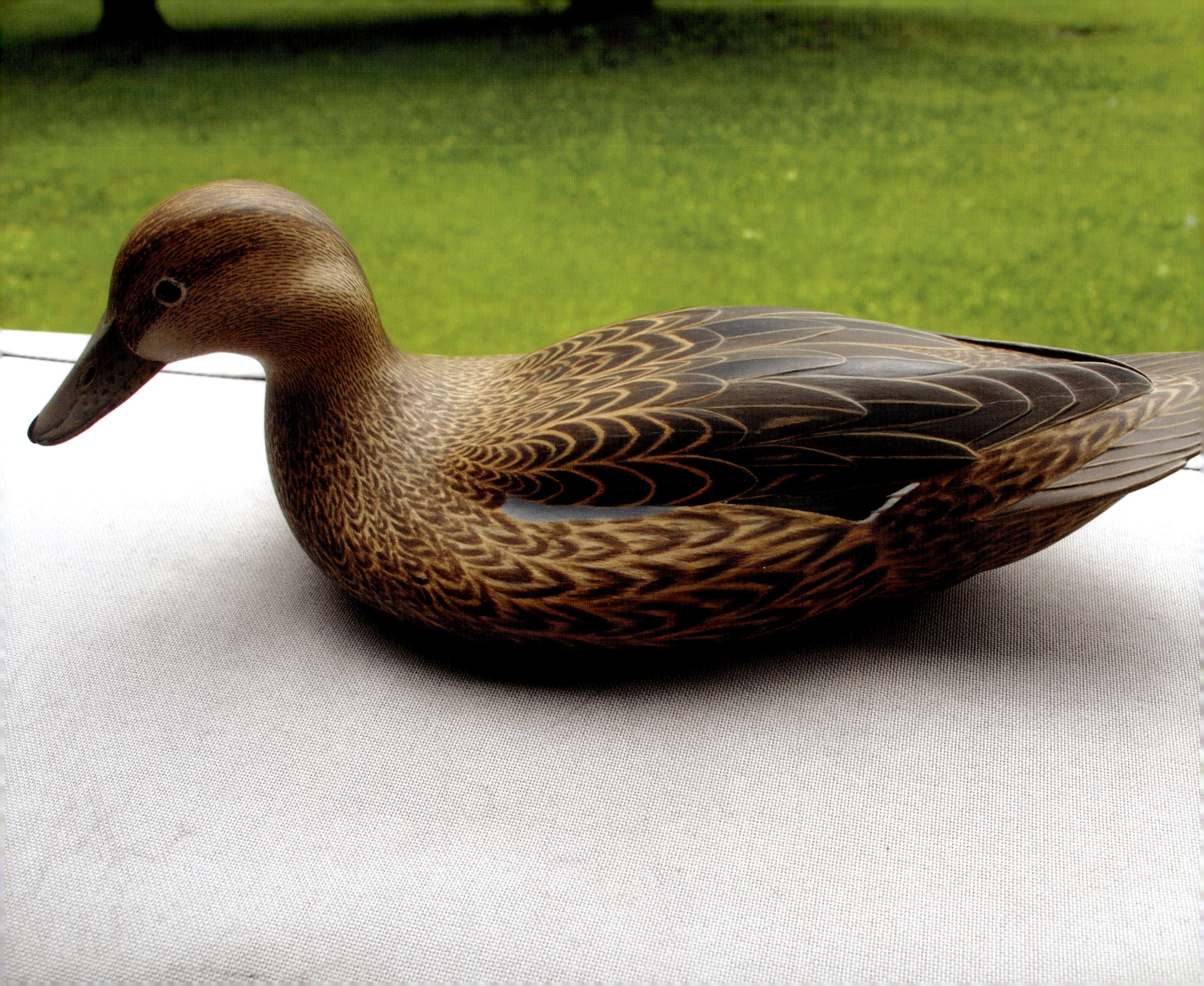

Opposite page: Dennis Treitler's green-winged teal hen

17 Dennis Treitler

Master Puddle Duck Decoy Carver

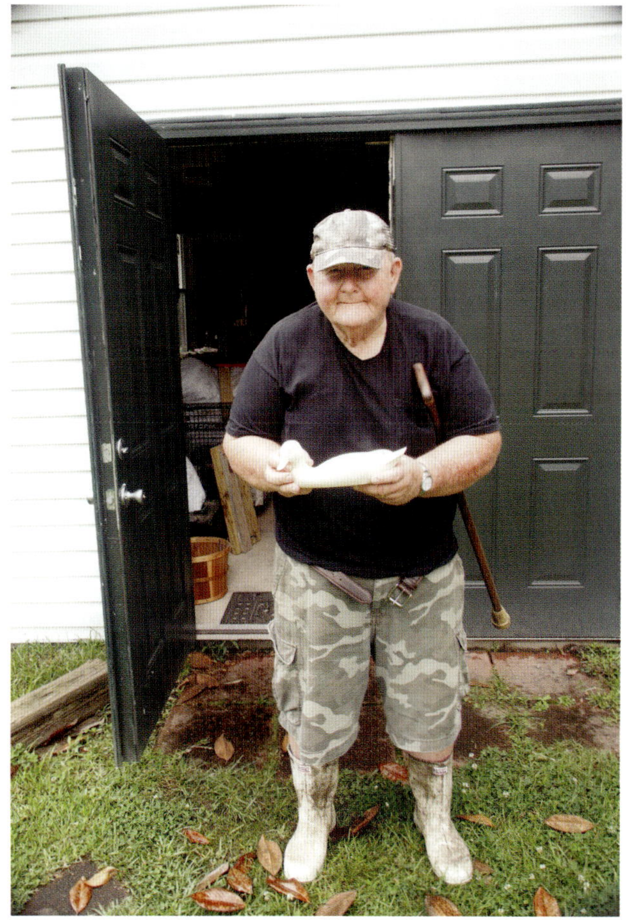

In appearance, Dennis Treitler is a cross between Santa Claus in shrimp boots and a stocky teddy bear, as is evident in photograph 1 showing him standing in front of his work shop. A third generation "marsh man" nicknamed "Outlaw Son," he is a friendly extrovert who lives to hunt, cook, and eat ducks, as well as carve decoys and make duck calls.

Dennis was born on February 23, 1946, and raised in New Orleans's Ninth Ward. He was the son and grandson of avid duck hunters. When he was five years old, Dennis started duck hunting with his father, a champion duck caller. The pair hunted over decoys carved by Clement "Tutu" Mackles (1859-1950), a market hunter and respected hunting decoy maker. Mackles's decoys fascinated Dennis, and at age six, he carved his first decoy. By age ten he was performing off-season repairs, like replacing broken bills on his father's decoys under Mackle's informal tutoring. In his early teens, Dennis started taking carving lessons from Francis "Slim" Uzee, an electrician and well-known decoy carver.[1] Dennis had a seventeen-mile bike ride, each way, to get to and from Uzee's carving lessons. Dennis was a diligent carving student but didn't care for school. At sixteen, he was selling decoys, and the following year, he dropped out of school and joined the Navy. Photograph 2 shows a mallard hen and 3 a drake that Dennis carved just before he left to go into the service. Note how beautifully the hen is painted. Over the years, Dennis worked in his father's bakery and later as a commercial fisherman until he retired in 2008. Before retiring, Dennis taught decoy carving at Delgado Community College and at St. Bernard Community College.

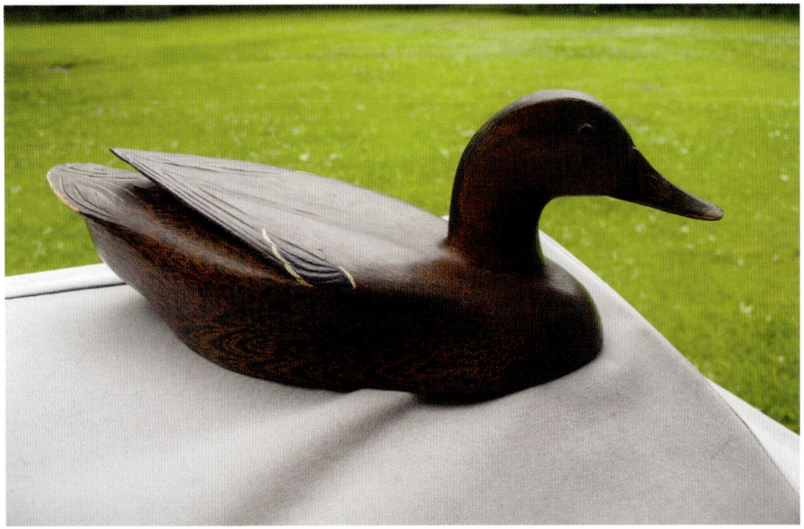

Above: (2) Dennis Treitler's mallard hen hunting decoy
Below: (3) Dennis Treitler's mallard drake hunting decoy

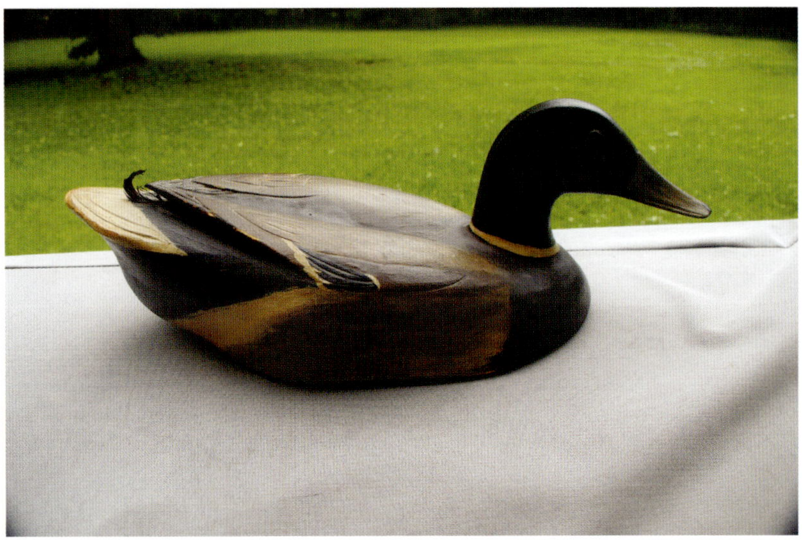

Since then he has been a professional decoy carver.

For many years it has been Dennis's ambition to carve the perfect decoy. Those that have collected his decoys believe that he has achieved that goal many times over, but Dennis remains unconvinced. He still strives to achieve perfection every time he meticulously carves and paints a decoy. Photograph 4 shows Dennis working on a new decoy in his workshop. He uses a pattern to rough-cut the decoy from a cypress or tupelo block of wood and then uses knives and sanding tools to finish and smooth the carving. Photograph 5 shows a detailed head, and photograph 6 an equally detailed decoy body carved by Dennis and awaiting painting.

Duck hunting has been his other passion since childhood. According to Dennis, the four must haves for a good duck hunt are: (1) ducks to shoot; (2) a good blind with wind at the hunter's back because ducks land into the wind; (3) someone who knows when and how to call ducks and; (4) hunters who are good shots. A good duck hunt also requires two tools: a good decoy spread and a duck call.

Dennis is an excellent duck caller and a great shot. He was so good that in the early days he thought he was exempt from the federal game limits. I strongly suspect that is how he got his "Outlaw Son" nickname. Dennis regularly killed enough wildfowl to feed his family, which meant twenty ducks per meal. He also poached alligators and he "shined" deer. Dennis's hunting prowess came to the attention of David Hall, the federal game warden in charge of Louisiana. Hall tried to catch Dennis with more than his limit of ducks and geese on many occasions. He came close a few times but never succeeded, so Hall tried a different approach. In the mid-1980s, Hall conceived a plan for converting poachers to law-abiding hunters through a program he called "Poach-

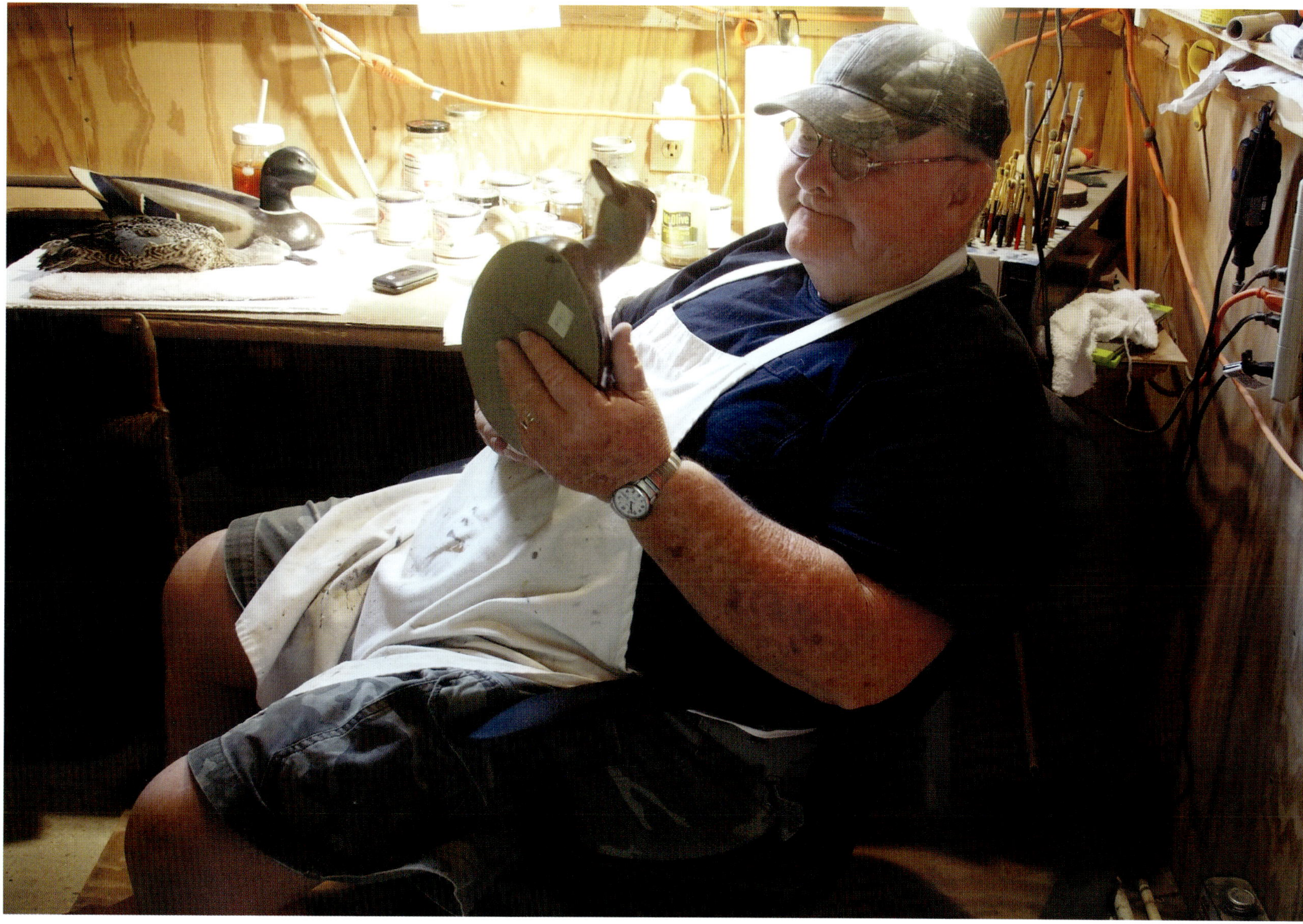

(4) Treitler in shop, admiring decoy he carved over forty years ago

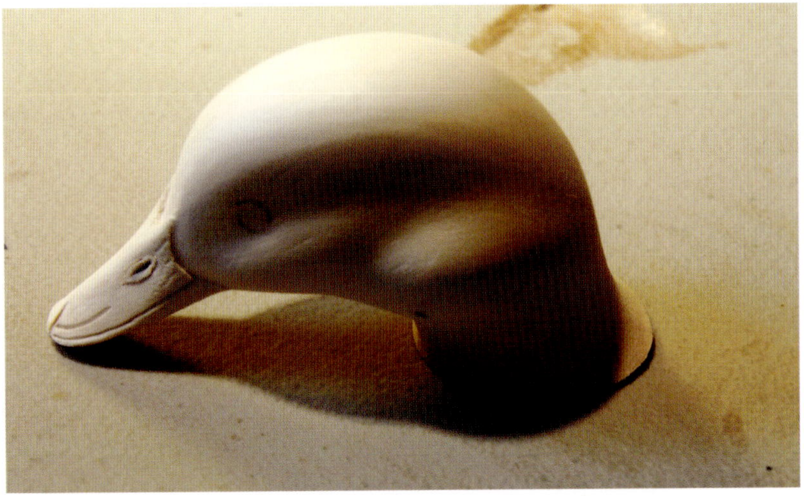

(5) Dennis Treitler's decoy head, work in progress
(6) Dennis Treitler's decoy body, work in progress

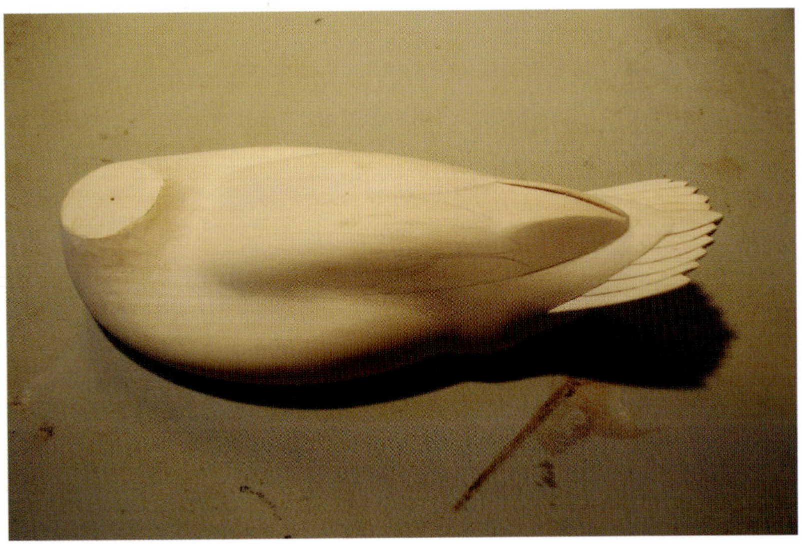

ers to Preachers," for which he decided to make Dennis the poster boy. Hall convinced Dennis that the combination of loss of habitat and overhunting would soon end wildfowl hunting in Louisiana and destroy a hallowed pastime that for many was a way of life. Dennis did not want that to be his legacy, so he gave up his "outlaw ways" and joined Hall's conservation efforts. Hall recorded a lengthy interview with Dennis that became a very effective anti-poaching message entitled "We Killed Ducks by the Thousands (Interview with a Game Poacher and Market Hunter)." Dennis is justifiably proud of his conversion and his part in conserving wildfowl hunting. His efforts continue to date.

Dennis's carving style, which he calls the "New Orleans School," was influenced by "Slim" Uzee, Mike Frady, and Bob Couret's Lifelike Lures, with just a touch of Mark Whipple. Dennis hunted in small, shallow freshwater ponds located in the marshes south and east of New Orleans and St. Bernard Parish. These ponds, also called "pot holes," were filled with duckweed, a favorite wildfowl food and a great attraction for mallards. Dennis's decoys have a flat bottom, are shaped like a triangle with rounded corners, and have an elevated tail that slopes down towards the head that is set above a projecting breast. This shape causes the decoy to appear to be swimming ahead but still relaxed. More importantly, it causes his decoys to float lower in the water and move about like real ducks. Some call his blocks "pot-hole" or "puddle decoys." These features and profile are clearly shown in photograph 7, which depicts a mallard drake and hen carved in the late 1970s.

Dennis is an excellent carver but an even better painter. Charlie Frank penned an article about Dennis that appeared in a 1975 edition of the *North American Decoys* magazine in

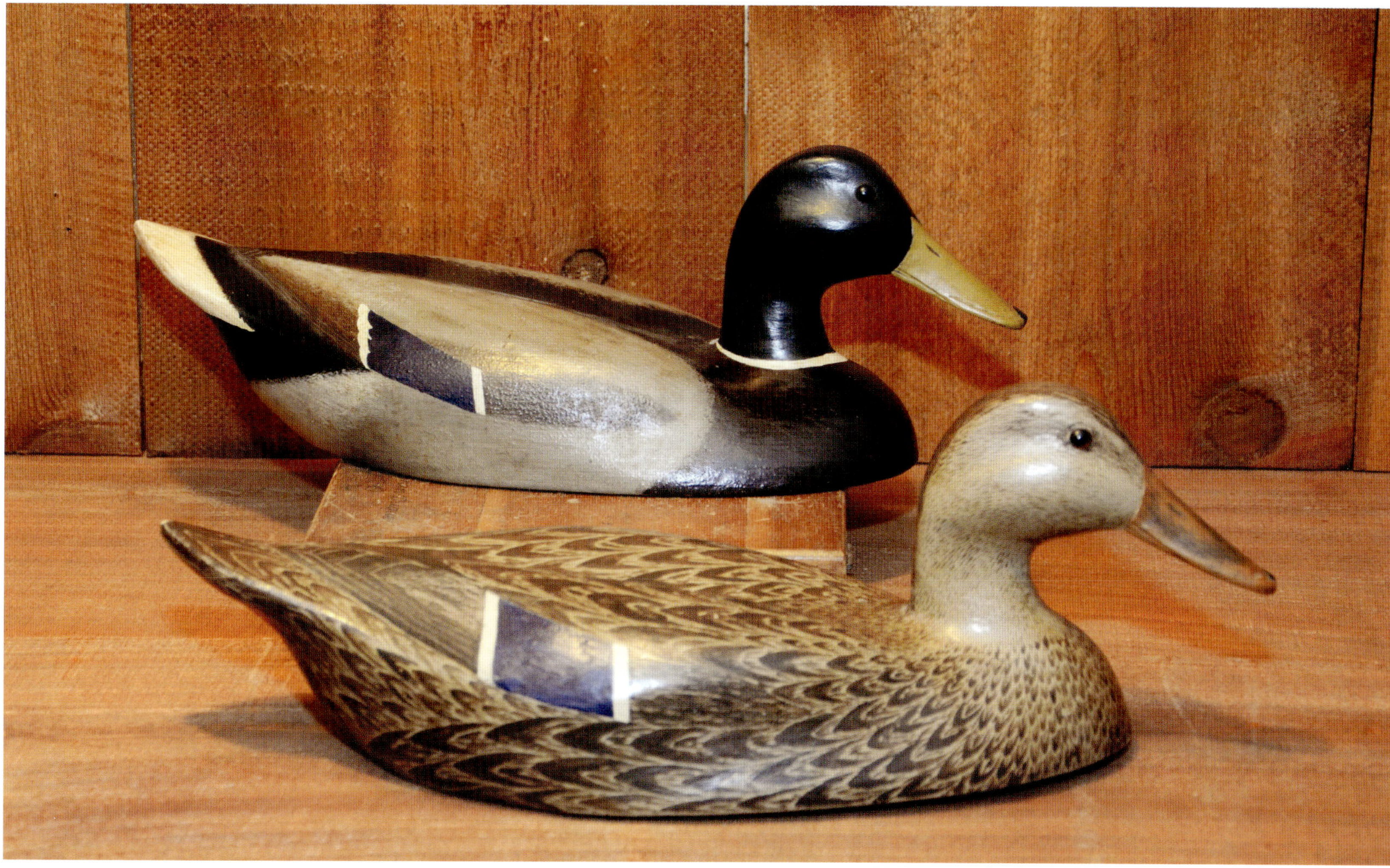

(7) Dennis Treitler's mallard pair, circa 1974

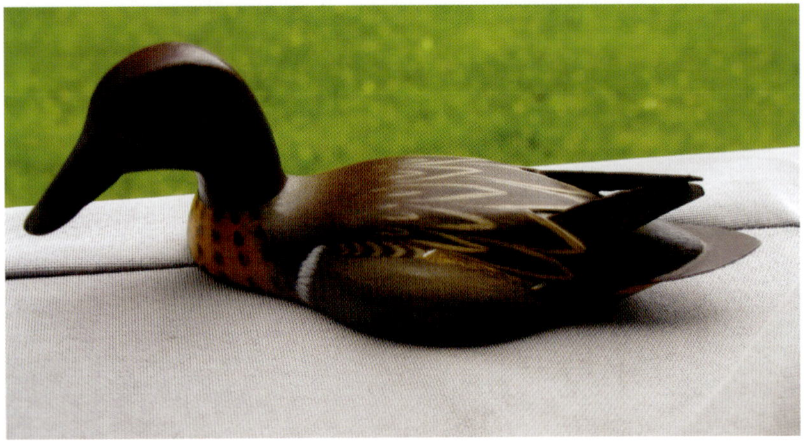

which he said about a pair of mallards, "These are probably the finest contemporary hunting decoys being made in Louisiana today"—very high but well-deserved praise, especially since Dennis's decoy carving and painting skills have continued to improve. Today, Dennis says he is carving decorative gunners but asserts that they are made to be hunted over. Photograph 8 shows a pair of teal that Dennis completed in the fall of 2015. One would be foolish to hunt over these two decoys, but Dennis insists that's their intended purpose. The green-winged teal that Dennis carved some years ago seems better suited for hunting than the blue-winged teal pair even though it, too, would be classified as a decorative gunner. That decoy is shown in photograph 9.

Above: (9) Dennis Treitler's green-winged teal drake

Below: (8): Dennis Treitler's blue-winged teal pair, circa 2015

In the past, Dennis carved his decoys from balsa and cypress wood but for some time he has used tupelo gum. He uses homemade patterns and starts by cutting out his decoys with a band saw. He uses Parker decoy paint mixed with Ronan paint, which is thicker. He avoids acrylics and oils because they fade and wash off.

In discussing the evolution of contemporary decoy carving from decoratives to decorative gunners to hunting slicks, Dennis had a single-word explanation: price. He noted that decoratives are very expensive despite lagging demand. I asked why he started

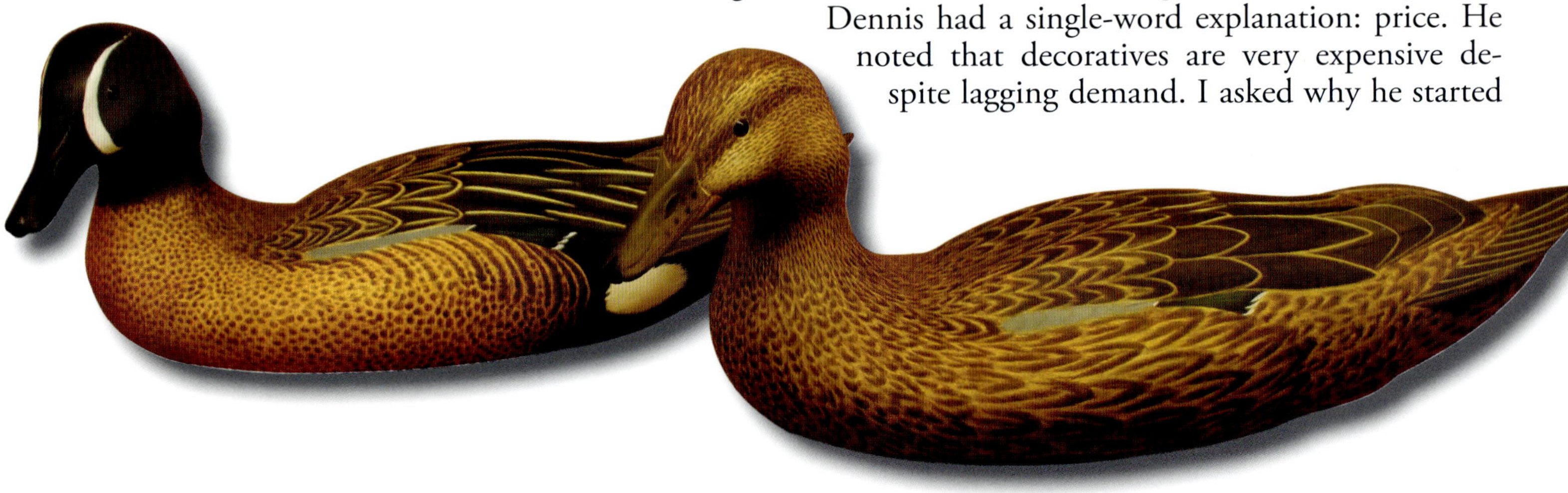

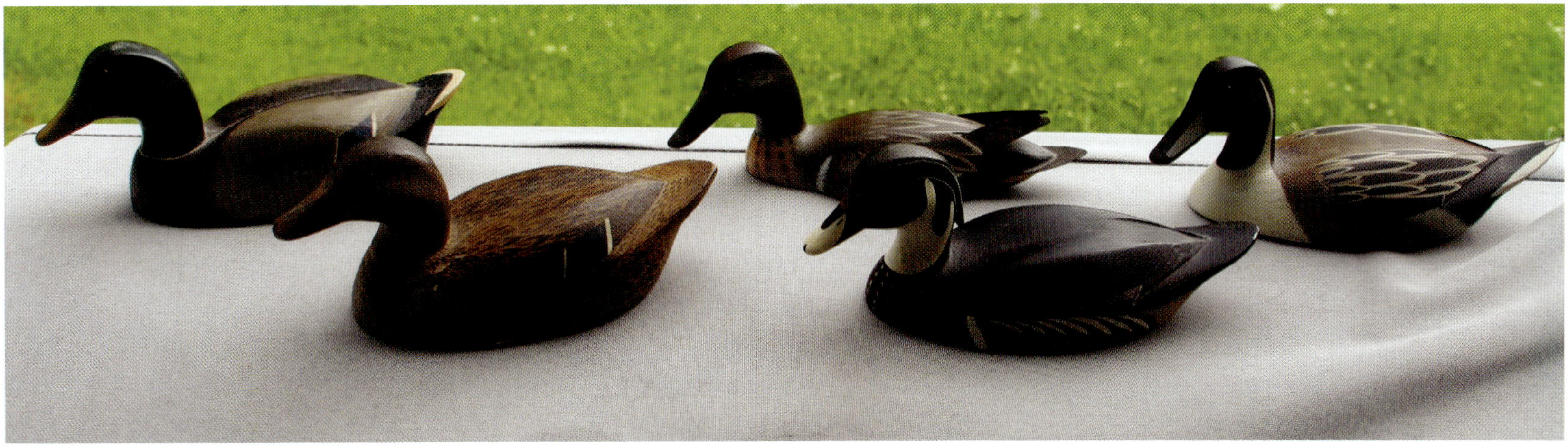

(10) Dennis Treitler's assortment of miniatures

carving miniatures, which are extremely popular with collectors, and he said candidly, "for economic reasons." Photograph 10 shows a full set of Treitler miniature decoys that are carved and painted with the same meticulous care as his full-size decoys.

Dennis inherited his father's decoy calling skill and has won many competitions. Listening to him demonstrate his duck calling prowess is a real treat. He is the Al Hirt of duck callers, and he makes his own calls, too. No discussion of Dennis would be complete without sharing his views on how to make duck calls. He makes his calls out of rubber or clear plastic hose and his reeds are made out of Mylar. When asked why he chooses such nontraditional material, he explains, "wood swells and splits and brass corrodes."

Dennis is one of my very favorite carvers, and a pair of his mallards has graced my collection for nearly forty years. He is one of Louisiana's best contemporary carvers, and his decoys rank among Louisiana's most collectible. He carves on a commission basis and has a full waiting list. He works slowly and very carefully. If you order one of his decoys, don't expect instant gratification, but it is certainly worth the wait.

Endnotes

1. Cheramie, et al., *Louisiana Lures and Legends*, 158.

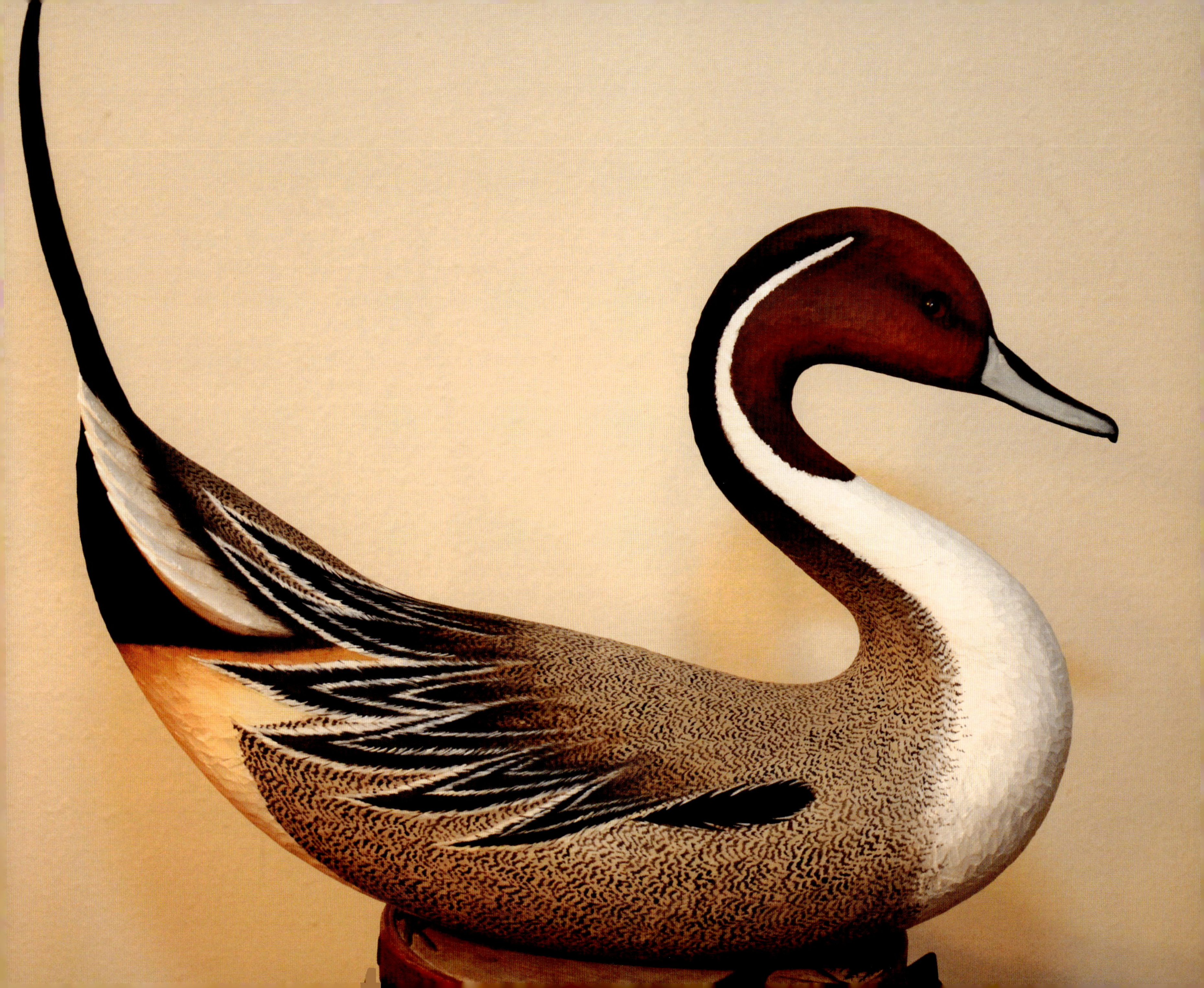

Opposite page: Chris Weaver's pintail drake

18 Chris Weaver

Versatile Carving Master

Chris Weaver is a certified dental technician, employed by the LSU Dental School in New Orleans. His family has lived in the city for many years. His avocations are hunting, fishing, and carving realistic looking wooden objects, including wildfowl decoys, life-size and larger fish, fishing lures, owls, and songbirds. Additionally, Chris is a superb wildlife painter.

Photograph 1 shows a fine decorative mallard drake. Photograph 2 shows a pair of decorative gunner blue-winged teal. Photograph 3 is a great looking decorative green-winged teal drake. Photograph 4 is a very nice wood duck drake. Photograph 5 is a superb pintail drake. This body of work alone proves that Chris is an exceptional duck decoy carver. The giant red snapper seen in photograph 6, the drum shown in photograph 7, and the paintings seen in photograph 8 and 9 prove that Chris is a fine and versatile flat artist.

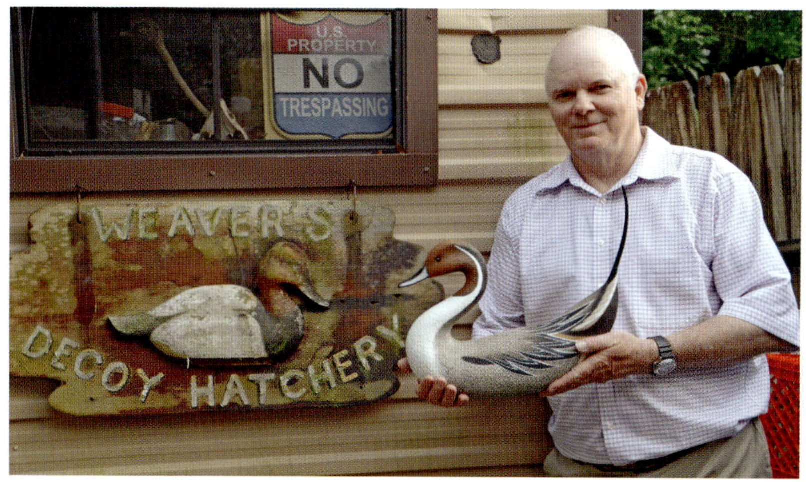

Chris comes by his carving skills, as well as his occupation, naturally. His father, Don Weaver Sr. was also a dental technician by profession and a prize-winning decoy carver. Don Sr. was one of the founding members of the Louisiana Wildfowl Carvers Guild (LWCCG) and its predecessor group dating back to a show at the St. Bernard Duck Calling Contest. From the earliest days, Chris accompanied his dad to these decoy carving events, including the monthly meetings.

Chris has a very good recollection of the Guild's early days and the even earlier events before its creation. He pro-

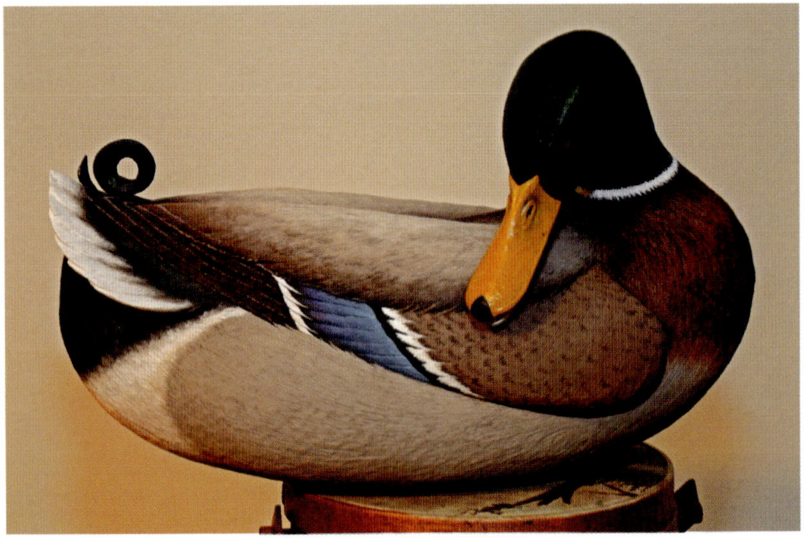

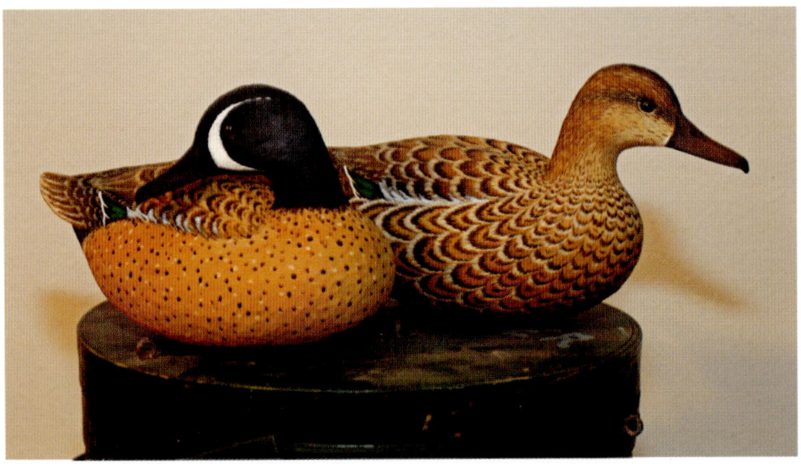

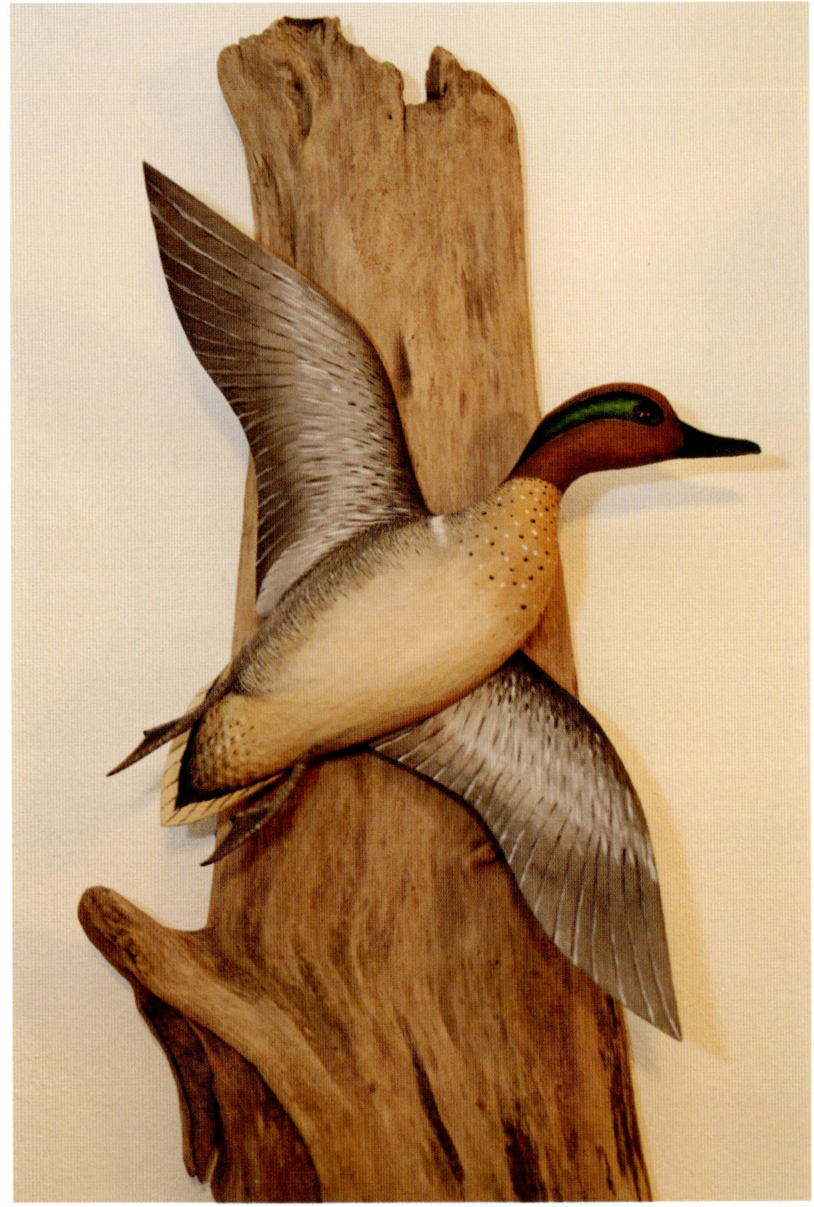

Chris Weaver decoys Top: (1) decorative mallard drake, Bottom: (2) chipped carved blue-winged teal pair, Right: (3) flying green-wing teal drake

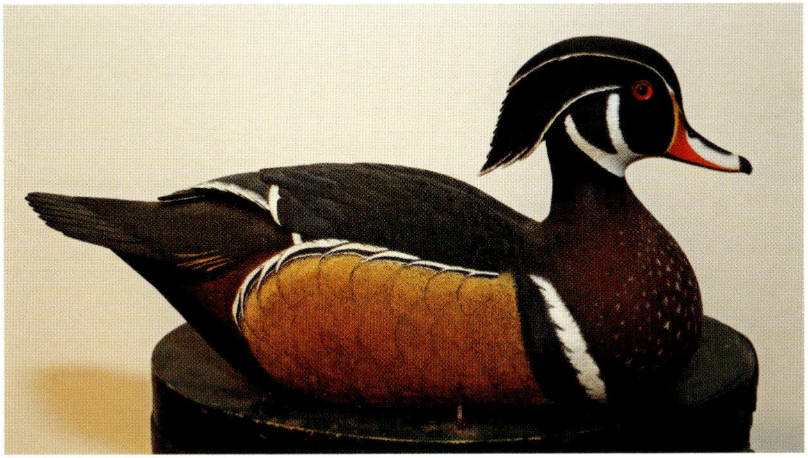

(4) Chris Weaver's decorative gunner wood duck drake

vided helpful information that went into this book's chapter on the LWCCG. More important, Chris is a wonderful person and a very talented carver who deserves to be in this book because of the quality and uniqueness of his work, especially the "chip carving" technique he learned from his father. It is sometime referred to as "relief carving." Photograph 10 shows a pair of green-winged teal carved in that style. Chris's peers regard him as an excellent decoy painter. I certainly share that view but also think his carving is equally exceptional.

Chris earned an associate degree as a certified dental technician from the LSU School of Dentistry and works in the school's lab creating very exacting things like bridges, teeth, crowns, and the like. The work requires excellent manual dexterity and the ability to produce small dental objects with no margin for error. Those skills are readily transferable to carving decoys, fish, and similar wooden objects.

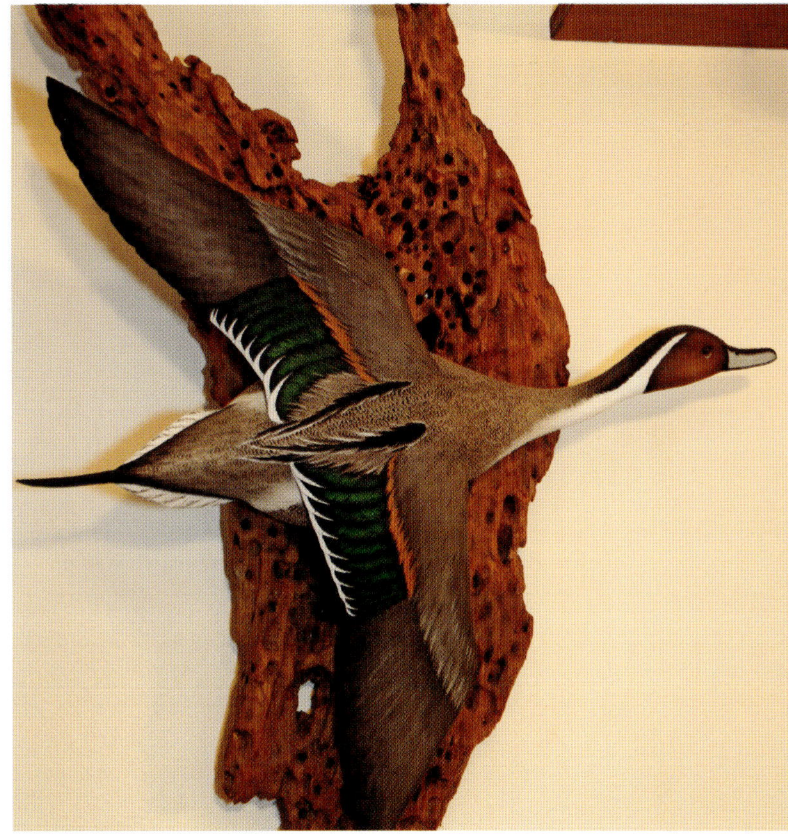

(5) Chris Weaver's flying pintail drake

It is important to note that Chris's father, Don, was also a dental tech with the same skill set. Chris, like his father, also became a first-rate wildfowl carver; it is hard to argue that he did not inherit the artistic gene from him.

It is no surprise that Chris caught the carving bug in 1974 when his father took him to the decoy carving competition that was put on by the carving club that morphed in

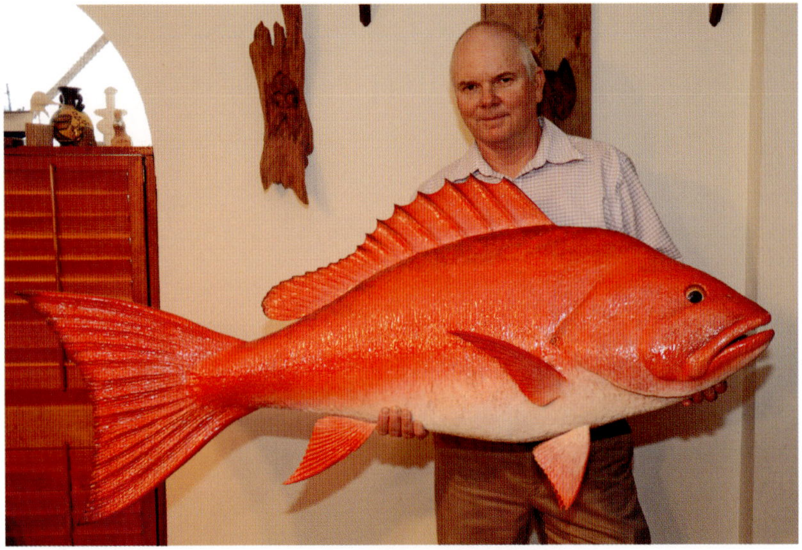

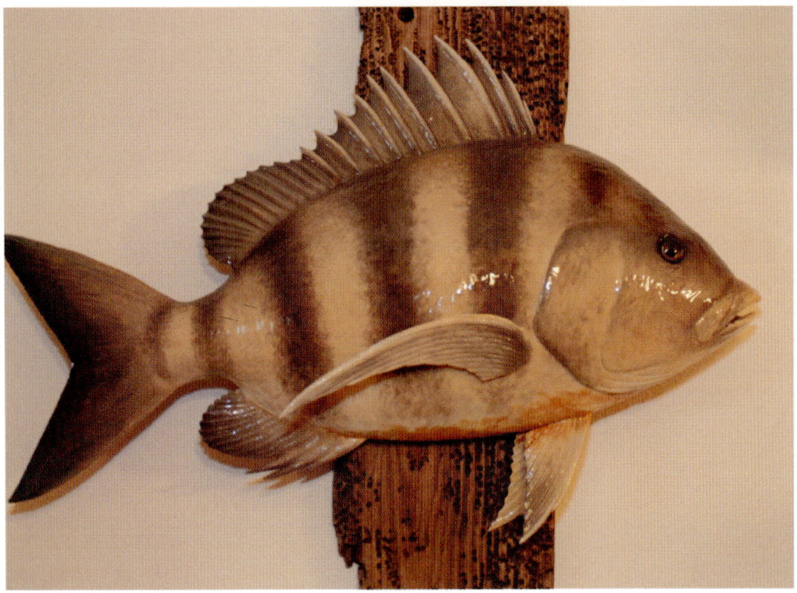

to the LWCCG several years later. Chris was fourteen years old and anxious to learn how to carve decoys. His father inspired and influenced his son and helped him when needed but Chris was largely self-taught. He readily acknowledges that he learned a great deal by watching his father.

It is fair to say that Chris Weaver was one of three charter members of the Junior Division of the LWCCG; Eric Hutchison was another. Early on, the Junior Division had a carving competition. Eric won first place, and Chris finished second.

Chris started carving miniatures and quickly became proficient enough that he was able to sell them for $3.00 apiece. He was also an avid hunter, and still is, so it's no coincidence that the original selling price of his miniatures was the same as the cost of a box of shotgun shells. Plastic decoys had largely replaced wooden ones at that time, so there was no need for Chris to carve decoys to hunt over nor was there much demand from his clients for wooden ones except for those produced using a unique carving style.

Don Weaver Sr. invented the "chip carving" technique he taught Chris. Don noticed that the paint on many wooden hunting slicks reflected the sun when afloat. This gave the decoy a shiny look that was very unnatural and caused ducks to flare off. Rather than change to non-glare paint, Don changed how he did the finish carving. Virtually all other decoy carvers sand their decoys smooth before painting them. Don felt that this was the source of the problem, so after he completed the rough finish, he used a knife and

Top left: (6) Chris Weaver's giant red snapper
Bottom left: (7) Chris Weaver's very large drum

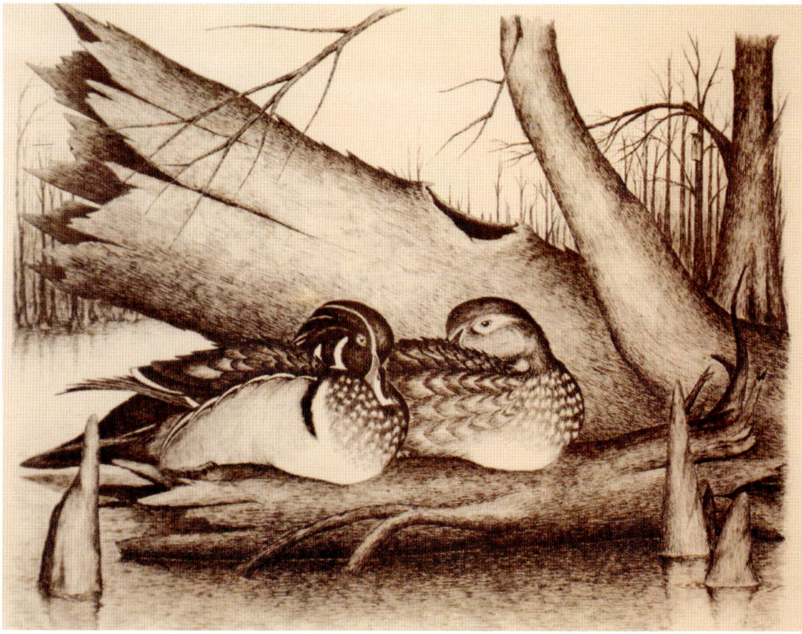

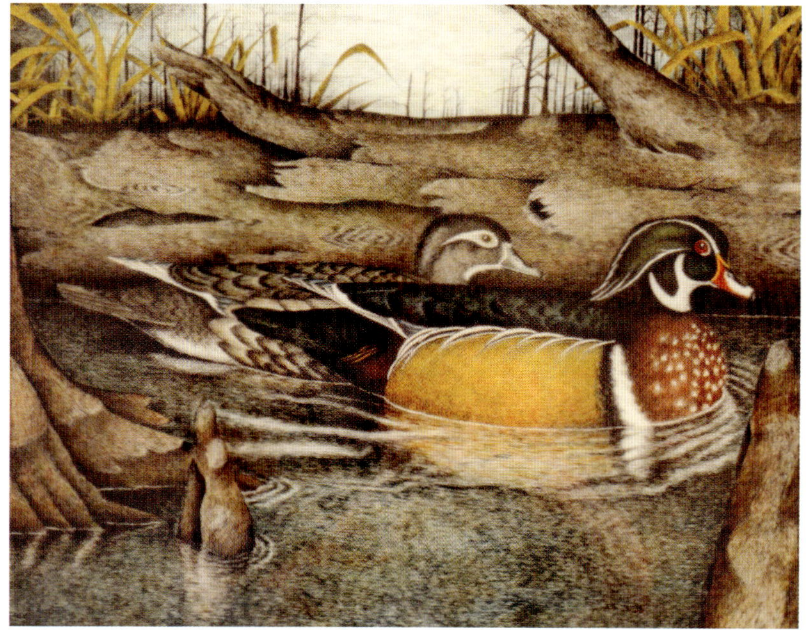

(8 & 9) Chris Weaver's wood duck pencil drawing and painting

cut away chips of wood until he was satisfied with the shape of the decoy. Then, he painted the decoy in his usual manner. He quickly discovered that a chip carved decoy's uneven surface did not look shiny or reflect the sun.

Chris has taken chip carving to a higher level by using that technique when carving decorative decoys as well as decorative gunners, as is evident in all of the decoy photographs that accompany this chapter but is likely most noticeable in the pair of chip carved green-winged teal seen in photograph 10. The appearance of a chip-carved decoy is visually appealing, and it is no wonder that carvers as prominent as Jett Brunet have used that carving style.

Chris's favorite carver is Tan Brunet. Chris says "Tan is a great painter whose decoys are more realistic than real ducks." Chris also likes the painting style of the Lafrance, Joefrau, and Frederick team. Nonetheless, if he could only buy one decoy from a contemporary carver, Chris said Tan Brunet would be his choice, "if he could afford it."

Chris has a nice workshop that adjoins his home. There, he carves his full-size decoys out of cypress that he personally harvests from trees naturally felled in the marsh. Chris uses tupelo gum for his miniatures. His decoys are painted in oils, and he does not use paint patterns; instead he looks at pictures and photographs of other carvers' decoys. The

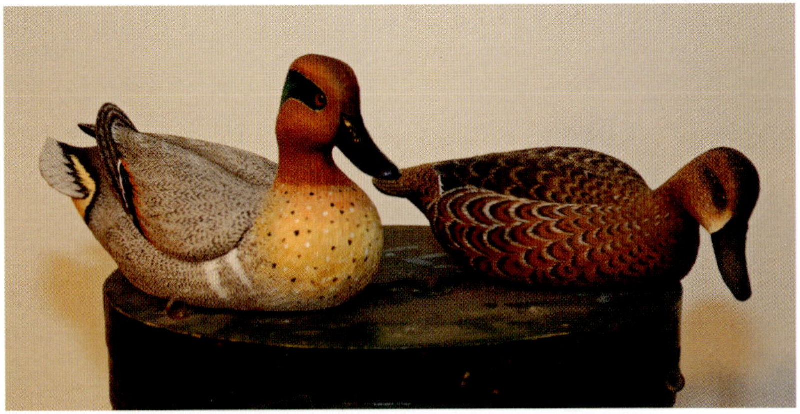

(10) Chris Weaver's unique chip-carved green-winged teal pair

size and shape of the wood he has to work with are important factors in determining species, sex, and pose of what he carves. Chris says sometimes "the wood just speaks to him."

Chris has also carved prize-winning fish, like the oversized red snapper shown in photograph 6. He also carves smaller decoys that are very well done, as photograph 11 illustrates. They take about a week to complete. His personal favorite is carving exotic birds and decoys in unique positions. The super preening pintail, seen in photograph 12, is a great example of a decoy in a unique position.

Chris works on commissions, and generally, it is the client who tells him what he wants carved. Chris charges $200 for hunting slicks and his prices go up from there depending on the complexity of what the client desires. He also takes commissions for wildfowl paintings. Even if you intend only to buy one his carvings, fish or fowl, do not miss viewing his paintings if you have the opportunity. They reflect Chris's deep love of and respect for nature. Chris does not get seller's remorse when he sells a piece of his art. Knowing that he can make another one keeps him from having any sense of loss.

Carving and painting are what Chris does for pleasure and to supplement his income. He doesn't carve decoys to win competitions. He has a laid-back personality. He is very approachable and enjoys helping his clients get the artwork they really want. If one catches a memorable fish, having Chris carve and paint a replica is almost certainly preferable to owning a taxidermist's stuffed one. Chris gives back by continuing to actively support the LWCCG. He was instrumental in getting the Guild to create a carving program for the Boy Scouts.

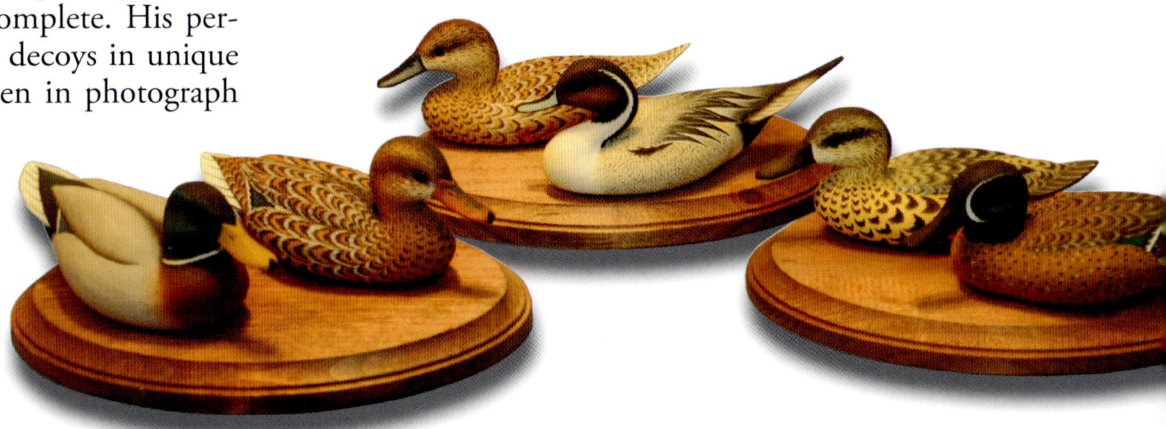

RIGHT: (11) Chis Weaver's assorted miniature decoys

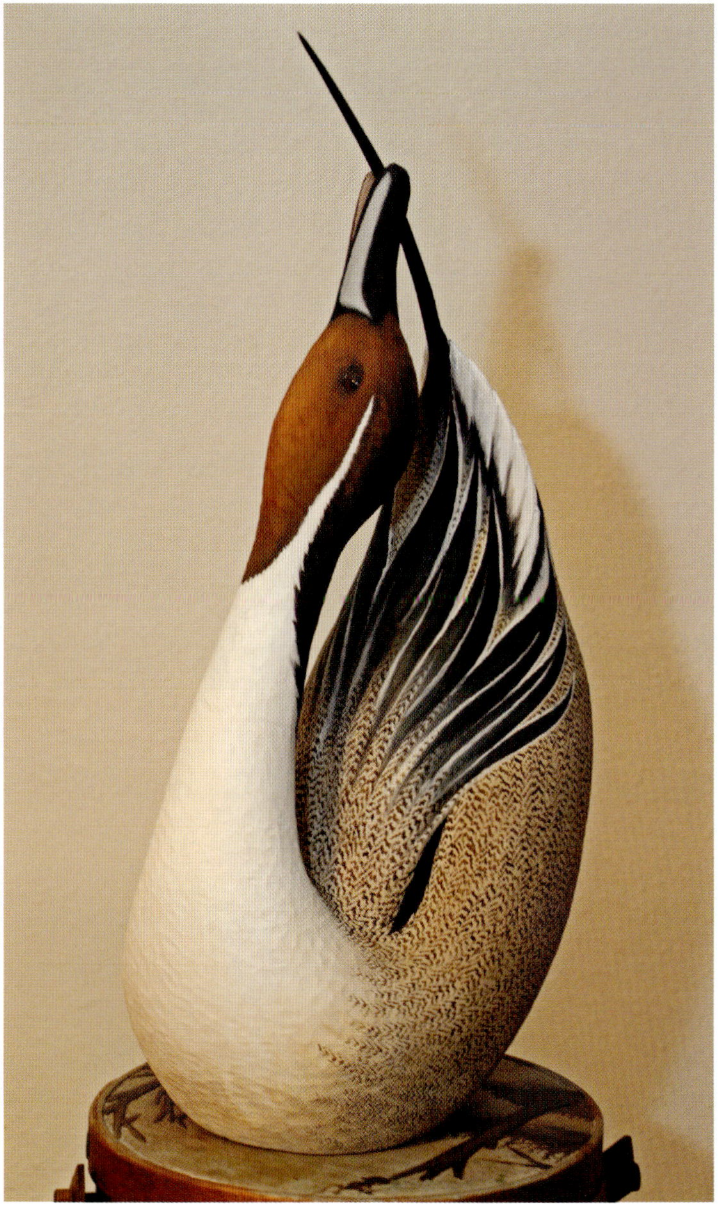

We spent a significant amount of time talking about duck and goose hunting and the future of wooden wildfowl decoys. Chris pointed out that the two are intimately related. The ever-increasing cost of good hunting leases, if available at all, and similar increases in the price of shotguns and shotgun shells has caused a significant decrease in the number of wildfowl hunters. This results in a decreased demand for hunting decoys, wooden or synthetic. It may have also reduced demand for mantle birds because, in time, there may be no hunts that evoke nostalgic memories. This has occurred in other areas of the country, including the Chesapeake Bay, where wildfowl hunting and decoy carving was once a way of life, as it remains in Louisiana today.

Three things cause me to strongly believe that this dire prediction will not come to pass, at least not in Louisiana. First, Chris said he was hunting over decoys he carved and fishing with lures he made, which he finds thrilling because it is "preserving the legacy." Second, a significant number of Louisiana carvers are experiencing increased demand for old-style hunting decoys. Third, there is a large number of decoy carving shows and competitions in Louisiana today and all seem to be very popular. Indeed, the legacy lives on.

LEFT: (12) Chis Weaver's preening pintail

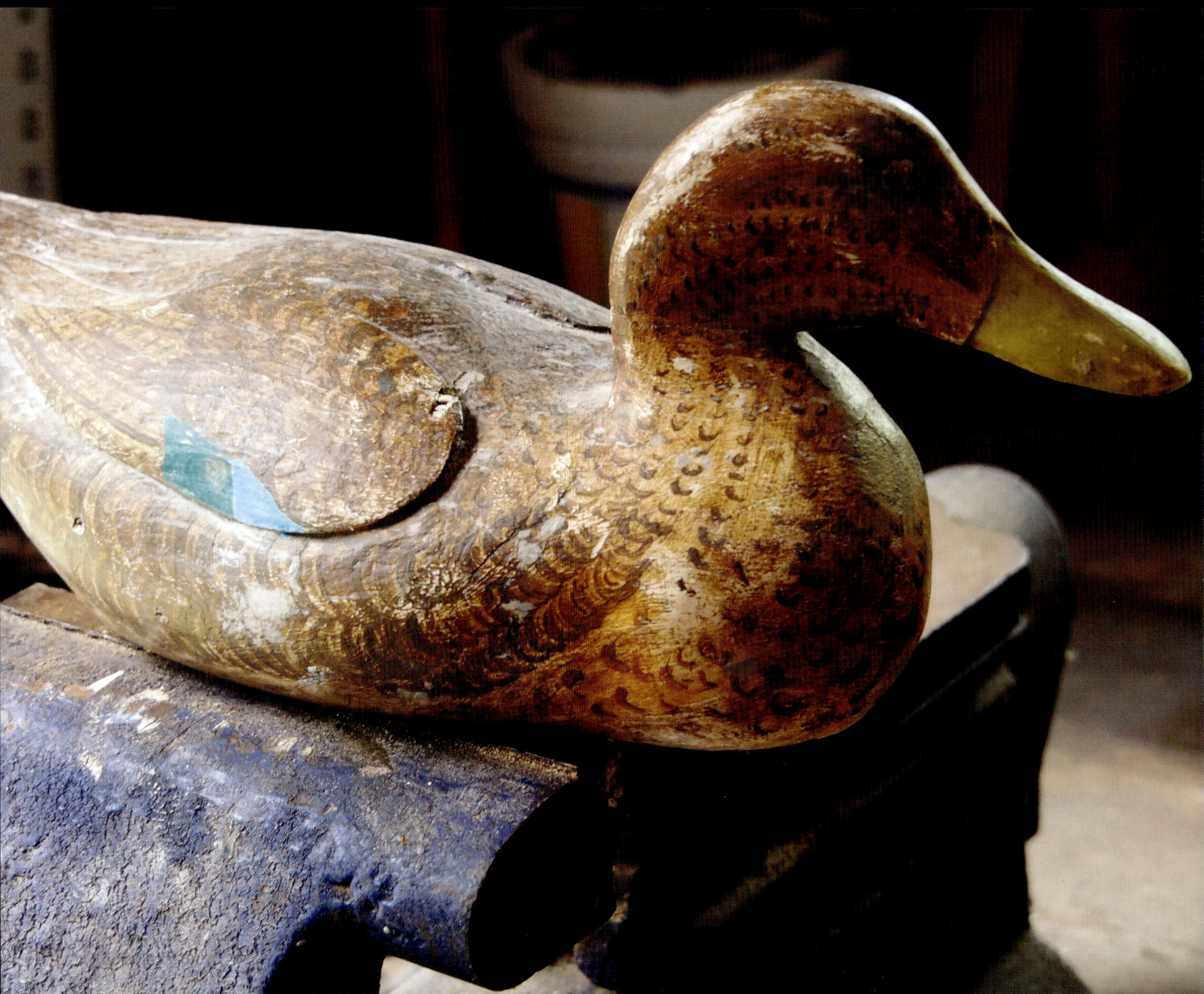

Opposite page: (2) One of Zeringue's well-worn "retired decoys" he carved early in his career

19 Rock Zeringue

Wildfowl Carver, Home and Boat Builder, Furniture Maker and Painter

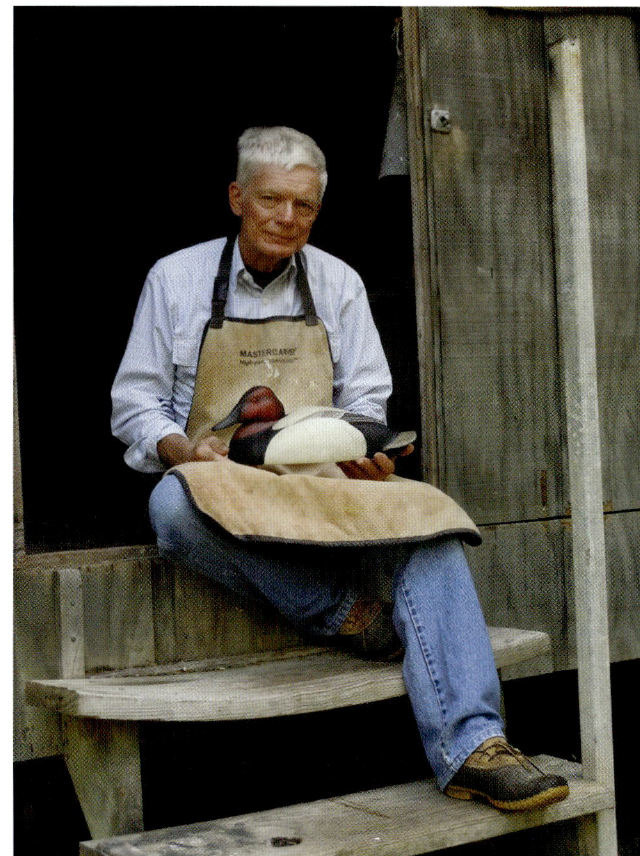

When describing Rock Zeringue, the following words are especially fitting: kind, unpretentious, friendly, multi-talented, artistic, compassionate, innovative, meticulous, and sportsman. He is a home and boat builder, painter, furniture maker, and an exceptionally versatile and accomplished decoy carver.

Rock was born in 1944 and graduated from Holy Cross High School in New Orleans. He attended the University of Southwestern Louisiana for two years but dropped out when Hurricane Betsy caused massive damage to New Orleans and Rock, a member of the Louisiana National Guard, was mobilized and sent home to help with the recovery. Later, he went to work for New Orleans Public Service Incorporated (NOPSI) and became the shift supervisor of a crew tasked with moving electricity from generators to various substations. Rock married his lovely wife, Sheila, in 1969 and the couple have two grown children. Rock speaks fondly of his wife, crediting her for raising two wonderful children and being the biggest fan of his artistic endeavors. He and Shelia were longtime residents of Kenner, Louisiana, but they decided years ago to move to Pearlington, Mississippi, and construct a home on some land that Rock owned. The planning and early construction started several years before Rock retired from Entergy (formerly NOPSI) in 1999 after thirty-five years of service. Rock and Sheila built their residence entirely by themselves. It is shown in photograph 1. Outbuildings,

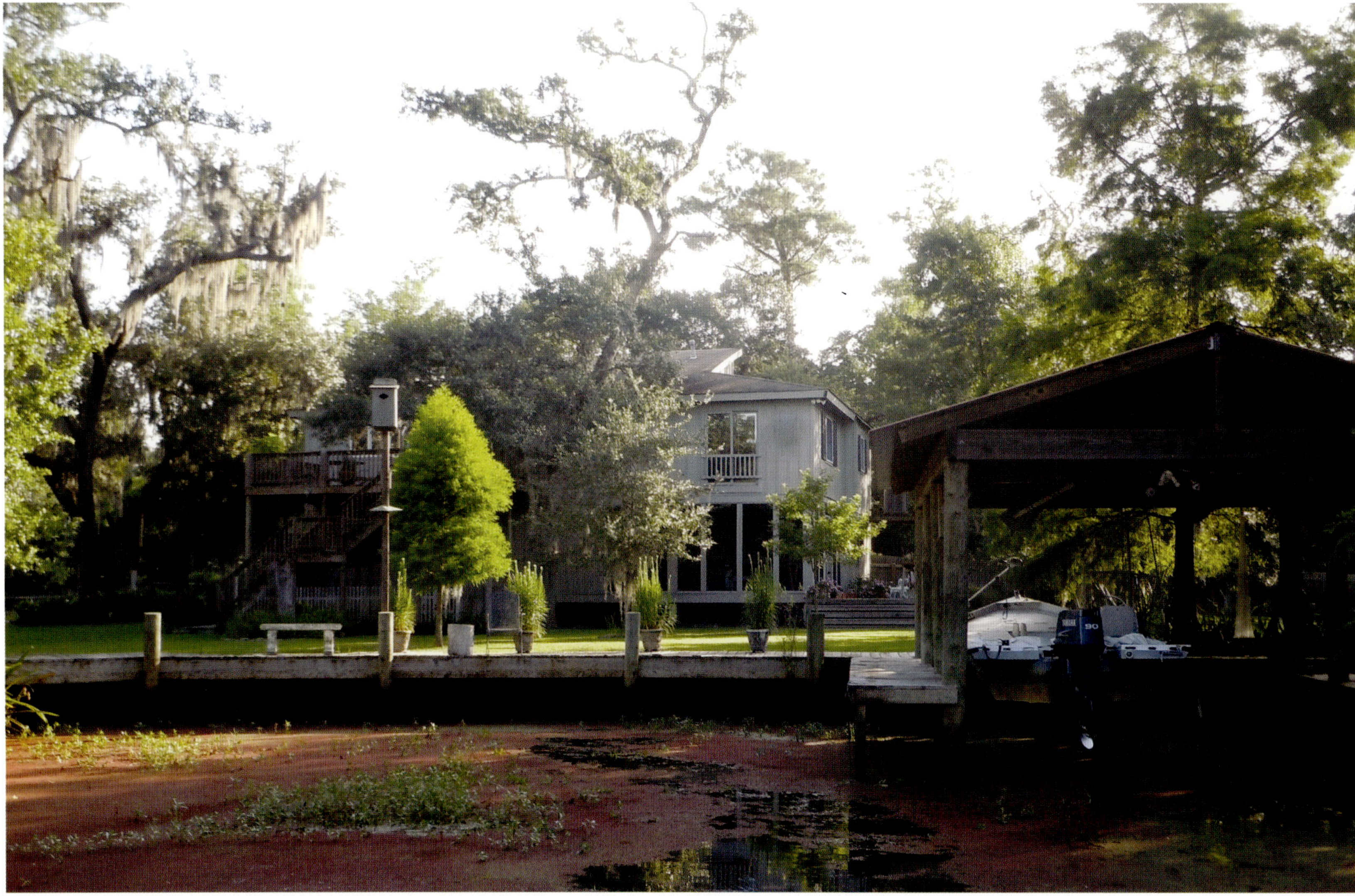

(1) Zeringue's waterside home and boat

including Rock's workshop and a large boathouse, were added later. As a completion bonus, Rock carved and gave Sheila an exquisite sinker cypress sideboard.

The Zeringue residence is located at the end of a canal that leads to the East Pearl River and the surrounding game-filled marshes. It is a perfect place for this outdoorsman and his wife to live, observe nature, and pursue both of their artistic endeavors; his decoy carving, other kinds of woodworking, and painting, and her photography. It allows Rock to make frequent observational forays into the marsh, armed with a camera and sketchpad. Rock now enjoys hunting wildlife with his camera rather than a shotgun in large part because of his love of and respect for nature.

In his younger days Rock was an avid duck hunter, and, for many years, he belonged to the Roseau Club on Rabbit Island at the mouth of the Rigolets. He "paid his dues" by building and repairing duck blinds, putting out the decoys, building pirogues and flatboats, and guiding club members.

Rock is a self-taught decoy carver; he made his own hunting rig when he was seventeen years old. In the beginning, he simply didn't know that anyone else carved decoys. A few years later Rock started hunting with an older gentleman, also a member of the Roseau Club and the regional distributor for Victor Majestic Decoy and Trap Co., which made plastic decoys. Rock brought his elder hunting companion to the duck blind, put out the decoys, and retrieved the downed birds. Rock believed that every decoy spread should include a number of poule d'eau, usually called coot in Louisiana. Victor Majestic didn't make poule d'eau decoys so Rock carved some out of balsa wood retrieved from old life rafts and gave them to the Roseau Club. They proved to be very effective and really launched Rock's career as a decoy carver. Photograph 2 (pg. 158) shows a decoy that Rock carved to hunt over early in his career. Photographs 3 and 3a shows some hunting slicks that he carved later.

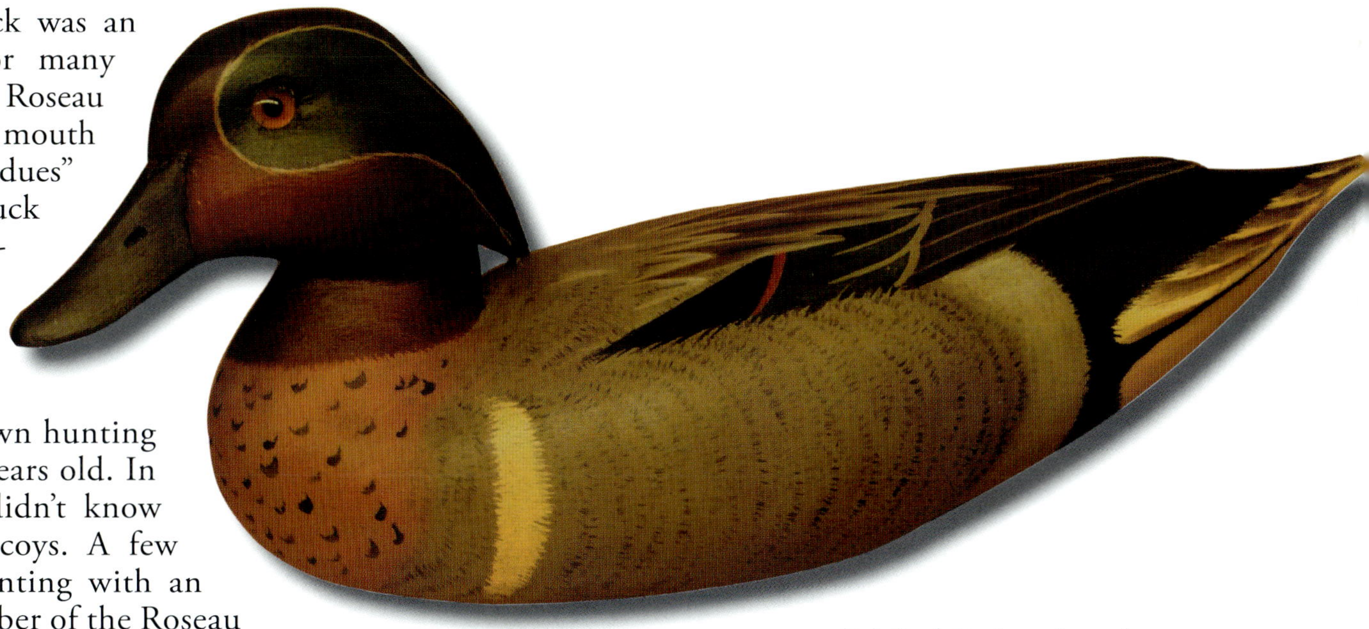

(3a) Rock Zeringue's modern green-winged teal drake gunner

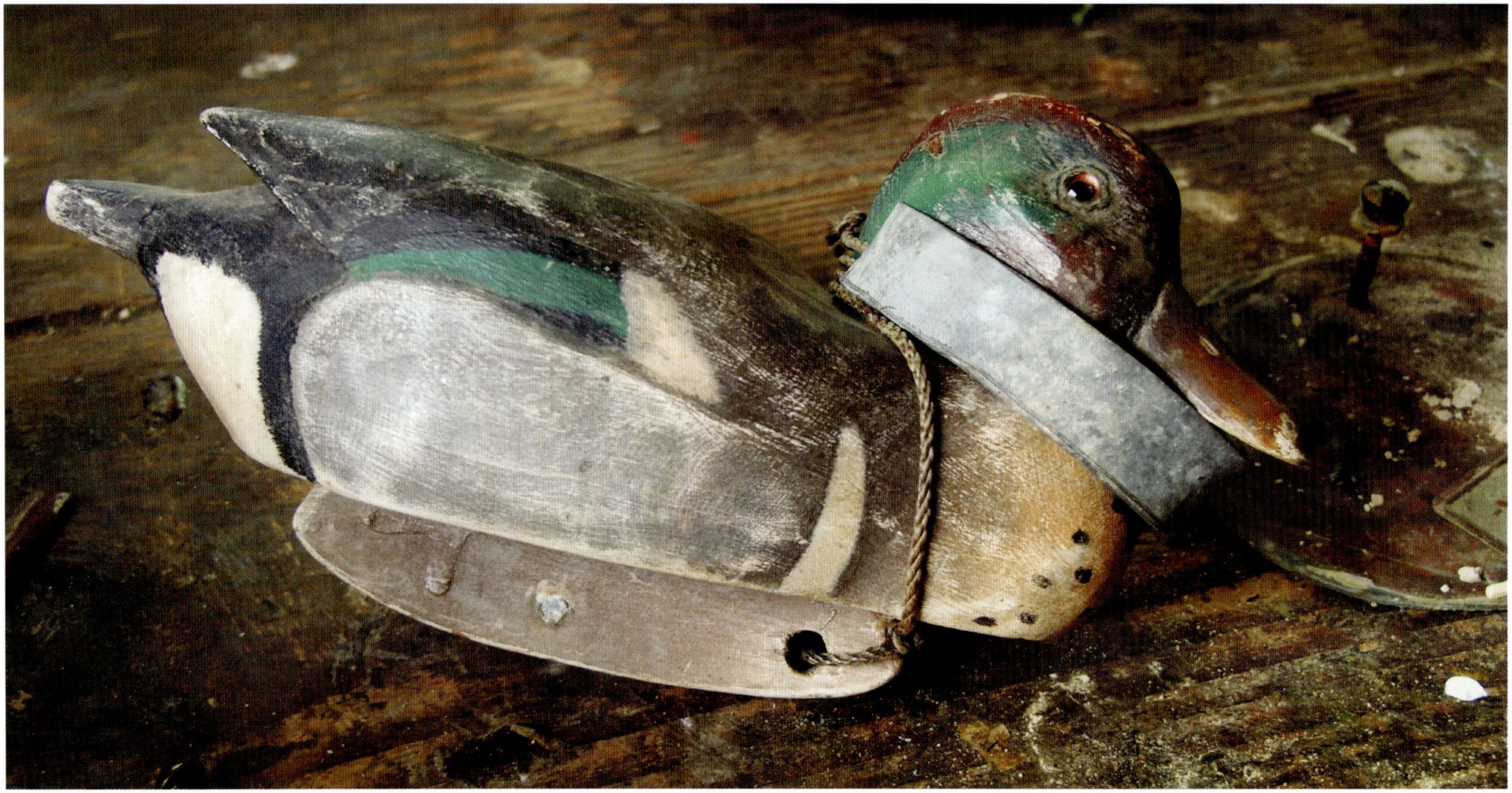

(3) A worn but working decoy carved by Zeringue

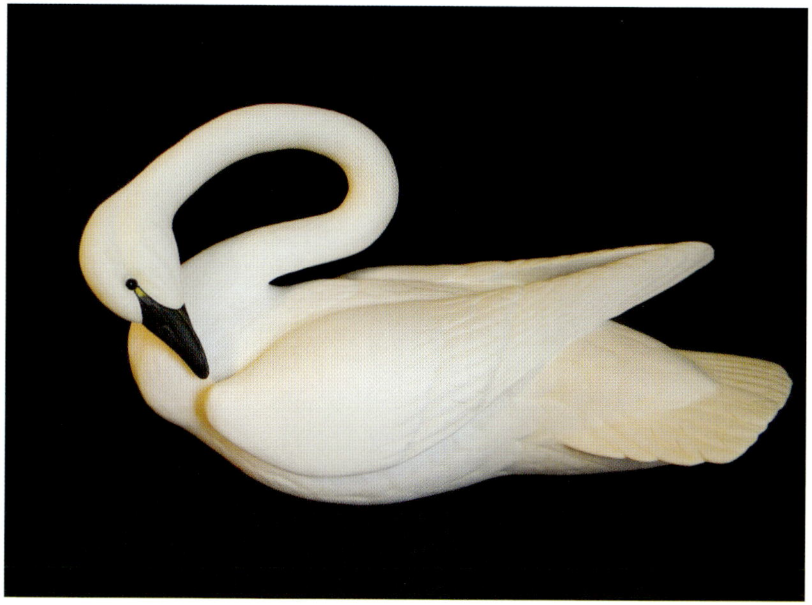

Left: (4) Rock Zeringue's preening decorative swan

Below: (5) Rock Zeringue's decorative pintail drake

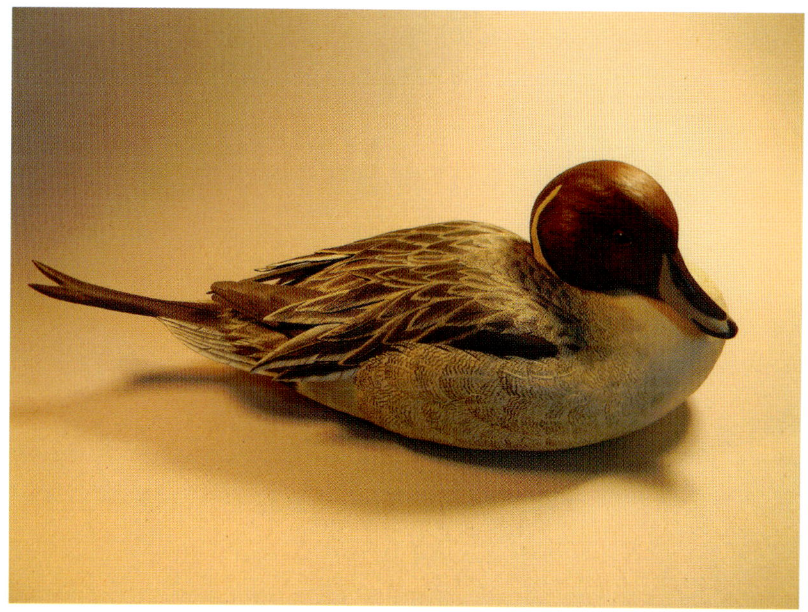

Rock started selling decoys in 1972. Interestingly, his first customer was Adler's Jewelry Store, which bought his decorative miniatures for $120 each. By then, Rock was getting advice from Al Muller, a highly respected New Orleans carver, and, later, from Mike Frady. Rock and Mike became very friendly, and Rock would harvest and trade cypress root for Frady's decoys. Some of Rock's proudest possessions are five personally inscribed decoys that Frady carved for him and Sheila

Rock rapidly progressed to carving decorative decoys that were commissioned by major corporations, like those shown in photographs 4, 5, and 6. Rock says, with a wry smile, that "my decorative decoys paid for our Pearlington home." Soon Rock's decoys were winning awards, but Rock dislikes competitive carving contests and has

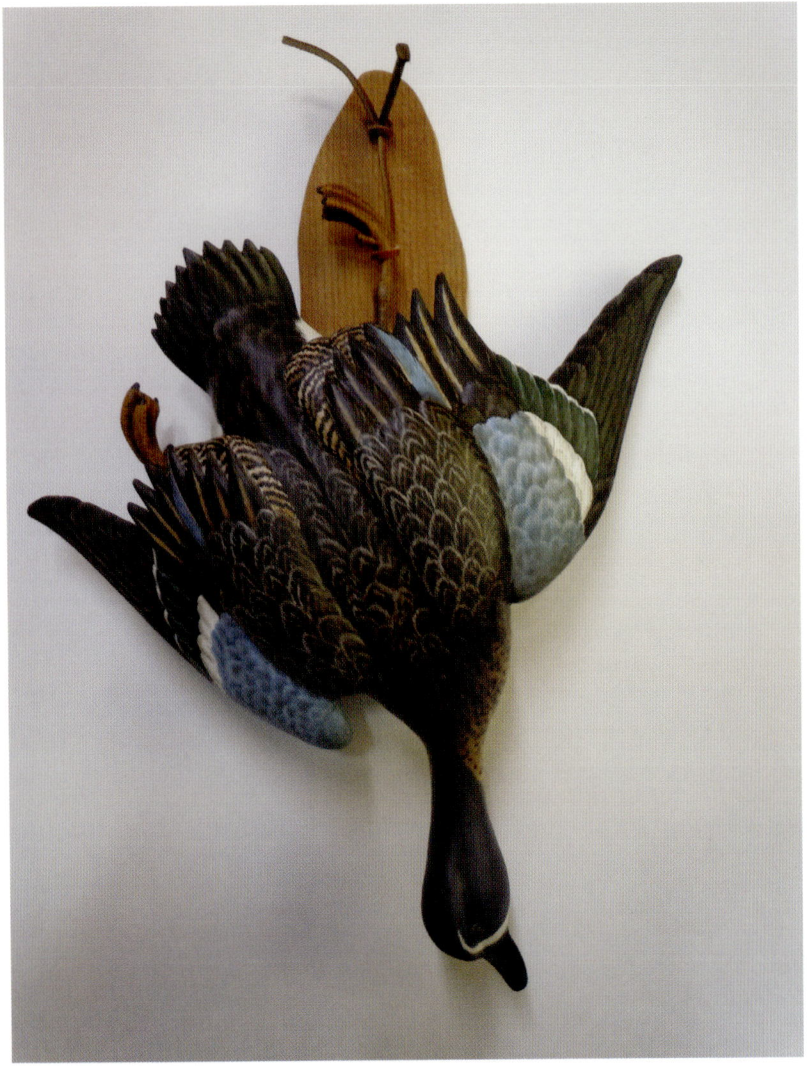

(6) Rock Zeringue's
decorative hanging blue-winged teal drake

rarely entered such events in recent years. However, he was very pleased to have had a number of his decoys on display during the 2008 *Birds of a Feather* exhibition at The Historic New Orleans Collection and even prouder that two of his decoys were retained as part of that prestigious organization's permanent collection.

Over time, Rock got burned out carving decoratives and turned his attention to carving slicks, which he calls "hunting birds," like those shown in photograph 3 and 3a, and decorative gunners, which he calls "contemporary birds," like those shown in photographs 7, 8, and 9.

Rock's hunting birds and his contemporary birds, if they are to be hunted over, have a unique feature, albeit not a visible one. As previously mentioned, wooden hunting decoys usually have two weak spots—the bill and the neck/body joint—that tend to break unless very carefully handled. Rock solved this problem by reinforcing these two areas. After completing the carving but before the decoy is painted, Rock drills one small hole that extends from the end of the bill into the decoy's head. Next, he drills another hole from the top of the decoy's head that extends into the body. Then, he takes two pieces of bamboo and drives one into each of the holes as shown in photograph 10. Finally, he cuts off the protruding pieces of bamboo and paints the decoy. Rock's innovation produces a decoy that has a stronger bill and a stronger neck/body joint than any other carver who doesn't use a functional reinforcing method. No wonder there is such a high demand for Zeringue's hunting decoys.

When asked why wooden decoys have again become popular, Rock explained that it's partly due to nostalgia and partly due to a belief that wooden decoys are more

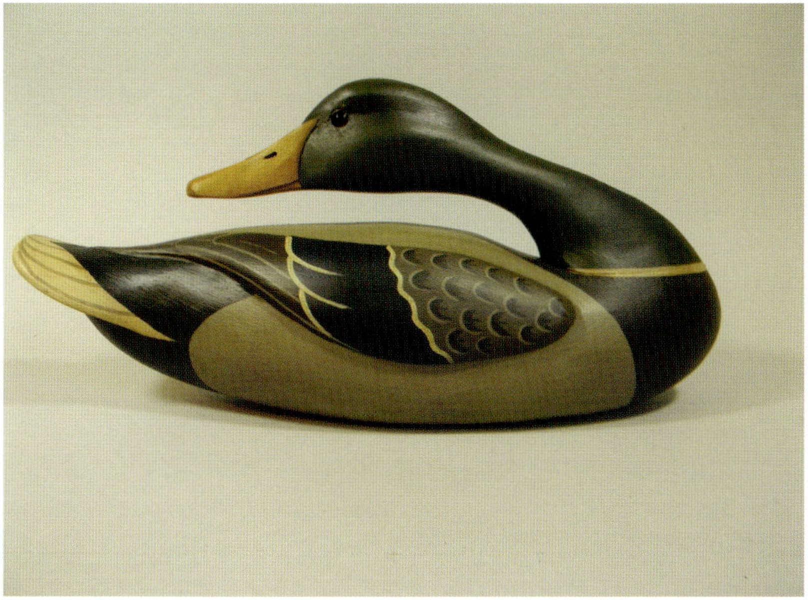

Left: (7) Rock Zeringue's modern preening mallard drake

Below: (8) Rock Zeringue's blue-winged teal drake hunting decoy

lifelike because they "ride the water" more realistically than plastic ones. Reason enough to pay $300 each for Rock's hunting decoys, provided you are a good enough shot to hit the ducks and not the decoys.

As with most contemporary carvers, Rock uses patterns and carves his decoys out of cypress or tupelo gum. He prefers cypress, which has been abundant until recent years. He reverently explains that cypress subtlety changes colors with every pass of his drawknife and produces images in the wood that leave him awestruck. Rock says that cypress has gotten scarce in the wild and now 95 percent of his decoys are carved out of tupelo gum, which is every bit as good as cypress for making decoys, just a bit more difficult to carve. Regardless of the wood used, Rock's decoys are a fine addition to anyone's hunting rig or display shelf.

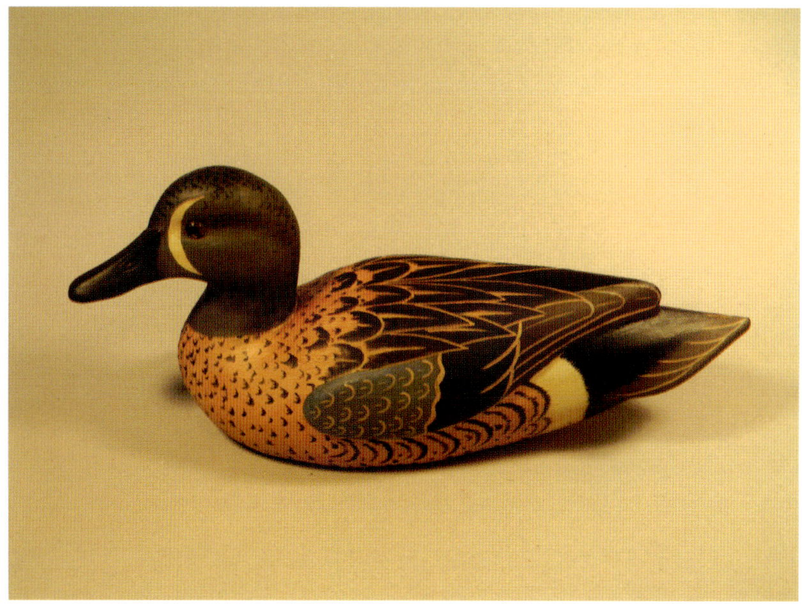

In recent years, Rock began painting wildfowl in the "nature morte" style favored by George Louis Viavant, the famous New Orleans painter of the 1920s. Rock's decoy carving friend, the late Mike Frady, was also an accomplished painter. It is thought that both men were inspired to take up painting by the many years they spent observing wildfowl in the coastal marshes of Louisiana and Mississippi.

Strangely enough, it was Rock's painting, coupled with his indomitable spirit, that saved the Zeringue's home, which was badly damaged by Hurricane Katrina when it came ashore at Pearlington on August 29, 2005. Rock and Sheila had evacuated before Katrina struck. Among the few things they were able to take with them was a painting that Rock had just finished for a married couple who lived in South Carolina. A few days after the storm struck, Sheila and Rock returned to Pearlington and saw that their home was devastated and uninhabitable. Rock and Sheila were quoted in the local newspaper five days after the storm as saying that they were leaving the coastal community and moving to higher ground because their home was beyond repair. Then, fate intervened; the Zeringues decided to drive to South Carolina and deliver the painting in person. The clients were so pleased with the painting and so touched when they heard about the damage to the Zeringues' property that they arranged for five volunteers to go to Pearlington and help the Zeringues clear away the debris and repair the damage. Thankfully, the Zeringues, aided greatly by this volunteer crew, did repair and rebuild. Now, nearly ten years later, life in Pearlington has returned to normal and Rock's artistic work is better than ever.

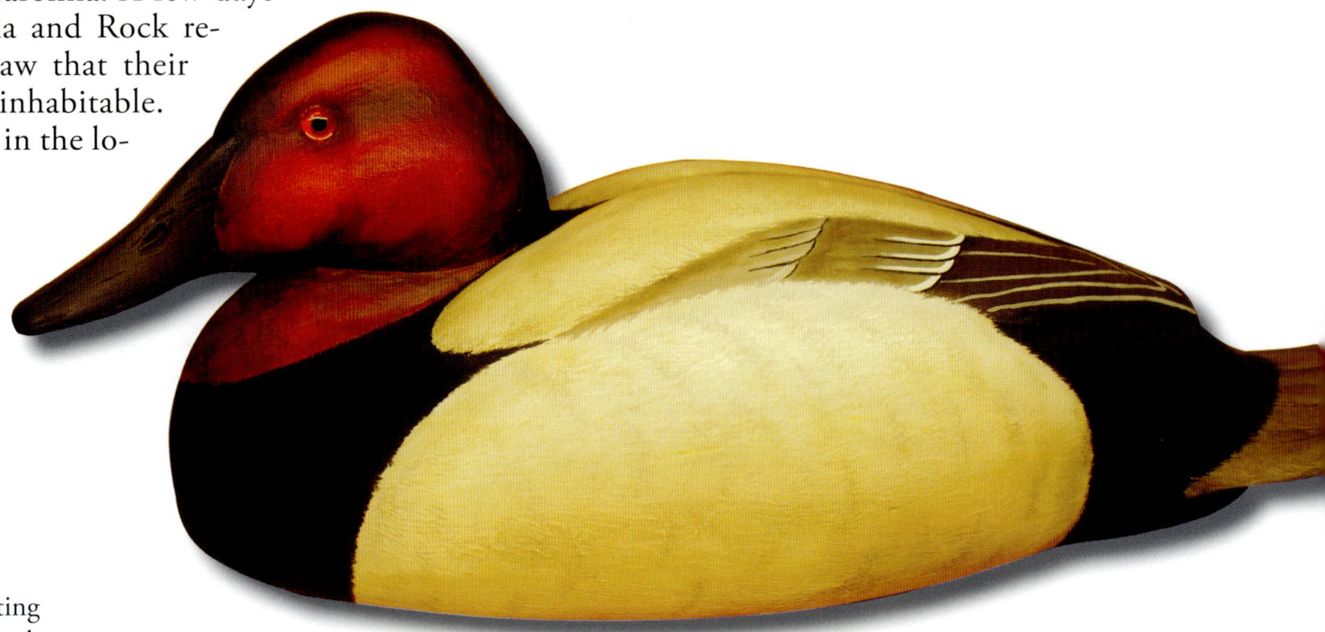

(9) Rock Zeringue's resting canvasback drake hunting decoy

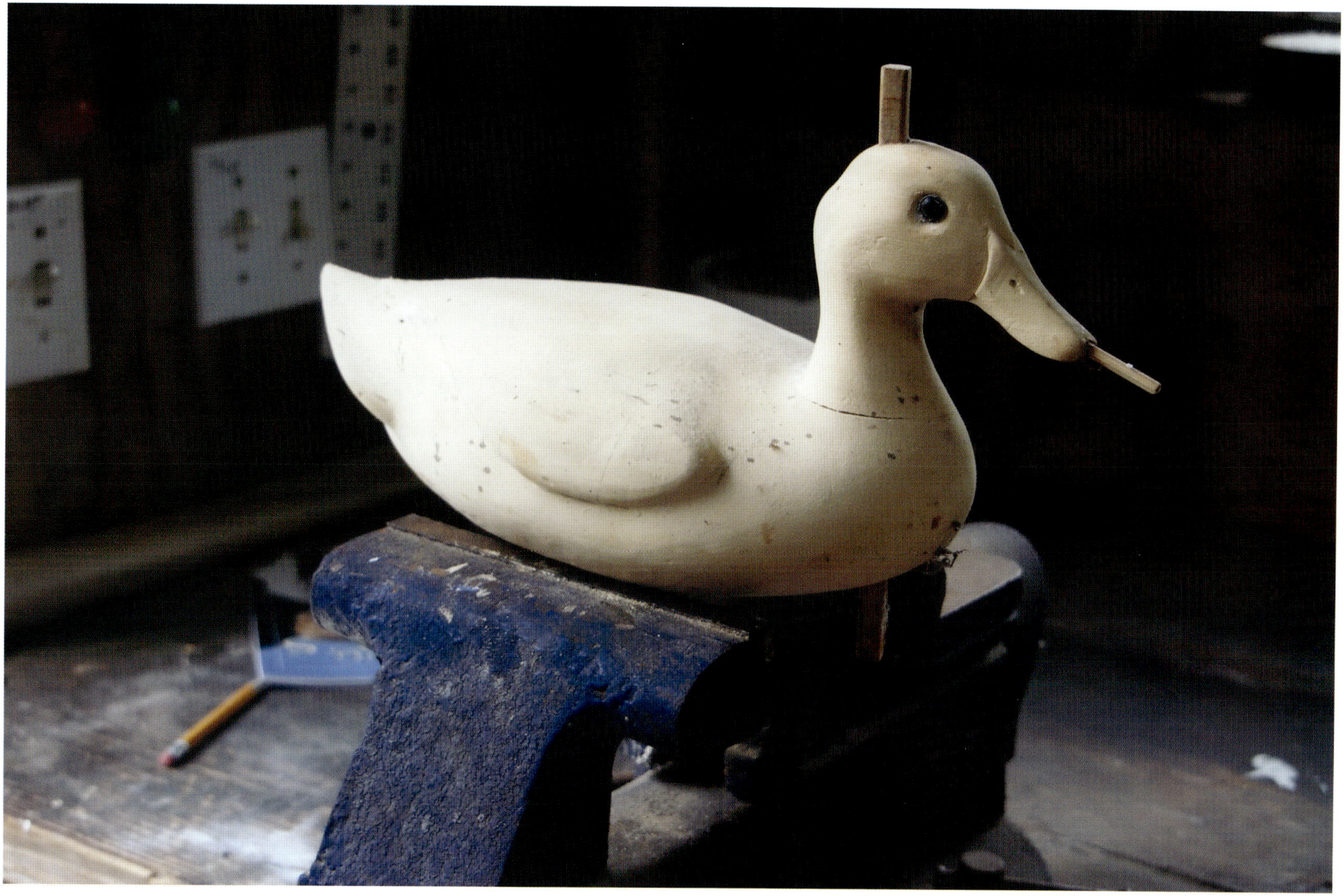

(10) An unpainted Zeringue decoy, note the "pegs" to reinforce the bill and neck

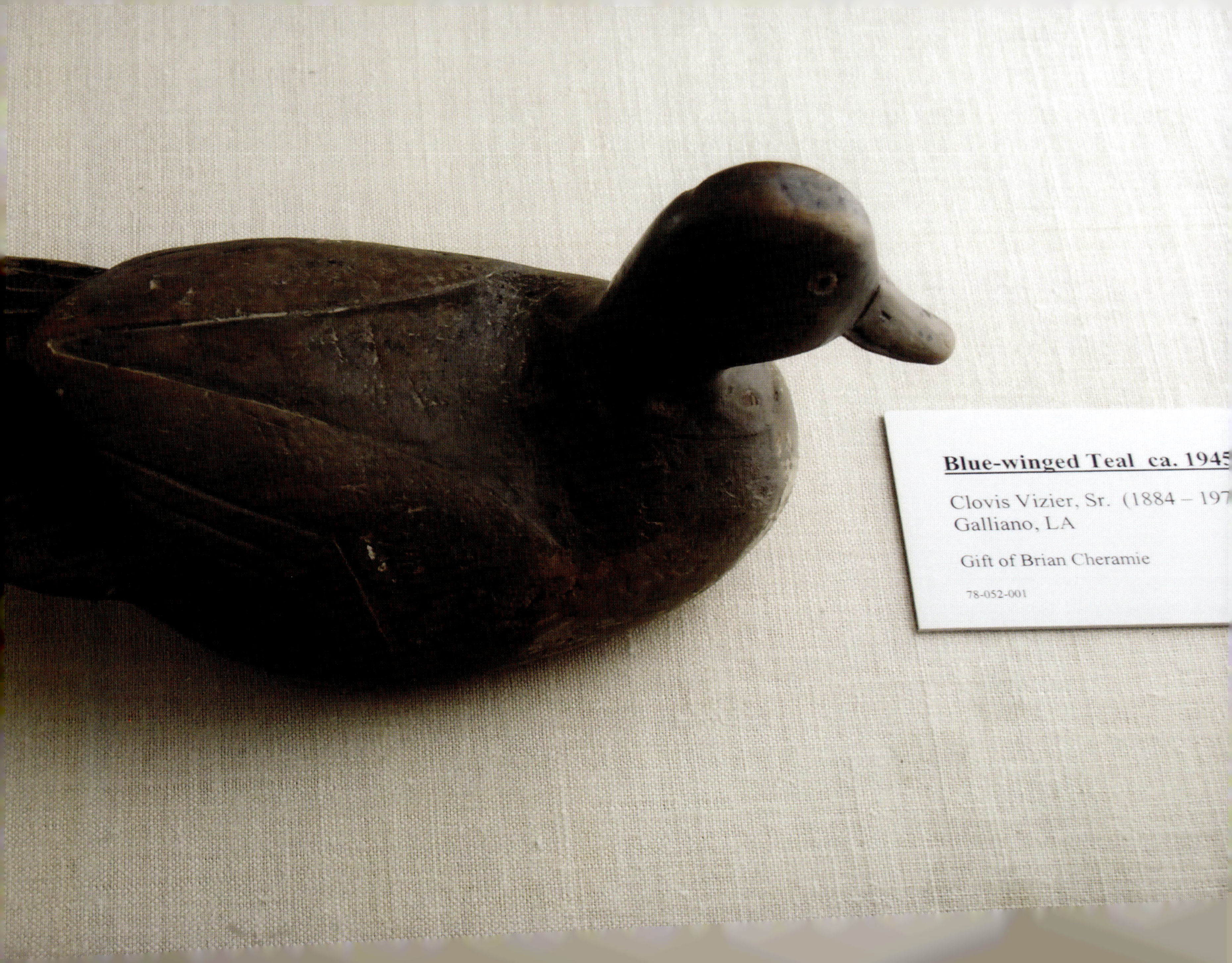
Blue-winged Teal ca. 1945
Clovis Vizier, Sr. (1884 – 197
Galliano, LA
Gift of Brian Cheramie
78-052-001

20 RESTORATION VS. COUNTERFEITING

Why write about restoration and counterfeiting old masters' decoys in a book about contemporary carvers and their decoys? [1]

Foremost, because it takes a skilled contemporary carver to create a counterfeit replica. Making copies of someone else's decoys isn't bad when done openly, and it can be quite beneficial in repairing and restoring old masters' works. But, when done for unscrupulous purposes, copying and passing off a counterfeit decoy as a genuine old master's hurts the buyer, the collectors' market, and the carver. It is generally agreed that decoy counterfeiting reduces the demand for and, hence, the selling price of the copied carver's work. By concealing the identity of the copying carver, it also prevents that carver from getting the recognition he or she deserves, thus negatively impacting the demand for and the price of that carver's decoys, as well. It is in the contemporary carvers' interests, as well as that of the collectors of their work, to prevent this from happening.

Old wooden hunting decoys are relatively fragile. They were frequently kept in burlap sacks or bushel baskets and were carried in those primitive decoy bags from their off-season storage place to the duck blind and back. No special care was used when handling the decoys because they only cost about $2.00 each when originally purchased. As a consequence, neck and bill breakage was common. Besides needing to repair broken parts or replace lead weights and anchor lines, it was also necessary to repaint the decoys periodically. Floating in the marsh was hard on the wooden decoy's paint and damage from shotgun pellets was not uncommon, as decoys sometimes fooled hunters as well as ducks. During the off-season, damage was repaired and the decoys that needed it were repainted, which usually meant a new coat was simply put over the old paint. If the decoy's owner was skilled enough, he or she would likely do it themselves. If not, the owner knew someone who was either the original or another skilled carver. If the broken decoy wasn't repaired or repairable, it was probably either used as firewood or kept in the storage shed until later discarded. The scenario changed in the 1970s, however, when there was an old hunting decoy renaissance in Louisiana.

Damaged decoys, some fifty years old or older, often wound up in the hands of collectors who wanted them repaired so they could be displayed. Besides fixing broken bills or necks and repainting the bird, collectors occasionally wanted more extensive work done, like replacing a decoy's head. Collectors needed to pay skilled contemporary carvers do this kind of work. Restoring the appearance of an old decoy preserves a valuable piece of art, just as a museum restores a fine painting. An artfully restored decoy can look as good as it did when it was new, but restoration experts agree that it should not look better. A very good example is the Lafrance trio's mallard hen that had the head replaced and then masterfully repainted by Bill Hanemann. This restored decoy is shown in photograph 1.

It is fair to call an old decoy that has undergone major repairs, like replacing a head, a "hybrid" decoy. When a hybrid has been renovated by a highly regarded contemporary carver, it is still very valuable but not as valuable as one of the old master's decoys that has not been extensively worked on, as long as its weathered condition is what one would expect of wooden folk art that is more than fifty years old.

Early on, the carver doing the restoration rarely signed the decoy or otherwise indicated it had been repaired. As a result, only a few with great expertise could tell the difference between a well-restored decoy and an unrepaired masterpiece by one of the great old carvers. Well-done restoration is a very good thing as long as there is full disclosure if the decoy changes hands. However, it also creates an opportunity for unscrupulous people to conceal the truth about the restoration and sell the decoy to a collector for the far higher price commanded by an unrepaired masterpiece. Unfortunately, there is a direct correlation between demand for and the value of old Louisiana masters' decoys and decoy counterfeiting.

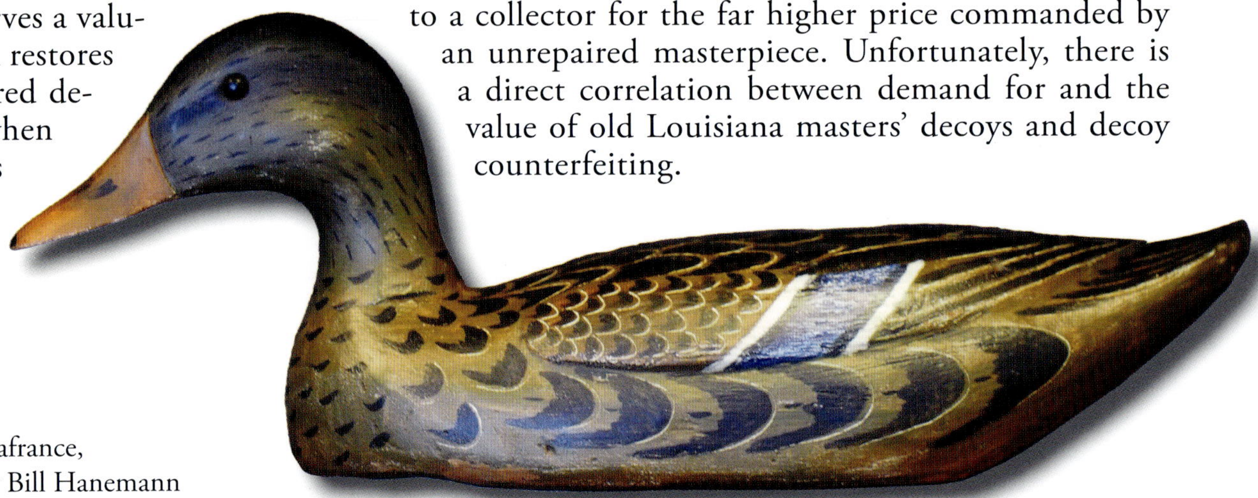

(1) Mallard hen, body by Lafrance,
head replaced and decoy painted by Bill Hanemann

On occasion, a decoy collector commissions a contemporary carver to create a "mate" for decoys carved by one of the old masters. Typically the collector asks that this mate be carved and painted in the same style as the genuine one. He also asks the carver to use distressing techniques to make it appear to be the same vintage as the genuine decoy. Upon completion, the newly carved mate is usually indistinguishable from the real thing because the contemporary carver is often as talented as the old master and usually has far better tools and paint to work with. A good contemporary carver has aging techniques and knows how to use them. Nonetheless, it is only a copy of the real thing. Photograph 2 is a mallard drake that was carved by Bill Hanemann as a mate for the mallard hen shown in photograph 1. This mallard drake is a counterfeit copy. If the person commissioning the decoy conceals its provenance and passes it off as the real thing to an unsuspecting buyer, that is fraudulent conduct.

If a decoy has had minor repair work done on it, like having a bill replaced or a broken neck repaired, or if the decoy has been repainted and the owner had the work done or knows that it had been done; should that information be given to a prospective purchaser if the owner decides to sell that decoy?

Without question, the answer is "Yes." Does it often go unannounced? In my experience the answer is again "Yes." This is wrong, even though the nondisclosure can be rationalized on the basis that such minor repair work was usual and should not substantially lower the value of the decoy.

What, if anything, should be told to a prospective buyer if the owner of the decoy has had major repair work done on it, like replacing the head, and then decides to sell it?

In these circumstances, the seller must disclose the fact that the decoy has a replaced head if that fact is known. Such a major change can materially lower the value of the decoy depending on how well the replacement was done. Concealment of a known material fact is fraud and may be a crime. Obviously, the same thing is true if the counterfeit, i.e. copied decoy, is sold after being represented as the real thing.

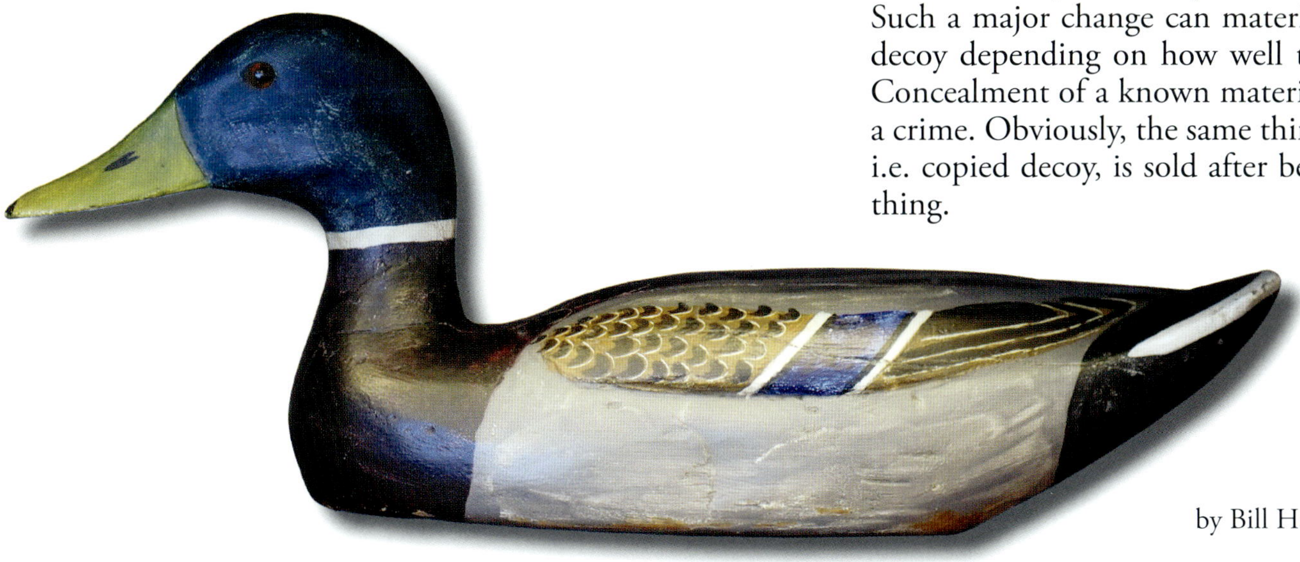

(2) Mallard drake
by Bill Hanemann in Lafrance Style

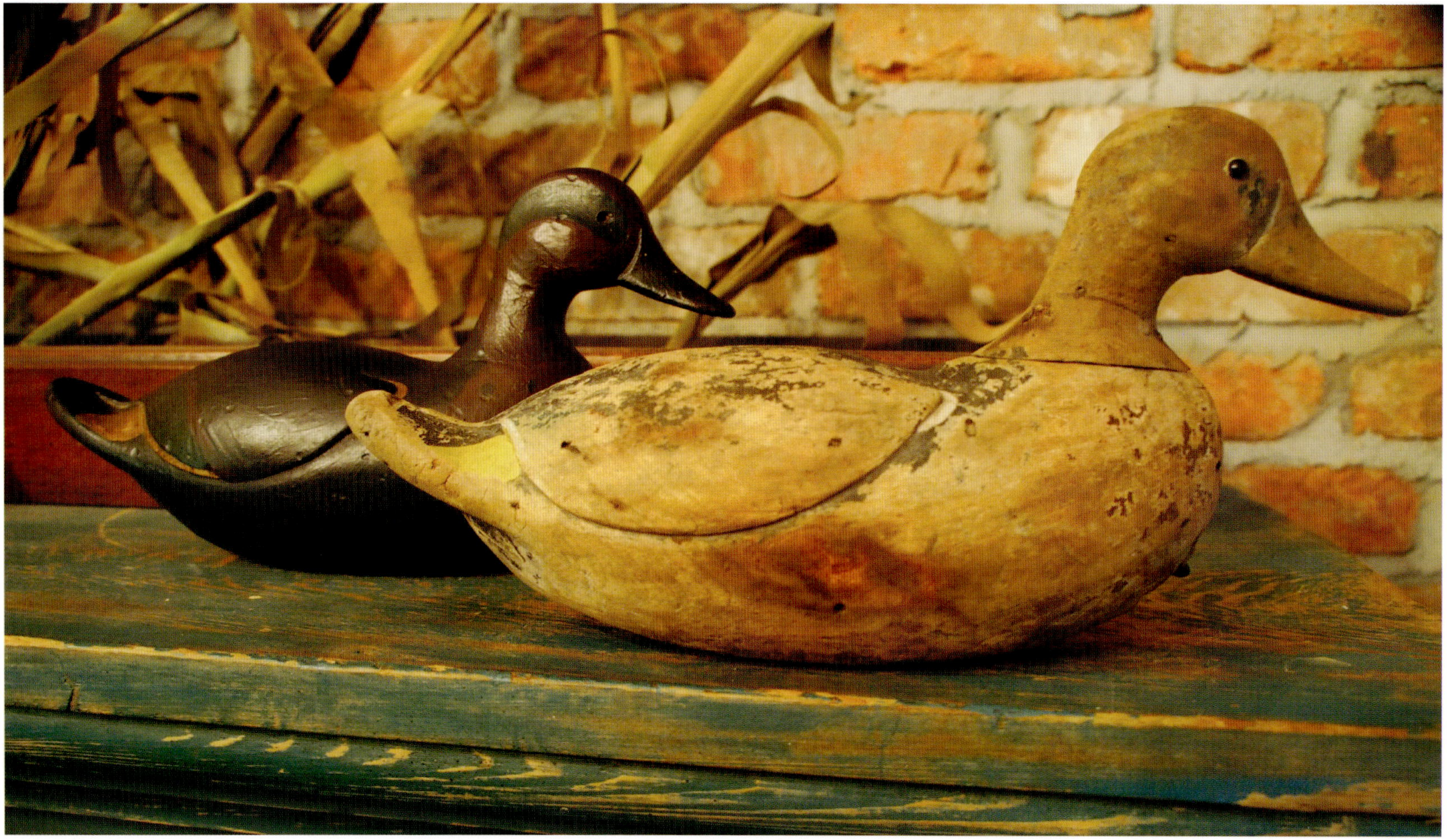

(3) Nicole Vidacovich teal on right; Bill Hanemann copy on left

How does this counterfeiting work in the decoy selling and/ or trading world?

Four things are essential. First is an uninformed and/ or gullible buyer, anxious to acquire a first-rate old decoy. Second is a knowledgeable and unscrupulous con-man who knows what decoys the buyer wants to buy. Third is a good contemporary carver willing and able to replicate the great masters' decoys for a fee and willing to forego signing the completed decoy if asked not to do so. Fourth is a market where demand for the old masters' decoys is great and the value of this unique artwork has substantially increased.

The previously mentioned books by Cheramie and Haid as well as Charlie Frank's *Wetlands Heritage* revived interest in old Louisiana hunting decoys, but, by then, essentially all of the old masters were either dead or, if alive, had quit carving, leaving few of their decoys for sale. Newcomers started collecting old Louisiana decoys, including many from out of state. These factors caused prices to rise dramatically. Sales of genuine old decoys in very good condition for $5,000 to $10,000 were not uncommon.

I know many very talented contemporary carvers and not one of them has ever knowingly carved a counterfeit decoy; that is carved a decoy in the style of an old master knowing the person commissioning the work intended to pass it off as an old master's decoys. Today, most carvers are just as anxious to stop counterfeiting as serious collectors. Fine contemporary carvers, including Bill Hanemann and Willie Badeaux, have helped me with this chapter. These two men carved the replicas needed to illustrate the counterfeiting problem and provided suggestions to help stamp out this fraudulent practice. It was mutually agreed that these copies would be labeled as such and signed by the carver otherwise they would not do the requested work.

Unfortunately, there are carvers out there who will make decoys that are virtually identical to a decoy carved by one of Louisiana's old masters. The fake is often so good that it can and does fool everyone except for the few true experts like Brian Cheramie and Bill Hanemann. That fake decoy is the essential ingredient that allows an unscrupulous person to sell that fake as the real thing. The carvers can stop this unlawful practice by refusing to create a copy of another carver's decoy. Failing to do so could make the carver an accomplice and could result in criminal sanctions if it can be shown that carver actually knew that his purchaser intended to pass off the copied decoy as the real thing. Civil liability, in the form of monetary damages, may be assessed against the copying carver if it can be shown that carver should have known the purchaser's intention to pass off the copy as the real thing to an innocent buyer.

I have been the victim of counterfeiters on more than one occasion and thus feel qualified to discuss the topic and describe how some of the more complex scams work. Likely, it was a kind of hubris that caused me to be victimized but it also gave me the experience and insight to help other collectors avoid being duped.

To help illustrate the counterfeiting problem I asked Bill Hanemann to carve a green-winged teal just like Nicole Vidacovich would have carved it and age it appropriately. I then asked Willie Badeaux to carve a pair of

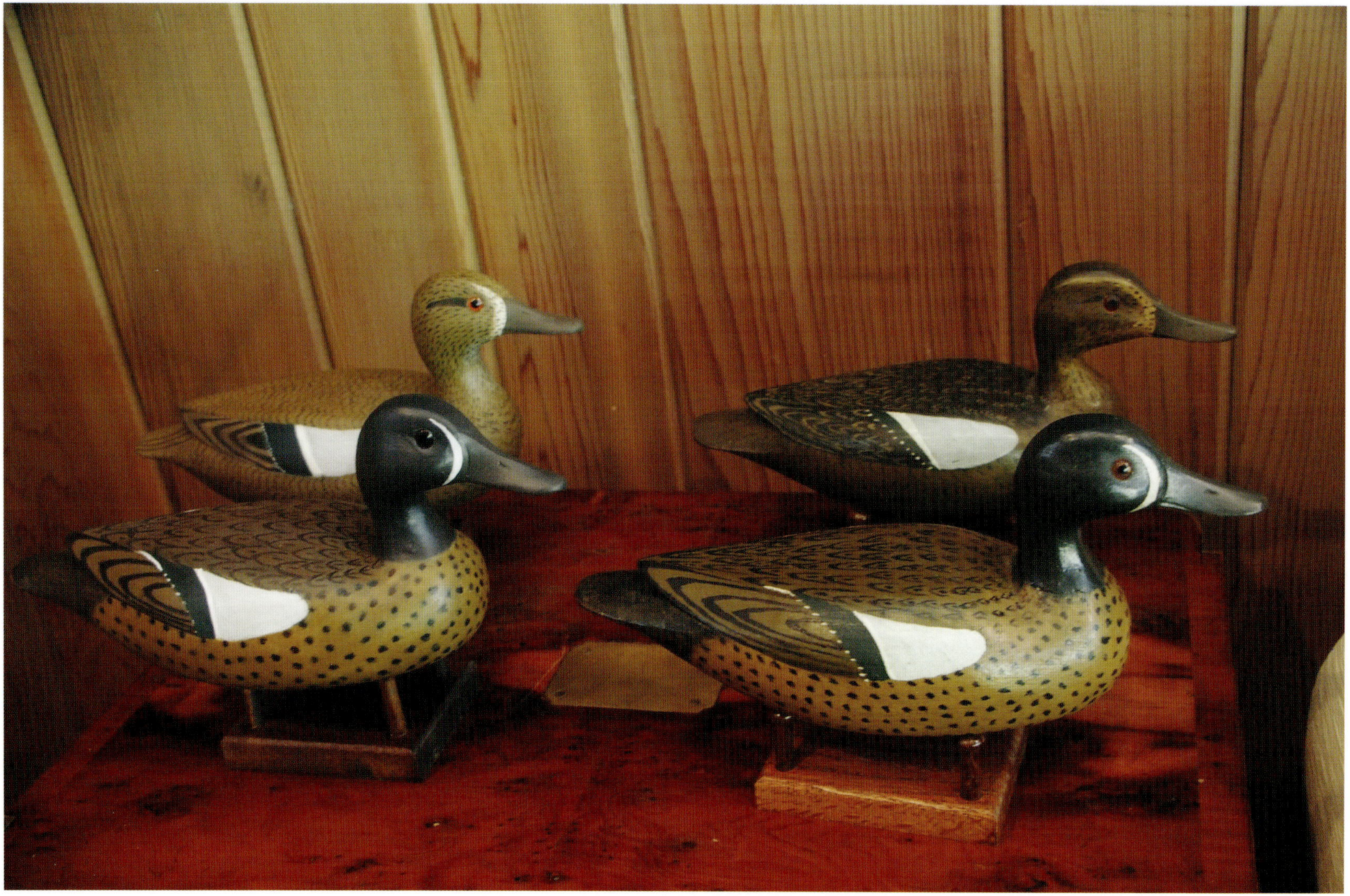

(4) Reme Roussel blue-winged teal pair on right; Willie Badeaux copies on left

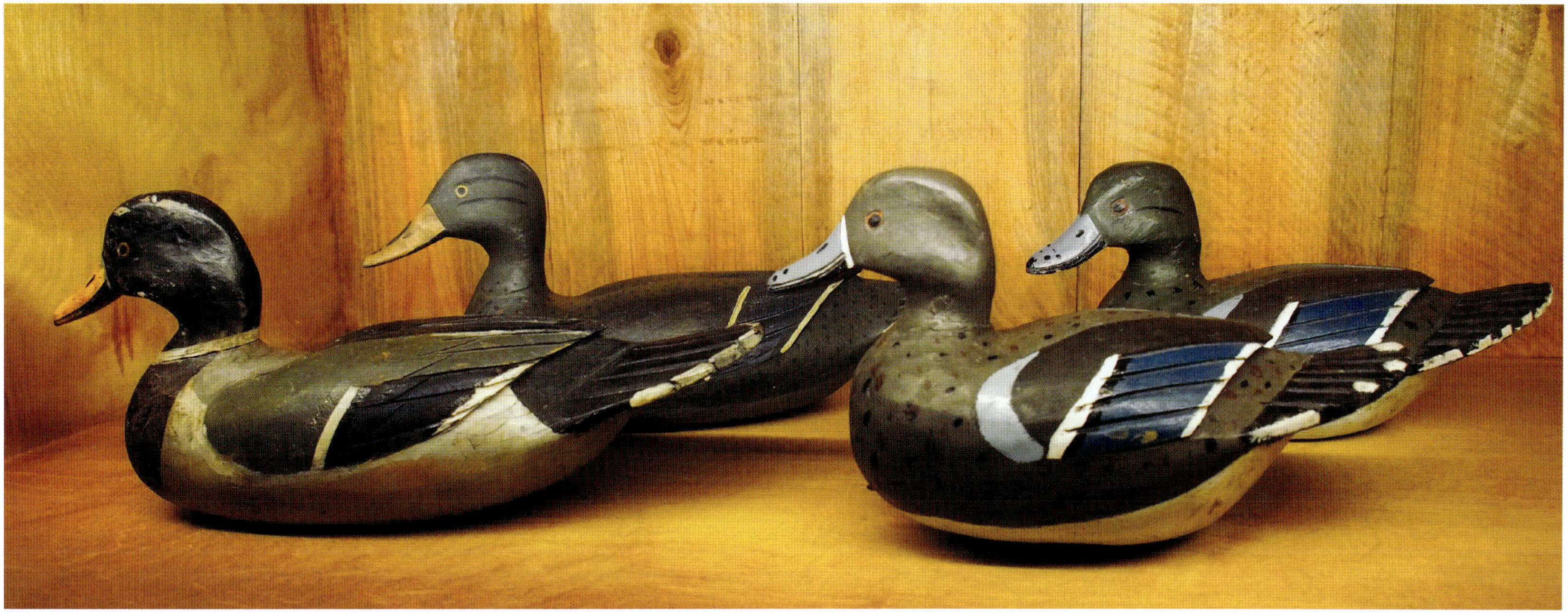

(5) Clovis Vizier mallard pair on left; unknown carver copies on right

blue-winged teal just like the ones Reme Roussel carved many years ago. The Vidacovich copy was then photographed alongside a genuine Vidacovich and is shown in photograph 3. Photograph 4 shows both the real and counterfeit Roussel copies. Photograph 5 depicts a pair of Clovis Vizier decoys and a pair of counterfeit copies that I was fooled into acquiring years ago. Your challenge is to identify the real decoys and the copies before reading their captions.

Meanwhile, let's discuss some complicated and hopefully informative counterfeiting schemes based on my own experiences. In the mid-1980s, a person calling himself a collector telephoned and asked for a meeting after telling me he had some decoys that I might be interested in buying or trading. I asked how he got my name and was told it came from another collector who was a close friend. With that entrée, he was invited to my office where I displayed most of my collection. He arrived with a sack of decoys, and after appropriate introductions, he invited me to inspect the decoys that he had brought. While I was doing this, he asked to look over my collection that was housed on shelves in an open display

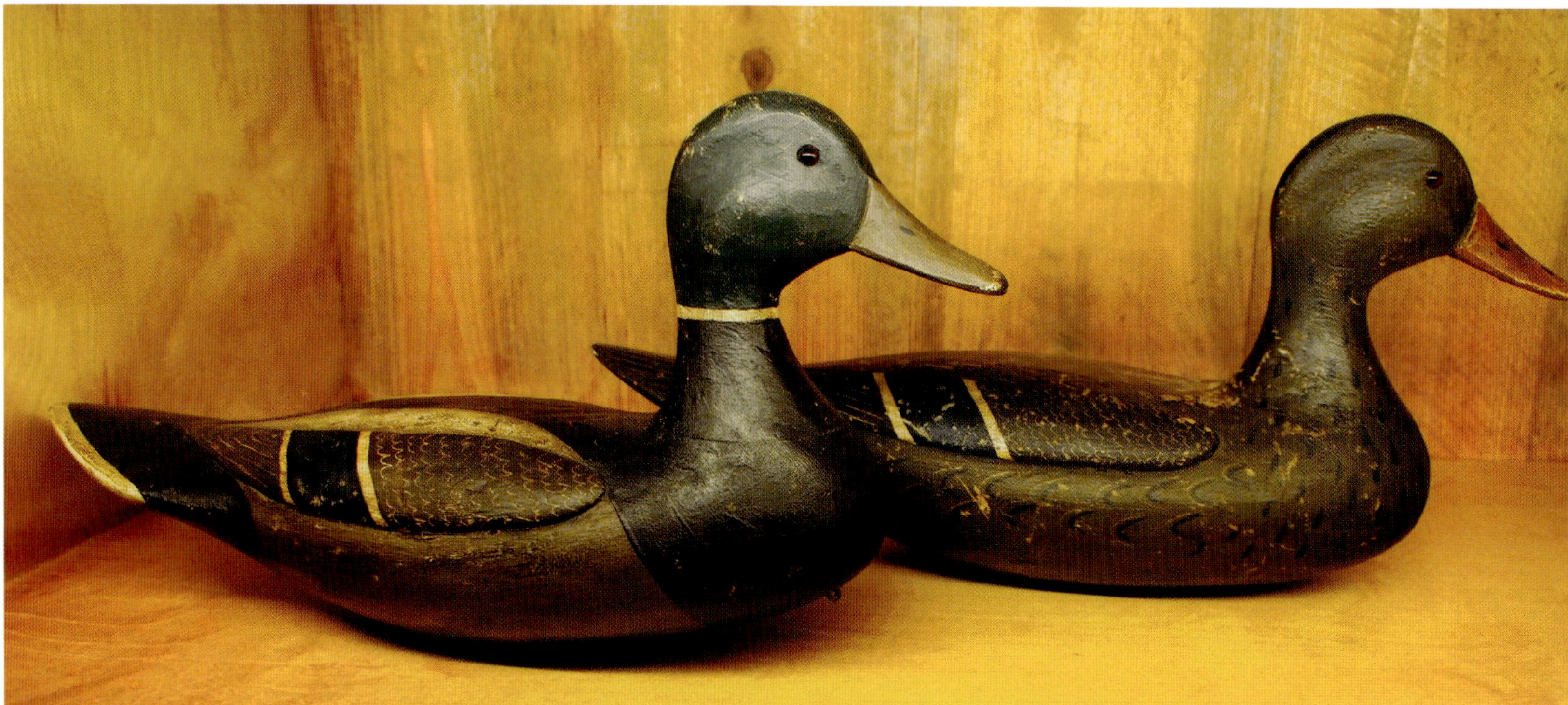

(6) Excellent copies of Gaston Isadore mallards by unknown carver

cabinet. I found one of his decoys very appealing and was told it was "a mint condition mallard hen carved by Charles Joefrau and painted by George Frederick" with an asking price of $900. After some haggling, I agreed to buy this very nice looking decoy that showed absolutely no wear for $800. I gave the collector my check and proudly put the decoy in my display cabinet. Before leaving, the collector asked if there were any other carver's decoys that I had an interest in buying or trading. I told him that I really wanted a Gaston Isadore decoy or, even better, a matched pair.

Several months later, the collector called me again to tell me that he had picked up a very nice pair of Isadore mallards from an old man from "down the river" and thought that I might be interested. I asked the price and was told we could discuss that when he brought the decoys in for me to examine. Arrangements were made to meet a few days later. At the appointed time, the collector arrived with three decoys, the most regal looking Gaston Isadore mallards I had ever seen and a fairly attractive teal by Xavier Bourg, another well-regarded old master carver. Gaston Isadore was born in 1857 and died in 1932. He lived and carved in Phoenix, a small hamlet on the Mississippi River south of New Orleans. He was a great carver and the relatively few decoys he made were all beautiful and highly prized by knowledgeable collectors. This pair was absolutely stunning as photograph 6 confirms. They did show some wear, not surprising since these decoys were between fifty and one hundred years old. I asked the selling price and was told they were not for sale but my new collector "friend" would trade his three decoys for my pair of Mossmeier mallards. Mossmeier lived in New Orleans and carved from 1920 until 1955. He carved even fewer decoys than Isadore. In fact, my mallards were, up to then, the only Mossmeier decoys I had ever seen. They were the centerpiece of my collection and were admired by knowledgeable collectors, who visited my office. I had no idea what my Mossmeier's were worth, but I was smitten and agreed to the trade.

For over thirty years my Gaston Isadore mallards and my Joefrau mallard hen graced my display case, until January 2015, when I gave up my law office when I completely retired. My decoy collection came home with me but the display case was too big to bring home so I left it in my office and put my decoys on a bookshelf in a bedroom long ago vacated by my son.

Some weeks later, I decided to have Bill Hanemann appraise a pair of Mark Whipple mallards because another collector, who was a friend, expressed an interest in buying them, and I wanted to find out what a fair price would be. Arrangements were made to visit Bill at his home, so he could examine and appraise the Whipples. I have known Bill since I first started collecting decoys. There is no dispute that he knows more about old Louisiana duck decoys and old carvers than any other person. He has repaired and restored hundreds if not thousands of old Louisiana decoys and helped curate virtually every Louisiana decoy exhibition held in any museum. He is the experts' expert when it comes to determining the authenticity of old Louisiana decoys.

I also decided to take my Gaston Isadore mallards along to have Bill "vet" these decoys and give me his views. After completing work on the Whipples, Bill turned his attention to the Isadore mallards. After carefully examining the decoys, Bill turned to me and sadly said, "Harvey, these decoys were not carved by Gaston Isadore but they are excellent copies—worth about $1,000 apiece." In other words, years earlier, I had traded a pair of Mossmeier mallards now worth at least ten times that amount for a pair of counterfeits. I was heartbroken, but things got worse.

Several weeks later, I was invited to a hunting camp cookout along with a number of decoy collectors and many excellent contemporary carvers. The collectors were asked to bring a decoy or two to "show and tell." I decided to bring the "Joefrau mallard" I had gotten from the same person who traded me the counterfeit Isadores. Wisely, I decided to show it to Bill first. Bill looked the decoy over and said quietly, "Harvey, this isn't a real Joefrau." I asked how he knew. He said years ago, he was given a decoy body that needed work and asked to carve and attach a new head in the Joefrau style and then restore and repaint the decoy, which he did. Bill told me that the body was indeed carved by Joefrau. That was some consolation. I had a great looking Hanemann/Joefrau decoy for what I paid years earlier and that eased the pain of being duped again. That decoy is shown in photograph 1. It also gave me the motivation to write this chapter and to suggest the following measures to help keep collectors from buying counterfeits.

First: Go to Bill Hanemann or someone with expertise like his and have the decoy that you are interested in buying vetted and appraised *before* you agree on anything. If the person offering the bird for sale refuses to allow such an inspection there is a very good chance it is not what it is represented to be. There are very few good quality old Louisiana decoys in circulation and being offered one for sale should be greeted with skepticism. As in my case, experienced collectors have bought fakes before without knowing it and are innocently ignorant about the decoy's real identity when they go to sell it years later. Decoy sellers are well advised to go to Bill or a person like him and get a certificate of authenticity if they expect to sell their decoys for top dollar. This is especially true if the decoy is going to be offered for sale at one of the national auction houses.

Charlie Frank discussed several scientific methods for detecting counterfeit decoys in his book *Wetland Heritage*. Most involve the use of radiographic equipment, including x-rays. I didn't appreciate how x-raying a decoy could be effective until I recently met Charlie's widow, Jean Frank, a lovely lady who knows almost as much about old Louisiana hunting decoys as her late husband did. She explained that the old carvers used either wooden pegs or square nails to join the decoy's head to its body. Additionally, she reminded me that an x-ray will also show if the wood is of different densities, as well as if fractures have been repaired. Almost all old Louisiana decoys were made of the same wood, either cypress or tupelo gum. This means if the x-ray shows that the decoy's head has a different wood density than the body, then that decoy is almost certainly not an original. Similarly, if the decoy's bill has wood of different densities, it has obviously been replaced. If the x-rays show that the decoy's head is secured to the body with round nails, at a minimum it shows that the head had been broken off at some time and then reattached at a later date. Other tell-tale signs of a repair job that would also likely show up on x-ray are fracture lines. If the decoy's head is secured to the body with round nails and the x-rays show a smooth head/body joint then the decoy is likely a counterfeit. If the asking price for the decoy is significant, having it x-rayed and interpreted by a knowledgeable radiologist is a prudent thing to do.

Second: Although previously discussed, it bears repeating, "counterfeit decoys" cannot be sold unless there is someone carving them. There is potential civil and criminal liability if the carver actually knows that the counterfeit is going to be misrepresented as having been carved by an old master or a well-known contemporary carver whose decoys command high prices. By agreeing not to sign or otherwise indicate that the decoy is a copy, the carver clearly becomes complicit in the scheme. Civil liability may attach if the carver should know that his client is likely to misrepresent who actually carved that decoy. If the carver is asked to carve a decoy in the style of an old master, distress the paint to make the decoy look old, and instructed to deliver it unsigned, what would a reasonable person (carver) think the purchaser intends to do with the decoy?

Third: Contemporary carvers routinely sign decoys they make with a burning tool, like a branding iron. This practice eliminates the identification problems that plague collectors of old decoys since neither the old masters nor their disciples who produced nearly identical decoys ever signed them. More is needed. Carvers making copies of another carver's decoys are urged to carve, burn, or otherwise indelibly sign their names on the bottom of the copy. Carvers, doing significant repair work and renovations are also urged to record what was done on the bottom of the decoys and then sign off on that work. As an alternative but less effective way to communicate, the carver can provide a written document that outlines the restoration work done on the decoy.

Counterfeiting hurts the carvers as much or more than the collectors. If the carver only produces unsigned copies of another carver's decoys, old or contemporary, he or she loses the opportunity to develop a recognizable style and an appreciative following. It takes an exceptionally talented artist to produce a copy of a decoy that is carved and painted like an old master's decoy and actually looks like the real thing when finished. Such skill would be in great demand if the carver's identity is known; but, demand for the actual carver's work is essentially lost if that identity is concealed. That cannot happen if the carver indelibly signs his name on the decoys he/she makes.

Endnotes

* How restoration affects the value of an old Louisiana hunting decoy is a very interesting topic but well beyond the scope of a book about contemporary Louisiana decoys and their carvers. Readers interested in that topic are referred to "Collector's Guide to Decoys" written by Linda and Gene Kangas. Although this book was published in 1992, its content is still very timely and informative, particularly chapter 8 "Fakes and Alterations."

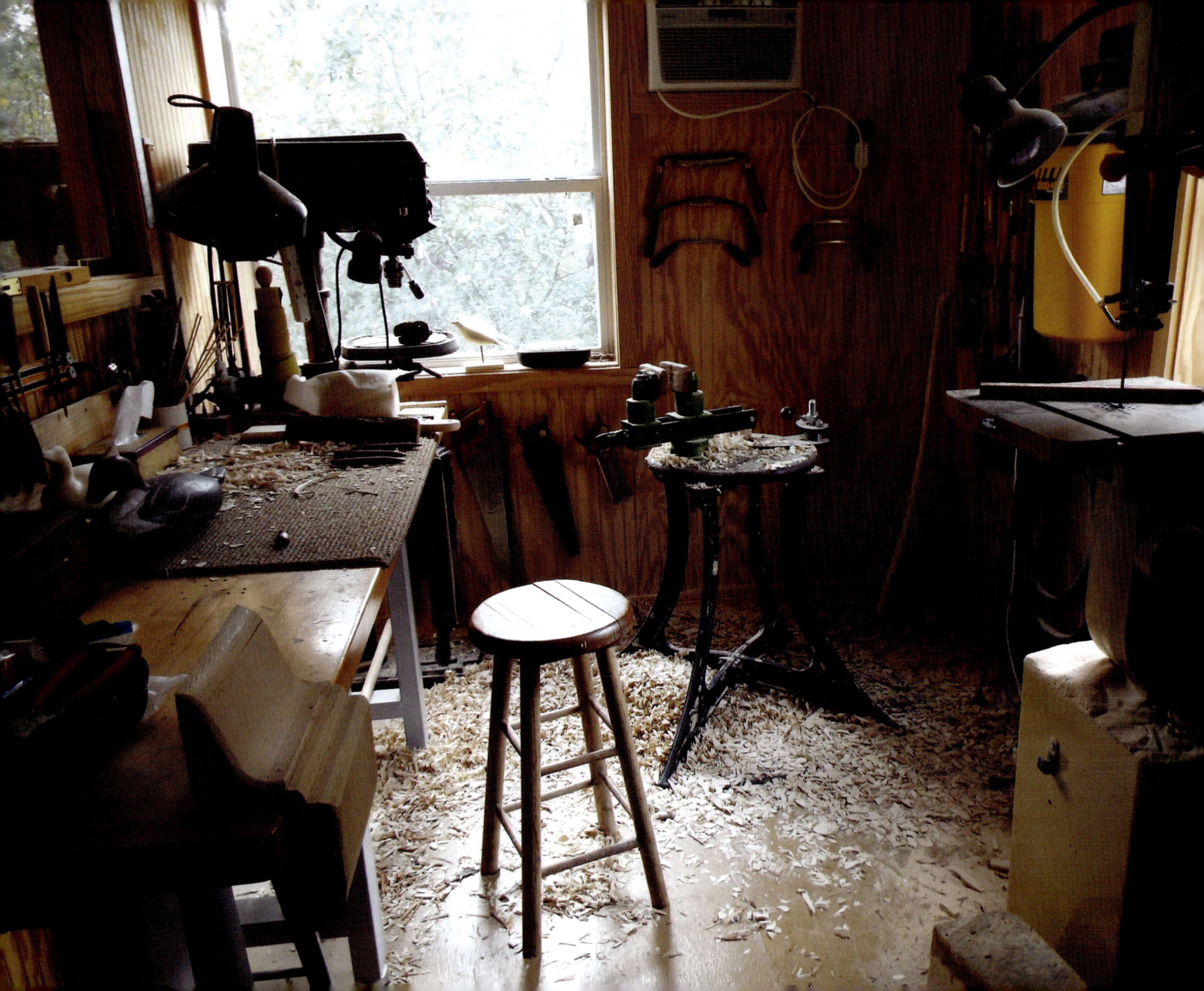

21 Burnishing the Legacy

The Louisiana Wildfowl Carvers and Collectors Guild

The origin and early years of the Louisiana Carvers and Collectors Guild are a bit murky. They can be traced to the confluence of two separate but ultimately related sources.

One source grew out of a small decoy show held by the St. Bernard Sportsman's League in 1973 in conjunction with the League's annual decoy calling contest, which was the main event. The carvers displaying decoys in the St. Bernard show included: Tan Brunet, Mike Frady, Ed Alba, Charlie Blaise, Bill Hanemann, Dennis Treitler, Clay Roberts, Donald Weaver Sr., Dr. Walter Mason, Roy Legaux, and Frank Ehret. These carvers did not regard the event as a formal competition but prizes were awarded for the decoys deemed best.

The other source was Charles Frank and Bill (then known as Billy) Hanemann and their frequent trips to remote areas of southeast Louisiana in search of indigenous decoy carvers and their decoys. The main purposes of the Frank-Hanemann expeditions are thought to be Frank's effort to prove Louisiana carvers produced fine and collectible decoys and also to add the better ones to his growing collection. These trips allowed Frank and Hanemann to get an up-close view of the older generation's carving and painting techniques. More important, it allowed these two men to form close and lasting friendships with many of the area's decoy carvers that later played an important role in the formation and growth of the LWCCG. Interestingly, Frank was also doing research for his influential book on Louisiana decoys on these trips. His findings on these forays helped him to write the text that forever changed the way people regarded wooden decoys made in Louisiana.

It took a few years for these sources to converge. Many of the carvers who displayed decoys in the St. Bernard Sportsman's League show were very concerned about the future of decoy carving in Louisiana. Wooden decoys were quickly becoming obsolete, replaced by less expensive, far lighter, and more durable synthetic ones. Motivated by a desire to preserve this important part of Louisiana's culture and heritage, as well as their income from selling decoys, these men held a meeting in October 1974 and decided to form a decoy carving club and display their work at a decoy show.

The club's first show was held at a mall in New Orleans East that no longer exists. Soon after this mall show, the newly formed carving club held a decoy carving competition. The year was 1975 and the competition was called "Wildfowl Sculpture." Fourteen carvers entered forty works of art. In the first competition, Frank Ehret's preening pintail and Don Weaver Sr.'s Canada goose took first and second place in the professional category, and Charlie Frank's hanging green-winged teal drake won first place in the semi-professional category. The emphasis of the first show was on old hunting decoys, even though the major East Coast carving competitions were featuring decorative decoys. Regardless, this first show was very successful and encouraged many older carvers to start making decoys again.

These results prompted the group to hold a second meeting at what is now Brother Martin High School on Elysian Fields in mid-town New Orleans. At this second meeting, the group adopted the name "Louisiana Wood Carvers Association" and elected Charlie Blaise as chairman. The group also decided to hold monthly meetings and put on a second decoy show and carving competition. Charlie Frank attended this second meeting and became very active in the club. In 1975, he was honored as the first winner of the club's Most Outstanding Member prize. This award was "intended to recognize the member who unselfishly devotes his time and efforts . . . for keeping alive the carving techniques and art forms of Louisiana decoy making and wildfowl carvings."[1] In 1976, Frank was a member of the Festival's Exhibition Committee and soon after that he became the chairman of that critically important committee.

The two sources had now converged with mutually beneficial results. Charlie Frank was an astute and very successful businessman as well as an avid hunter, decoy collector, and ever-improving wildfowl carver. He was also an effective leader who got things done for the club. For many years he prudently managed the club's fiscal affairs and played a key role in securing essential corporate financial support that funded the prize money awarded to the winners of the club's carving competitions. Frank's first book, *Louisiana Duck Decoys*, published in 1975, cemented the symbiotic relationship between he and the Carver's Association. The book conclusively proved that Louisiana's wooden decoys were beautiful, valuable, and collectible as folk art. The book also proved to be an invaluable resource for the people who attended the Association's decoy shows and wanted to learn more about Louisiana carvers and their decoys. As a result, the book was immensely popular. It generated a great deal of publicity, piqued public interest, and caused many people to start attending the Association's decoy shows.

Before the 1976 show and contest, held in the grand ballroom at the now-closed Fontainebleau Hotel, the club decided that the name "Louisiana Wood Carver's Association" did not sufficiently describe its major purpose of preserving and promoting decoy carving in Louisiana. The name was then changed to the Louisiana Wildfowl Carvers and Collectors Guild, which has now been in use for forty years. Twenty-nine professional carvers entered 155 items in the second year of competition. Tan Brunet won Best of Show honors.

Ed Alba, one of the carvers in the original St Bernard show, was elected president of the Guild in 1976 and 1977, but Charlie Frank quickly became its de facto leader. The year 1977 was one of significant progress, as the Guild was formally incorporated and received a charter from the Louisiana Secretary of State. This action was probably taken to assure continuity of the organization and ease corporate governance, and to allow the Guild to obtain tax-exempt status.

Alba reported that by 1977 the Guild had "stabilized at about 120 members."[2] The name of the Guild's annual show was changed from "Wildfowl Sculptures" to "Wildfowl Festival." The program for the Guild's third annual show and carving competition lists some sixty participating artists as compared to the fourteen that competed in the first show held two years earlier. The emphasis of that show was on decorative wildfowl carvings and was held at the Jung Hotel, another now-closed hotel in downtown New Orleans. The 1977 Wildfowl Festival was the first to award a cash prize for the Best of Show winner and was the first and probably the last contest to be judged by the competitors, all seeking to win the $3,000 awarded the Best of Show carver.

The Wildfowl Festival's transition from hunting decoys to decorative decoys was a natural result of what was happening at the premier East Coast shows and competitions. In the late 1970s, the "Cajun Conquistadors," led by Tan Brunet and Jimmie Vizier, left their Bayou Lafourche homes, traveled to Maryland, and began winning these exceptionally competitive national events and the significant cash prizes they came with. Tan and his Cajun colleagues proved to be among the very best carvers in this country, and, in 1978, Tan Brunet won the Ward World Championship. Moreover, collectors thronged to those shows and bought a lot of decoys at far higher prices than they sold for in Louisiana. In due course, decorative decoys helped jump start the interest in, and demand for, Louisiana decoys as art objects and not just hunting lures.

In 1978 the Guild put on its fourth annual Wildfowl Festival. It featured seventy-five artists, including such familiar names as Willie Badeaux, Michael Frady, Bill Hanemann, Eric Hutchison, Mitchell LaFrance, Jimmy Vizier, Rock Zeringue, Charlie Frank, and Tan Brunet, the reigning Ward World Champion carver. Willie Badeaux won a $300 cash price for the Best of Show Competition Grade Decorative Decoy in the Professional Category. Three thousand people attended the two-day show.[3]

In 1981, the seventh annual Festival was held at the University of New Orleans gymnasium. The cover page of the program for that year carried the name "Gulf South Championship Wildfowl Carving Competition." It drew major financial support from the oil and gas industry that funded the purchase award that went to the Best of Show winner as well as lesser cash awards. By endowing the purchase awards, major companies, like Phillips Petroleum, received the winning wildfowl while the carver got the cash prize. It is debatable whether the carver got the best of that arrangement. It is known that Phillips acquired a wonderful and very valuable decoy collection. It is also known that the winning carvers were often able to sell their decoys for more than the purchase prize. In 1981, that perceived problem was solved, if not entirely eliminated, when the purchase award was increased from $2,000 to $10,000. Later, it was raised to $14,000.

The seventh annual show in 1981 had 172 carvers participating. That number included forty-nine from out of state. While out-of-state carvers may have participated in earlier festivals, that information was not provided in the programs of earlier festivals.

Out-of-staters have played a significant role in the LWCCG's contests. From 1984 through 1986 a Louisiana carver won the $10,000 purchase prize awarded for the outstanding full-size decorative decoy. In 1984 it was Willie Badeaux; in 1985 it was Dick Bonner; and in 1986 it was Phil Galatas. Galatas repeated this achievement in 1990 and again in 1992, but a Louisiana carver did not win the top prize again until 2004 when Richard Reeves captured the $14,000 purchase award with a beautiful pair of widgeons.

The Guild's most important development in the 1980-1981 period was almost certainly the creation of an irrevocable trust that served as the receptacle for the substantial sums that the Guild had accumulated from entry, exhibitor and admission fees, sponsorships, auction proceeds, and other past and future revenues. The Whitney National Bank was named as the trustee and the trust document limited annual distributions to the amount earned each year. This money was used to fund the annual festival. This arrangement permanently assured the Guild's financial future.

A year later, another important development occurred. In 1982, the Guild led an initiative that resulted in decoy carving being recognized as an art form worthy of display in Louisiana's state museums. It is incongruous that Louisiana took so long to feature decoy carving in its museums when they had achieved that status in other decoy carving states' museums about twenty years earlier. The Wildfowl Festival in 1982 was the first to create a category for "flat art," better known as painting and photography. The Guild promoted flat art and the ninth annual Festival held in 1983 had a significant increase in the number of painters participating. The president's message in the program for that Festival quotes the Guild's motto, which was and presumably still is "To help preserve the folk art associated with waterfowling."[4]

It also appears that Tan Brunet had stopped competing as a professional carver in the Guild's festivals after 1981 except for an occasional appearance in the head whittling contests. This is certainly understandable since that incomparable carver ultimately won five Ward World Championships in 1977, 1978, 1981, 1982, and 1983, as well as Best of Show awards in three different categories in the Guild's 1980 festival, a feat later matched by Tan's son, Jett. It is also likely that Tan did not want to compete against his sons, Jett and Jude, or his best friend Jimmy Vizier—all exceptional carvers. However, Brunet did enter the 1982 flat art competition as a painter, and for many years he remained very active in the Guild and was one its foremost leaders.

The Brunet family, along with Willie Badeaux, were the dominant carving forces in the Guild from 1975 to the early 1980s. The Brunets were succeeded in that lofty status by Dick Bonner and his son Mike, along with Carl and Reagan Danos. At the twelfth festival, in 1986, Dick Bonner won the $10,000 Best in Gulf South Purchase Award for his decorative life-size wildfowl carving and son Mike won a $2,000 purchase award for the Best in Gulf South Competition Grade Decorative Decoy Pairs. Meanwhile, the Danos brothers took home ten various colored ribbons in the Competition Grade Decorative Decoy Category; four more in the Decorative Life-Size Wildfowl Carving Category, including three blue ones; and two more in the Shooting Stool Category. Fittingly, Tan Brunet was the master of ceremonies for the Guild's tenth annual festival, a role he filled with warmth and good humor for a number of years. In 1985, Willie Badeaux reconfirmed his status as one of Louisiana's very best carvers by winning the $10,000 purchase award for the Best in Gulf South Decorative Life-Size Category.

The year 1986 was a tough year financially for the Guild because economic problems adversely impacted a number of its major sponsors. The oil and gas industry was depressed due to low oil prices. The space industry was shut down on account of the Challenger tragedy. New Orleans was still hurting as a result of the 1984 World's Fair, which for the most part was a financial disaster. The negative effect of these pervasive economic problems on the Guild and on the 1986 festival cannot be overstated. In 1985, the Guild listed 385 members, and 285 carvers participated in that year's festival. In 1986, the Guild listed only 142 members, and that year's festival had only 205 participating carvers. Nonetheless, the Guild put on a successful festival in 1986 largely as a result of the earnings generated by the Guild's trust fund. It is noteworthy that Jett Brunet won two Best of Show blue ribbons in the two major categories previously won by his father, Tan.

Festival Chair Charlie Frank called 1990 a "banner year" for the Guild, when over five thousand people attended that year's festival. By 1991, the Guild's membership had increased to 248 members. Prize money was up and new flat art divisions were added, including fish and pyrographics.

The Guild held its nineteenth annual festival in 1993. Jett Brunet won Best of Show. Carl Danos won a blue ribbon for his competition grade decorative black duck, and Mike Bonner won a blue ribbon for his canvasback in the same category. Jude Brunet and Richard Reeves won multiple ribbons. Reagan Danos won Best of Show in the Gulf South Shooting Stool Category as well as the second place ribbon in that category. The 1993 festival featured 159 carvers from twenty states and Canada.

The twentieth annual festival, held in 1994, marked Charlie Frank's twentieth year as chair of the Guild's festivals. That year also marked the death of Wayne Frady to whom the twentieth festival was dedicated. Jett Brunet won Best of Show honors in both the Competition Grade Decorative Decoy (in tank) as well as the Decorative Life-Size Carving; a very impressive achievement considering the competition, which included Richard Reeves, Jude Brunet, and Russel Martin—three Ward World Champion Carvers.

The twenty-fifth annual Wildfowl Festival in August 1999 moved to the Alario Center, a newly completed facility in Westwego (a suburb of New Orleans) after being held for over twenty years at the University of New Orleans gym. By 1999, the Guild had nearly three hundred members. The previous year's show had 178 registered competitors, who entered 640 items. Willie Badeaux won the Competition Grade Decorative Pair $4,000 purchase award for a greater scaup drake and hen. Carl Danos's mallard drake took home the $500 purchase award in the Shooting Stool Gunner category. Mike Bonner took the blue ribbon for winning the Decorative Miniature Wildfowl Carving category.

The popularity and financial success of the Wildfowl

Festivals allowed the Guild to engage in diverse activities that greatly contributed to Louisiana's wildfowl legacy and tradition. The Guild's flat arts presentations, particularly the junior painting program headed up by Joan (Mrs. Dick) Bonner, and the photography competitions, drew a large number of participants. Later shows included non-wildfowl items like miniature boats and fish. Perhaps the Guild's most important accomplishment was creating and maintaining the most successful decoy carving junior development program in the country, as evidenced by the many carving competitions won by Louisiana teenagers in this state and nationally.

Inspired by the success of the LWCCG, carving clubs were formed in other parts of Louisiana, and they held annual carving competitions and shows in Baton Rouge, Houma, and Larose. These shows were well supported and well attended; however, the Baton Rouge and Houma events differed somewhat from the LWCCG's annual Wildfowl Festival. The Baton Rouge and the Houma shows feature old and new hunting decoys while the Larose show, now about forty years old, focuses on contemporary decoys and styles, including wildfowl sculptures like the LWCCF's Wildfowl Festival. Contemporary carvers who specialize in old-style hunting decoys, such as Cal Kingsmill, Bill Hanemann, Rock Zeringue, and Dennis Treitler, are very popular at the Baton Rouge show; while decoys produced by decorative carvers like Carl and Reagan Danos are in great demand at their hometown contest and show in Larose.

Regardless, the LWCCG's annual Wildfowl Festival was and still is Louisiana's decoy carving "Superbowl." Between the late 1970s and early 2000s, the Guild's Festivals continued to attract some of the nation's very best carvers, many from Louisiana. They drew big crowds and offered increasingly larger cash purchase prizes. The later Festivals featured more diverse competition categories, like oil and watercolor paintings and different kinds of model boats, as well as decoy carving and painting exhibitions.

For many years, the Guild has held meetings on the last Wednesday of every month at the Piccadilly Cafeteria on Clearview Parkway in Metairie, Louisiana. These meetings regularly drew and continue to draw crowds of fifty or more members and invited guests, who have "show and tell" opportunities, like displaying new carving, burning, and painting tools and techniques, recently carved decoys, and newly collected old ones. The Guild's monthly meetings are congenial and informative affairs. They continue to date and follow the same format.

The Guild's thirty-first annual Festival, held August, 12-14, 2005 at the Alario Center was memorable for a number of reasons. The cover of that Festival's program featured a picture of Richard Reeves's stunning pair of widgeons that had won the 2004 Best in Gulf South Life-Size Decoratives and the $14,000 purchase award that went with it. Charles Frank announced that the thirty-first would be his last as festival chair after nearly thirty years in that position. He submitted his chairman's report in the program for that year and signed off as "Chairman Emeritus." The thirty-first Festival was a great success financially and artistically. Then, just over two weeks later, tragedy struck.

On August 29, 2005, Hurricane Katrina hit. Levees gave way and flooded much of Greater New Orleans. Hurricane winds and rains also struck coastal communities in southeast Mississippi. This storm and the ensuing flooding badly damaged or completely destroyed 75 percent of the homes of Louisiana's carver members. Katrina put the LWCCG on life support. A highly respected and influential board member wanted to dissolve the Guild, terminate the trust, and distribute the assets to various charitable and educational entities. A small group led by Richard Reeves fought to save the Guild while also struggling to rebuild their lives and homes. By nature, Louisiana carvers are a resilient group. Carl Danos told a prominent collector from out of state, "Rebuilding is what we do." With President Richard Reeves leading the charge, the Guild was resurrected, despite formidable resistance, and put on a Wildfowl Festival in 2009 with very limited resources. That show was very successful and convinced the skeptics that the Guild could flourish and again put on high-quality festivals in the post-Katrina era with Richard Reeves at the helm.

Today, the LWCCG and its annual festivals, now held at the Castine Center in Pelican Park in Mandeville, Louisiana, are bigger and better than ever, even though virtually all of the out-of-state clubs that served as early models for the LWCCG are no longer in existence. The LWCCG is the second largest organization devoted to wildfowl art in the country with over four hundred members. The annual Wildfowl Festival distributes some $40,000 in prize money, the largest amount awarded by any decoy competition in the United States.

Louisiana carvers, including many of those featured in this book, dominate not only the LWCCG's annual festivals and other competitions in this state but also major national events put on by the Ward Foundation in Ocean City, Maryland, and the annual competitions held in Easton, Maryland. For example, Richard Reeves, immediate past president of the LWCCG, won the Best of Show award in the 2015 Ward Foundation contest. In fact, Louisiana has more Master Carvers than any other state. To earn Master Carver status a contestant must win a first, second, or third place in the Ward World Championship at an annual Foundation competition or two Best of Show awards in the Ward's advanced category.

When Charles Frank died in 2011 at age eighty-nine, the LWCCG lost a long time leader and guiding force, but the Guild continued under the able leadership of Reeves and his successor Gene Hebert. The ongoing success of the LWCCG and its carvers is a fitting tribute to Frank, who devoted a major part of his life promoting Louisiana decoys and their carvers. Louisiana decoy collectors have also greatly benefitted from Frank's numerous books, articles, and lectures on the beauty and value of Louisiana decoys and are also deeply indebted to him.

While Charlie Frank was the Guild's operational and financial guiding light, Tan Brunet was and remains its artistic heart and soul. Richard Reeves said that the LWCCG's Wildfowl Festivals could not have achieved their lofty status without Tan Brunet, who encouraged his carving colleagues from Louisiana and elsewhere to compete in the Festival's contests. Tan Brunet is a warm and friendly man in addition to being a multi-year Ward World Champion carver. Just spending time talking to him is a special treat. Reeves, himself a multi-year Ward World Champion, calls Tan Brunet the "LWCCG's Artistic Ambassador" to the decoy world and the best decoy carver who ever lived.

The LWCCG's most important achievement is not just promoting, exhibiting, and keeping wildfowl art alive, but also, in the process, enhancing Louisiana's long history of decoy carving by teaching and encouraging the creation of irresistible lures to hunt over and exquisitely beautiful wooden sculptures to be displayed and enjoyed.

Endnotes

1. 1976 Louisiana Wodcarvers Association Festival Program.
2. 1978 LWCCG Festival Program.
3. Programs are available for all of the Wildfowl Festivals from 1976 until 2004. It is believed that the vital statistics from each of those competitions will soon be put on the Guild's website. It was thought important to discuss the activities of the Guild and the Festival results in the early years in some detail to illustrate what the Guild was doing and how the Festivals were growing in size, scope, and popularity. From here on, the focus will be confined to significant developments in the ensuing years. Those interested in specifics like the competition sites and winners, membership numbers, and number of participating carvers and attendees are directed to the programs until that information is posted online.
4. 1983 LWWCG Festival Program.

Featured Carvers' Contact Information

A major reason for writing this book is to promote the art and tradition of decoy carving in Louisiana by spotlighting a number of the state's very best contemporary decoy carvers. That objective can be best accomplished by buying their wildfowl art. The following list of those carvers and their contact information is solely intended to enable prospective collectors to communicate with those carvers. It should be understood that as of the summer of 2016 inclusion on this list does not assure that every carver is now or in the future will be carving decoys for sale to the public, although that is the author's fervent hope.

Gary Badeaux
(985) 758-3531

Willie Badeaux
(985) 758-7612

Dick Bonner
(504) 254-9984

Mike Bonner
(504) 254-9984

"Tan" Brunet
judebrunet @yahoo.com

Jett Brunet
jettbrunet@yahoo.com

Jude Brunet
judebrunet@yahoo.com

Carl Danos
(985) 691-7206

Reagan Danos
(985) 691-3171

Ronnie Flynn
(985) 643-8793

Bill Hanemann
(228) 216-0910

Eric Hutchison
(504) 339-4048

Cal Kingsmill
(504) 256-9708

Roy Legaux Sr
(504) 277-0180

Richard Reeves
(504) 810-1199

Dennis Treitler
(985) 290-3468

Chris Weaver
(504) 390-5498

Rock Zeringue
(228) 533-7604

Selected Bibliography

Books

Barber, Joel. *Wild Fowl Decoys*. New York: Derrydale Press, 2000.

Cheramie, Brian, Charles Connor, Mark Riseling, and Troy Glasgow. *Lures and Legends: The Decoy Collection of Brian Cheramie and Period Photography of David L. Hall*. Golden Meadow, La.: REM Corporation, 1997.

Earnest, Adele. *The Art of the Decoy: American Bird Carvings*. New York: C.N Potter, 1965.

Frank, Charles, Jr. *Louisiana Duck Decoys*. Gretna, La.: Pelican Publishing, 1975.

Frank, Charles, Jr. *Wetland Heritage: The Louisiana Duck Decoy*. Gretna, La.: Pelican Publishing, 1985.

Kangas, Gene. *Decoys: A North American Survey*. Spanish Fork, Utah, Hillcrest Publications, 1983.

Kangas, Linda and Gene Kangas. *Collector's Guide to Decoys*. Radnor, Pa.: Wallace-Homestead Book Co., 1992.

Periodicals

Frank, Charles, Jr. "Cal Kingsmill, Creating Louisiana decoys in the Image of the Legends." *Decoy Magazine*. May/June 2000.

Greenwald, Erin. "Louisiana's William Hanemann." *Hunting and Fishing Collectibles Magazine*. 10, no. 6 (November-December 2010).

Gurtner, George. "'An Endangered Species:' Cal Kingsmill's decoys." *New Orleans Magazine*. August 2010.

International Wildfowl Carvers Association. *Wildfowl Carving Competition Magazine*. 1993.

Other

1996-97 Decoy Collector's Guide.

LWWCG Festival Programs.

Packard, Morgan. "The Call of the Hunt." myNew Orleans.com. Dec. 2006.